AN INTRODUCTION TO
THE GOSPEL OF JOHN

THE ANCHOR BIBLE REFERENCE LIBRARY is designed to be a third major component of the Anchor Bible group, which includes the Anchor Bible commentaries on the books of the Old Testament, the New Testament, and the Apocrypha, and the Anchor Bible Dictionary. While the Anchor Bible commentaries and the Anchor Bible Dictionary are structurally defined by their subject matter, the Anchor Bible Reference Library will serve as a supplement on the cutting edge of the most recent scholarship. The series is open-ended; its scope and reach are nothing less than the biblical world in its totality, and its methods and techniques the most up-to-date available or devisable. Separate volumes will deal with one or more of the following topics relating to the Bible: anthropology, archaeology, ecology, economy, geography, history, languages and literatures, philosophy, religion(s), theology.

As with the Anchor Bible commentaries and the Anchor Bible Dictionary, the philosophy underlying the Anchor Bible Reference Library finds expression in the following: the approach is scholarly, the perspective is balanced and fair-minded, the methods are scientific, and the goal is to inform and enlighten. Contributors are chosen on the basis of their scholarly skills and achievements, and they come from a variety of religious backgrounds and communities. The books in the Anchor Bible Reference Library are intended for the broadest possible readership, ranging from world-class scholars, whose qualifications match those of the authors, to general readers, who may not have special training or skill in studying the Bible but are as enthusiastic as any dedicated professional in expanding their knowledge of the Bible and its world.

David Noel Freedman
GENERAL EDITOR

CONTENTS

Foreword xi
Editor's Preface xvii
Acknowledgments xix
Abbreviations xxi

Editor's Introduction   1

General Selected Bibliography   15

Chapter 1. An Overview of Johannine Studies   26
   Excursus: Narrative Approaches to the Fourth Gospel 30

Chapter 2. The Unity and Composition of the Fourth Gospel   40
   The Problem 40
   Possible Solutions 42
   The Theory Adopted in This New *Introduction* 62
   Excursus: Theories of Johannine Community History 69
   Summary 85
   Bibliography 86

Chapter 3. Johannine Tradition: Relation to the
      Synoptics and Historicity   90
   The Value of the Information Found Only in John 91
   The Question of Dependence on the Synoptic Gospels 94

The Historical Value of John in Reconstructing
    Jesus' Ministry   104

Bibliography   111

Chapter 4. Proposed Influences on the Religious Thought
    of the Fourth Gospel   115

Gnosticism   116

Extrabiblical Hellenistic Thought   127

Traditional Judaism   132

Summary   142

Bibliography   144

Chapter 5. Echoes of Apologetics and the Purpose
    of the Gospel   151

Apologetic against Adherents of John the Baptist   153

Apologetic against Jews   157

Apologetic against or Rivalry with Other
    Adherents of Jesus   175

Purpose: Encouragement to Believing Christians,
    Gentile and Jew   180

Bibliography   183

Chapter 6. The Author, the Place, and the Date   189

The Author   189

The Place of Composition   199

The Date of the Written Gospel   206

Bibliography   215

Chapter 7. Crucial Questions in Johannine Theology   220

Ecclesiology   221

Sacramentalism   229

Eschatology   234

Christology   249

Son of Man   252

Wisdom Motifs   259

Summary   265

Bibliography   267

Chapter 8. The Language, Text, and Format of the Gospel:
Some Considerations on Style   278

The Original Language of the Gospel   278

The Greek Text of the Gospel   281

The Poetic Format of the Gospel Discourses   284

Notable Characteristics in Johannine Style   287

Bibliography   292

Chapter 9. The Outline of the Gospel   298

The General Outline of the Gospel   298

The General Outline of the Book of Signs   300

The General Outline of the Book of Glory   307

Bibliography   316

Editor's Conclusion   317

Author Index   327

Subject Index   333

Biblical Citations Index   349

FOREWORD

THE SUDDEN DEATH of Father Raymond E. Brown, S.S., on August 8, 1998, was a major loss to the Church and to the world of biblical scholarship. We are fortunate to have this book—his last major scholarly contribution—appear posthumously.

Raymond Edward Brown was born on May 22, 1928, in the Bronx, New York. His family moved to Florida in 1944, and it was there that he decided to be priest. He was ordained in 1953 for the diocese of St. Augustine, but during his seminary career at the Sulpician seminaries in Baltimore he became attracted to biblical studies and to the work of the Sulpician Fathers. The Society of St. Sulpice is a community of diocesan priests founded in 1641 in France for the purpose of initial and ongoing formation of Catholic priests. The Sulpicians arrived in the United States in 1791 at the invitation of John Carroll, the first bishop of the U.S., and founded the first Catholic seminary in the country, St. Mary's Seminary and University in Baltimore, Brown's alma mater. Even as a student Brown's extraordinary talents were recognized and encouraged. His bishop released him to the Sulpicians, and he was promptly assigned to teach high school at St. Charles College in Catonsville, Maryland. This position allowed him to begin doctoral studies at the Johns Hopkins University in Baltimore where he became a student of the world-renowned scholar, William Foxwell Albright, who was known as "the dean of biblical archaeologists." Brown finished his dissertation in 1958 (later digested and published as *The Semitic Background of the Term "Mystery" in the New Testament* [Facet Books, Biblical Series 21; Philadelphia: Fortress Press, 1968]), a work that was to demonstrate his longstanding interest in combining Near Eastern and Old Testament studies with the study of the New Testament.

Brown was also fortunate at that time to be invited to work on the Dead Sea Scrolls in Jerusalem from 1958–59 where he and fellow doctoral student and friend, Father Joseph A. Fitzmyer, S.J., toiled diligently to create a preliminary concordance of these exciting archaeological documents. When his return from Jerusalem, the Sulpicians assigned Brown to teach at St. Mary's Seminary and University in Baltimore, where he taught for twelve years, until 1971. During those years Brown did what most Sulpicians do: he taught and mentored future Roman Catholic priests. It was also a time, however, when he began work on the commentary that was to thrust him into the limelight of modern biblical scholarship, the two-volume Anchor Bible commentary on the Gospel of John (*The Gospel According to John* [AB 29, 29A; Garden City, NY: Doubleday, 1966, 1970]).

Father Brown's Sulpician superiors recognized his enormous scholarly talent and, fortunately, encouraged a placement where he could expand his range of experience and sphere of influence. In 1971 he moved to New York where he accepted a joint professorship at the Jesuit Woodstock College and Union Theological Seminary. When Woodstock closed, Brown accepted a full-time position at Union Theological, where he taught as Auburn Distinguished Professor of Biblical Studies for twenty years, until his early retirement in 1990. Upon his so-called "retirement," which was actually a cessation of teaching duties in order to be fully invested in research and publication, he took up residence at St. Patrick Seminary in Menlo Park, California, another Sulpician institution. It was there that he died on August 8, 1998, of cardiac arrest, after experiencing difficulty breathing. His funeral liturgy was celebrated on August 17, 1998, at the Sulpician chapel in Catonsville, Maryland, on the site of the former seminary where he had begun his teaching career forty years earlier. He was laid to rest at the Sulpician cemetery there on the campus that has become Charlestown Retirement Community.

A brief summary of major achievements gives an overview of his extensive career. His doctorate from Johns Hopkins gave him his primary credential in the scholarly world, but Brown was a consummate seeker of knowledge. Among his earned degrees were an earlier pontifical doctorate in theology from St. Mary's Seminary and University (S.T.D., 1955) and a licentiate in Sacred Scripture from the Pontifical Biblical Institute in Rome (S.S.L., 1963), as well as degrees from The Catholic University of

America (B.A. 1948; M.A. 1949). From the publication of his first dissertation in 1968 to the present volume, he published dozens of books, large and small, and hundreds of articles and book reviews. The final figures have yet to be tallied. Many of his books continue to be translated into foreign languages. A full bibliography of his works is in preparation as part of a scholarly symposium to be held in October 2003 at the recently inaugurated Raymond E. Brown Center at St. Mary's Seminary and University.

Brown received many honors in his career, including more than forty honorary doctorates, and the distinction of being the first person to serve as president of the three most prestigious societies for New Testament study: the Catholic Biblical Association (1971–72), the Society of Biblical Literature (1976–77), and the Society for the Study of the New Testament (1986–87). In an oft-quoted article, *Time* magazine named him "probably the premier Catholic Scripture scholar in the U.S." Pope Paul VI named Brown the only American member of the Pontifical Biblical Commission (1972–78), and he achieved this distinction again when Pope John Paul II named him in 1996 until his death. He was also inducted into Phi Beta Kappa, the American Academy of Arts and Sciences, and the prestigious British Academy. Many of his publications won book awards, and to his death, he remained in demand as a popular lecturer. His massive volumes on the birth and death of Jesus, respectively, *The Birth of the Messiah* (New York: Doubleday, 1977; new updated edition, 1993) and *The Death of the Messiah* (2 vols.; New York: Doubleday, 1994) stand as classic contributions to New Testament studies. They have both been enormous best-sellers, and scholars will interact with them for decades to come.

Brown's most lasting contribution to biblical scholarship, to which this latest volume now belongs, is his analysis of the Johannine literature. He remained fascinated with John for his entire career. As Professor Moloney points out, Brown's two-volume commentary on John remains a lasting testimony to his exegetical prowess. It demonstrates the skills of a master exegete whose talent has been appreciated both by scholars and generations of preachers. Not only is it a fine exposition of the text, but it is filled with an enormous amount of background material that fleshes out the Johannine world. A measure of the lasting power of this commentary is that more than thirty years after its publication Johannine scholars continue to remain in dialogue with it. It is most appropriate, then, that his final major contribution—the present volume—brings Brown's scholarly career full circle.

I hasten to note that the commentary was not Brown's sole contribution to Johannine studies. Two other books demonstrated his creative approach to the Johannine world. Perhaps his most intriguing analysis is found in the monograph, *The Community of the Beloved Disciple* (New York: Paulist Press, 1979). There Brown attempted to reconstruct a history of the Johannine community based upon his interpretation of the critical texts. He acknowledged in the introduction the precariousness of his venture: "I warn the reader that my reconstruction claims at most probability; and if sixty percent of my detective work is accepted, I shall be happy indeed" (p. 7). His complex theory, which met with considerable interest, tried to demonstrate how John's Gospel and the Letters of John revealed a community caught up in serious internal christological debates with profound ramifications. Later he published the Anchor Bible commentary on the Johannine epistles (*The Epistles of John* [AB 30; New York: Doubleday, 1982]) where he continued to expound his understanding of what he termed "a theological life-and-death struggle with a Community at the end of the first century" (p. xv). These works, accompanied by many articles on Johannine topics, provide a deep treasure of exegetical gold that can still be profitably mined. His contribution to Johannine studies, however, extended even farther afield. A day or two before his death his small, popular book, *A Retreat with John the Evangelist* (Cincinnati: St. Anthony Messenger Press, 1998), appeared. It is his most whimsical treatment of the Johannine literature, but one thoroughly grounded in scholarly depth. In it he gives the evangelist a hypothetical persona and makes himself the interviewer of this literary creation who guides the reader through the biblical text on a seven-day retreat. The result is as entertaining as it is illuminating.

Upon Brown's untimely death, many scholars wondered whether he had other projects that might yet appear. His magisterial *An Introduction to the New Testament* (Anchor Bible Reference Library; New York: Doubleday, 1997) had been published the year before his death, but it was always his custom to have some project "in the wings." As executor of Brown's estate, I was charged with reviewing his research to ascertain the state of affairs. I was aware, along with his publisher and a small number of other colleagues and friends, that he had begun work on revising his

IN MEMORIAM

Raymond E. Brown, S.S.

1928–1998

THE ANCHOR BIBLE REFERENCE LIBRARY

An Introduction to the Gospel of

JOHN

RAYMOND E. BROWN, S.S.

Edited, updated, introduced, and concluded by

Francis J. Moloney, S.D.B.

ABRL

DOUBLEDAY

New York   London   Toronto   Sydney   Auckland

THE ANCHOR BIBLE REFERENCE LIBRARY
PUBLISHED BY DOUBLEDAY
a division of Random House, Inc.
1745 Broadway, New York, New York 10019

THE ANCHOR BIBLE REFERENCE LIBRARY, DOUBLEDAY,
and the portrayal of an anchor with the letters ABRL are
trademarks of Doubleday, a division of Random House, Inc.

Book design by Leslie Phillips

LIBRARY OF CONGRESS CATALOGING-IN-PUBLICATION DATA
Brown, Raymond Edward.
An introduction to the Gospel of John / by Raymond E. Brown;
edited by Francis J. Moloney.—1st ed.
p. cm. — (The Anchor Bible reference library)
Includes bibliographical references and index.
ISBN 0-385-50722-4
1. Bible. N.T. John—Introductions.   I. Moloney, Francis J.   II. Title.   III. Series.
BS2615.52 .B76 2003
226.5'06—dc21   2002073475

1   3   5   7   9   10   8   6   4   2

influential Anchor Bible commentary on the Gospel of John. Happily, an investigation of his laptop computer revealed multiple electronic files. Among them was a massive introduction (already some 400 manuscript pages) to the projected revised commentary, and some very preliminary revisions of several early sections of the commentary. It became apparent rather quickly that only the introduction was in a shape to be published, but it needed some editing and updating. The question then became: Who could appropriately edit this manuscript for publication?

There were several excellent candidates for the job; the field of Johannine studies is populated with many talented experts. After careful thought and consultation, I finally conversed with Andrew Corbin of Doubleday and suggested the name of Father Francis J. Moloney, S.D.B., of the Catholic University of America. The reasons were multiple. First, I knew from personal conversations with Father Brown that he had a great deal of respect, both personally and professionally, for Professor Moloney. He particularly enjoyed his work on the Gospel of John. Second, Moloney is a scholar who has remained open to and has utilized the newer scholarly methods of biblical studies and the more traditional historical-critical methods. Brown himself had grown in his methodological approach to the biblical text, especially in his latter years. For instance, he was already moving in the direction of incorporating more narrative-critical insights into his revised commentary, albeit sporadically. In my judgment, Moloney exhibits the kind of methodological balance that characterized Brown's own work. Finally, I suspected that, if he agreed to the task, Moloney would tackle it with enthusiasm and efficiency. Fortunately for all concerned, he graciously agreed to the request, with the full approval and cooperation of Andrew Corbin and Doubleday. Although the task proved to be a bit more than anticipated, Professor Moloney endured and accomplished the feat in near record time. He gave the scholarly world a preview of the result in his Presidential Address to the Catholic Biblical Association meeting in Cleveland, Ohio, on August 3, 2002, when he lectured on the topic, "Raymond E. Brown's new *Introduction to the Gospel of John.*" As readers will see, although the book remains substantially Father Brown's, Moloney has done an outstanding job of editing the text, updating the bibliographies, and fleshing out other areas in the manuscript that were either sketchy or remained to be developed. I could not be happier with the final product.

I am pleased now, as provincial of the U.S. Province of Sulpicians, to express publicly my sincere gratitude to Professor Moloney and to Mr. Corbin for their hard work and cooperation on this project. I also thank all those at Doubleday, both current and former employees, who worked closely with Father Brown in the production of his monumental works. He greatly appreciated this special publishing relationship. In particular, I thank Professor David Noel Freedman, editor of the entire Anchor Bible Series and a friend of Father Brown's, for his unfailing support over the years. This volume, a contribution to the Anchor Bible Reference Library, is a most fitting capstone to an incredibly productive career in Johannine studies. I am confident that Father Brown himself would be pleased. Johannine scholars, and all interested readers, now have the final statement of a master interpreter of the Gospel of John and the Johannine literature. Readers will see, and be able to judge for themselves, where Brown grew in his understanding of the Fourth Gospel, where he altered his stance somewhat, and where he remained thoroughly convinced of his earlier understanding. It is my opinion, based upon the sketchy revisions of his commentary left behind, that had he lived, Brown would have produced a considerably changed and nuanced commentary on John. Alas, what we have in this remarkable volume—properly dubbed "magisterial" by Professor Moloney—are his summary thoughts on introductory matters to the Fourth Gospel, and these will have to suffice. Readers will not be disappointed, as a master interpreter once more leads them into the mysterious landscape of the magical Gospel called John.

August 28, 2002   Ronald D. Witherup, S.S., Ph.D.
                                              Sulpician Provincial House
                                              Baltimore

EDITOR'S PREFACE

ISSUES TRADITIONALLY dealt with in a preface will be found in the "Editor's Introduction," which follows the abbreviations. I am using this space merely to instruct the reader of this *Introduction* on some of the more technical aspects which emerge when an editor takes over the almost completed work of a distinguished scholar.

The abbreviations that follow refer only to the *Introduction*. A fuller list, containing many of the abbreviations found below, but not all of them, can be found on pp. xiii–xviii of Brown's 1966–70 Commentary. Over the years, and in many publications, Brown developed a singular way of referencing his work. Against much current practice, he eliminates repetition in his text and his bibliographical lists. Generally, studies found in the General Bibliography and the specialized bibliographies that follow each chapter are never given in full in the text. Occasionally Brown even abbreviates a title in his bibliographies. On the whole I have sought to maintain that system. However, in places where I felt that the reader deserved a less cryptic reference or confusing abbreviation, I have provided fuller indications. I have also provided full detail for all the works cited in the bibliographies. I trust that these decisions will make the reading of this *Introduction* an easier experience.

On almost every occasion where I have introduced new material, I have attempted to indicate this to the reader. However, this process appeared unnecessary when I was adding bibliography or introducing reference to discussions that have appeared since 1998, the year of Brown's untimely death. Readers will be aware that bibliographical references from 1997 onward (and even some earlier ones) necessarily come from the hand of the editor.

ACKNOWLEDGMENTS

I WOULD LIKE TO THANK Ronald Witherup, S.S., and Andrew Corbin, for asking me to take on this task. There were times when "thanks" were not the sentiments uppermost in my mind. However, they are now, for two reasons. First, this task has forced me to "think Johannine" all over again. Working long hours on someone else's incomplete text was an interesting way back into that thought-world. Secondly, it has allowed me to do a substantial piece of work to honor the memory of Raymond E. Brown. As I prepared this volume, I was struck by the immense influence that his work has had on me over the three decades of my professional life as a biblical scholar, however much I may have begged to differ as the years went by. In publicly recognizing all I have received from him, and thanking God for the gift of Ray Brown, I have no doubt that I express the sentiments of many scholars of my generation who have had the good fortune to learn from him in many ways. He was not only the premier New Testament scholar of our time, but also a consummate gentleman and an outstanding and generous colleague.

Finally, I am grateful to the resources and the staff of the Woodstock Library, Georgetown University, Washington, DC, and to the Sisters of the Visitation, Georgetown, who have provided me with rest and sustenance during the brief intervals that interspersed my long hours in that fine library.

Francis J. Moloney, S.D.B.
The Katherine Drexel Professor of Religious Studies
The Catholic University of America
Washington, DC

ABBREVIATIONS

AB	Anchor Bible
ABD	*Anchor Bible Dictionary*
ABRL	Anchor Bible Reference Library
AGAJU	Arbeiten zur Geschichte des Antiken Judentums und des Urchristentums
AJBI	Annual of the Japanese Biblical Institute
AnBib	Analecta Biblica
ANRW	W. Haase and H. Temporini, eds., *Aufstieg und Niedergang der Römischen Welt: Teil II: Principat—Religion* (Berlin: Walter de Gruyter, 1979–84)
ATANT	Abhandlungen zur Theologie des Alten und Neuen Testaments
ATR	*Anglican Theological Review*
BBB	Bonner Biblische Beiträge
BBET	Beiträge zur Biblischen Exegese und Theologie
BD	The Beloved Disciple
BDM	R. E. Brown, *The Death of the Messiah. From Gethsemane to the Grave. A Commentary on the Passion Narratives in the Four Gospels* (2 vols.; New York: Doubleday, 1994)
BEJ	R. E. Brown, *The Epistles of John* (AB 30; New York: Doubleday, 1982)
BETL	Bibliotheca Ephemeridum Theologicarum Lovaniensium
BETS	*Bulletin of the Evangelical Theological Society*
BibIntS	Biblical Interpretation Series
Bib	*Biblica*
BibOr	*Bibbia e Oriente*
BibLeb	*Bibel und Leben*
BibRev	*Bible Review*
BibTod	*The Bible Today*

BINT	R. E. Brown, *An Introduction to the New Testament* (ABRL; New York: Doubleday, 1997)
BJRL	*Bulletin of the John Rylands Library*
BK	*Bibel und Kirche*
BMAR	R. E. Brown and J. P. Meier, *Antioch and Rome: New Testament Cradles of Catholic Christinaity* (New York: Paulist, 1983)
BNTE	W. D. Davies and D. Daube, eds., *The Background to the New Testament and Its Eschatology. Studies in Honour of C. H. Dodd* (Cambridge: Cambridge University Press, 1956)
BR	*Biblical Research*
BSac	*Bibliotheca Sacra*
BSRel	Biblioteca di Scienze Religiose
BT	Bible Translator
BTB	*Biblical Theology Bulletin*
BThSt	Biblisch-theologische Studien
BWANT	Beiträge zur Wissenschaft vom Alten und Neuen Testament
BZ	*Biblische Zeitschrift*
BZNW	Beihefte zur Zeitschrift für die neutestamentliche Wissenschaft
CahRB	Cahiers de la Revue Biblique
CBEGJ	R. A. Culpepper and C. C. Black, eds., *Exploring the Fourth Gospel. In Honor of D. Moody Smith* (Louisville: Westminster/John Knox, 1996)
CBET	Contributions to Biblical Exegesis and Theology
CBQ	*Catholic Biblical Quarterly*
ch., chs.	Chapter, chapters
CINTI	W. Klassen and G. F. Snyder, eds, *Current Issues in New Testament Interpretation* (New York: Harper, 1962)
CJOC	J. Neusner, ed., *Christianity, Judaism and Other Greco-Roman Cults. Studies for Morton Smith at Sixty* (4 vols.; SJLA 12/1–4; Leiden: E. J. Brill, 1975)
ConBNT	Coniectanea Biblica, New Testament Series
CS	*Chicago Studies*
CSEL	Corpus Scriptorum Ecclesiasticorum Latinorum
CTR	*Criswell Theological Review*
DBSup	L. Pirot, A. Robert, H. Cazelles and A. Feuillet, eds., *Dictionnaire de la Bible: Supplément* (Paris: Letouzey, 1928–)
DR	*Downside Review*
DSS	The Dead Sea Scrolls
EB	Études Bibliques
ECW	O. Cullmann, *Early Christian Worship* (SBT 10; London: SCM Pressm 1953)

EH	Eusebius, *Ecclesiastical History*
EPJ	M.-É. Boismard and A. Lamouille, *Un Évangile Pré-johannique* (EB; Paris: Gabalda, 1993–)
EQ	*Evangelical Quarterly*
ErbAuf	*Erb und Auftrag*
EstBib	*Estudios Biblicos*
EstEccl	*Estudios Ecclesiásticos*
ETL	*Ephemerides Theologicae Lovanienses*
EvJean	M.-É. Boismard, et al., eds, *L'Évangile de Jean* (RechB 3; Louvain: Desclée de Brouwer, 1958)
ExpTim	*Expository Times*
FB	Forschung zur Bibel
FGFN	F. van Segbroeck, C. M. Tuckett, G. van Belle, and J. Verheyden, eds, *The Four Gospels 1992: Festschrift Frans Neirynck* (3 vols.; BETL 100; Leuven: Leuven University Press, 1992)
FJJ	M. C. de Boer, ed., *From Jesus to John: Essays on Jesus and New Testament Christology in honour of Marinus de Jonge* (JSNTSup 84; Sheffield: Sheffield Academic Press, 1993)
FRLANT	Forschungen zur Religion und Literatur des Alten und Neuen Testaments
FTS	Frankfurter theologische Studien
GCS	Die griechische christliche Schriftsteller der ersten drei Jahrhunderte
GP	R. T. France, D. Wenham, and C. Blomberg, eds, *Gospel Perspectives* (6 vols.; Sheffield: JSOT, 1980–86)
GTRH	H. Cancik, H. Lichtenberger, and P. Schäfer, eds., *Geschichte, Tradition, Reflexion: Festschrift für Martin Hengel zum 70. Geburtstag* (3 vols.; Tübingen: J. C. B. Mohr [Paul Siebeck], 1996)
HBT	*Horizons in Biblical Theology*
HNT	Handbuch zum Neuen Testament
HOAJL	L. Hartman and B. Olsson, eds., *Aspects of Johannine Literature* (CnBNT 18; Uppsula: Almquist & Wiksell, 1987)
HTR	*Harvard Theological Review*
IBS	*Irish Biblical Studies*
IEJ	*Israel Exploration Journal*
ITQ	*Irish Theological Quarterly*
JBap	John the Baptist
JBL	*Journal of Biblical Literature*
JETS	*Journal of the Evangelical Theological Society*
JohSt	A. Feuille, Johannine Studies (New York: Alba House, 1964)
JSNT	Journal for the Study of the New Testament

JSNTSup   Journal for the Study of the New Testament Supplement Series
JSOT   Journal for the Study of the Old Testament
JT   F.-M. Braun, *Jean le Théologien* (EB; 4 vols; Paris: Gabalda, 1959–72). They are confusingly numbered; here 1 (= 1959), 2 (= 1964), 3 (= 1966), 4 (= 1972)
JTS   Journal of Theological Studies
KBW   Katholisches Bibelwerk (Stuttgart)
KGB   D. Luhrmann and G. Strecker, eds., *Kirche Festschrift für Günther Bornkamm zum 75. Geburtstag* (Tübingen: J. C. B. Mohr [Paul Silbeck], 1980)
LD   *Lectio divina*
LumVie   *Lumière et Vie*
LXX   The Septuagint
MAMJ   J. P. Meier, *A Marginal Jew* (3 vols; New York: Doubleday, 1991–2001)
MD   *La Maison-Dieu*
NJBC   R. E. Brown, J. T. Fitzmyer and R. E. Murphy, eds., *The New Jerome Biblical Commentary* (Englewood Cliffs: Prentice Hall, 1989)
NHL   Nag Hammadi Library in English
NovT   *Novum Testamentum*
NovTSup   Supplements to Novum Testamentum
NRT   *Nouvelle Revue Théologique*
NT   New Testament
NTAbh   Neutestamentliche Abhandlungen
NTAuf   J. Blinzler, O. Kuss, and F. Mussner, eds., *Neutestamentliche Aufsätze. Festschrift. J. Schmid* (Regensburg: Pustet, 1963)
NTD   Das Neue Testament Deutsch
NTE   R. E. Brown, *New Testament Essays* (2nd reprint; New York: Paulist Press, 1982)
NTP   W. C. van Unnik, ed., *Neotestamentica et Patristica: eine Freundesgabe Herrn Professor O. Cullmann überreicht* (NovTSup 6; Leiden: E. J. Brill, 1962)
NTS   *New Testament Studies*
OT   *Old Testament*
PIBA   *Proceedings of the Irish Biblical Association*
PL   J. P. Migne, ed., *Patrologia Latina*
PRS   Perspectives in Religious Studies
RB   *Revue Biblique*
RechB   Recherches Bibliques
RExp   *Review and Expositor*

RevSR	*Revue des Sciences Religieuses*
RHPR	*Revue d'Histoire et de Philosophie Religieuses*
RivBib	*Rivista Biblica*
RSR	*Recherches de Science Religieuse*
Rthom	*Revue Thomiste*
RTP	*Revue de théologie et de philosophie*
SacPag	J. Coppens, A. Descamps, and E. Masseux, eds., *Sacra Pagina. Miscellanea Biblica Congressus Internationalis Catholici de Re Biblica* (2 vols., Gembloux: Duculot, 1959)
SB	La Sainte Bible—"Bible de Jérusalem" traduite en Français
SBFLA	Studii Biblici Francescani Liber Annuus
SBLDS	Society for Biblical Literature Dissertation Series
SBLMS	Society for Biblical Literature Monograph Series
SBLSP	Society for Biblical Literature Seminar Papers
SBLSymS	Society for Biblical Literature Symposium Series
SBS	Stuttgarter Bibelstudien
SBT	Studies in Biblical Theology
ScEccl	*Sciences Ecclésiastiques*
ScotJT	*Scottish Journal of Theology*
SFG	F. L. Cross, ed., *Studies in the Fourth Gospel* (London: Mowbray, 1957)
SJLA	Studies in Judaism in Late Antiquity
SNTSMS	Society for New Testament Studies Monograph Series
SNTU	Studien zum Neuen Testament und seiner Umwelt
SQE	P. Benoit, M.-É. Boismard, et al., *Synopse des Quattres Évangiles* (3 vols.; Paris: Cerf, 1972–77)
SRSR	*Studies in Religion/Sciences Réligieuses*
ST	*Studia Theologica*
StEv	*Studia Evangelica* (Papers for the Oxford International Congress of NT Studies, published at Berlin: Akademie Verlag, in the series TU): I = TU 73 (1959); II = TU 87 (1964); III = TU 88 (1964); IV = TU 102 (1968); V = TU 103 (1968); VI = TU 112 (1973); VII = TU 126 (1982)
TANZ	Texte und Arbeiten zum neutestamentlichen Zeitalter
TD	*Theology Digest*
TDNT	G. Kittel and G. Friedrich, eds., *Theological Dictionary of the New Testament* (10 vols.; Grand Rapids: Eerdmans, 1964–76)
TG	*Theologie und Glaube*
THKNT	Theologischer Handkommentar zum Neuen Testament
TLZ	*Theologische Literaturzeitung*
TNTS	*Twelve New Testament Studies*

TRev	*Theologische Revue*
TRu	*Theologische Rundschau*
TS	*Theological Studies*
TU	Texte und Untersuchungen
TV	*Theologische Versuche*
TZ	*Theologische Zeitschrift*
v., vv.	verse, verses
VigChr	*Vigiliae Christianae*
WBC	Word Bible Commentary
WMANT	Wissenschaftliche Monographien zum Alten und Neuen Testament
WUNT	Wissenschaftliche Untersuchungen zum Neuen Testament
ZKT	*Zeitschrift für katholische Theologie*
ZNW	*Zeitschrift für die neutestamentliche Wissenschaft und die Kunde der älteren Kirche*
ZTK	*Zeitschrift für Theologie und Kirche*

AN INTRODUCTION TO

THE GOSPEL OF JOHN

EDITOR'S INTRODUCTION

IN HIS 1966 PREFACE, the late Raymond E. Brown apologized for "yet another commentary" on the Gospel of John by rightly pointing to the brilliance and eloquence that had been dedicated to commentary upon this Gospel over the first 50 years of the twentieth century (Loisy, Bauer, Lagrange, Hoskyns, Bultmann, Lightfoot, Dodd, to mention only some of the luminaries). He suggested that he wished to produce two volumes of synthesis, directed by three principles:

1. The desire to present a "moderately critical theory of the composition of the Gospel."
2. The conviction that the Fourth Gospel "is rooted in historical tradition about Jesus of Nazareth."
3. "Sincere confessional commitment to a theological position is perfectly consonant with a stubborn refusal to make a biblical text say more than its author meant it to say."[1]

His magisterial commentary reflects these principles on every page. Its ongoing life as one of the most reliable and used commentaries on the

---

1. All citations from R. E. Brown, *The Gospel According to John* (2 vols.; AB 29–29a; Garden City: Doubleday, 1966–70), vi. All future references to Brown's commentary will be indicated by the title *John*, and the page number. The volume will not be given, as the page numbers continue across the two volumes. Other references will be given in full, or in a form explained above in the Abbreviations, or by a brief indication of the name of the author and the work. In this last case, full details will be found in either the General Bibliography (pp. 15–25) or in the specialized bibliographies that conclude each section.

Fourth Gospel indicates that his commitment to these issues has underlined their importance. Yet much has changed in scholarly biblical criticism since 1966, especially under the first two above-mentioned principles. The third principle is perhaps—gratefully—more strongly in place, thanks to the contributions of Raymond Brown and his contemporaries across all the Christian traditions.

The hardworking, astute mind of Raymond Brown was well aware of newer directions. He turned toward a reworking of his commentary once he retired from his position as the Auburn Distinguished Professor of New Testament at Union Theological Seminary, New York. I recall chatting with him at the meeting of the Society of Biblical Literature in Philadelphia, Pa., in 1997. I was honored when asked if I would send him studies I had published in less widely available journals. He informed me then that he was working toward a new edition of his commentary. But the God whom Ray Brown served so well had other ideas.

I was therefore delighted to be approached by Ronald Witherup, S.S., the Provincial of the Sulpician Fathers in the USA, and subsequently by Andrew Corbin of Doubleday, asking me to take in hand the work that Ray had left behind. A review of the unfinished script was called for, to see if the completion of a second edition of his superb commentary was possible. On downloading the script from Ray's computer, it became obvious that the only extensive work carried out was on his magisterial *Introduction*. Brown had retouched other sections of his work, here and there, and made occasional notes on recent bibliography that called for attention. The commentary proper was still as it had appeared in its original dress. The translation, the detailed studies of each chapter and verse retain their fresh and lively significance in contemporary Johannine studies, and will continue to guide both scholars and students for years to come.

However, a new *Introduction to the Gospel of John* from R. E. Brown was in an advanced stage of preparation, and it appeared opportune to work further on the unfinished text that it might be prepared for publication.[2] It is thus a privilege to have worked through this new *Introduction*, so that it can be placed side by side with Brown's classic com-

---

2. A briefer "introduction" to the Fourth Gospel from Brown's pen can be found in his recent BINT, 332–82.

mentary on the Fourth Gospel. May it further enhance what remains one of the most significant studies on the Fourth Gospel of the twentieth century, and give it continued life into the twenty-first century.

Without wishing to lessen the importance of a firsthand encounter with the pages that follow, some general remarks concerning Brown's second edition of his *Introduction* are in order. The new *Introduction* continues Brown's concern to follow the major attempts across the twentieth century to trace the history of a gospel until it became the Gospel of John.[3] This issue has become less central in much contemporary Johannine scholarship. Many scholars, especially in English-speaking circles, have turned to what can be loosely called a narrative critical approach to the text as we now have it.[4] Side by side with an emerging interest in the Fourth Gospel as a unified narrative, however, there has been considerable interest in rediscovering the history of the Johannine community. Brown has been a leading figure among those who have attempted to rediscover this history.[5]

Brown rightly refuses to neglect the historical-critical question of the development of a Gospel that was the result of a long process, however unified the final form of the narrative may appear to be. For Brown, many of the tensions, both literary and theological, can still best be understood by coming to grips with the various stages in the development

---

3. Brown consistently refers to stages in the development of the final form of the tradition as "gospel," and to the final form itself as "the Gospel."

4. More attention needs to be devoted by English-speaking scholars to the work of a newer generation of German-speaking scholars who are associating themselves with many of the newer methods of approach to the Gospel of John. Especially significant is the work of M. Labahn, *Jesus als Lebensspender. Untersuchungen zu einer Geschichte der johanneischen Tradition anhand ihrer Wundergeschichten* (Berlin: de Gruyter, 1999); Idem, *Offenbarung in Zeichen und Wort. Untersuchingen zur Vorgeschichte von John 6,1–25a und seiner Rezeption in der Brotrede* (Tübingen: J. C. B. Mohr [Paul Siebeck], 2000); and K. Scholtissek, *In ihm sein und bleiben: Die Sprache der Immanenz in den Johanneischen Schriften* (Herders Biblische Studien 21; Freiburg: Herder, 2000). They are not alone, however. See the surveys of K. Scholtissek, "Neue Wege in der Johannesauslegung. Ein Forschungsbericht I," *TG* 89 (1999): 263–95; Idem, "Neue Wege in der Johannesauslegung. Ein Forschungsbericht II," *TG* 91 (2001): 109–33.

5. See his seminal work, *The Community of the Beloved Disciple.*

of a gospel, which eventually became the Gospel. The classical approaches to this question, from J. H. Bernard down to R. Bultmann and more recent developments of these methods, are skillfully surveyed. One might wonder if there is still need for such a survey at the turn of the third millennium. Scholars continue to debate possible theories of composition, and Brown was able to include the recent work of scholars like U. C. von Wahlde in the United States and I. Dunderberg in Europe in his survey. Since then Udo Schnelle and his students Michael Labahn and Manfred Lang in Germany, John Painter in Australia, and Paul Anderson in the United States, continue to ask penetrating questions about these matters, and propose thought-provoking answers.[6] However committed a newer generation may be to the impact a text makes upon a reader (the world in front of the text), the serious consideration of what may have generated that text (the world behind the text) must still be part of the biblical scholar's activity. Brown's clear and fair presentations of the various theories clear the ground for what many will regard as the most significant new element in this new *Introduction*.

In the 1966 commentary, before his work on the history of the Johannine community, Brown had suggested a five-stage theory for the development of the Gospel.[7] Since that time, much has been done, and especially by Brown himself, to reconstruct the history of the Johannine community. In this new edition, Brown associates a theory of composition, distilled from the strengths and weaknesses of those who have gone before him, with the more recent speculations upon the history of the community. This process leads him to propose a three-stage development that produced the Gospel as we now have it. Brown's modified the-

---

6. See U. Schnelle, *Antidocetic Christology in the Gospel of John. An Investigation of the Place of the Fourth Gospel in the Johannine School* (trans. L. M. Maloney; Minneapolis: Fortress Press, 1992); M. Labahn, *Jesus als Lebenspender,* and especially his *Offenbarung in Zeichen und Wort;* M. Lang, *Johannes und die Synoptiker. Eine redaktionsgeschichtliche Analyse von Joh 18–20 vor dem markinischen und lukanischen Hintergrund* (FRLANT 192; Göttingen: Vandenhoeck & Ruprecht, 1999); J. Painter, *The Quest for the Messiah. The History, Literature and Theology of the Johannine Community* (2nd ed.; Edinburgh: T. & T. Clark, 1993); P. N. Anderson, *The Christology of the Fourth Gospel. Its Unity and Disunity in the Light of John 6* (Valley Forge: Trinity Press International, 1997).

7. See *John,* xxxiv–xxxix.

ory reduces the gospel's development to three stages, akin to all the Gospels.[8] The reader must pay careful attention to the pages that follow, but Brown's 1998 proposal may be summarized as follows:

Stage One: As with all the Gospels, the Gospel of John had its origins in the ministry and teaching of Jesus, witnessed to by a disciple.

Stage Two: Again, in a fashion similar to the development of the Synoptic Tradition, for several decades Jesus was proclaimed in the postresurrectional context of a Christian community. It is at this stage that the BD, not one of the Twelve, but a disciple and a witness to the life and ministry of Jesus, played a crucial role.[9] He was the link between the first and the second stage of the Gospel's development. The bulk of this lengthy period (several decades) would have been marked by the oral transmission of the tradition of the BD. There may have been something written toward the end of this stage.

Stage Three: There are two moments in this final stage. The first is the creative writing of a remarkable storyteller, whom Brown calls "the evangelist." This person is *not* the BD, but faithfully, and indeed brilliantly (see chs. 9, 11, 18–19), receives the tradition of the BD and communicates it through a coherent theologically-motivated story, containing signs, discourses and narratives. He is the author of the bulk of the Gospel. To cite Brown: "If in Stage Two the Beloved Disciple was a major instrument of the Paraclete-Spirit in bearing witness, by producing the gospel in Stage Three the evangelist was the instrument of the Paraclete-Spirit."[10] Brown suggests that the evangelist may have worked and reworked the story, but we cannot be sure of this. Finally "the redactor" produced the Gospel as we now have it. This figure is responsible for such features as the Prologue (1:1–18), the Epilogue (21:1–25), and shifting certain blocks of material within the evangelist's story from one place to another. Contrary to Bultmann and his many followers, the redactor was not responsible for

---

8. Brown's original five-stage theory was widely criticized as too complex. He has regularly pointed out that the first two of those "stages" were not literary: the activity of Jesus (Stage One) and the preaching of the first disciples (Stage Two). He has now subsumed these two stages into his new Stage One. For some further brief remarks on this "new" three-staged process of growth, see my remarks in the Conclusion.

9. On the BD, see Chapter Six, pp. 189–99.

10. See below, p. 81.

making the Gospel of John more acceptable to the so-called "greater Church." He did not introduce material on traditional eschatology and Sacraments to correct a more radically realized and existentialist reading of the Jesus story. The redactor is in deep sympathy with the evangelist who, in his own turn, has brilliantly rendered the traditions passed on by the BD into the narrative forms which produced the Gospel.

Yet, Brown, marking a serious shift of position from his earlier understanding of the development of the Johannine Gospel, comments as he concludes his reflection upon the relationship between the evangelist and the redactor:

> Even though I think there was both an evangelist and a redactor, the duty of the commentator is not to decide what was composed by whom, or in what order it originally stood, nor whether these composers drew on a written source or an oral tradition. One should deal with the Gospel of John as it now stands, for that is the only form that we are certain has ever existed.

The influence of contemporary Johannine scholarship is apparent in this position. How seriously this affirmation would have influenced a complete commentary on the Gospel of John from Brown is speculation.[11]

Closely related to the issue of the history of the development of the gospel lies the question of the relationship of the Gospel of John to the Synoptic tradition. The influence of the Louvain school upon contemporary scholarship is given its full importance. The figures of Gardner-Smith and Dodd dominated these discussions for most of the twentieth century. Gardner-Smith and Dodd asked whether it is easier to explain the similarities between the Gospel of John and the Synoptic Gospels *without* a theory of dependence, or to explain the differences between the two (?) traditions *with* one. They opted for the former position, and Dodd's classical study insisted that there are common, shared traditions between John and the Synoptics, but no *literary* dependence of one upon the other.[12] This position has been eroded by an increasing number of scholars who, under the influence of F. Neirynck and his school in Louvain, claim that the Gospel of John depends upon one, two, or even all

---

11. However, see my own speculations in the Conclusion.

12. C. H. Dodd, *Historical Tradition in the Fourth Gospel* (Cambridge: Cambridge University Press, 1965). On Gardner-Smith, see pp. 8–9.

three of the Synoptic Gospels.[13] However, in the end, Brown comes down—less securely than in his earlier commentary—upon a theory of *literary independence* from the Synoptic tradition. With great lucidity, after evaluating all the possibilities, Brown points out that to accept that the evangelist and/or the redactor drew directly from Mark, Matthew and Luke, as F. Neirynck claims, would mean that the evangelist (and the redactor?), writing in the eighties and nineties of the first century, would have known and accepted all three Synoptic Gospels as authoritative Christian documents. If this were the case, it would make them the earliest Christian authors to know and use them in this fashion. This is hardly likely to be the case. The better option remains that of Gardner-Smith and Dodd. All four Gospels draw on independent traditions, but Brown shifts ground here. In a fashion similar to the recent work of Udo Schnelle, Brown suggests that John did not think he was inventing the literary form of "Gospel." There was probably some cross-influence, most likely during Brown's "Second Stage" (but one cannot be sure of this), especially from the emerging Lukan tradition.[14] As Brown points out and subjects to careful analysis, a common use of shared ancient traditions raises the historical question. Is it possible that there may be in the Gospel of John more genuine historical data about Jesus and his world than is often allowed? The lofty theological nature of the Johannine story cannot and must not be downplayed, but it should not lead scholars to affirm uncritically that this Gospel has lost all contact with the world and person of Jesus of Nazareth.

The chapter dedicated to the background and the possible influences

---

13. Less influential, because of its complexity, is the theory of M.-É. Boismard, especially as it has been developed in M.-É. Boismard and A. Lamouille, *L'Evangile de Jean. Synopse des Quatres Evangiles en Français III* (Paris: Cerf, 1977). For Brown's assessment of this contribution, see below, pp. 59–62. Boismard's contribution is evidence of a long-standing insistence that the Gospel of John was influenced by the Synoptic tradition (especially the Lukan tradition).

14. See Schnelle, "Johannes und die Synoptiker," FGFN, 3.1799–1814. Since Brown's work, Michael Labahn (*Jesus als Lebensspender*) has proposed that the influence may have been in the form of "secondary orality." Depending upon Walter Ong's study of orality, Labahn suggests that there may have been an oral tradition that grew from the existing Synoptic Gospels. The fourth evangelist, aware of the existence of the Synoptic Gospels, would reflect this "secondary orality," but not literary dependency. See Chapter Three, below.

on the Johannine tradition may strike some readers as a restatement of Brown's 1966 position. In many ways this is true. He rejects the possible influence of Gnostic, Hermetic and any other extrabiblical Hellenistic thought (especially Philo). No stone is left unturned, however, as he sifts through the evidence, and in the end, I detect a slight change of position. In a way that I would personally like to see broadened,[15] Brown accepts, for example, that there is a certain mutuality between Philo and John. He continues to reject any direct "influence." He suggests a certain commonality that arises from a way of developing biblical motifs in a partially Jewish, partially Greek world, where Hellenistic thought had taken root. One senses Brown's awareness that the world receiving the text of the Gospel of John may have influenced the way it was written. He still turns, however, to Judaism as the Gospel's most formative element. Nevertheless, there is a shift of focus. In 1966 Brown wrote confidently of "Palestinian Judaism." He now broadens his base, and suggests that a number of different Jewish worlds played into the stream that formed the Gospel of John: the Old Testament, Jewish practices and the Jewish thought world of the time. This world and its thought can be notoriously difficult to identify, but is probably best reflected by the DSS. Brown now speaks of a *more broadly based* "traditional Judaism," defined as a Judaism that took its main inspiration from what we call the OT without conscious adoption of large amounts of extrabiblical Hellenistic philosophy and theology.[16]

Perhaps the most significant single contribution that this new *Introduction* will make is found in Chapter Six. There Brown discusses the purpose of the Gospel, and traces hints of apologetic. Following Schnackenburg, he warns that exegetes should be careful not to trace signs of an apologetic theme that may have crept into the gospel during its formation. He suggests that some aspects of apologetic pertain to the contexts out of which the Gospel developed rather than its purpose. This

---

15. See my Conclusion.

16. I draw the reader's attention to the use of the expression "conscious" and "large amounts" in my paraphrase of Brown at this point. It is beyond scientific control to estimate what was "conscious" or not in the composing and writing practices of an ancient author. Similarly, we do not know what "quantities" of sources an author may have consciously used. These are modern questions, and the nature of the Gospel of John should guard us from asking such questions of it.

principle is crucial to the nuanced treatment of a number of issues. Brown questions the exaggerated anti-Baptist polemic often found in this Gospel, rejects an antidocetic tendency,[17] accepts that the Gospel is written to encourage crypto-Christians to take the step into full commitment to the Johannine Jesus, but condemns those whose faith is insufficient.

Crucial to this chapter, however, is a completely updated and documented study of the use of "the Jews" in the Fourth Gospel. This is Brown at his best. He begins with the difficulties that existed between the historical Jesus and some Jews of his time, through the various stages of the development of the Gospel and the history of the community across the latter half of the first Christian century. Brown identifies "the Jews" as hostile Jews whose *role in the story* is to demonstrate implacable rejection of Jesus, and its consequences, both for Jesus and for themselves. However, this identification by "role" is followed by no less that eight "riders" that clarify and circumscribe this position. Both the survey of scholarship and Brown's careful presentation of his own position are a pleasure to read, and will do much to clear the air in this urgent and necessary debate.

The discussion of the author, the place and the date of the Gospel, in its final form, is identical to the position Brown took in 1966. Ongoing debates, especially the recent interest in northern Transjordan, are critically evaluated. Brown's history of the Johannine community allows for a geographical move from Palestine to Ephesus, where the Gospel finally saw the light. He allows that northern Transjordan may have been part of that journey, and has thus left its mark in the Johannine story. In Chapter Seven Brown continues the basic structure of his 1966 commentary, but looks further into several Johannine theological questions. As in his 1966 volume, he continues to treat ecclesiology, sacraments, eschatology and wisdom as the crucial issues. Although the themes are the same, and Brown's approach is the same, these sections have been totally rewritten and brought up to date. What was lacking in the 1966 commentary, however, was a discussion of Johannine Christology. This has now been remedied with a brief account of the major questions of Johannine Christology, and a detailed study of the Johannine Son of Man. Given my per-

---

17. Wrongly, in my opinion. See Schnelle, *Antidocetic Christology in the Gospel of John.*

sonal interest in this particular Johannine question,[18] I was delighted to see Brown singling out "the Son of Man" for special attention. There are some places where Brown's understanding of the Johannine Son of Man Christology and my own overlap; there are other places where they do not.

My major difficulty lies in Brown's acceptance of the widely held idea that the determining feature of the Johannine Son of Man is his ascent into and descent from heaven.[19] The only place where the theme of the ascent and descent of the Son of Man is present is 3:13. Unless, as does Brown, one reads the Johannine use of ὑψωθῆναι as indicating not only crucifixion, but also ascension and return to the Father. This is certainly the meaning of the expression in Philippians 2:9, but John 3:14 and 12:33 insist that *just as* (καθώς) the serpent was lifted up *so also* (οὕτως) must the Son of Man be lifted up (3:14), and that the lifting up of the Son of Man indicates the way in which he was to die (12:33: ποίῳ θανάτῳ ἤμελλεν ἀποθνῄσκειν). In the Fourth Gospel, the expression has nothing to do with the return to the Father, but affirms that on the cross Jesus is both lifted up on a stake and exalted.[20] It anticipates the theology of the revelation of the glory of God and the return of the Son to the glory that was his before the world was made (see 17:24) that undergirds the Johannine passion narrative, the "hour" of the glorification of Jesus, the Son of Man (12:23; 13:31–32).[21] But once 3:14, 8:28 and 12:32 are removed from the ascent and descent of the Son of Man, and by association, also 12:23 and 13:31–32, which deal with the revelation of the glory of God on the cross and the glorification of the Son of Man by means of it (see 11:4), 3:13 is the only remaining Johannine Son of Man saying explicitly linking the expression with ascent and descent. It is probable, but not certain, that 6:62 implies the ascent of the Son of Man. The rhetorical nature of

---

18. See Moloney, *Son of Man*.

19. For the most recent study, which is fundamentally flawed by the acceptance of the ascent and descent of the Son of Man as the key to the meaning of the expression in John, see M. Sasse, *Der Menschensohn im Evangelium nach Johannes* (TANZ 35; Tübingen: Francke Verlag, 2000).

20. This was conclusively argued many years ago by W. Thüsing, *Die Erhöhung und Verherrlichung Jesu im Johannesevangelium* (2nd ed.; NTAbh XXI.1/2; Münster: Aschendorff, 1970).

21. A further important exegetical question, which can only be mentioned here, is the need to distinguish between the revelation of the "glory" of God (the primary task of Jesus), the glory possessed by the Son because of his presence with the Father

that unfinished question from Jesus to his disciples after the bread of life discourse is enigmatic, to say the least. In 1:51, often brought into this discussion, it is the angels who ascend and descend upon the Son of Man who remains, one supposes on the basis of the link with Gen 28:12, firmly located on earth. Thus, with the exception of 3:13 (and perhaps 6:62), all other Son of Man sayings are either about the Cross (3:14; 6:27, 53–54; 8:28; 12:23, 27, 32–33; 13:31–32; 19:5 [?]), the revelation of the heavenly (1:51) in one who can be seen, heard and believed in (9:35–38), a revelation that produces judgment (5:27).

However much rethinking I must do with 3:13 and 6:62, I would continue to claim that the Johannine use of the Son of Man points to the revelation of God in the human event of Jesus of Nazareth, especially in the event of the cross. Only a human being can be crucified, and John never speaks of the crucifixion of the Son. But neither would he dream of placing on the lips of Jesus: "Father, glorify the Son of Man in your presence with the glory that was his before the world was made" (see 17:5).[22] In this, the Johannine use of the expression of "the Son of Man" comes into the Fourth Gospel from the primitive tradition, and especially its association with the passion predictions (see Mark 8:31; 9:31; 10:33–35; and parallels). But its focus upon the human figure and experience of Jesus opens the door to the regular patristic use of the expression, in conjunction with "Son of God" to stress Jesus' humanity.

I have raised these, and several other critical questions, without altering Brown's text, by means of editorial notes. I trust that the reader of this new *Introduction* will find Brown's lucid presentation of the data, and his own understanding of it, side by side with my probing of this understanding, an interesting experience of the many possible interpretations that seem to emerge when one approaches this timeless text with attention and respect.

---

before, during and after the story of Jesus of Nazareth, and the glorification of Jesus, who returns to the Father by means of the "hour" of the cross and resurrection. It is around this final aspect of the Gospel's Son of Man Christology that "glory" language gathers. For some further reflections and the basic bibliography surrounding this question, see Moloney, *Signs and Shadows*, 190–91 n. 49.

22. On the need to distinguish the Johannine "Son (of God)" and "Son of Man" Christologies, see Moloney, *Son of Man*, 208–20. For an attempt to roll them together, see Sasse, *Der Menschensohn*, 248–62.

The final chapters cover traditional areas for any introduction: the Greek language and text of the Gospel, and some of its stylistic features (Chapter Eight), and an outline of the Gospel (Chapter Nine). These Chapters have been considerably updated by Brown, and I have updated them even further. I have added some pages on stylistic features that have emerged over recent years as Johannine scholarship has turned steadily toward the evaluation of the Gospel's literary worth, but that are not mentioned by Brown.[23] Finally, Brown's script for Chapter Nine only provided an outline for the Gospel down to 12:50. I have exercised considerable license in my presentation of the literary shape and theological message of the Book of Glory (13:1–20:31) and the Epilogue (21:1–25). As I will point out at that stage, there would probably be points where Brown and I differ in our understanding of the literary structure of the second half of the Gospel. Brown's structure of 13:1–17:26 may have continued to rely on his diachronic understanding of the prehistory of Jesus' final encounter with his disciples. A synchronic reading of the text as we now have it has shaped mine.[24] But we would be in basic agreement over its theological message.

The editing and updating of this text, received unfinished from the hand of one of the greatest Johannine scholars of the twentieth century, has been a daunting experience. At all times I wished to respect the greatness of Brown's contribution. Yet, by the time this book sees the light of day, he will have been deceased some 5 to 6 years. This has led me to make a number of decisions. In general, I have only touched up Brown's text. At times I had to finish sentences, find details for footnotes only sketched in, and track down bibliography mentioned without any detail. I regarded as my major task the preparation of a text that genuinely reflected Brown's thought as he was penning this study, his final contribu-

---

23. It should not be imagined that older Johannine scholarship disregarded this feature of the Johannine narrative, nowadays so much at center stage. See, for example, the important perceptive study of H. Windisch, "Der johanneische Erzählungsstil," in *"EUCHARISTERION." Studien zur Religion und Literatur des Alten und Neuen Testaments Hermann Gunkel zum 60. Geburtstag dargebracht von seinen Schülern und Freunden* (2 vols.; FRLANT 19; Göttingen: Vandenhoeck & Ruprecht, 1923), 2.174–213.

24. But see my Conclusion for some suggestions of newer directions already foreshadowed by Brown's unfinished work.

tion to a lifetime of interest in matters Johannine. It would have been presumptuous on my part to have taken the text further than Brown himself had dared to go in 1998.[25]

But I could not allow the intervening 5 to 6 years to go unmentioned. Brown would have been the first to insist on this. I have thus had recourse to a series of editor's notes, in which I add more recent discussions that further elucidate, or perhaps question, what is found in Brown's text. I have also used the editor's notes to add, and sometimes briefly summarize, recent important bibliography. In three places I have written extensive new material. Two of them take the form of excursus. One is dedicated to narrative critical approaches to the Gospel of John, inserted into Brown's chapter on contemporary Johannine studies.[26] Brown made mention of these newer methods, but did not offer any description. Indeed, his harsh remarks (which I left in the text), the result of some overambitious claims of early narrative critics about the end of historical-critical scholarship, called for this excursus, in the light of the amount of fine narrative critical work done on the Gospel of John since 1998. Narrative criticism is only one of the several newer methods being used in contemporary Johannine scholarship,[27] but it is by far the most important *addition to* (not replacement of) the historical-critical approach so capably wielded by Brown. The second excursus is a brief presentation of various theories concerning the history of the Johannine community, including Brown's own important contribution to this discussion. In a footnote to the script I received, Brown promised that the second edition of the commentary would contain an appendix providing this sketch. My excursus is an attempt to provide material that may have appeared in this unwritten appendix. Third, as mentioned above, I took it upon myself to complete the second half of the final chapter, detailing the outline and the major themes of 13:1–21:25.

My other major contribution has been a widespread updating of all bibliographies, from the following General Bibliography to the detailed bibliographies following each section of the new *Introduction*. Like Brown, I make no claim to have provided exhaustive bibliographies. They

---

25. But see my few suggestions in the Conclusion on the directions he may have taken.

26. See below, pp. 30–39.

27. See, for example, Moloney, *"A Hard Saying,"* 259–79.

are selective, but will provide readers sufficient information to investigate further questions that may particularly arouse their interest or concern. The bibliographies provide information down to the middle of 2001. In addition to following Brown's practice of placing a General Bibliography at the beginning of the volume, and providing more specialized bibliographies at the end of each chapter, I have also followed his practice of giving only abbreviated reference to works found in either the general or the more specialized bibliographies. The reader will need to have recourse to those bibliographies for detail. However, I have removed his sometimes cryptic references from within the text (a sign of the unfinished nature of the script I received) and placed them in footnotes. When reference is made to a book or article not found in either the General Bibliography or the specialized bibliographies, I provide full details in the footnotes.

There may be times where the reader may not be sure where Brown ends and Moloney begins. I have attempted to make it clear *on every occasion* when I invade Brown's argument. My Conclusion to this volume indicates where I would like to see Brown's argument develop further. It may be pure speculation, but I suspect there are hints in the unfinished script as Brown left it that suggest he may have been about to chart newer Johannine waters.[28]

---

28. A series of coincidences have led me to the task of editing (and largely rewriting) Brown's "John, The Gospel of," in the *New Catholic Encyclopedia* (18 vols.; New York: McGraw-Hill, 1967–88), 7.1080–88 (1967), work with students with his BINT (1997), and now edit his final work in this *Introduction* (1998). My first impressions were that Brown had shifted very little over a period of 30 years. There was rigidity in his approach, and the grid he used to discuss introductory questions. But a closer familiarity with the text of the *Introduction* suggested to me that some major changes of direction may have emerged from a completely rewritten commentary on the whole Gospel. Like most of us, Brown would have gone back to rewrite his *Introduction* once he had finished his commentary! Some of these changes of direction will be suggested in my Conclusion. I am, however, aware of the danger that I may be reading too much of myself into my interpretation of Brown.

GENERAL SELECTED BIBLIOGRAPHY

No ATTEMPT HAS BEEN MADE to provide a complete Johannine bibliography. Many of the classical studies of the twentieth century are still represented as Brown often focuses upon these contributions. Nevertheless, recent works, down to mid-2001, receive the most attention. Thus there are books and articles mentioned here, published since 1996, which are not mentioned in the text of the *Introduction*. I introduced them when I sensed that they were relevant to Brown's discussion. I have left the work basically as Brown constructed it, but more recent important bibliography which, for obvious reasons, could not be considered by Brown, had to be included in the list that follows. A number of excellent critical surveys of contemporary Johannine scholarship are found in the first section of this General Bibliography. Those surveys will inform readers of the considerable amount of contemporary interest in the Gospel of John, and the newer directions that are emerging from this interest. Readers looking for more complete bibliographies should consult the annual *Elenchus Bibliographicus* of *ETL*. Another rich resource has been the *Elenchus Bibliographicus* of *Biblica*, but that publication has fallen sadly behind (it presently only covers publications up to 1996). Bibliographies for specific areas of Johannine research (e.g., sources, community history, author, theology, etc.) are found after the respective Chapters of this volume.

BIBLIOGRAPHIES AND ANALYSES OF LITERATURE/STUDIES ON JOHN

Volumes explicitly dedicated to listing bibliographies will be marked with an asterisk (*).

Ball, D., "Some Recent Literature on John: a Review Article," *Themelios* 19 (1993): 13–18.

Becker, J., "Aus der Literatur zum Johannesevangelium (1978–1980)," *TRev* 47 (1982): 279–301, 305–47.

*Belle, G. van, *Johannine Bibliography 1966–1985* (BETL 82; Leuven: Peeters, 1988).

Beutler, J., "Literarische Gattungen im Johannesevangelium. Ein Forschungsbericht 1919–1980," *ANRW* 2.25/3 (1985): 2506–68.

———, "Méthodes et Problèmes de la recherche johannique aujourd'hui," in J.-D. Kaestli, J.-M. Poffet and J. Zumstein, eds., *Communauté johannique et son histoire* (Geneva: Labor et Fides, 1990): 15–38. Reprinted in German in *Studien*, 191–214.

Brown, R. E., "The Gospel according to John—An Overview," *Chicago Studies* 37 (1998): 5–15

Carson, D. D., "Selected Recent Studies of the Fourth Gospel," *Themelios* 14 (1989): 57–64.

Davies, M., "Which is the Best Commentary? XI: The Fourth Gospel," *ExpTim* 99 (1987–88): 73–78.

Devillers, L., "Études sur les écrits johanniques," *RThom* 96 (1996): 453–78.

Edwards, R. B., "John and the Johannines. A Survey of Some Recent Commentaries," *Bible Translator* 43 (1992): 140–51.

Gourges, M., "Cinquante ans de recherche johannique, de Bultmann à la narratologie," in *"De bien des manières." La recherche biblique aux abords du XXIᵉ siècle* (eds. M. Gourges and L. Laberge; LD 163; Paris: Cerf, 1995), 229–306.

Haenchen, E., "Aus der Literatur zum Johannesevangelium 1929–1956," *TRu* 23 (1955): 295–335.

Howard, W. F. and C. K. Barrett, *The Fourth Gospel in Recent Criticism and Interpretation* (4th ed.; London: Epworth Press, 1955).

Käsemann, E., "Zur Johannesinterpretation in England," *Exegetische Versuche und Besinnungen* (2 vols.; Göttingen: Vandenhoeck & Ruprecht, 1960, 1964), 2.131–55.

Koester, C. R., "R. E. Brown and J. L. Martyn, Johannine Studies in Retrospect," *BTB* 21 (1991): 51–55.

Kysar, R., *The Fourth Evangelist and His Gospel* (Minneapolis: Augsburg Press, 1975).

———, "The Fourth Gospel: A Report on Recent Research," *ANRW* 2.25/3 (1985): 2389–2480.

Lémonon, J. P., "Chronique johannique (1981–1992)," *LumVie* 41 (1992): 95–104.

Léon-Dufour, X., "Où en est la recherche johannique?" in Marchadour, *Origine* (1990): 17–41.

Lindars, B., "Some Recent Trends in the Study of John," *The Way* 30 (1990): 329–38.

*Malatesta, E., *St. John's Gospel 1920–1965* (Rome: Biblical Institute Press, 1967).

Menoud, P.-H., *L'Évangile de Jean d'après les recherches récentes* (Neuchâtel: Delachaux, 1947).

———, "Les études johanniques de Bultmann à Barrett," *EvJean*, 11–40.

*Mills, W. E., *Bibliographies for Biblical Research IV: The Gospel of John* (Lewiston, NY: Mellen, 1995).

*Moda, A., "Quarto Vangelo: 1966–1972," *RivBib* 22 (1974): 53–86.

Moloney. F. J., "The Gospel of John: A Survey of Current Discussion," *Compass Theology Review* 11 (1977): 20–25.

———, "Revisiting John," *Scripture Bulletin* 11 (1977): 9–15.

———, "Where Does One Look? Reflections on some recent Johannine scholarship," *Salesianum* 62 (2000): 223–51.

Nielsen, H. K., "Johannine Research," in Nissen and Pedersen, eds., *New Readings*, 11–30. (See under "Essay Collections" for full details)

*Rábanos Espinosa, R. and D. Muñoz León, *Bibliografía Joanica 1960–1986* (Madrid: Consejo Superior de Investigaciones Scientificas, 1990).

Robinson, J. A. T., "The New Look on the Fourth Gospel," *StEv* 1.338–50. Also in *Twelve New Testament Studies* (London: SCM Press, 1962), 94–106.

Schlumberger, S., "Quelques études récentes sur Jean," *Foi et Vie* 86 (1987): 91–94.

Schmithals, W., *Johannesevangelium und Johannesbriefe. Forschungsgeschichte und Analyse* (BZNW 64; Berlin: de Gruyter, 1992).

Schnackenburg, R., "Neuere englisch Literatur zum Johannesevangelium," *BZ* 2 (1958): 144–54.

———, "Entwicklung und Stand der johanneischen Forschung seit 1955," in de Jonge, *L'Évangile* (1977), 19–44.

Schnelle, U., "Perspektiven der Johannesexegese," SNTU 15 (1990): 59–72.

———. "Ein neuer Blick: Tendenzen gegenwärtigen Johannesforschung," *Berliner Theologische Zeitschrift* 16 (1999): 21–40.

Scholtissek, K., "Johannine Studies: A Survey of Recent Research with Special Regard for German Contributions," *Currents in Research: Biblical Studies* 6 (1998): 227–59.

———, "Neue Wege in der Johannesauslegung: Ein Forschungsbericht I," *TG* 89 (1999): 263–95. (Revised and updated version of "Johannine Studies," above.)

———, "Johannes auslegen I: Forschungsgeschichte und methodische Reflexionen," SNTU 24 (1999): 35–84.

————, "Johannes auselegen II. Methodische, hermeneutische und einleitungswissenschaftliche Reflexionen," SNTU 25 (2000): 98–140.

Simoens, Y., "L'évangile selon Jean. Positions et propositions," *NRT* 122 (2000): 177–90.

Smalley, S. S., "Keeping up with Recent Studies XII. St. John's Gospel," *ExpTim* 97 (1985–86): 102–108.

————, "The Johannine Literature. A Sample of Recent Studies in English," *Theology* 103 (2000): 13–28.

Smith, D. M., "Johannine Studies," in *The New Testament and Its Modern Interpreters* (eds. E. J. Epp and G. W. Macrae; Atlanta: Scholars, 1989), 271–96.

Thyen, H., "Aus der Literatur zum Johannesevangelium," *TRu* 39 (1974): 1–69, 222–52, 289–330; 42 (1977): 211–70; 43 (1978): 328–59; 44 (1979): 97–134.

Untergassmair, F. G., "Das Johannesevangelium. Ein Bericht über neuere Literatur aus der Johannesforschung," *TRev* 90 (1994): 91–108.

*Wagner, G., *An Exegetical Bibliography of the New Testament: John and 1, 2, 3 John* (Macon, GA: Mercer Press, 1987).

Walter, L., "Regards sur la recherche johannique. Deux ouvrages récents," *Esprit et Vie* 102 (1992): 215–20.

Ward, A. M., "The Fourth Gospel in Recent Study," *ExpTim* 81 (1969–70): 68–72.

COMMENTARIES AND GENERAL STUDIES

Anderson, P. N., *The Christology of the Fourth Gospel. Its Unity and Disunity in the Light of John 6* (Valley Forge: Trinity Press International, 1997).

Ashton, J., *Understanding the Fourth Gospel* (Oxford: Clarendon Press, 1991).

Bacon, B. W., *The Fourth Gospel in Research and Debate* (New York: Moffatt, 1910).

————, *The Gospel of the Hellenists* (New York: Holt, 1933).

Barclay, W. *The Gospel of John* (2nd ed.; 2 vols.; The Daily Study Bible; Philadelphia: Westminster Press, 1956).

Barrett, C. K., *The Gospel According to St. John* (2nd ed.; Philadelphia: Westminster Press, 1978).

Bauer, W. *Das Johannesevangelium erklärt* (HNT 6; Tübingen: J. C. B. Mohr [Paul Siebeck], 1933).

Beasley-Murray, G. R., *John* (WBC 36; Waco, TX: Word, 1989).

Becker, J., *Das Evangelium nach Johannes* (2 vols.; Ökumenischer Taschenbuchkommentar 4/1–2; Gütersloh/München: Mohn/Echter, 1979–1981).

Ball, D. M. *'I Am' in John's Gospel. Literary Function, Background and Theo-

logical Implications (JSNTSup 124; Sheffield: Sheffield Academic Press, 1996).

Bernard, J. H., *A Critical and Exegetical Commentary on the Gospel According to St. John* (ed. A. H. McNeile; 2 vols.; Edinburgh: T. & T. Clark, 1928).

Beutler, J. *Martyria: Traditionsgeschichtliche Untersuchungen zum Zeugnisthema bei Johannes* (FTS 10: Frankfurt: Josef Knecht, 1972).

Bittner, W. J., *Jesu Zeichen im Johannesevangelium: Die Messias- Erkenntnis im Johannesevangelium vor ihrem jüdischen Hintergrund* (WUNT 2.26; Tübingen: J. C. B. Mohr [Paul Siebeck], 1987).

Blank, J., *The Gospel according to John* (NT for Spiritual Reading; New York: Crossroad, 1981).

Boer, M. C., *Johannine Perspectives on the Death of Jesus* (CBET 17; Kampen: Kok Pharos, 1996).

Boismard, M.-É, and A. Lamouille, *L'Évangile de Jean. Commentaire* (SQE 3; Paris: Cerf, 1977).

Bouyer, L., *The Fourth Gospel* (Westminster, MD: Newman, 1964).

Braun, F.-M., *Jean le Théologien, 1: Jean le Théologien et son Évangile dans l'Église ancienne*, 1959; 2: *Les grandes traditions d'Israël*, 1964; 3: *Sa théologie: Le mystère de Jésus-Christ*, 1966 (Paris: Gabalda).

Brodie, T. L., *The Gospel According to John. A Literary and Theological Commentary* (New York: Oxford University Press, 1993).

Brown, R. E., *The Community of the Beloved Disciple. The Life, Loves, and Hates of an Individual Church in New Testament Times* (New York: Paulist Press, 1979).

Bühner, J.-A., *Der Gesandte und sein Weg im 4. Evangelium: Die kultur- und religionsgeschichtlichen Grundlagen der johanneischen Sendungschristologie sowie ihre traditionsgeschichtliche Entwicklung* (WUNT 2.2; Tübingen: J. C. B. Mohr [Paul Siebeck], 1977).

Bultmann, R., *The Gospel of John* (Philadelphia: Westminster Press, 1971). From the 18th German ed. of 1964, and the supplement of 1966. Original 1941.

Burge, G. M., *The Anointed Community. The Holy Spirit in the Johannine Community* (Grand Rapids: Eerdmans, 1987).

Carson, D. A., *The Gospel According to John* (Grand Rapids: Eerdmans, 1991).

Casey, M., *Is John's Gospel True?* (London: Routledge, 1996).

Cassidy, R. J., *John's Gospel in New Perspective. Christology and the Realities of Roman Power* (Maryknoll: Orbis, 1992).

Charlesworth, J. H., *The Beloved Disciple. Whose Witness Validates the Gospel of John?* (Valley Forge: Trinity Press International, 1995).

Cullmann, O., *Early Christian Worship* (SBT 10; London: SCM Press, 1953).

————, *The Johannine Circle: Its place in Judaism, among the disciples of Jesus and in early Christianity: A study in the origin of the Gospel of John* (London: SCM Press, 1976).

Culpepper, R. A., *Anatomy of the Fourth Gospel.* (New Testament Foundations and Facets; Philadelphia: Fortress Press, 1983).

————, *John, The Son of Zebedee. The Life of a Legend* (Studies on the Personalities of the New Testament; Columbia: University of South Carolina Press, 1994).

————, *The Johannine School: An Evaluation of the Johannine School Hypothesis Based on an Investigation of the Nature of Ancient Schools* (SBLDS 26; Missoula: Scholars Press, 1975).

Doohan, L., *John. Gospel for a New Age* (Santa Fe: Bear, 1988).

Dodd, C. H., *The Interpretation of the Fourth Gospel* (Cambridge: Cambridge University Press, 1953).

————, *Historical Tradition in the Fourth Gospel* (Cambridge: Cambridge University Press, 1963).

du Rand, J. A., *Johannine Perspectives* (Part 1; South Africa: Orion, 1991).

Ellis, P. F., *The Genius of John* (Collegeville: The Liturgical Press, 1984).

Ernst, J., *Johannes. Ein theologisches Portrait* (Düsseldorf: Patmos Verlag, 1991).

Fortna, R. T., *The Fourth Gospel and its Predecessor: From Narrative Source to Present Gospel* (Studies in the New Testament and its World; Edinburgh: T. & T. Clark, 1989).

————, *The Gospel of Signs: A Reconstruction of the Narrative Source Underlying the Fourth Gospel* (SNTSMS 11; Cambridge: Cambridge University Press, 1970).

Haenchen, E., *John* (2 vols.; Hermeneia; Philadelphia: Fortress Press, 1984).

Hanson, A. T., *The Prophetic Gospel. A Study of John and the Old Testament* (Edinburgh: T. & T. Clark, 1991).

Hengel, M. *Die johanneische Frage. Ein Lösungsversuch mit einem Beitrag zur Apokalypse von Jörg Frey* (WUNT 67; Tübingen: J. C. B. Mohr [Paul Siebeck], 1993).

————, *The Johannine Question* (London: SCM Press, 1989).

Hoskyns, E., *The Fourth Gospel,* (ed. F. N. Davey; 2nd ed.; London: Faber & Faber, 1947).

Käsemann, E., *The Testament of Jesus according to John 17* (London: SCM Press, 1966).

Keil, G., *Das Johannesevangelium. Ein philosophischer und theologischer Kommentar* (Göttingen: Vandenhoeck & Ruprecht, 1997).

Koester, C. R., *Symbolism in the Fourth Gospel. Meaning, Mystery, Community* (Minneapolis: Fortress Press, 1995).

Kysar, R., *John's Story of Jesus* (Philadelphia: Fortress Press, 1984).

———, *John* (Minneapolis: Augsburg Press, 1986).

———, *John the Maverick Gospel* (rev. ed.; Louisville: Westminster John Knox Press, 1993).

Lagrange, M.-J., *Évangile selon Saint Jean* (EB; 8th ed.; Paris: Gabalda, 1948).

Léon-Dufour, X., *Lecture de l'Évangile selon Jean* (4 vols.; Paris: Seuil, 1987–96).

Lightfoot, R. H., *St. John's Gospel* (ed. C. F. Evans; Oxford: Clarendon Press, 1956).

Lindars, B., *The Gospel of John* (New Century Bible; London: Oliphants, 1972).

Loisy, A., *Le Quatrième Évangile* (1st ed.; Paris: Picard, 1903; 2nd ed.; Paris: Nourry, 1921).

Macgregor, G. H. C., *The Gospel of John* (Moffatt Commentaries; New York: Doubleday, 1929).

Maier, G., *Johannes-Evangelium* (2 vols.; Neuhausen-Stuttgart: Hänssler, 1984).

Malina, B. J., and R. L. Rohrbaugh, *Social Science Commentary on the Gospel of John* (Minneapolis: Fortress Press, 1998).

Manns, F. *L'Evangile de Jean à la lumière du Judaïsme* (SBFLA 33; Jerusalem: Franciscan Printing Press, 1991).

Marrow, S. B., *The Gospel of John: A Reading* (New York: Paulist Press, 1995).

Marsh, J., *Saint John* (Harmondsworth: Penguin Books, 1968).

Martyn, J. L., *History and Theology in the Fourth Gospel* (2nd ed.; Nashville: Abingdon Press, 1979).

Mateos, J., and J. Barreto, *El Evangelio de Juan* (Madrid: Cristiandad, 1979).

Menken, M. J. J., *Old Testament Quotations in the Fourth Gospel. Studies in Textual Form* (CBET 15; Kampen: Kok Pharos, 1996).

Mlakuzhyil, G., *The Christocentric Literary Structure of the Fourth Gospel* (AnBib 117; Rome: Biblical Institute Press, 1987).

Mollat, D., *Introductio in exegesim scriptorum sancti Joannes* (Rome: Gregorian University, 1961).

Moloney, F. J., *Belief in the Word: Reading John 1–4* (Minneapolis: Fortress Press, 1993)

———, *Signs and Shadows: Reading John 5–12* (Minneapolis: Fortress Press, 1996)

———, *Glory not Dishonor: Reading John 13–21* (Minneapolis: Fortress Press, 1998)

———, *The Gospel of John* (Sacra Pagina 4; Collegeville: The Liturgical Press, 1998).

———, *The Johannine Son of Man* (2nd ed.; BSRel 14; Rome: LAS, 1978).

Morris, L. *The Gospel according to John* (Rev. ed.; New International Commentary on the New Testament; Grand Rapids: Eerdmans, 1995).

Neyrey, J. H., *An Ideology of Revolt: John's Christology in Social-Science Perspective* (Philadelphia: Fortress Press, 1988).

Obermann, A., *Die christologische Erfüllung der Schrift im Johannesevangelium. Eine Untersuchung zur johanneischen Hermeneutik anhand der Schriftzitate* (WUNT 2.83; Tübingen: J. C. B. Mohr [Paul Siebeck], 1996).

O'Day, G. R., "John," in *New Interpreter's Bible* (12 vols.; eds. L. E. Keck et al; Nashville: Abingdon Press, 1995), 9.493–865.

Painter, J., *The Quest for the Messiah* (2nd ed.; Edinburgh: T. & T. Clark, 1993).

Pancaro, S. A. *The Law in the Fourth Gospel: The Torah and the Gospel, Moses and Jesus, Judaism and Christianity according to John* (NovTSupp 42; Leiden: E. J. Brill, 1975).

Perkins, P., *The Gospel According to John* (Chicago: Franciscan Herald Press, 1978).

Petersen, N. R. *The Gospel of John and the Sociology of Light. Language and Characterization in the Fourth Gospel* (Valley Forge: Trinity Press International, 1993).

Potterie, I. de la, *La Verité dans Saint Jean* (2 vols.; AnBib 73–74; Rome: Biblical Institute Press, 1977).

Prete, B., *Vangelo secondo Giovanni* (Milano: Rizzoli, 1965).

Rensberger, D. K., *Johannine Faith and Liberating Community* (Philadelphia: Westminster Press, 1988).

Richardson, A., *The Gospel According to Saint John* (Torch Commentaries; London: SCM Press, 1959).

Ridderbos, H. N., *The Gospel according to John. A Theological Commentary* (Grand Rapids: Eerdmans, 1997).

Robinson, J. A. T., *The Priority of John* (London: SCM Press, 1985).

Sanders, J. N., and B. A. Mastin, *The Gospel According to St. John* (New York: Harper, 1968).

Schlatter, A., *Der Evangelist Johannes* (3rd ed.; Stuttgart: Calwer Verlag, 1960).

Schnackenburg, R., *The Gospel according to St. John/Das Johannesevangelium* (3 vols. in English; 4th vol. [Supl.] in German; 1968–82; 1984; New York: Crossroad; Freiburg: Herder).

Schneider, J., *Das Evangelium nach Johannes* (Berlin: Evangelische Verlagsanstalt, 1976).

Schnelle, U., *Antidocetic Christology in the Gospel of John: An Investigation of the Place of the Fourth Gospel in the Johannine School* (Minneapolis: Fortress Press, 1992).

————, *Das Evangelium nach Johannes* (THKNT 4; Leipzig: Evangelische Verlagsanstalt, 1998).

Scholtissek, K., *In Ihm Sein und Bleiben. Die Sprache der Immanenz in den johanneischen Schriften* (Herders biblische Studien 21; Freiburg: Herder, 2000).

Schuchard, B. G., *Scripture within Scripture. The Interrelationship of Form and Function in the Explicit Old Testament Citations in the Gospel of John* (SBLDS 133; Atlanta: Scholars Press, 1992).

Schulz, S., *Das Evangelium nach Johannes* (12th ed.; Neue Testament Deutsch 4; Göttingen: Vandenhoeck & Ruprecht, 1972).

Schwank, B., *Evangelium nach Johannes* (St. Ottilien: Eos, 1996).

Scott, M., *Sophia and the Johannine Jesus* (JSNTSup 7; Sheffield: JSOT Press, 1992).

Segalla, G., *Giovanni* (Nuovissima Versione della Bibbia; Rome: Edizioni Paoline, 1976).

Simoens, Y., *Selon Jean* (3 vols.; Collection IET 17; Brussels: Institut d'Études Théologiques, 1997).

Smalley, S.S., *John—Evangelist and Interpreter* (2nd ed; Carlisle, UK: Paternoster Press, 1998).

Smith, D. M., *John* (Proclamation Commentaries; Philadelphia: Fortress Press, 1986).

————, *The Theology of the Gospel of John* (New Testament Theology; Cambridge: Cambridge University Press, 1995).

Stibbe, M. W. G., *John* (Readings: A New Biblical Commentary; Sheffield: JSOT Press, 1993).

————, *John as storyteller: narrative criticism and the Fourth Gospel* (SNTSMS 73; Cambridge: Cambridge University Press, 1994).

Strachan, R. H., *The Fourth Gospel: Its Significance and Environment* (3rd ed.; London: SCM Press, 1941).

Strathmann, H., *Das Evangelium nach Johannes* (10th ed.; Neue Testament Deutsch, Göttingen: Vandenhoeck & Ruprecht, 1963).

Talbert, C. H., *Reading John. A Literary and Theological Commentary on the Fourth Gospel and the Johannine Epistles* (London: SPCK, 1992).

Tasker, R.V.G., *Gospel according to St. John* (New ed.; London: Tyndale, 1971).

van den Bussche, H., *L'Évangile du Verbe* (2 vols.; Brussels: Pensée Catholique, 1959–1961).

————, *Jean: Commentaire de l'Évangile Spirituel* (Bruges: Desclée de Brouwer, 1967).

Vouga, F., *Le cadre historique et l'intention théologique de Jean* (Paris: Beauchesne, 1977).

Wengst, K., *Bedrängte Gemeinde und Verherrlichter Christus: Der historischer Ort des Johannesevangeliums als Schlüssel zu seiner Interpretation* (2nd ed.; BThSt 5; Neukirchen-Vluyn: Neukirchener Verlag, 1983).

Westcott, B. F., *The Gospel According to St. John* (Reissued by A. Fox; London: Clarke, 1958). Original 1880.

Wikenhauser, A., *Das Evangelium nach Johannes* (2nd ed.; Regensburg: Pustet, 1957).

Wilckens, U., *Das Evangelium nach Johannes* (NTD 4; Göttingen: Vandenhoeck & Ruprecht, 1998).

Witherington, B., III, *John's Wisdom: A Commentary* (Louisville: Westminster John Knox Press, 1995).

Zumstein, J., *Kreative Erinnerung. Relecture und Auslegung im Johannesevangelium* (Zürich: Pano Verlag, 1999).

ESSAY COLLECTIONS

Ashton, J., *The Interpretation of John* (2nd ed.; Edinburgh: T. & T. Clark, 1997).

————, *Studying John. Approaches to the Fourth Gospel* (Oxford: Clarendon, 1994).

Barrett, C. K., *Essays on John* (Philadelphia: Westminster Press, 1982).

Beutler, J., *Studien zu den johanneischen Schriften* (Stuttgart: KBW, 1998).

Borgen, P., *Logos was the True Light and Other Essays on the Gospel of John* (Relieff 9; Trondheim: Tapir, 1983). Of the eleven essays, seven were reprinted in his *Philo, John and Paul* (Brown Judaic Studies 131; Atlanta: Scholars Press, 1987).

Braun, F.-M., *L'Évangile de Jean* (Recherches Bibliques 3; Bruges: Desclée de Brouwer, 1958).

Collins, R. F., *These Things Have Been Written: Studies on the Fourth Gospel* (Louvain Theological and Pastoral Monographs 2; Louvain: Peeters, 1990).

Chicago Studies 37 (1998): 5–57: *John: A Gospel for Today's Church.*

Cross, F. L., ed., *Studies in the Fourth Gospel* (London: Mowbray, 1957).

Culpepper, R. A., and C. C. Black, eds., *Exploring the Gospel of John. In Honor of D. Moody Smith* (Louisville: Westminster John Knox Press, 1996).

Culpepper, R. A and F. F. Segovia, eds., *The Fourth Gospel from a Literary Perspective* (Semeia 53: Atlanta: Scholars Press, 1991).

Feuillet, A., *Johannine Studies* (Staten Island, NY: Alba House, 1964).

Hartman, L., and B. Olsson, eds., *Aspects on the Johannine Literature* (ConBNT 18; Stockholm: Almqvist & Wiksell, 1987).

Jonge, M. de, *Jesus, Stranger from Heaven and Son of God* (Missoula, MT: Scholars Press, 1977).

————, ed., *L'Évangile de Jean. Sources, rédaction, théologie* (BETL 44; Gembloux: Duculot, 1977).

Kaestli, J.-D., J.-M. Poffet, and J. Zumstein, eds., *La communauté johannique et son histoire* (Geneva: Labor et Fides, 1990).

Lindars, B., *Essays on John* (ed. C. M. Tuckett; Leuven: Peeters, 1992).

Marchadour, A., ed., *Origine et posterité de l'Évangile de Jean* (LD 143; Paris: Cerf, 1990).

Martyn, J. L., *The Gospel of John in Christian History. Essays for Interpreters* (New York: Paulist Press, 1978).

Moloney, F. J., *"A Hard Saying." The Gospel and Culture* (Collegeville: The Liturgical Press, 2001), 107–180.

Morris, L., *Studies in the Fourth Gospel* (Grand Rapids: Eerdmans, 1969).

Neirynck, F., *Evangelica II* (BETL 99; Leuven: Peeters, 1991), 571–711.

Nissen, J. and S. Pedersen, eds., *New Readings in John. Literary and Theological Perspectives: Essays from the Scandinavian Conference on the Fourth Gospel: Århus 1997* (JSNTSup 182; Sheffield: Sheffield Academic Press, 1999).

Orton, D. E., ed., *The Composition of John's Gospel. Selected Studies from Novum Testamentum* (Leiden: E. J. Brill, 1999).

Porter, S. E., and C. A. Evans, eds. *The Johannine Writings* (Sheffield: Sheffield Academic Press, 1995).

Priest, J. E., ed., *Johannine Studies. Essays in Honor of Frank Pack* (Malibu CA: Pepperdine University Press, 1989).

Richter, G., *Studien zum Johannesevangelium* (ed. J. Hainz; Regensburg: Pustet, 1977).

Rose, M., *Johannes-Studien. Interdisziplinäre Zugänge zum Johannes-Evangelium. Freundesgabe der Theologischen Fakultät der Universität Neuchâtel für Jean Zumstein* (Zurich: Theologischer Verlag, 1991).

Segovia, F. F., *"What is John?" Readers and Readings of the Fourth Gospel* (SBLSymS 3; Atlanta: Scholars Press, 1996).

————, *"What is John?" Volume II. Literary and Social Readings of the Fourth Gospel* (SBLSymS 7; Atlanta: Scholars Press, 1998).

Smith, D. M., *Johannine Christianity: Essays on Its Setting, Sources, and Theology* (Columbia: University of South Carolina, 1984).

Stibbe, M. W. G., ed., *The Gospel of John as Literature. An Anthology of Twentieth Century Perspectives* (New Testament Tools and Studies 17; Leiden: E. J. Brill, 1993).

Studies in John: Presented to Professor Dr. J. N. Sevenster on the Occasion of His Seventieth Birthday (NovTSup 24; Leiden: E. J. Brill, 1970).

1

An Overview of
Johannine Studies

◆

CHRISTIANITY HAS ENTERED a third millennium, supplying an apt context for reflection on how in its history it has treated one of its principal foundational documents. While this Gospel was known throughout most of the second century, it is noteworthy that the earliest preserved commentaries on John were by Gnostic Christians who would later be classified as heretics. A major contribution of the work that Irenaeus, bishop of Lyons, began writing ca. 180 against the Gnostic heretics was to clarify the orthodoxy of this Gospel (often by appealing to the First Epistle of John for non-Gnostic readings of Johannine thought) and its pedigree as having come from an eyewitness of Jesus' ministry—one whom Irenaeus identifies as John the (beloved) disciple who had reclined on Jesus' breast during the Last Supper. The next centuries saw substantial commentaries on John by Origen and Chrysostom in the East, and by Augustine in the West. The Church Fathers were particularly perceptive about John since often they were well attuned to its symbolism. The "high Christology" of the Gospel that stressed Jesus' divinity and its personal portrayal of the Spirit as the Paraclete won for John prominence in the debates over the Trinity. Medieval theologians and mystics drew special inspiration from this evangelist known as "John the divine [*ho theologos* = the theologian]" and from his work, which Clement of Alexandria dubbed as "the spiritual Gospel." Sacramental debates both before and after the Reformation drew on statements in chs. 3 and 6: "born/begotten of water and Spirit" (3:5); "My flesh is true food, and my blood, true drink" (6:55); "It is the Spirit that gives life; the flesh is useless" (6:63).

Because it was thought to stem from the closest of Jesus' companions, the Fourth Gospel, with its three Passovers and numerous journeys back and forth from Galilee or the Transjordan to Jerusalem, most often supplied the historical and chronological framework for studies of the life of Jesus. Yet, as early as the second century the sharp differences of John from the Synoptic Gospels caused some to reject John. At the end of the eighteenth century and throughout the nineteenth century, the historical issues posed by these differences were the subject of far more skeptical treatment. By the beginning of the twentieth century, radical scholars had knocked John from its pedestal of prominence as the most reliable Gospel and cast it down to the level of the least reliable with nothing historical to contribute. Similarly "John the divine" lost his halo when the rationalist preference for a totally human depiction of Jesus dismissed John's emphasis on the divine Word-made-flesh as fanciful deification. Not all who examined John by the historical criteria applied to other books went that far, but the overall thrust of what were then new forms of investigation were skeptical, much to the discontent of churches that used John as a major component in theology, spirituality, and liturgy.

By the first part of the twentieth century many critical scholars, centrist as well as radical, had given up the idea that the Fourth Gospel was written by John son of Zebedee,[1] and recognized that the Gospel as it

---

1. *Editor's Note:* The tradition that the Fourth Gospel is the work of John, the Son of Zebedee had its defenders throughout this period (e.g., Westcott, W. Sanday. *The Criticism of the Fourth Gospel. Eight Lectures on the Morse Foundation, delivered in the Union Seminary, New York in October and November, 1904* [Oxford: Clarendon Press, 1912]; J. Donovan, *The Authorship of the Fourth Gospel* [ed. E. F. Sutcliffe; London: Burns Oates & Washbourne, 1936]). See, however, the powerful rejection of Sanday's claims by Bacon, *The Fourth Gospel in Research and Debate.* However modified to cater to the literary and theological issues raised above, authorship by John, the son of Zebedee, still receives energetic support (e.g., Morris, Barclay, Carson, Ridderbos).

now exists is a good distance removed from the theological atmosphere of the ministry of Jesus. The main concern was how such a Gospel came into being. Various source theories flourished—sometimes sources akin to those postulated for the Synoptic Gospels, sometimes unauthentic sources (fabricated miracle collection, Greco-Roman syncretistic religious poetry, partially colored by Jewish components). The unity of Johannine thought dissolved as scholars saw in the aporias (inconsistencies, lacks of sequence) the sign of competing hands. The religious background of the writers (sources and/or Gospel) was sought in Philonic Alexandrian thought, Greco-Roman neoplatonism, Gnosticism, or even Hinduism or Buddhism. Increasingly a date well into the second century was assigned to the Gospel. Representing a wide range of views, German-speaking scholarship was particularly fruitful in the twentieth century, e.g., Bultmann, Käsemann, Haenchen, Schnackenburg, Becker, Schneider, Schwank, Schulz, and Thüsing. More consistently centrist in their approach to John, scholars in the United Kingdom produced a remarkable series of commentaries and studies, e.g., Westcott, Bernard, Hoskyns, Barrett, Dodd, R. H. Lightfoot, J. N. Sanders, and Lindars. While applying increasingly sophisticated judgmental criteria, most often they recognized substantial historical and theological content in John, thus keeping it vital as a font of spiritual and liturgical growth.

A series of discoveries in the decades of the 1930s through the 1960s made centrism more plausible. Papyri of John written in the second century militated against a very late dating. The DSS found at Qumran showed that Hebrew- and Aramaic-speaking Jews in Palestine shared vocabulary and thought patterns similar to those of John, thus reopening the plausibility that the Gospel's tradition originated in the Palestine area. Greater attention was paid to disputes, dramatis personae, and places in the Gospel; and again many of those indicated favored the Jewish world of Palestine in the first century, so that theories of dependence on Greco-Roman or Philonian philosophy have waned. Indeed, a number of scholars with different approaches thought they could detect the history of a community of Christians that would make sense of John's outlook—a community stemming from disciples of Jesus (and previously of JBap), who were Judeans and hence different from the Galilean main body of the Twelve, and whose particular missionary activity (e.g., among Samaritans) and struggles with the leaders in the synagogues shaped their thought in a way different from many other Christians.[2] The discovery of fourth-century A.D. Coptic treatises in Egypt, many of them translations of second—century Gnostic Greek writings, greatly increased our knowledge of Gnosticism. Some who were already inclined to find in John a Gnostic background have claimed to detect parallel developments of thought in John and several of these treatises; but were John to have been found among them, it would stand out as uniquely different in its subject matter and style of narration. Scholars debate whether or not the Johannine writer(s) drew on the Synoptic Gospels, but it stands far closer to them than to any of the Coptic documents from Egypt.

In the last part of the twentieth century the burgeoning application of new hermeneutical approaches to the NT affected the interpretation of John. Sometimes extravagant claims have been made for these new approaches as if they supplied messianic deliverance from a barren past totally concerned with sources and reconstructions. But when seen as complementary enrichment rather than rejection or cataclysmic replacement, these approaches have filled out Johannine study in a fascinating way. Throughout the twentieth century more and more attention was paid to John's writing technique with its artistic misunderstandings, double meanings, and poetic structures; rhetorical criticism has made that study more systematic so that the evangelist's dramatic skills in characterization have been newly appreciated as means of reaching out to his readers/hearers of all times, drawing them into contact with Jesus as the source of life. Many past practitioners of what is described without necessary distinction (or even dismissed) as historical criticism made a conscious effort to distinguish between the prehistory of the Gospel and the final product, recognizing that only the latter actually exists before our eyes and therefore it is the primary duty of the commentator to interpret that.[3] Fascination with reconstructing exactly John's sources still continues, but many doubts have been raised about the surety of diagnostic method and the theological relation of the sources to the goal stated in

---

2. On theories concerning the history of the Johannine community, see below, pp. 69–76.

3. *Editor's Note:* For a presentation of the increasingly widespread narrative approaches to the Gospel, see the Excursus ("Narrative Approaches") below, pp. 30–39.

the extant Gospel. Various literary critical studies are bringing the scales of interpretation back to a better balance by emphasizing the importance of following the logic of the text itself. For instance, contrary views are not seen primarily as an indication of different origins or as changing community outlook but as a deliberately inclusive technique. Reader-response criticism has emphasized that, once written, the Gospel has a life of its own, so that fresh meaning is achieved by the interaction of a text and new generations of readers—meaning that should have some relation to what was intended by the original author.[4]

All this points to ever-enriching Johannine research. I hope that this second edition of my *Introduction to the Gospel of John,* enriched by another third of a century of research from writers of all schools since the first edition, will prepare new readers to appreciate the wealth of John.[5] In the first edition of his great commentary (1955), C. K. Barrett characterized the fourth evangelist as "perhaps the greatest theologian in the history of the church." More cautiously in his second edition (1978), he rephrased: "perhaps, after Paul, the greatest theologian in the history of the church." But Paul was known as *ho apostolos* "the apostle"; of the NT authors only John was known as *ho theologos.* I would contend that, properly evaluated, the twentieth century has not weakened John's right to be called par excellence *"the* theologian," nay even "the divine."

Excursus: Narrative Approaches to the Fourth Gospel[6]

A FEATURE OF THIS NEW INTRODUCTION to the Gospel of John from Brown is his insistence upon the importance of interpreting the text as it

---

4. *Editor's Note:* For a comprehensive survey of the many newer approaches to the Fourth Gospel, see the two articles of Scholtissek, "Johannes auslegen I," and "Johannes auslegen II" in the General Bibliography. See also the brief description of the processes of *Relecture* and *Ré-édition* in Chapter 8, pp. 291–92.

5. *Editor's Note:* Brown's original text made reference to a second edition of his commentary. This has been modified, but I trust his hope that what is reproduced in this volume will "prepare new readers to appreciate the wealth of John" will be realized.

6. The following excursus is entirely the work of the Editor. See also Moloney, *John,* 13–20. For more detailed reflections, see Moloney, "Narrative Criticism of the

finally came down to us. Contemporary narrative criticism, starting from that presupposition, claims that it is possible to identify a strong narrative unity across the Fourth Gospel. In assessing that narrative unity, however, the world behind the text must never be lost from view, but narrative critics concentrate upon the world in the text, attempting to show how the story has been designed and told in order to influence the world in front of the text.[7] Biblical scholarship has gradually come to appreciate more fully that there are more than two "worlds" involved in the interpretation of an ancient text. Historical-critical scholarship has devoted almost 200 years to the rediscovery of the *world behind the text,* so that there be no abuse of the *world in the text.* Contemporary critics are devoting more attention to the world *in front of the text* as there is now a greater interest in approaching each single document, however limited and flawed it might be, as a work of art.[8]

Contemporary Gospel studies are showing an increasing interest in what has come to be known as narrative criticism. Adapting and applying theories of narrative developed by literary theorists, Old Testament scholars were the first to seize upon this possible approach, given the large amount of narrative text found within the pages of the Bible. New Testament critics have not been slow to follow.[9] Behind each "story" there

---

Gospels," in *"A Hard Saying,"* 85–105. See also the studies of Culpepper and Stibbe and the three-volume narrative commentary by Moloney (*Belief in the Word, Signs and Shadows, Glory not Dishonor*) in the General Bibliography.

7. Brown, along with many of his contemporaries, who have worked so hard—often against heavy opposition from fundamentalist Christians—were concerned that the undeniable achievements of their scholarship was being disregarded by the contemporary interest in the narrative as such. This explains his caustic remark, recorded above: "Sometimes extravagant claims have been made for these new approaches as if they supplied messianic deliverance from a barren past totally concerned with sources and reconstructions." This happens when narrative critics refuse to ask or answer historical questions. What follows will indicate that the achievements of historical-critical scholarship are an essential part of sound narrative critical approaches to the Fourth Gospel. Brown himself recognizes this as he comments, "But when seen as complementary enrichment rather than rejection or cataclysmic replacement, these approaches have filled out Johannine study in a fascinating way."

8. See S. M. Schneiders, *Interpreting the New Testament as Sacred Scripture* (2nd ed.; Collegeville: The Liturgical Press, 1999).

9. On the Fourth Gospel, see Culpepper, *Anatomy;* Moloney, *Belief in the Word* 1–22; Stibbe, *John as storyteller.*

is a *real author* who has a definite person or group of people in mind as he or she tells the story. Thus, there is an intended *real reader*. Neither of these figures can be found *in* the story itself. One produces it and the other takes it in hand to read it, or listens to it. An author constructs a narrative as a means to communicate a message to an audience. The Fourth Gospel is one such writing, but it is something more. The real author, whoever he (or she) might have been, is long since dead, as are the original recipients of the book. However, the Gospel still has a widespread readership. There is something about this book that has generated interested readers for almost 2,000 years.

Although the real author and the real reader(s) do not play an active role in the events of the narrative, they leave their traces. Narratives have deliberately contrived plots and characters that interact throughout the story along a certain time line, through a sequence of events. An author devises certain rhetorical features to hold plot and character together so that the reader will not miss the author's point of view. These rhetorical features are *in* the narrative. Although narrative theoreticians dispute the exactness of the scheme, one can broadly claim that the communication between a real author and a real reader who are *outside* the text takes place through an implied author, a narrator, a narratee and an implied reader who are *inside* the text. However obscure the details of the concrete situations of the original real author and the original real reader(s) may be, we still have the text, and much can be gleaned from it. This language may sound overly complex, but it reflects everyone's reading experience. Whether or not one knows who the historical author is or was, and whether or not a story was directed specifically to the reader who has it in hand, any reader senses the presence of a storyteller, called throughout this commentary "the narrator," and behind the narrator hides an author who is directing affairs. A lost letter picked up by a disinterested third party quickly tells the reader something of the person writing the letter. The rhetoric of the letter also reveals something of the author's understanding of and approach to the reader. The person who has found the letter knows neither the real author nor the original intended reader, but the real reader—the person who picked up the letter from the pavement—is able to identify the communication attempted by the letter. The person who found the letter traces an author "implied" and a reader "implied" by the letter. Indeed, a very beautiful letter may even move the "eavesdropper." When that happens, a mutuality is established between the reader "implied" by the letter and the real reader of the letter. One does not have to be part of the original communication process between the original writer of the letter and its original reader to be moved and inspired by the power of the emotions expressed by the letter. The literary form of a letter is very different from the sometimes complex literary shape of a narrative, especially one that was written almost 2,000 years ago. However, the process of communication between an author and a reader takes place in both. Contemporary narrative approaches to the Gospels attempt to enter into the process of communication between an author and a reader whom we do not know, and who are long since dead, so that the contemporary reader might be moved and inspired by the passionate convictions of the author.

Not ignoring historical questions that lie "behind" the text of the Gospel, narrative critics focus upon the literary features found in the narrative of the Fourth Gospel. Much attention is given to the literary shape of each section of the story; the way each section follows logically from what went before and leads directly into what follows; the roles of the various characters in the story; the passing of time; unresolved puzzles that emerge, forcing the reader to look further into the narrative to tie these puzzles together; the consistency of the underlying point of view of an author who has shaped and told a story of the life of Jesus in a way unparalleled by any other early Christian writing. Like the reader who "eavesdropped" on the letter found on the pavement, and was moved by the sincerity and power of the emotions communicated by the letter, we are "eavesdropping" on an ancient story of Jesus. "Eavesdropping" on this particular story, however, has been going on for some time, and it has served as an inspiration for Christians from all walks of life for almost 2,000 years. Via the literary features of the storytelling, narrative critics trace the communication taking place *in the narrative* between an author and a reader.

We must allow ourselves to be seduced by the perspective of the author—but which author? It is possible for an author to write a narrative that communicates a point of view that is not a reflection of his or her own situation in life, humor, personality, or personal experience. As George Steiner has correctly remarked: "Aristophanes may, at heart, have been the saddest of men—the which proposal is itself a piece of romanticised inversion. Our persuasion that some deep turbulence of spirit and sexuality attended the composition of *King Lear* and *Timon of Athens* may be nothing but trivial rationalisation. We have no shred of evidence either way." [10] There is, therefore, an author *in the text* of the Fourth Gospel, just as there was an author *in the text* of the letter described above. Whatever the perspective of a historical flesh-and-blood author may have been, we can only claim to trace the theological point of view of an author in the text itself. Such an author is generally called *the implied author*. This feature of any narrative is not a historical person, however well the point of view may or may not reflect the choices of that figure from the past who should be called *the real author*. Unlike some contemporary narratives, it can generally be assumed (but never proved) that the real author *of* and the implied author *in* New Testament narratives speak with the same voice. It is difficult to imagine that such a passionate book as the Fourth Gospel is anything but the communication of a historical person's deeply held and passionate belief in what God has done in and through Jesus.

Like the historical author of the book, now long since dead and beyond our knowledge and scientific control, the flesh-and-blood historical first real readers are outside our control. We cannot be sure of the reception that this passionate story of Jesus received. The ongoing existence of the Gospel demonstrates that it was received, treasured, and passed on, but the evidence of the Johannine Letters indicates that the readers did not always agree on what the author wanted to communicate. Indeed, they quickly broke into argument, and even division, over the christological and Christian significance of the Gospel. This is understandable. How I might respond to a narrative in any of the Gospels may vary from day to day, depending on any number of circumstances. We are well aware of the numerous circumstances that affect, for better or worse, the reading process. Yet, *within the narrative* there is a reader addressed by the implied author, as there was an identifiable reader implied by the letter described above. As the narrative unfolds, the reader is gradually provided with information and experiences that such a reader cannot avoid. This reader is shaped by the desires of the author and emerges as the text unfolds. This reader does not suffer from the vagaries that can impinge upon the reading process. Critics speak of a literary construct within the narrative itself, whose responses are totally controlled by the implied au-

---

10. G. Steiner, *Real Presences. Is there anything* in *what we say?* (London: Faber & Faber, 1989), 169.

thor. Such a "reader" is generally called *the implied reader.* The implied reader is not a historical person. Historically there are only real readers. The implied reader is produced by the unfolding narrative. By tracing the developing knowledge and experience of the implied reader as each page of the text is opened, I am better able to appreciate the temporal flow of the narrative and grow in my appreciation of the unfolding narrative. Stanley Fish has described the use of the implied reader by a narrative critic as follows:

> The basis of the method is a consideration of the *temporal* flow of the reading experience, and it is assumed that the reader responds in terms of that flow and not to the whole utterance. That is, in an utterance of any length, there is a point at which the reader has taken in only the first word, and then the second, and then the third, and so on, and the report of what happens to the reader is always a report of what happened *to that point.*" [11]

As each page of the Fourth Gospel is opened, much is learnt about Jesus and the Father who sent him, but there is still more to learn from those parts of the story that lie ahead. Only when the author has signed off from the telling of the story (cf. 20:30–31) does the reader come to rest. But the citation from Fish needs expansion, as it does not fully exhaust the experience of the readers of ancient, canonical texts like the Fourth Gospel. The reader gradually emerges from the unfolding narrative, shaped by the author, knowing only what has been read so far, and the reader is able to move backward to recall events already narrated. But it is impossible that the reader in a Christian Gospel has no knowledge or experience of the story of Jesus of Nazareth and Christian life and its practices. The direct importation of literary scholarship into New Testament studies has sometimes presupposed such a "virginal" reader, but this is unrealistic. The author of the Fourth Gospel takes it for granted that the reader knows many things already. The implied reader knows Greek!

The reader in the Fourth Gospel is able to understand double meanings behind Greek words (e.g., 3:3–5, 14; 8:28; 12:32), subtle ironies (e.g., 9:28–29; 19:14–15) and language that was used in the sacramental life of

---

11. S. Fish, *Is There a Text in This Class? The Authority of Interpretative Communities* (Cambridge: Harvard University Press, 1988), 26–27.

the community (3:3, 5; 6:51–58; 19:35). References to Jesus' resurrection are taken as understood from quite early in the story (cf. 2:22). Much more than a knowledge of the syntactically correct and simple Greek of the text of the Fourth Gospel (cf. Barrett, *St. John*, 5–11) is presupposed of its reader. The unexplained use of certain Jewish messianic categories (e.g., 1:19–51), religious customs (e.g., 2:6; 5:9; 6:4; 7:2; 10:22) and the geography of Palestine (e.g. 5:2; 18:1; 19:17) indicates that such things are taken as known. The reader knows everything that the author does not explain. The reader in the Fourth Gospel story may be credited with a knowledge of the Jesus story, but its Johannine form is being presented to bring the reader (or listener) to accept a particular point of view. The reader knows that Jesus died on a cross, but the author of this Gospel insists that this death is both a "lifting up" (cf. 3:14; 8:28; 12:32) and a glorification (11:4; 12:23). Indeed, on two occasions the author of the Fourth Gospel does not hesitate to tell the reader why the story is being written in this particular way (19:35; 20:30–31).

But one must recognize that every word of the Gospel is historically and culturally conditioned. The fact that it is written in koiné Greek is prima facie evidence of this truth. There is inevitably something "strange" and "foreign" about the biblical text which demands that we wrestle with it. First-century history and culture must play a part in interpretation. The Fourth Gospel, like all biblical texts handed down to us by Jewish and Christian tradition, is a difficult text, and a great deal of this difficulty comes from its strangeness when read in our present cultural context. The original readers of the Gospel are an important point of reference in following the interplay between author and reader in the text. Adela Yarbro Collins has rightly insisted that we:

> give more weight to the original historical context of the text. This context cannot and should not totally determine all subsequent meaning and use of the text. But if . . . all meaning is context bound, the original context and meaning have a certain normative character. I suggest that Biblical theologians are not only mediators between genres. They are also mediators between historical periods. . . . Whatever tension there may be between literary- and historical-critical methods, the two approaches are complementary.[12]

---

12. A. Yarbro-Collins, "Narrative, History and Gospel," *Semeia* 43 (1988): 150, 153.

Every narrative generates a reader as it unfolds, but it would be a mistake to think that one has performed one's task of interpretation once one has traced the temporal flow of a narrative through the experience of an emerging reader. Such a use of literary techniques will still only tell us how an author achieves an effect. But there are other elements that must be kept in mind for a sound, critical reading of an ancient, normative text. The world behind the *text* must be respected and studied, in order to understand its strange distance from our world and our concerns, and despite Brown's interest in the final form of the Gospel, his *Introduction* remains a fresh and fascinating analysis of that world.[13] But a narrative approach also asks: how does the reader *in the text* who emerges as this ancient story of Jesus unfolds speak to the knowledge and experience of the twenty-first-century Christian reader *of the text?* There is a context that unites the original and all subsequent readers of the Gospel of John: a context generated by Christian faith, a community of believing readers. The secret of the lasting value of a narrative lies in the mutuality that is created between the implied reader *in the text* and the real reader *of the text,* and the common context of Christian belief helps this mutuality. A story that tells of Jesus the Christ should appeal to Christians. Nevertheless, there are libraries of Christian books that have not! What is it in the Fourth Gospel that has generated its ongoing readership? There must be an understanding and respect for the world behind the text, which shaped the reader *in the text,* but there is more. When I read a good novel for the first time, I become the implied reader. I become part of the story, caught in its characters, events, time and places as the pages turn. This is the case with any good book, but in a classic there is an even deeper relationship between the reader in the text and the reader of the text. It is the mutuality generated between the implied reader *in the text* and the real reader *of the text* which makes any given text a classic. As David Tracy has said: "The classic text's real disclosure is its claim to attention on the

---

13. Closely associated with the recent trend toward a more *synchronic* reading of the Johannine text, but devoting important attention to the *diachronic* questions of changing situations in the original context that produced that text, are the more recent interpretative paradigms of *relecture* and *réécriture.* For a summary, see below, pp. 391–92. See also, for a fuller description, K. Scholtissek, *In ihm sein und bleiben. Die Sprache der Immanenz in den johanneischen Schriften* (Herders Biblische Studien 21; Freiburg: Herder, 2000), 131–39.

ground that an event of understanding proper to finite human beings has here found expression."[14]

The practice of reading and the community of readers that have produced the Bible is an example of that truth. The Fourth Gospel can lay claim to being a Christian classic. As we continue to read the Fourth Gospel after nearly 2,000 years of reading, in a variety of contexts, we can be sure that there has been a mutuality between its implied and real readers. The unfolding narrative of the Fourth Gospel raises problems that the reader will solve through the ongoing reading of the story of Jesus. Did these solutions speak to the members of the Johannine community, the original intended readers who were part of the world of the narrative of the Gospels in a way that the contemporary real reader can never be? They read Greek, or at least understood it as it was read; they caught the subtleties of double meanings and ironies. None of this can be taken for granted for most contemporary readers of the Fourth Gospel. Do the questions raised and the solutions offered by this story of Jesus still speak to real readers at the beginning of the third millennium? Is this text a classic? Does its ongoing claim to a readership rest upon "the ground that an event of understanding proper to human beings has here found expression" (Tracy)? Narrative critical *theory* rightly distinguishes between an implied reader who emerges from the unfolding narration, the intended reader, for whom the narrative was originally written (for whom it was originally "intended" by a real author), and the real reader, whoever, wherever and whenever he or she may take the text in hand. Reading *practice* does not make such neat distinctions. Our experience of reading is that some stories speak to us, while others do not.

Although Brown never managed to complete his commentary upon the text, he shows in his new *Introduction* that he is convinced that readers at the turn of the second and third millennia still find that their response to this Gospel, in dialogue with the experience of almost 2,000 years of Christian life, resonates with the experience of the implied reader and the original readers in the Johannine community. There is a further aspect to contemporary narrative and reader-response approaches to the Gospel of John which Brown mentions, but does not attempt to involve in his *Introduction*. Nor should he! Sometimes we may

---

14. D. Tracy, *The Analogical Imagination: Christian Theology and the Culture of Pluralism* (New York: Crossroad, 1981), 102.

have a further response that is independent of the implied reader, and thus outside the control of the author. It is unavoidable that our response, either of empathy or antipathy, will be the result of our privileged position as the recipients of almost 2,000 years of the Christian practice of reading the Gospels. As Honoré de Balzac's narrator informs his implied reader at the beginning of *Père Goriot:* "You may be certain that this drama is neither fiction nor romance. *All is true,* so true that everyone can recognise the elements of the tragedy in his own household, in his own heart perhaps."[15]

The Johannine story of the life, teaching, death and resurrection of Jesus is told in a way that touches the reader's experience. Two thousand years of Christian history are a fair indication that generation after generation of Christian readers have "entered the fictional contract" of the Fourth Gospel; they have become one with the implied reader.[16] But Brown has provided a new Introduction to the Fourth Gospel that rounds off decades of masterly concern with the world behind and in the Johannine text. There is a theoretical distinction between various elements that combine to form a satisfactory reading experience, and a contemporary interpreter attempts to create a meeting of horizons among the worlds behind the text, in the text, and in front of the text. Traditional critical scholarship and a contemporary literary approach are combined to create a space where a satisfied Christian reader is born. Brown's firm grip and clear exposition of the worlds *behind and in the text* will serve a new generation of scholars and readers *in front of the text* each time they turn to the Gospel of John.

---

15. H. de Balzac, *Old Goriot* (Penguin Classics; Harmondsworth: Penguin Books, 1951), 28. Stress in original.

16. See S. Chatman, *Story and Discourse. Narrative Structure in Fiction and Film* (New York: Ithaca, 1978), 150.

2

The Unity and Composition

of the Fourth Gospel

❖

The Problem

Is THE FOURTH GOSPEL as it now stands the work of one person?[1] The solution commonly accepted before the advent of biblical criticism was that this Gospel was the work of John son of Zebedee, written shortly before his death. I shall discuss the identity of the author in the section devoted to this issue below;[2] but even if we lay aside the question of identity, there are features in the Gospel that offer difficulty for any theory of unified authorship. Too often, as Teeple has pointed out, difficulties have been created by not respecting the intention of the author, so that complicated hypotheses have been constructed where simple explanations were available.[3] Still, making every allowance for that, scholars find these major difficulties:

First, there are differences of Greek style in the Gospel. I refer the

---

1. I shall exclude from this discussion the Story of the Adulteress in 7:53–8:11, not found in the earliest Greek witnesses. See *John*, 335–36.

2. See Chapter Six.

3. Teeple, "Methodology."

reader to my original (1970) discussion of ch. 21. The passage differs from the rest of the Gospel in small stylistic details that betray difference of authorship.[4] The Prologue is written in a carefully constructed, interlocking poetic pattern found but rarely in the Gospel proper. Moreover, the Prologue employs important theological terms not found elsewhere in the Gospel, for example, *logos* ("Word" personified), *charis* ("grace" or "covenant love"), *plêrôma* ("fullness").

Second, there are breaks and inconsistencies in sequence. Too much has been made of the geographical and chronological "jumps" in John, whereby without any indication of a transition one chapter may be situated in a different locale from that of the previous chapter. Such jumps would be crucial only if the Gospel were an attempt to give us a complete account of the ministry of Jesus, but 20:30 and 21:25 state specifically that the account in the Gospel is incomplete. However, even if one is careful not to impose upon the evangelist a modern passion for chronology, there are still seeming contradictions in the present order of the Gospel. In 14:31, Jesus concludes his remarks at the Last Supper and gives the command to depart; yet this is followed by three more chapters of discourse so that the departure does not seem to take place until 18:1. In 20:30–31 we are given a clear conclusion to the Gospel: the evangelist sums up his narration and explains the purpose he had in writing; yet this is followed by another, seemingly independent, chapter with another conclusion. There also seems to be a twofold conclusion to the public ministry in 10:40–42 and 12:37–43,[5] although here the evidence is not as clear. The disciples of JBap, who were present when he identified Jesus and explained his mission in 1:29–34, do not seem to understand anything about Jesus in 3:26–30. After Jesus' first sign at Cana (2:11), he works signs in Jerusalem (2:23); yet his next miracle at Cana is apparently designated as his second sign (4:54), as if there were no signs intervening. In 7:3–5, his brothers speak as if Jesus had never worked signs in Judea, despite the Jerusalem signs just mentioned and another miracle in ch. 5. At the Last Supper, Peter asks Jesus where he is going (13:36, also 14:5); yet in the same setting in 16:5 Jesus complains that no one has asked him, "Where are you going?" Throughout ch. 3, Jesus has been at Jerusalem, which is in Judea; yet in mid-chapter (3:22) we are suddenly told that he

---

4. See *John*, 1077–82.
5. See the discussion in *John*, 414–15.

came into Judea. Some of these difficulties may be explained away, but not all of them. It appears that in John we have on the one hand the elements of a planned and cohesive outline,[6] and on the other, elements that seem to indicate alterations, insertions, or reeditings. On the one hand there are dramatic scenes that betray minute editorial care (ch. 9, and the trial before Pilate in 18–19); on the other, there are scenes that lack finish and organization (chs. 7–8).

Third, there are repetitions in the discourses, as well as passages that clearly do not belong to their context. At times, the evangelist's economy of style is truly impressive, but at other times what has been said seems to be repeated over again in only slightly different terms. Although this repetition could be pedagogic, to many it appears to be the result of two different traditions of the same words (a phenomenon akin to what we find in the traditions of the Pentateuch). For example, what is said in 5:19–25 with an emphasis on realized eschatology appears again and, in part almost verbatim, in 5:26–30 with an emphasis on final eschatology.[7] What is said and what happens in 6:35–50, where Jesus presents his revelation as the bread of life, is almost the same as what is said and what happens in 6:51–58, where Jesus presents his body as the bread of life. What is said in 14:1–31 in the Last Discourse is largely said all over again in 16:4–33. In addition to these duplications, there are sections of discourse that apparently do not belong to their context. Who is speaking in 3:31–36, John the Baptist or Jesus, or even the evangelist? The context would indicate John the Baptist, but the words are appropriate to Jesus, and some have suggested that it forms a final comment from the evangelist. Another discourse that is possibly not in its original sequence is 12:44–50, where we find Jesus making a public proclamation when we have just been told that he went into hiding (12:36).

Possible Solutions

DIFFICULTIES SUCH AS THOSE SAMPLED above have caused many scholars to abandon the traditional picture of the composition of the Gospel by one person from memory. With much oversimplification, I shall group

---

6. See Chapter Nine, below.
7. See Chapter Seven, below.

below modern alternative explanations under three headings. These solutions are not necessarily mutually exclusive; they may be, and often are, combined.

Theories of Accidental Displacements

Perhaps the simplest solution to difficulties found in John is to rearrange parts of the Gospel. From the time of Tatian (ca. 175) to the present day, scholars have thought that by moving passages around they could put John into consecutive order. Their usual presupposition has been that some accident displaced passages and destroyed the original order, thus creating the confusion that we now find. Since there is absolutely no evidence in the textual witnesses for any order other than that which we now possess, it must be assumed that this accidental displacement happened before the Gospel was published. And generally it is conjectured that it took place after the death or in the absence of the evangelist; for were he available, he could easily have restored his original order.

The amount of rearrangement that has been proposed varies considerably. Many scholars who do not otherwise favor rearrangement, for example, Wikenhauser, will at least support a reversal of order between chs. 5 and 6 in order to obtain better geographical sequence. (Unfortunately, we have no proof that the evangelist shared this geographical interest.) Bernard in his commentary supports a fairly extensive rearrangement, affecting not only chs. 5 and 6, but also the whole of 15 and 16 in the Last Discourse, and parts of 3, 7, 10, and 12. Bultmann carries rearrangement even further, so that individual verses and parts of verses are affected; for example, in one part of his rearrangement, the order of verses is 9:41; 8:12; and 12:44. Wilkens and Boismard are others who tend toward frequent rearrangement to reach the original order.

Rearrangement does solve some problems of the Gospel. That it does not solve them all means that often it has to be combined with another explanation of the composition of the Gospel, for example, the source or edition theories to be discussed below. It is important to note, however, that there are serious objections to any theory of displacement and rearrangement:

First, there is a danger that the rearrangements will reflect the interests of the commentator, which may not be the same as the interests of the evangelist. It is possible that the rearrangements will destroy a sequence that was intended, at least by the final editor of the Gospel. For instance, if the section on JBap in 3:22–30 seems to break up what might be a better sequence between 3:1–21 and 3:31–36 (so Bernard), may one not argue that the passage was inserted in its present location precisely to remind the reader of the baptismal significance of the words in 3:1–21, a significance that might otherwise be missed? Geographically, ch. 6 does go better before ch. 5, but the evangelist might have intended the bread theme of ch. 6 to be followed immediately by the water theme in 7:37–38 in order to echo the story of the Exodus where God gave Israel bread from heaven and water from the rock. If one comments on the Gospel as it now stands, one is certain of commenting on an ancient Gospel as it really existed at the final moment of its publication. If one indulges in extensive rearrangement, one may be commenting on a hybrid that never existed before it emerged as the brain child of the rearranger. One can exaggerate this objection: for instance, Bultmann has unfairly been accused of commenting on the Gospel according to Bultmann, rather than on the Gospel according to John. The German title of his commentary, moreover, *Das Evangelium des Johannes* (rather than the more usual *nach Johannes* or *Johannesevangelium*) has been interpreted by some to indicate Bultmann's firm assurance that he has found the real Gospel of John behind the Gospel as it has been transmitted to us. But this is to read too much into a perfectly acceptable wording.

Second, rearrangements are based on the thesis that the Gospel does not make satisfactory sense as it now stands; but many commentators, like Hoskyns, Barrett, and Dodd, are convinced that the present order does make sense. As Dodd famously commented:

> I conceive it to be the duty of an interpreter at least to see what can be done with the document as it has come down to us before attempting to improve upon it. . . . I shall assume as a provisional working hypothesis that the present order is not fortuitous, but deliberately devised by somebody—even if he were only a scribe doing his best—and that the person in question (whether the author or another) had some design in mind, and was not necessarily irresponsible or unintelligent.[8]

---

8. Dodd, *Interpretation*, 290.

This claim lies at the heart of contemporary literary approaches, where the interpreter's responsibility is seen as making sense out of the narrative as it has been preserved in the storytelling and in the literary and liturgical traditions of Christianity (see, for example, Culpepper, Stibbe, Moloney). Generally, if we respect the evangelist's limited purpose, the Gospel is an intelligible document in its present form; and we can reasonably assume that this form of the Gospel made sense to the one who had the final responsibility for the Gospel's appearance. But suppose that we had to reckon with the possibility that while this editor put the Gospel in the order that seemed best to him, he was not in a position to know the original order of the manuscript and had to settle for what he has given us. Then a real question is whether with our modern scientific tools almost 2,000 years later we are able to establish a more original order than was possible for a contemporary editor. That no great assurance marks this task is demonstrated in the sharp differences among the proposed elaborate rearrangements.

Third, theories of displacement do not always offer an adequate explanation of how the displacement took place. If the Gospel was written out on a scroll, any theory of displacement is difficult. Scrolls tend to lose their outermost leaves, but confusion of leaves within the roll is not plausible. It has been suggested that a scroll came apart into separate sheets when the joints where the sheets were glued together came loose. But we must remember that often in such scrolls the columns of writing overlap the joints, and if a joint comes apart, the sheets can be easily matched.

More recently scholars have suggested that the original form of the Gospel was a codex or book, a form in which detached sheets are a greater hazard. But even if sheets became detached, the original order could have easily been restored for those sheets that did not both begin with a new sentence and end at the conclusion of a sentence (because incomplete sentences would provide a clue to the sequence of the sheets). Only pages that were units in themselves would pose a problem. This observation has led the advocates of the displacement theory to calculate how many letters would be on the recto and verso of a codex leaf. Units that became displaced would have to be of such a length or a multiple thereof. J. H. Bernard does a creditable job of computing this for the displacements he proposes in John, and F. R. Hoare has given a strong exposition of the possibilities of this approach.[9] One might ask, however, how great would be the mathematical likelihood of finding in a manuscript of John such a large number of units that would not overlap on to other leaves. One might also ask in how many proved cases in antiquity did such large-scale, accidental displacements take place before the work was published.

If a theory of displacement of regular units has at least some plausibility, one cannot say the same for a theory of displacement of lines. That Bultmann never explains how the displacement he posits could have taken place is, as Easton, "Bultmann's," has noted, a great weakness. His rearrangement is supposed to be so patently better than the existing order of the Gospel that the dislocations may be said to have been demonstrated exegetically. But many will not be so easily convinced. Was the Gospel written on small bits of papyrus, often containing no more than a sentence? This seems to be the only way to explain the dislocations that Bultmann posits. Any theory of damage to a scroll or a codex would leave us with broken sentences that became detached, but in Bultmann's theory the displacements are always composed of complete sentences.

In summary, the theory of accidental displacement seems to create almost as many problems as it solves. The solution to our problem would appear to lie in the direction of a more deliberate procedure.

Theories of Multiple Sources

If the fourth evangelist combined several independent sources, some of the stylistic differences, as well as the lack of sequence and the presence of duplications, can be accounted for. In the recent forms of the source theory it is customarily supposed that the evangelist composed none of the sources himself but received them from elsewhere. It is also usually proposed that these sources were written, for oral sources would have been rendered in the evangelist's own style and thus be more difficult to discern. (We may note, however, that Noack has been a strong proponent of a theory in which the entire Gospel arose from oral tradition.) Sometimes a theory that conceives of the Gospel as the composite of a combination of sources has been joined with a theory that views the Gospel as having undergone several editions or redactions—but such a composite

---

9. Bernard, *St John*, 1.xxviii–xlii; F. R. Hoare, *The Original Order and Chapters of St John's Gospel* (London: Burns Oates & Washbourne, 1944).

theory can become quite complicated. For instance, in the early part of the twentieth century one German scholar arrived at six combinations of sources and redactions. A complete history of the source theories may be found in the surveys of Johannine literature (see the General Selected Bibliography, following the Editor's Introduction, above); in the period before 1950 the names of Hirsch, Spitta, and Wendt were associated with such theories.

Macgregor, Morton, McLeman. An interesting example of the use of modern tools is supplied by two books by Macgregor and Morton,[10] and by Morton and McLeman,[11] which employ statistical analysis. *Structure* proposed that the Gospel was composed by joining two sources, J^1 and J^2. The former, the longer source, is characterized by short paragraphs; the latter has long paragraphs. Although both sources belong to the same general sphere of theological persuasion, there is some stylistic evidence that they are from different hands. J^2 contains ch. 4, most of 6, 9–11, 14–16. Such a breakdown of the material does not in itself solve the principal problems mentioned above, and so a theory of multiple editings was part of the picture. *Genesis* seeks to refine the method by arguing for a codex form and stressing computerized stylometry (sentence length + counting important but common words) with the sources now designated P^1 and P^2. In general the authors have not entered a debate with the theories of most contemporary scholars who they are convinced are ill-equipped to appreciate their statistical arguments and therefore are not open to conviction.

Bultmann. The most influential form of the source theory proposed in the twentieth century was that of Bultmann, who distinguishes three principal sources:

1. *Semeia-Quelle* or signs source: John narrates a select number of Jesus' miracles, and these constitute the main narrative sections in the first part of the Gospel (chs. 1–13). Bultmann suggests that these were excerpted from a larger collection of signs attributed to Jesus. The indication of borrowing from a source is found in the

---

10. *Structure* (1961).
11. *Genesis* (1980).

enumeration of signs in 2:11 and 4:54, and in the mention of various signs in 12:37 and 20:30. The latter passage states that Jesus performed many other signs not written down in this Gospel. Bultmann thinks that the story of the call of the disciples in 1:35–49 may have constituted the introduction to the signs source. This source was written in a Greek that betrays strong Semitic affinities (verb before subject, absence of connective particles, etc.). It was composed among Christians converted from among followers of JBap and was originally used as a mission document to persuade their former confreres to follow Jesus.[12] Since Bultmann does not believe in the miraculous, and since he finds this source somewhat more developed than the Synoptic narrative material, he attributes to it little real historical value for reconstructing the career of Jesus of Nazareth.[13]

2. *Offenbarungsreden* or Revelatory Discourse Source: It was from this source that the evangelist drew the discourses attributed to Jesus in the Gospel. The source began with the Prologue and contained poetic discourses written in Aramaic. The Syriac Odes of Solomon is a surviving example of this type of literature. The theology of the source was an early Oriental Gnosticism as professed by a group like the followers of JBap and later by the Mandaean writings.[14] The source was translated into Greek either by the evangelist himself or by another, but the poetic format was maintained. The main task of the evangelist was to Christianize and to demythologize the discourses: He placed them on the lips of Jesus and thus gave them a historical setting. What was once said by the Gnostic figure of Original Man is now said by Jesus the Revealer; what once referred to any son of perdition now refers to Judas (17:12); no longer does 12:27 refer to a general conflict with the demonic lower world, but to the

---

12. In subsequent variant theories of the signs source/Gospel, the idea that it was a mission document has continued. For Bultmann the evangelist was himself a former follower of JBap, and so the source he used was not totally alien to his background. Nevertheless his theology was so different that the source can scarcely be described as harmonious with Johannine tradition (as it is in other source theories).

13. The Greek text of the reconstructed signs source may be found in Smith, *Composition*, 38–44.

14. See below, Chapter Four, pp. 119–27.

passion of Jesus. Additions and changes introduced into the source material are betrayed by their departure from the poetic format.[15]

3. *The Passion and Resurrection Story:* Although this narrative had much in common with the passion story underlying the Synoptic Gospels, Bultmann insists that the fourth evangelist drew on non-Synoptic material. The style of this source is not clearly defined, but it was written in a Semitizing Greek.[16]

In Bultmann's theory, the evangelist wove these three sources together with ingenuity, making them the vehicle of his own thought. He himself had belonged to a Gnostic group of disciples of JBap and had converted to Christianity. His Greek, as evidenced in the additions and connecting passages, shows less Semitic influence than that of his sources.[17] However, in some way the work of the evangelist fell into disorder; the lines of the discourses were mixed up, and a great number of displacements resulted. Therefore Bultmann posits a final stage in the evolution of the Gospel, namely, the work of the Ecclesiastical Redactor. This figure had both a literary and a theological task. First, he tried to put the work of the evangelist into proper order. He succeeded in part, but he still left many displacements. (To some extent, Bultmann himself has finished the task of the Redactor by moving verses around to restore the original order). The second task of the Redactor was the more important theological one. The evangelist's work was still too Gnostic to be accepted by the church at large. For instance, it made no mention of the sacraments or of the second coming. The Ecclesiastical Redactor, a type of primitive *censor librorum*, added sacramental references, e.g., to the water of baptism in 3:5, to the flesh and blood of eucharist in 6:51–58, and symbolically to both baptism and eucharist in 19:34b–35. He added references to final eschatology and the last day in passages like 5:28–29 and 12:48. In historical details the Redactor tried to harmonize John with the Synoptic tradition. Thus he won acceptance by the church for the Fourth Gospel.

The evaluation of Bultmann's theory as representative of the source theories is difficult. Many of the highly disputable and weak points in

---

15. A Greek text of the reconstructed Revelatory Discourse Source is found in Smith, *Composition*, 23–24, and an English text in Easton, "Bultmann's," 143–54.

16. For the reconstructed Greek text, see Smith, *Composition*, 48–51.

17. For the details of his style, see Smith, *Composition*, 9–10.

such a reconstruction of John are personal to Bultmann's own form of the source theory; other shortcomings are common to all source theories. Among the former are the postulated Gnostic influence, the presupposed nonsacramental character of the evangelist's work, and his exclusive interest in realized eschatology; these contentions shall be examined later. I have already pointed out the difficulties in the elaborate displacement hypothesis advanced by Bultmann. The portrait of the Ecclesiastical Redactor is particularly subject to doubt. It seems at times that the additions credited to him have been determined by a form of circular reasoning where one rather arbitrarily decides what fits the theological outlook of the evangelist and attributes what is left to the Redactor.

But aside from these peripheral difficulties, what are we to say about the signs source and the Revelatory Discourse Source? The quasi-poetic format of the Johannine discourses has been accepted by many;[18] one need not pattern it on a collection of Gnostic poems, however, for it resembles the discourse style of personified Wisdom in the OT. The enumeration of signs in several Gospel passages is at first sight a more impressive argument and has influenced a number of people who have worked with sources (Boismard; Fortna). Yet other suggestions for the numbers "first" (2:11) and "second" (4:54) are possible. Does such an enumeration reflect an earlier and simpler (oral?) stage of the Gospel outline where 4:54 was the second sign after the Cana sign of 2:1–11 or was there a truly independent signs source? Literary critics have pointed out that there are a number of further connections between the two Cana miracle stories that link them. The enumeration of the two stories is there to focus the reader's attention upon the repetition, and may not have even been present in a hypothetical and reconstructed source.

Major difficulties militate against a source theory of the Bultmann type:

First, in John signs and discourses are closely woven together. Dodd has shown impressively that the discourses that accompany the signs are interpretations of the signs.[19] Ch. 6 is a perfect example of this, for the Bread of Life Discourse interprets the multiplication of the loaves. This is such a consistent feature of chs. 2–12 that, although one might posit that the evangelist has shaped the discourses as a commentary on the signs, it

---

18. See below, Chapter Eight, pp. 284–87.
19. Dodd, *Interpretation*.

seems incredible that the signs and discourses came from totally inde-pendent pre-Gospel sources. An exception may be claimed, however, for the two Cana signs which are not accompanied by interpretative dis-courses.[20] These two signs remain the best argument for the existence of some sort of signs source. The argument, however, is a two-edged sword. For Heekerens, *Zeichen-Quelle,* they (plus ch. 21) are the whole Signs Source, and are so different that they were added by a redactor to the complete Gospel.[21]

Second, embedded in the discourses are sayings of Jesus which, by comparison with those in the Synoptics, have every reason to be consid-ered as belonging to a primitive tradition of the words of Jesus. Dodd has shown this convincingly.[22] This means that, in part at least, the discourses consist of traditional sayings and explanatory developments based on them. The supposed pre-Christian collection of poetic Revelatory Dis-courses then becomes a superfluous hypothesis.

Third, the stylistic differences among the various sources are not veri-fiable. E. Schweizer isolated thirty-three peculiarities of Johannine style.[23] His work was supplemented by Jeremias and Menoud, and has been brought to its fullest development by Ruckstuhl and Dschulnigg, whose list has reached 153 (of which, interestingly, only thirty-eight are found in 1 John). In response to objections, the diagnosis has become increas-ingly sophisticated.[24] These Johannine peculiarities appear in material

---

20. Yet in some ways the discourse in 5:19–47 can be seen as a comment not only on 5:1–15 but also on 4:46–54. See *John,* 198.

21. Heekerens, *Zeichen-Quelle.*

22. Dodd, *Tradition.*

23. Schweizer, *Ego Eimi.*

24. Objection: Redactors might have imitated the evangelist or one another and thus have the same stylistic peculiarities. Response: Increasingly to select Johannine peculiarities that are theologically meaningless and scarcely deliberately imitable, so that several writers would betray themselves by stylistic differences (which are not found). Objection: A school of writers might share the same style. Response: No other ancient school of writers betrays the uniformity of style found in John. Objec-tion: Some of the claimed Johannine peculiarities were common to koine Greek and could accidentally have been employed by several Johannine writers. The latter (when used in the same way as in John) have been eliminated from the list of peculi-arities and indeed in Ruckstuhl and Dschulnigg, *Stilkritik,* peculiarities are chosen that are lacking in 32 other writings of the period 100 B.C. and A.D. 150.

from all three of the sources posited by Bultmann, as well as in the material attributed to the evangelist himself, and even in some of the material attributed to the Ecclesiastical Redactor (although Ruckstuhl has pressed his arguments too far here).[25] Now, we grant that in incorporating the sources into one work, the evangelist would introduce common elements of style. However, if we remember that, according to Bultmann's hypothesis, one of the sources was originally in Aramaic poetry and another was in Semitizing Greek, and the evangelist himself wrote in a less Semitized Greek, the commonness of Johannine peculiarities in all three is inexplicable. As P. Parker has remarked, "It looks as though, if the author of the Fourth Gospel used documentary sources, he wrote them all himself."[26] Smith's sympathetic study of Bultmann concludes that the arguments of Schweizer and Ruckstuhl present obstacles that Bultmann's answers have not removed.[27] As we shall see below, others refined the source theory precisely because of this difficulty.

Fourth, there are no really convincing parallels in pre-Christian antiquity for the types of sources that Bultmann has postulated. The hypothesis of collected miracles of Jesus has been invoked in discussion of pre-Synoptic material,[28] but nothing so systematic as the signs source as proposed for John. The Odes of Solomon has been proposed as a parallel to the Revelatory Discourse Source, but the similarity of this collection of hymns is more to the Prologue than to the discourses. Of course, Bultmann joins the Prologue and the discourses as one source, but the poetry of the Prologue is quite different from that of the discourses. Becker has sought parallels for the Discourse Source from a wider field of Gnostic

---

25. Although he works with Bultmann's source analysis, Reim, *Studien*, corrects Bultmann's failure to detect OT background for ideas in the Revelatory Discourse Source—a correction that blurs the line between the source and the evangelist to whom Bultmann attributed the use of the OT. Borgen, "John's Use," presses OT usage to an even sharper critique of the source theory.

26. Parker, "Two," 304.

27. See Smith, *Composition*, 108.

28. See P. J. Achtemeier, "Toward the Isolation of Pre-Markan Miracle Catenae," *JBL* 89 (1970): 265–91; ibid, "The Origin and Function of the Pre-Markan Miracle Catenae," *JBL* 91 (1972): 198–221. The proposed Hellenistic and rabbinic parallels for Jesus' miracles (Apollonius of Tyana as described in Philostratus' Life; Ḥoni and Ḥanina in rabbinic writings) come from a later period and are not systematic collections. See MAMJ 2.536, 576–88.

literature.[29] That parallels for isolated portions of John may be found in individual passages in the Nag-Hammadi Gnostic, Mandaean, and Hermetic literature is true.[30] But this does not mean that there is a good example of a collection of discourses such as Bultmann proposes. I cannot help but judge that the theory suffers from almost insuperable difficulties.

Fortna. In 1970, R. T. Fortna, having profited from the objections to Bultmann's analysis, proposed another reconstruction of the narrative source underlying John.[31] In 1988, he adjusted his proposal into a very subtle source hypothesis.[32] Fortna presents us with a two-stage approach to John: an older basic source document and a later redactor who is the evangelist (so that the third or final hand whom many regard as post-evangelist disappears). The source, a "gospel of signs," consisted entirely of narrative (seven signs plus passion and resurrection); it can be discovered in its entirety, for the evangelist respected the source and did not dismantle it when he made his additions and changes—it was known and beloved by the readers he envisaged for his Gospel. The evangelist also added all the discourse material, but Fortna does not concern himself with an analysis of that material. The additions can be detected by the aporias (intrusions, sudden turns, non sequiturs, and even contradictions) created by the evangelist when he did his work. Fortna thinks he can discern both the theology of the source (e.g., miracles simply as proof of messiahship; death as fulfilling prophecy) and new dimensions added by the evangelist (e.g., miracles as manifesting Jesus' identity and glory; crucifixion as lifting up and salvific).

Although Fortna states he would be happy if half of what he proposes is convincing,[33] his exegesis of the existing Gospel depends very heavily on the exactitude of his reconstruction of the source. That causes hesitation: (a) On p. 56, below, I present a comparative scheme of various suggested sources. They disagree quite radically at times, and if I offered

---

29. Becker, *Reden.*

30. See below, Chapter Four, pp. 119–27.

31. *The Gospel of Signs.* Already in this book Fortna attempted to justify his source according to the criteria offered by E. Schweizer and E. Ruckstuhl.

32. Fortna, *Fourth.*

33. Fortna, *Fourth,* xii.

more reconstructions, readers would find even further disagreement. Such divergence causes me to doubt that we have the scholarly tools to do what Fortna has done.[34] (b) Some of what he sees as aporias or awkwardness may be only in the eye of the beholder; moreover the posited original source may have had considerable awkwardness in transitions and phrasing. (c) The thesis that the evangelist drew heavily on the source for the theology he developed but drew all the discourse material, which also is harmonious with his theology, from elsewhere is not fully plausible. (d) By not considering the discourse material, Fortna avoids an area that has forced many to posit a third stage—redaction after the Gospel was written—for there are inconsistencies of sequence and theology in the discourses. Although Fortna's thesis has become the best known source approach to John, it has been subjected to careful criticism by Lindars.[35] Carson contends that while it is not unlikely that the fourth evangelist used sources, their existence has not been demonstrated with any significant degree of probability; and if they exist they have not been isolated with great precision.[36] This sentiment is increasingly shared by recent more literary approaches that treat the text as a unified utterance, whatever its sources may or may not have been.

Modern variations. One component of Bultmann's theory has had relatively little acceptance: the Revelatory Discourse source. Yet there are variant discourse source theories, e.g., Schenke proposes as a source a "Dialogue of Jesus with the Jews" that supplied material for chs. 3–12,[37] and that the evangelist rearranged into the existing discourses to meet the needs of his community. The other three components of the Bultmannian source theory (none original with him) have had wider acceptance continuing through the 1990s (often without the theological orientation attributed to them by Bultmann): a Passion narrative source, a collection of signs/miracles, and the work of a redactor. Leaving the Passion Narrative to one side, let us look at some of the recent variations.

---

34. In BDM 2.1492–1524, M. L. Soards shows the great differences among thirty-five reconstructions of the pre-Marcan passion narrative.

35. Lindars, *Behind the Fourth Gospel.*

36. Carson, "Source," 428.

37. Schenke, "Dialog." It would have covered the coming of the one sent for salvation and judgment, the witness he bore, and the unbelief of "the Jews."

Variations in the signs source theory. The accompanying table lists various scholars' hypotheses about contents.[38] (I include editing theories wherein the first edition is substantially a collection of signs.)

- Although most of these scholars count seven, they are not at one in whether to count 21:1–14. *Yes:* Fortna, Heekerens; *No:* J. Becker, Bultmann, Corsani, Nicol, von Wahlde; *Indefinite:* Schnackenburg.[39] There is no explicit reference to the number "seven" in John.
- Beyond miracles, most would include in the source other narratives (dialogues), JBap's disciples, Samaritan, etc. *Yes:* J. Becker, Bultmann, Fortna, Nicol (probably), Teeple, von Wahlde; *No:* Heeckeren. A Passion Narrative is included by Fortna, Teeple, and von Wahlde.
- They disagree whether the signs source/Gospel came from outside, alien circles or from the Johannine community tradition. *Alien:* J. Becker; *No:* Dunderberg, Fortna, Nicol, von Wahlde.
- They disagree as to whether the miracles should *in globo* be considered fictional. *Yes:* J. Becker; Bultmann; *No:* Corsani, Nicol, von Wahlde.
- They disagree whether the signs source/Gospel had an essentially objectionable Christology (e.g., *theios anēr*;[40] wonder-worker) so that the Johannine writer who took it over had to correct it radically, or a Christology to which he was not totally hostile and which with modifications he could build on and supplement. *Radically objectionable:* J. Becker; Bultmann, Heekerens; *No:* Fortna, Dunderberg; Nicol, von Wahlde.

---

38. Neirynck, "Signs Source," offers more detailed comparisons covering particularly Spitta (1910 commentary), Fortna, Pesch, Boismard, and Heekerens. Kysar, *Fourth Evangelist,* 26–27, compares Teeple, Fortna, Nicol, Schnackenburg, and Becker. Carson, "Current," 416–17, compares Bultmann, Becker, Schnackenburg, Nicol, Fortna, Teeple, and Temple. Comparisons are difficult because in ongoing writing authors change opinions.

39. The Gospel does not refer to it as a sign, and it is added after an indication that John has finished citing from the signs (20:30–31). Bauckham, "Beloved" 40, chooses the flow of blood and water from the dead Jesus' side attested by an eyewitness (19:34–35) as the seventh sign.

40. The existence of a *theios anēr* concept and Christology and the validity of using it in relation to Jesus' miracles have been seriously questioned. A. Pilgaard (in *The*

J. Becker

Resembles Bultmann's contents: Seven miracles: four in Galilee (+ Jbap [1:19–34.] first disciples [1:35–51; Samaritan]); three in Jerusalem (+ beginning of Tabernacles; 12:37–43; 20:30–31). Origin in peripheral Christianity. Signs not real events; Jesus is Hellenistic wonder-worker; gets major reinterpretation in the Gospel.

Bultmann

First disciples (1:35–49); Cana (2:1–12); Samaritan (parts of 4:4–40); Official at Cana (4:46–54); Multiplication and Walking on Water (6:1–25); to Jerusalem (7:2–10); Bethesda pool (5:2–18); Moses argument (7:19–23); Blind man (9:1–38); Crosses Jordan (10:40–42); Lazarus (11:2–19, 33–44); Endings (12:37–38; 20:30–31).

Dunderberg

A basic document with miracles and other material; marked by Johannine theology and themes; similar to the Synoptic tradition but no clear knowledge of Synoptic Gospels.

Fortna

A gospel: Seven miracles in different arrangement (catch of fish followed two Cana miracles); material in ch. 1; Samaritan; passion and resurrection.

Heekerens

Three-miracle source (chs. 2; 4; 21), Elijah-Elisha type, stemming from Samaria, originally in Aramaic, translated into Semitized Greek; added by the redactor (!) to (an unrecoverable) basic Document that he was editing.

Nicol

Seven miracles (chs. 2; 4; 5; 6; 9; 11) + 20:30–31; possibly first disciples and Samaritan narratives. Not a *theios anēr* theology, but Jesus as divine Messiah. Historical deeds later interpreted symbolically.

Schnackenburg

In the course of his commentary he became more and more convinced of the existence of a signs source which contained the seven miracles found in chs. 1–11, and (ultimately) ch. 21; no strong theological orientation.

Teeple

Seven miracles preceded by testimony of JBap and first disciples, and interspersed by purification of Temple, Nicodemus, and Samaritan; + passion material. Written after A.D. 75; Hellenistic deification of Jesus.

von Wahlde

A gospel composed in Judea ca. A.D. 70–80. Miracles with much dialogue material, a passion, and resurrection appearance to Magdalene; a low Christology; Moses typology; Jesus is Messiah, Son of God. Signs not symbolic till later editions.

The diversity shows how hard it is to do such pre-Johannine reconstruction. Bittner has done a meticulous study of Johannine miracle tradition, rejects all signs-source proposals.[41] This study has now been further reinforced by the remarkable survey and negative assessment of van Belle.[42] This Source is also rejected by Dschulnigg, Lindars, Noack, Schulz, Smalley, Schnelle and Labahn, among others. Marguerat presents what I regard to be the most objective analysis of the evidence: "The Johannine community was familiar with miracle stories of diverse provenance. The evangelist made a selection with an eye towards his gospel project, without limiting himself to one source or one provenance."[43]

Variations in the redaction theory. Here are some of the issues on which proponents differ in their interpretation of the (hypothetical) redactor:

- Almost all posit that the redactor's style and theology differ from the (Johannine) work he is editing (most often the work of the evangelist). They are not in agreement, however, on whether the difference in theology is radical. Does the adapting complement or correct? What were his theological interests?
- Is the redactor a fellow disciple of the evangelist, part of the same school?
- How extensive was the work of the redactor compared to that of the writer of the document he was redacting? Thyen, and his pupils Langbrandtner and Heekerens, attributed so much reshaping in

---

New Testament and Hellenistic Judaism [ed. P. Borgen and S. Giversen; Arhus: Arhus University Press, 1995], 101–22) gives a balanced discussion and ample bibliography. His conclusion (122): "In my opinion the use of Hellenistic concepts of *theioi andres* as a model for the early Christian christology without further qualification confuses rather than clarifies this question." See also Holladay, C. H., *THEIOS ANER in Hellenistic Judaism. A Critique of the Use of this Category in Christology* (SBLDS 40. Missoula: Scholars Press, 1977), and B. Blackburn, *Theios Anêr and the Markan Miracle Traditions. A Critique of the Theios Anêr Concept as an Interpretative Background of the Miracle Traditions Used by Mark* (WUNT 2.40; Tübingen: J. C. B. Mohr [Paul Siebeck], 1991).

41. Bittner, *Jesu*, 2–14.
42. van Belle, *The Signs Source.*
43. Marguerat, *"La source,"* 93.

terms of order, material, and theology to the redactor that he became the evangelist or principal author.[44]

- Is the redactor the author of one or more of the Johannine epistles or of the same mindset? Did the redactor do his work before or after the writing of the epistles?

Theories of Multiple Editions

The pattern common to these theories is that one basic body of Gospel material has been edited several times to give us the present form of John. There is no agreement on the number of editions or on whether the editions were all done by the same man; but generally at least two editors (sometimes distinguished as the evangelist and the redactor) are posited, and the later of the two is often associated with the writer of the Johannine epistles. E. Schwartz, J. Wellhausen, and H. H. Wendt were among the earlier proponents of this approach. The modern proponents cover a spectrum from positing a rather complete rewriting of the earliest edition to minor tinkering. At the minor tinkering end the supposition is that the first edition was already truly a gospel. The more radical the rewriting the closer the editing theory comes to a source theory; for if there was an original edition to which a great deal of material was subsequently added, even to the point of giving the original a totally new orientation, we are not far from the combination of two sources.[45] Only when the additional material has come from the same author who composed the original work do we get a decisive variation, a variation that frees the editing theory from the objections about stylistic consistency that undermine the source theory.

Wilkens. A good example of an editing theory that attributes rewriting to the same author (the BD) is that of W. Wilkens. He proposes three stages:

---

44. This was Thyen's view in the 1970s ("Johannes 13"), but by the 1990s ("Johannes und die Synoptiker") he had given up source critical work, moving toward what we would call literary criticism.

45. I treated Fortna under Sources and I treat von Wahlde here (because he speaks of editions and says we know nothing about the author of the first edition); but they are quite similar in many points.

1. The *Grundevangelium* consisted of the narratives of four Galilean signs and three Jerusalem signs—thus like a book of signs (20:30).
2. The evangelist added seven discourses to the signs. These discourses had their own prehistory for which the evangelist was responsible.
3. This collection of signs and discourses was turned into a Passover Gospel by the transposition of three stories from Passover week into an earlier setting (2:13–22; 6:51–58; 12:1–7), thereby extending the Passover motif throughout the Gospel. Then there was a considerable rearrangement of verses and breaking up of discourses. These editions represented the work of the evangelist's whole lifetime; a final redactor made some additions, for example, in ch. 21.

There are some important contributions in Wilkens's theory, of which I have given only the barest outline. The suggestion (originally his father's) about the transposition of scenes from Passover has a certain validity. Moreover, this theory, which accepts the authorship of the BD,[46] who was an eyewitness, is more adaptable to the presence of historical tradition than is Bultmann's theory. However, in Wilkens's theory the process of editing consisted in adding material and rearranging it but never in rewriting what was originally written; that does seem to be a curious way of editing one's own work.

Parker is less radical than Wilkens. He suggests two editions of John. The second would have involved the addition of passages like 2:1–12; 4, 6, and 21, excerpts concerned largely with Galilee. Thus, Parker arrives at a first edition that was a Judean gospel, in harmony with his theory that the evangelist was a Judean disciple.

Boismard. A major exponent of the edition theory has been M.-É. Boismard. In the 1960s he maintained that John son of Zebedee was responsible for the central plan of the Gospel and for its tradition. He either wrote or supervised the writing of the basic Gospel and was responsible for two or more reeditions that introduced slight changes of plan and different formulations of the same material. Then there was a final redac-

---

46. See Chapter Six, below.

tion by Luke,[47] who gathered together all the strands of Johannine material into the Gospel as we now know it.

By the time of the third volume of SQE (1977), Boismard was diagnosing four stages in the writing of John.

1. *Document C* was a complete gospel stretching from JBap to the resurrection, much more archaic than Mark. It was written in Aramaic in Palestine about the year 50; and although at certain points it would have been closer to the Synoptics than to final John, C cannot be distinguished systematically in vocabulary and style from subsequent stages of Johannine composition. It may have been written by the BD (most likely either John of Zebedee or Lazarus). The Christology was primitive, with no pejorative attitude toward the world or the Jews, even though there was strong Samaritan influence.

2. *Jean II-A*, also in Aramaic, is to be dated ca. 60–65 and reflects the work of Presbyter John of Papias renown, a Palestinian Jew. II-A added miracles to C, exhibits wisdom Christology, has Lucan affinities (but drew upon none of the Synoptics in their final form), and introduces hostility toward the Jews and the world.

3. *Jean II-B* was written in Greek thirty years later by the same Presbyter John who had now moved to Ephesus and who also wrote the epistles. He greatly changed the order of the material from the geographical orientation of Jean II-A to a pattern of eight weeks. Whole sections of II-A were replaced by (sometimes parallel) passages with Synoptic affinities since by this time the editor knew all three Synoptic Gospels in their final form (and favored Luke-Acts). He knew both the Pauline letters and the Qumran material, and stressed Jesus as a preexistent figure, clearly superior to Moses.

4. *Jean III* is a final John redacted by an unknown Jewish Christian in Ephesus in the second century. He added duplications from earlier editions and from the Johannine epistles, rearranged chapters, stressed final judgment, modified anti-Judaism and clarified the Christology in the direction of monotheism (17:3: "the one true God").

---

47. Boismard sought to prove this identification of the redactor from the Lucan characteristics he found in the style of ch. 21 and in the additions to the Prologue. He has since given up the identification.

By way of judgment on this particular approach, let me remark that the thesis of two Aramaic editions, and the diagnosis of the elaborate plans of the various editions will probably gain few followers. Nevertheless, one cannot but both gasp at and admire Boismard's confidence in writing a commentary on each of the four editions!

In the 1990s Boismard launched a new endeavor producing EPJ. He had always depended on patristic references to John as a major guide to the original text,[48] but now from Chrysostom's commentary and homilies on John he (and A. Lamouille) set about to reconstruct a Greek pre-Johannine gospel (which I designate Pjg). This Pjg was combined with another parallel form of Johannine gospel tradition to give us the canonical Gospel we now know. One cannot judge that everything in Pjg was more ancient than duplicate material in the other parallel form, but in Boismard's theory Pjg is a relatively faithful guide to the primitive Aramaic document.

Boismard's approach to editing, in all its forms, takes into account many features in the thought of the Gospel (e.g., different Christologies, different attitudes toward "the Jews," echoes of Palestine and Ephesus). It can account for the breaks of sequence in the present form of the Gospel, which was caused by the editor's insertion of new matter into the original outline. Such a theory can also explain repetitions, for the editor may have included variant forms of the same words. Unattached portions of discourse might be explained by a desire to preserve a morsel of tradition without being able to find an ideal place to insert it. The objection of similar style leveled against the source theories is less applicable here where the material used in the various editions has come from one man and his disciple. Those passages of the Gospel where the Greek style does betray a difference of hand, for example, ch. 21, can be explained by positing a final redaction by another hand.

Boismard's thesis has been subjected to searching criticism.[49] In my judgment, the chief fault of such a theory of editing is the temptation to reconstruct too exactly the history of the editions. The problems in John are obvious, and it is possible that various editings caused these problems, but we must preserve our skepticism about any commentator's attempt to tell us down to the half-verse what belongs to what edition.

---

48. See below, Chapter Eight, pp. 283–84.
49. For example, Neirynck, *Jean;* Robert, "Un examen."

After Boismard have come other simpler edition theories, so that the twentieth century has ended with both source and edition theories thriving.

von Wahlde. Writing in 1989 and later, and using outlooks about the signs and the Jews for discriminating, he distinguished three editions. The first edition, probably composed in Judea before 90, was a gospel stretching from the baptism to the resurrection, but concentrating on Jesus' signs and the reactions to them. The second edition, composed about 90 when the Jewish Christian Johannine community was being expelled from the synagogue, stressed the Spirit, and treated the grounds of belief and how "the Jews" refused to believe. The signs now took on a symbolic value; there was stress on witnesses; and Jesus was presented as equal to God. The third edition, reflecting the inner-community split visible in 1 John, was the work of someone who shared the theology of the author of 1 John.

Dunderberg. His *Johannes*, appearing in 1994, proposed a relatively simple theory of editing. Working chiefly with chs. 1–9, he detects a basic document (= a gospel) that involved both narrative and discourse and then a later Johannine redaction.[50] His chief interest is the thesis that the basic document shows no direct dependence on the Synoptic tradition, but the redaction does. The way the redactor includes what he takes over from the Synoptics sometimes betrays a polemic purpose (hostility to Jewish authorities), an apologetic interest (shifting blame from Peter to Judas), and an ironic tone of superiority over the Synoptic tradition (improving on it). While I might not agree with Dunderberg on his use of a Synoptic criterion for detecting the hand of the redactor, this simplified picture of two-step composition is manageable.

The Theory Adopted in This New *Introduction*

SOME OBJECT TO A READING of the Gospel in its present order without imposing rearrangements. They object that such an approach attains only to the meaning given to passages in the final edition of the Gospel,

---

50. In the later chapters of John, with varying degrees of likelihood he would attribute to the redactor John 21, all the BD passages, and chs. 15–17.

and hence perhaps only to the meaning of a subordinate editor (redactor) rather than to the meaning of the evangelist. Yet, if one thinks of the final editor as someone loyal to the evangelist's thought, there will be very few times when editing has completely changed the original meaning of a passage. I prefer to run that risk rather than by ingenious rearrangement run the much greater risk of imposing on passages a meaning they never had. Naturally, where there is reason to suspect that in the formative history of the Gospel a passage had another setting and meaning, I shall mention it with proper qualifications as to the certainty with which the original position can be reconstructed. But that speculation will remain secondary; primary consideration should be given to the passage as it now stands. More recent commentary turns more easily to a commentary on the text of the Gospel in its present order than did Johannine scholars who have developed theories of displacement or editions. The above detailed analysis shows the rich activity produced by that period, and although less dominant, still being importantly pursued in some circles (von Wahlde, Painter, Dunderberg, Labahn). However, there are serious hermeneutical, theological and literary considerations that have swung interpreters back to a "reading" of the text as we have it. There are no signs in the textual traditions that received and passed on the Johannine text that there had ever been a text in the life of the church other than the one we now have.[51] There are hundreds of small, and often important, problems with the text as it has been handed down by a large variety of textual traditions that need to be resolved by the interpreter.[52] However, theologically, the early church received and transmitted our present Gospel of John as a part of what eventually came to be known as a "New Testament," a word of God to be used by the faith community for the proclamation of the Church's foundational experiences and beliefs concerning Jesus Christ. This fact must be respected. Second, despite the attempts of some more radical scholars who attempt to read against the text in a more freewheeling fashion, there are increasing indications that the narrative of the Fourth Gospel makes sense in its present order.

---

51. See V. Salmon, *Quatrième Évangile. Histoire de la tradition textuelle de l'original grec* (Paris: Letouzey, 1969).

52. For example, see *John*, 6–7, 282, 372, 1056, for discussions of the punctuation of 1:4 and the textual difficulties in 6:51, 9:5 and 20:31. See also Chapter Eight for issues concerning the Johannine Greek text.

Where once scholars felt that the tensions and aporias in the text called for rearrangement or for theories of redaction (and no doubt there were a number of editions before the appearance of the Gospel in its final form), nowadays they focus more intensely on the need to recapture the narrative design imposed upon the material by the author. It is the literary and theological world of a late first-century church that should determine this matter, not the "common sense" or the sense of right order that may appeal to a scholar at the turn of the third Christian millennium. The very existence of the text of the Fourth Gospel is evidence of the practice of reading and listening that has gone on for two thousand Christian years. This demands respect from the interpreter. That being said, however, the following theory concerning the development of the finished text of the Fourth Gospel is proposed.

In the original edition of this commentary (1966) I posited five stages in the composition of the Gospel. I believed them to be minimal, for I am convinced that the full details of the Gospel's prehistory are far too complicated to reconstruct. Nevertheless, a number of reviewers found counting up to five very difficult and complained about the complexity of my approach. In one way I found that amusing since I was counting as stages moments of origin and development (activity of Jesus and subsequent preaching about him by his disciples) that most scholars suppose for all four canonical Gospels and that only those who think the written Gospel is totally fictional would reject. But rather than engage in a defensive debate, let me rearrange the same approach into three stages. Beyond hoping that this will be less difficult for the arithmetically challenged, I can then make it clearer how this treatment of John resembles the standard approach to the other Gospels.[53] Naturally, the difficulties mentioned in the first section of this chapter have guided what I propose here, and the previous solutions mentioned have all contributed to my tentative solution.

Stage One: Origin in the Public Ministry or Activity of Jesus of Nazareth

Jesus did things of note, orally proclaimed his message, and interacted with others (e.g., JBap and Jewish religious figures). He chose compan-

---

53. For the three-stage approach to Gospels, see BINT 107–11.

ions who traveled with him and saw and heard what he said and did. Their memories of his words and deeds supplied the raw "Jesus material." These memories were already selective since they concentrated on what pertained to Jesus' proclamation of God, not the many trivia of ordinary existence (or elements of the "actual Jesus"). Both the Synoptic and the Johannine Gospel traditions sprang from this matrix. How can this be when the end products, Mark/Matthew/Luke compared to John, are so different? Part of the answer may stem from the fact that Jesus had disciples who had different religious backgrounds.[54] (This observation reflects the principle that what is received is received according to the mind-set of the recipient.) The Twelve were all or mostly Galileans (e.g., those who fished on the shore of the Lake and collected taxes), and their way of understanding Jesus and their recollections of his ministry in Galilee are enshrined in Mark (drawn upon by Matthew and Luke) and Q (the sayings tradition common to Matthew and Luke).[55] Quite differently, however, John speaks of followers of JBap who became disciples of Jesus at the Jordan, of Jesus' frequent activity in Jerusalem on the occasion of feasts that brought him there, and of Judean followers.[56] One of those disciples, later to become known as the Beloved Disciple,[57] could have been a particular vehicle for the preservation of this different body of Jesus material. Inevitably some of the material would be similar to that to be preserved in the Synoptic Gospels if he traveled with Jesus to Galilee (and the Galilean disciples did come to Jesus for the Passover time in which Jesus died), but the same events could have been seen from a different perspective.

The differences of John from the Synoptic Gospels are in terms not only of what is recounted but also of theological tone and language. After the discovery of the DSS we are in a better position to realize that the Jewish groups of Jesus' time had different attitudes toward the Law, the Jeru-

---

54. I am suggesting only that the roots of some of the differences lie in this Stage One; the differences increased and multiplied in Stages Two and Three to be described below.

55. On this, see the important essay of J. P. Meier, "The Circle of the Twelve: Did it Exist During Jesus' Public Ministry?" *JBL* 116 (1997): 635–72.

56. We are not dealing with two hermetically sealed bodies of tradition: Some of the Galilean disciples are remembered by name in John, as are some Galilean scenes (Cana miracles, multiplication of loaves, walking on water).

57. See below, Chapter Six, pp. 189–96.

salem Temple and its cult, and the immediacy of God's decisive action for Israel, as well as different ways of phrasing their religious aspirations. Similarly, Jews of different religious backgrounds could have comprehended Jesus differently and appreciated different aspects of his message. For instance, both Gospel traditions, Synoptic and Johannine, remember that Jesus spoke in the patterns of the Wisdom Literature of the OT, but the Synoptics recall Jesus speaking in parables while John recalls his speaking in the language of personified Wisdom.[58] Many parallels with the Qumran (DSS) literature (light and darkness, truth and falsehood, Spirit of Truth, etc.)[59] have been traced in John. It is possible that the followers of JBap may have been the channel whereby such Qumran theological language came into the Johannine picture.[60]

Stage Two: Proclaiming Jesus in the Postresurrectional Context of Community History.

In the decades between Jesus' lifetime and the writing of the Gospels, some developmental features were common in the proclamation of the Jesus tradition, e.g., a more perceptive faith enlightened by the resurrection, adaptation to the background of those being evangelized, and the influence of the life experience both of the proclaimers and the communities whom they converted. From the internal evidence of John, those who proclaimed Jesus during this period and those who accepted that proclamation may have formed a particularly close-knit community with a peculiar history. This history shaped the Jesus material in a way very different from the shaping of the Synoptic tradition shared by a larger group of Christians. If, presumably in different areas, the authors of

---

58. See below, Chapter Seven, pp. 259–65.

59. Although there are verbal parallels between John and Qumran, they are not frequent or systematic enough in my judgment to warrant positing that the Johannine writers had seen Qumran documents. More likely, the influence was mediated by persons who had indirect knowledge of the kind of Jewish thought found at Qumran.

60. *Editor's Note:* Care must be taken in understanding the significance of this affirmation. The relationship between JBap and the Qumran community may not have been direct, as has been suggested. See the balanced survey of MAMJ, 2.24–27, 69–71. Meier concludes that JBap is one of a number of manifestations (and the Qumranites were another) of "a wider religious phenomenon."

Matthew and of Luke independently used Mark and Q, those two documents must have circulated widely and represented something like common Christian tradition. The ancient claims that Mark drew on Peter may be a figurative translation of Mark's preserving the preaching outline common to the apostles (= the most prominent of the Twelve, best represented by Peter). The Johannine community would have had contact with these Christians of the "larger church" (see John 10:16), and so some of the undeniable similarities between John and the Synoptics may be traced to Stage Two as well as Stage One, i.e., to the tradition-shaping stage. As will become evident, I think this more plausible than Johannine dependence on the written Gospels (Stage Three below).

Yet the differences between John and the Synoptics outweigh the similarities. How might that situation be explained, in part,[61] through a Johannine community history that differed from the history we can discern behind the Synoptic Gospels? For instance, in none of the Synoptics does Jesus have a Samaritan following.[62] Yet in John a whole community of Samaritans comes to believe in Jesus as the Savior of the world (4:42); and Jesus is accused of being a Samaritan (8:48). This suggests that the community reflected in the Fourth Gospel brought into membership a number of Samaritans—thus a composite membership of Jews and Samaritans not present in the communities evangelized by the Twelve.[63] This may have contributed to John's frequent generalizing hostile and

---

61. Unique factors in the theology of John were shaped by other factors also, as pointed out in discussing Stage One and Stage Three.

62. In Matt 10:5, Jesus forbids his disciples to go into any city of Samaria; in Luke 9:52–54 Samaritan villagers refused to offer Jesus hospitality, so that James and John wanted to call fire from heaven down on them. For possible Samaritan influence on John, see the Bibliography in *John*, 188–89, further supplemented in Moloney, *John*, 135–36.

63. Notice that John 4:38 insists that the conversion of the Samaritan village was not the work of the previous disciples of Jesus who included members of the Twelve. Acts 8:14 reports that first evangelizing of Samaria was not by the apostles (= the Twelve). In "Change in Christology: New Testament Models and the Contemporary Task," ITQ 63 (1998): 33–50, especially 41, J. F. McGrath confusingly classifies such proposed influence of Samaritan converts on Johannine Christology as "syncretistic." The Samaritans would have become full members of the Johannine community and eventually no more foreign to its development than the original Jewish members.

alienated reference to "the Jews," since for the Samaritans (who were not Jews) this language would have been natural. Their presence may also help to explain the emphatic Johannine appreciation of Jesus as a Moses-like figure (1:17; 3:13–14; 5:45–46; 6:32; etc.).[64] Just as Moses had spoken to God, heard from God, and seen God's plans, so the Johannine Jesus never says or does anything by himself: all that stems from his preceding presence with God.

Indeed one may say that John's picture of Jesus combines a Moses image with that of personified divine Wisdom who was with God before creation, an image that made the use of "God" language for Jesus more forceful in John than in the other Gospel traditions. There is nothing in the Synoptics, for instance to match "The Word was God" (1:1) and "My Lord and my God" (20:28). As a result the focus of the struggle between Johannine believers and other Jews was not primarily that Jesus was a sinner who broke the Law but that he was being exalted as God (5:18; 10:33). In the eyes of their opponents these Christians no longer adhered to the fundamental principle, "The Lord our God is one" (Deut 6:4). Thus, confessing faith in Jesus led to the expulsion of Johannine Christians from the synagogues (9:22, 34; 16:2), an expulsion that would have been facilitated if there were Samaritans in their midst (8:48).[65] Being os-

---

64. The Samaritans rejected the Davidic heritage but venerated Moses; and although the Johannine Jesus is descended from David (7:42), he is not someone who at one moment in his life was crowned or recognized as the Davidic king. In one major point, the Johannine Jesus is unlike Moses: he did not have to go up (the mountain) to God; he was already with God before the world began (17:5).

65. *Editor's Note:* At various moments in the first century A.D., Christians of various backgrounds were unwelcome or maltreated in synagogues (Mark 13:9; Acts 22:19; 2 Cor 11:24), but the expulsion of Johannine Christians as a group by the local synagogue(s) may have come earlier than elsewhere. It has already taken place by the time the Fourth Gospel was written, and is no longer even an issue when 1, 2 and 3 John were written. Notice that the evidence for the synagogue expulsion is internal to John. Once widely accepted in Johannine studies (especially under the influence of J. L. Martyn and K. Wengst) as the crucial piece of external evidence to guide the dating and the theological perspective (especially as regards "the Jews") of the Gospel, it is increasingly accepted that there is no need to invoke the *Birkat ha-mînîm* or synagogue blessing (really a curse) against deviants as was frequently done in the past. The idea that it was a universal Jewish decree against Christians is almost certainly wrong and the dating of that blessing to A.D. 85 is dubious. In his *Dialogue* (ca. A.D. 160) Justin states that those who believed in Christ were cursed in the synagogues

tracized may have induced members of the Johannine community no longer to think of themselves as "Jews" and (in addition to the Samaritan influence mentioned above) caused the alienation apparent in expressions like "feast of the Jews" (i.e., not our feast: 5:1; 6:4; etc.) and "their Law" (15:25). Seemingly in the course of expulsion the Johannine Christians were interrogated by synagogue authorities and challenged to defend their claims about Jesus. This would explain the strong legal tone in John (testimony, witness, marshaling of proofs). If preaching shaped the Synoptic traditions, a type of courtroom defense had an impact on the Johannine tradition (see 1:19–27; 5:31–47). One can detect the traces of arguments over the exegesis of biblical passages (6:31–33; 10:34–36).

Excursus: Theories of Johannine Community History[66]

THE AFFIRMATIONS MADE in the final paragraphs of the section above presuppose a theory of the history of the Johannine community. Similar affirmations will return in the further development of Brown's understanding of the second stage of the Gospel's development. The major players in this discussion, and Brown's own understanding of that history, call for a brief presentation before proceeding further with the explanation of his understanding of the second stage of the composition of the Fourth Gospel. It depends heavily upon his theory of the growth of the Johannine community.

(16:4; 47:4; etc.). For a survey of the debate, with his own suggestions, see P. van der Horst, "The Birkat ha-minim in Recent Research," *ExpTim* 105 (1994–95): 363–68. For a valuable study of the Christian view of their Jewish counterparts in the second century, see J. M. Lieu, *Image and Reality. The Jews in the World of Christians in the Second Century* (Edinburgh: T. & T. Clark, 1996).

66. *Editor's Note:* The following excursus (pages 69–85) is my work in its entirety. In the manuscript as Brown left it, he promised: "In Appendix I, I shall discuss various theories of Johannine community history; my approach is laid out in Brown, *Community*." This Appendix was never written, but a summary from the pen of Brown himself can be found in BINT, 373–76. I am taking over my survey of the question, found originally in Moloney, "Revisiting John," 9–15. Other surveys can be found in the General Selected Bibliography. See especially the studies of Koester, "R. E. Brown," U. Schnelle, "Perspektiven," and D. M. Smith, "Johannine Studies." See also Painter, *Quest,* 66–87.

J. Louis Martyn.[67] Martyn has been the most significant figure in developing an understanding of the history of the Johannine community. In 1968, in an important book, *History and Theology in the Fourth Gospel,* he attempted to link the growth of the Johannine Christology with the experience of a particular Christian community working its way through the final breach between the synagogue and the emerging Christian church. He carried these suggestions further in a number of studies, the most important of them being "Source Criticism and Religionsgeschichte in the Fourth Gospel" (1971), and "Glimpses into the History of the Johannine Community. From Its Origin to the Period of Its Life in Which the Fourth Gospel Was Composed" (1977). Martyn arrived at a three-staged development in the community's development.

1. *The Early Period.* This period covers the years before 70, until the 80s. Using John 1:35–49 as a test passage, Martyn claims that the Gospel began with a series of homilies that attempted to present Jesus to the Jews as the Messiah. Jesus is shown as the fulfillment of the messianic hopes of Israel, and thus could be acclaimed with all the traditional messianic titles. Any convert from Judaism into the Christian group would have little difficulty in living the new faith within the world of Torah and synagogue. Martyn uses the expression "Christian Jews" to describe the community at this stage of its life. The homilies were eventually gathered, and roughly formed what is identified by some as the signs source.

2. *The Middle Period.* A second stage within the development of the community was marked by two traumatic experiences. First, the synagogue became suspicious, demanded discussion and midrashic debate over the claims of Jesus, and eventually used the *Birkat ha-mînîm* to force confessing Christians from their midst. This process of midrash, confession and expulsion is dramatically acted out in the account of the experience of the man born blind in John 9. Some of the "Christian Jews" remained within the synagogue, hiding their real identity (see 12:42–43). Martyn uses the expression "Jewish Christians" to describe those excluded from the syna-

---

67. As well as Martyn, *History and Theology,* see ibid. "Glimpses into the History of the Johannine Community. From Its Origin through the Period of Its Life in Which the Fourth Gospel Was Composed," in de Jonge, *L'Évangile,* 149–75.

gogue. The second trauma was caused by the threat of physical persecution and death (see 1:11; 10:28–29; 15:18; 16:2). In this situation, the community began to see itself as "not of this world" (see 17:1–26), hated by the world (see 15:18–16:3; 16:33).

3. *The Late Period.* This period is complex. The Johannine community, gradually developing its identity, addressed the Christian Jews who remained in the synagogue. They were told that there could be no middle way. The community also addressed itself to other Jewish Christians who had been scattered because of the persecution. They were regarded as the "other sheep" (10:16), promised that they would eventually be one flock under one Good Shepherd.

Martyn attempted to trace the social, historical and religious crises that lay behind the growth of the Johannine community. The association of a developing theology and Christology with this growth is not his major concern, although not entirely absent.

Georg Richter.[68] Richter devoted his short career (he died of cancer at 56 years of age) to the development of the Gospel from its beginnings to the final edition. He argued for an original basic written Gospel (*Grundschrift*) that had been reworked by various groups, with varying Christologies, arising within the community. Martyn's interest was strongly focused upon the external factors that shaped the community and its Gospel, while Richter argued that the Gospel indicates that various christological points of view were at play *within* the group. On this basis, he traces four moments in the Gospel's development:

1. *The Mosaic-prophet Christians.* This group of Johannine Christians understood Jesus as the fulfillment of the promise made to Moses in Deut 18:18: "I will raise up for them a prophet like you from among the brethren; and I will put my words in his mouth, and he shall speak to them all that I command him." This Christology can

---

68. The best synthesis of Richter's position from his own pen can be found in G. Richter, "Präsentische und futurische Eschatologie im 4. Evangelium," in *Gegenwart und kommendes Reich: Schulergabe Anton Vögtle zum 65. Geburtstag* (eds., P. Fiedler and D. Zeller; Stuttgart: KBW, 1975), 117-51. See also A. J. Mattill, "Johannine Communities Behind the Fourth Gospel: Georg Richter's Analysis," *TS* 38 (1976): 294-315.

be found in 1:29–34; 6:14 and 7:31. Jesus is not a Davidic Messiah. He was chosen from among men to be the Messiah. This group produced the *Grundschrift* after they were put out of the synagogues of northern Palestine, Syria and Transjordan.

2. *The Son-of-God Christians.* A part of the earliest community reworked the *Grundshrift* as they began to establish themselves in a non-Jewish world. Jesus was now regarded as a Son of God, a man from heaven who brings eschatological salvation *now*. A split occurred at this stage, as not all the community followed this development. A Son-of-God Christology, however, finds its way into a further reworking of the *Grundschrift* in such places as 1:1–13; 8:27–28; 12:16; 13:7; 14:20, 26). Richter regarded the writer of this revised version of the *Grundshrift* as "the Evangelist."

3. *The docetic Christians.* This group carried the Son-of-God Christology of the evangelist to its extremes, and claimed that Jesus was not genuinely human. They made no direct contribution to the Gospel, but we know of their existence from the evidence of the last stage of the Gospel's growth, during which polemical anti-docetic material was introduced into the story. The docetic group also broke with the mainstream Johannine community, to follow its own christological development.

4. *The antidocetic redaction.* The Gospel's final stage was a revision that attacked any hint that of docetism (stage 3). See especially 1:14–18; 19:34–35. The same tendency is reflected in, for example, 1 John 4:2–3 and 2 John 7. The Christology that results from this final redaction lies somewhere between the Mosaic prophet of the *Grundschrift* and the Son-of-God idea of the evangelist. The anti-docetic redaction pulled back from some of the positions taken by the evangelist.

Richter moved toward the Johannine epistles for evidence of his final, anti-docetic, stage in the development of the Gospel. His concern throughout is the intersection between history and theology in the development of the final form of the Gospel.

Wolfgang Langbrandtner.[69] Langbrandtner begins his attemnpt to retrace the history of the Johannine community with the Johannine epistles. A fea-

---

69. Langbrandtner, *Weltferner Gott oder Gott der Liebe*, 373–404.

ture of Langbrandtner's contribution is his introduction of the influence of early Gnosticism. He traces three stages in the community's history:

1. *Grundschrift.* In contrast to the suggestions of both Martyn and Richter, Langbrandtner claims that the earliest form of the Gospel was Gnostic and dualistic, written some time after 80 C.E. This earliest composition attempted to present Jesus thematically. For example, 1:1–13 is determined by the themes of soteriology and Christology; ch. 3 by the theme of the human being and its possibilities, ch. 6 by faith, and so on. At this stage of the life of the community (still present in the final form of the Gospel) there is a strong anti-signs tendency. Miracles were regarded as useless for faith.

2. *Redaction.* Some time about 100 C.E. a polemical anti-Gnostic and anti-docetic rewriting of the *Grundschrift* took place. The redactor looked to a historical figure, an aged and revered man of authority in the community, as the authority for this redaction. He called this figure "the Beloved Disciple." The redactor was not the BD, but added this figure to the story to add support to the anti-Gnostic and anti-docetic redaction. At this stage, all the historical, fleshly, elements came into the Gospel, along with the so-called "ecclesial" elements: sacramental hints, ethics, and a traditional "end-time" eschatology.

3. *The Letters.* The epistles were written in the order of 2 John, 3 John and finally 1 John. They reflect a gradual development toward a more rigidly "ecclesial" line of thought, also called "early Catholicism." The redactor went further in this direction, while those who refused to accept this line left the community and eventually made their way into full-blown Gnosticism. There were others, however (like the Diotrephes of 3 John) who claimed that there was too much ambiguity in the development of the community's thought and discipline. They demanded greater order and discipline.

All three scholars whose theories are outlined above contributed importantly to a discussion which, in many ways, reached in zenith in the work of Brown, *The Community of the Beloved Disciple.* Some clear lines were already appearing. Both Martyn and Richter agreed that the earliest community adopted a simple Jewish-Christian Christology, and regarded the development of a more exalted Christology (a Son-of-God Christology) as the reason for the break with the synagogue. Both regard the introduction of the *Birkat ha-mînîm* as a significant moment in the parting of the ways between the synagogue and Johannine Christianity. Langbrandtner has no interest in this development. He claimed that the community went back no further than the 60s of the first Christian century and had never had contact with the early Christologies outlined by Martyrn and Richter. Yet Langrbrandtner correctly insists that the story of the experiences of Johannine community reaches beyond the evidence of the Gospel, and that the epistles are a further source of information for the ongoing directions taken by the various factions that can been seen behind the development of the Johannine traditions.

Raymond E. Brown. Brown makes full use of both the Gospel and the epistles to rediscover "the Community of the Beloved Disciple."[70] He argues, always aware that this form of scholarship remains hypothetical, that one can trace four stages in the community's growth.

1. *Before the Gospel.* An original group, beginning with a circle of ex-disciples of JBap. Shows a typically early Christian "low" Christology. At this stage, the figure of the BD is important. He is an ex-disciple of JBap, a follower of Jesus from the start of his ministry, but *not* one of the Twelve. This outstanding historical personality, the "father" of the community, serves as a link between the historical Jesus and the Johannine community.

2. *When the Gospel was written.* After the admission of Samaritan and other anti-Temple groups, a conflict with "the Jews" begins. This leads to a "higher" Christology, eventually leading to the use of the absolute *Ego Eimi* and the idea of the preexistence of Jesus. As the Gospel is written, the community takes an increasingly determined stance against those they would regard as nonbelievers: "the world," "the Jews," and adherents of JBap. Also included in the list of "nonbelievers" were so-called "crypto-Christians." These were Jews who believed, but remained in the synagogue (see 12:42–43), and Jewish Christians who would not confess the high Johannine Christology. In general terms, they might be regarded as Christians who followed the less charismatic line of the so-called "greater Church," exemplified by the Jerusalem Church and its leader, James.[71]

---

70. Brown, *Community.*
71. See below, Chapter Five.

3. *When the letters were written.* The community, having taken a closed stance against those outside their ranks, began to suffer from internal divisions. These divisions grew out of variant possible interpretations of the Johannine Gospel. A study of the letters reveals at least two groups. Both appear to be looking back to the Gospel as their inspirational document, but they interpret it differently. In the areas of Christology, ethics, eschatology and pneumatology, the letters show a historicizing, more conservative, approach than the Gospel. They are moving more in the direction of the so-called "greater church," while the "opponents" are accused of dehistoricizing, eliminating the obligations that ethics and a true life in the Spirit should produce. They were moving in the direction of what was later known as docetic Gnosticism.

4. *After the letters were written.* The final moment in the history of the community is its separation and dissolution. The group behind the letters merges with the greater church. This can already been seen in the writings of Ignatius of Antioch (c. 110). Johannine Christology has been accepted, but a Paraclete-dominated ecclesiology and ethics have been lost. The "opponents" take the Gospel and their interpretation of it into Gnosticism. This can be seen from the strong presence of the Johannine Gospel in the literature of the Gnostic sects.

This brief excursus indicates scholarly reflection upon the history of the Johannine community that guided Brown to the development of his own hypothesis. On the basis of this hypothesis, he has developed his three-stage theory of the development of the Fourth Gospel. It lies behind the following suggestions as he further develops his understanding of what took place in his so-called "second stage" as the community proclaimed Jesus in the postresurrectional context of the community's history.[72]

Expulsion from the synagogue had several side effects that eventually would leave their mark on the Fourth Gospel. First, the Johannine Christians in their self-estimation made a great sacrifice in bravely confessing

---

72. *Editor's Note.* I now resume Brown's text, after the necessary introduction of the survey of theories surrounding the development of the Johannine community, concluding in Brown's own theory, promised but not completed in the original Brown typescript. For critical reaction to these "histories" of the Johannine community, see Moloney, "Revisiting John," 11–15, and the works mentioned above in note 67.

Christ even when they knew the penalty. Consequently they had nothing but contempt for others who believed in Jesus but did so secretly and thus avoided punishment. Those people valued human respect over God's glory (12:42–43; cf. 9:22–23; 19:38; one may pause to reflect that in the eyes of the people thus castigated the Johannine Christians were surely deemed to be unnecessarily brash and rude [e.g., 9:27–28] when prudent gradualism might have been more persuasive). No other Gospel is so judgmental about the inadequate faith of other followers of Jesus, equating it with disbelief (6:60–66; 8:31ff.). Consequently the Johannine community struggled on several fronts: with Jews who did not believe in Jesus and with Jews and others who did believe but deficiently. Moreover, since in the Johannine tradition the first followers of Jesus were disciples of JBap, John shows acute awareness of disciples of JBap who did not accept Jesus (3:25–26). Although JBap is venerated as a man sent by God (1:6), John is careful to stress the limitations of his role: not the light but only a witness to it (1:8); not the bridegroom but the best man (3:29); one who must decrease while Jesus increases (3:30).

Expulsion had cut the Johannine Christians off from the rich Jewish liturgical life, and to compensate for that the Johannine tradition emphasized a strong motif of replacement: Jesus takes the place of many of the institutions of Judaism. In a play on the imagery of the Tabernacle or desert tent where the Lord God was present, the Prologue proclaims that the Word became flesh and "tented" among us (1:14). The body of Jesus is raised up in place of the destroyed Temple sanctuary (2:19–22). If the Sabbath was a day on which human beings are not to work, nevertheless, people are born and die on the Sabbath—work peculiar to God; and the Son has received from the Father the right to give life and judge on the Sabbath (5:10, 20–21). The theme of manna was associated with Passover; and Jesus, not the manna, is the true bread come down from heaven (6:4, 31–35). Tabernacles in popular celebration was a feast of water and light; and on that feast Jesus proclaims himself as the source of living water and the light of the world (7:2, 37–38; 8:12). Hanukkah or Dedication celebrated the reconsecration of the great altar of holocausts in the Temple, and on that feast Jesus speaks of himself as the one whom the Father has consecrated and sent into the world (10:22, 36).[73]

---

73. *Editor's Note.* I have let this paragraph on "replacement" stand in Brown's discussion of the community's relationship to the "institutions of Judaism." However,

In my hypothesis this stage was very formative in Johannine thought patterns and shaping of the tradition. Over a period lasting perhaps several decades, under the influence of the developments in community life just described, the Jesus material from Stage One was sifted, selected, thought over, and molded into the form and style of individual stories and consecutive sayings. Contacts with other Christians brought a familiarity with the way the Jesus tradition was being shaped and proclaimed among them.[74] The Beloved Disciple probably played a major role in guiding the community through its vicissitudes and helping it to acquire theological perspective. In fact it is probably in this period that he became "Beloved," since the depth of insight that he gained was seen as a mark of Jesus' special selection and love. Nevertheless, in the preaching, teaching, and witness-bearing that marked Stage Two there had to be more than one man. As evidence of that, in the final Gospel there are units of Johannine material, like ch. 21, that are different in style from the main body of material.

Much of the transmission during this Stage Two was oral, and B. Noack has stressed the influence of oral tradition on the later, written Gospel, although his conclusions may be somewhat exaggerated. Goodwin has noted interesting indications that some of John's citations of the OT are from memory, a conclusion that also points toward oral transmission.[75] Yet, toward the end of this second stage, written forms of what was preached and taught may have taken shape. If one looks through pages 66–78 in this chapter, possibilities emerge like a signs source or

---

more recent scholarship questions the use of the term "replacement." There is a real sense of the Johannine Christology bringing to perfection what took place in the great festive "memories" of God's saving actions. However, the memory of the God of Israel, and the Jewish symbols used (life and judgment, manna, light, water, shepherds and the consecrated place of encounter between God and human beings) retain their place in the Johannine theology. For a reading of John 5–10 along these lines, see Moloney, *Signs and Shadows*. Much depends upon the exegesis of the two "gifts" of God in 1:17. Does the gift that comes through Jesus Christ *surpass* or *replace* the gift of the Law that came through Moses?

74. Later I shall explain that I do not think the fourth evangelist knew Mark's Gospel, but he was aware of the type of tradition enshrined in Mark.

75. C. Goodwin, "How Did John Treat his Sources?" *JBL* 73 (1954): 61–75. Many more commentators point to orality in the background, e.g., Collins, "Figures"; Lindars, *Behind the Fourth Gospel* (Johannine homilies).

Fortna's "Gospel of Signs." I doubt that we have the ability to isolate in detail pre-Gospel written sources or to distinguish them from possible early editions of the Gospel not written by the evangelist (Boismard's Document C).

Stage Three: The Writing of the Gospel

Here I would detect the work of two figures, the evangelist and the redactor. The "evangelist" is the writer who composed the body of the existing Gospel,[76] and "redactor" refers to another writer who made some additions after the evangelist had completed his work. Who was the evangelist and who was the redactor? It may help at this juncture to advise readers that in my judgment the answer that best fits the evidence is that they were disciples of the Beloved Disciple who probably was dead by the time the Gospel was written.[77] Let me emphasize that in positing two hands in Stage Three, with the evangelist responsible for a form of the gospel before the existing canonical Gospel, I am not proposing to indulge in constructing a hypothetical pre-Gospel text (whether source or edition) in the manner of Fortna or Boismard—something that would belong to Stage Two. What I contemplate is working entirely on the level of the existing Gospel but assigning parts of it to different hands. True, it is hypothetical to posit such a division of labor; yet in my judgment the theory of two contributors best explains the difficulties described on pp. 40–42.[78] In this theory, the contribution of the evangelist is far more notable and influential; and if one wants to use the language of author, he is truly the author of the Fourth Gospel.

---

76. It is impossible to say whether he physically wrote the gospel himself or used the services of a scribe. Most probably he wrote in Greek (Chapter Eight, pp. 278–81). Since in this hypothesis the final (canonical) Gospel contained more than the work produced by the evangelist, in this discussion I shall use lowercase "gospel" to refer to what the evangelist completed, and keep the upper case for the existing work.

77. For further detail, see below, Chapter Seven.

78. *Editor's Note:* Brown adds a long parenthesis to his introduction at this point, claiming that he makes this distinction as a "theoretical explanation of the origins of the Gospel." He affirms, however, that the distinction would not have influenced his commentary on the text. Under the influence of more narrative approaches, he had decided to base his second edition "on the Gospel as it now stands."

THE EVANGELIST

The work of the evangelist is important in all the Gospels. Evangelists were not just collectors of material; rather, by selecting, editing, arranging, and expounding, each one of the four produced a coherent theological presentation of Jesus adapted to the needs of the envisioned audience. The Johannine pre-Gospel relationships described in Stage Two left indelible marks on the tradition; but the evangelist was not writing to explain what had happened between the Johannine community and the synagogue, or the followers of JBap, etc.[79] He was not addressing either "the Jews" or Christians of inadequate faith. He was writing to encourage the faith of his own community and like-minded Christians. He expressed the purpose of his gospel in this way: "That you may have faith that Jesus is the Messiah, the Son of God, and through this faith you may have life in his name" (20:31).

To accomplish that purpose the evangelist called on remarkable skills. Some of what I shall describe may already have been part of the tradition that came down to the evangelist from Stage Two, but the end product is not haphazard in its techniques and betrays a deliberate hand. Stories of Jesus' miracles, probably those most used in preaching, were developed into superb dramas of christological import, e.g., ch. 9.[80] The sayings of Jesus were woven into lengthy discourses of a solemn and poetic character, much like the discourses of personified Wisdom in the OT, as the evangelist carried through the Jesus/Wisdom theme from an earlier Stage. The techniques of Johannine storytelling, such as misunderstanding and irony, were introduced, or at least developed, from Stage Two in the way we now know them. Various factors contributed to the welding of sign and interpretative discourse. This was not necessarily an artificial joining, for probably even in Stage One miracles had often carried with them words of explanation. But now the evangelist's goal demanded

---

79. In response to Painter, *Messiah* 67, note 101, it is one thing to suggest that the history of the Johannine community can be read out of the Gospel by a type of detective work (something I affirm), but is entirely different to suggest that the evangelist set out to write a history of the community in the guise of a Gospel (something I firmly deny).

80. See E. K. Lee, "The Drama of the Fourth Gospel," *ExpTim* 65 (1953–54), 173–76; Culpepper, *Anatomy of the Fourth Gospel.*

longer explanation and a more unified arrangement. Let me concentrate on several aspects of the evangelist's work.

Structure. Two sentences of the Prologue summarize well the flow of the Gospel by describing the activity of the Word: "To his own he came; yet his own people did not accept him. But all those who did accept him he empowered to become God's children" (1:11–12). If the Prologue was a community hymn, then this division of Jesus' activity was well fixed in the community's outlook, and the evangelist took it over into his gospel.[81] The first sentence of the Prologue summary covers the first half of the existing gospel (1:19–12:50), which describes the public ministry of Jesus and his "signs," ending with a harsh judgment culled from Isaiah on the nonbelievers (who in the Gospel context are clearly Jesus' fellow Jews). They have been blinded and numbed, and so they have not been converted (12:37–41).[82] But now Greeks (= Gentiles) have come asking to see Jesus, and their arrival signals that the hour has come for his glorification through return to the Father. The second sentence of the Prologue summary covers the second half of the gospel (13:1–20:31), which deals with those who do accept him and who thus become God's children—a new "his own" whom he loves to the very end (13:1) and whom in ascending to heaven he will assure that "my Father" is "your Father" (20:17). The Last Discourse (13:31–17:26)[83] is a magnificent address to those of all time who would be Jesus' disciples.

Theological function of signs. Instead of the many miraculous acts of power described in the Synoptic Gospels, the Fourth Gospel chooses a few incidents that serve as "signs" because they reveal heavenly truth about Jesus and what he has brought from God. In performing these

---

81. Beginning the story of Jesus with JBap and ending it with crucifixion, burial, and resurrection (appearances) was to a great extent dictated by fact, and is the backbone of all four Gospels. Disciples first encountered Jesus after his baptism by JBap and, except for fleeing at the time of crucifixion, were witnesses from then on. (See the qualification for being one of the Twelve in Acts 1:21–22.) How to divide that span and the theological import given to the divisions varied with each evangelist.

82. In the discussion of the redactor, I shall raise the possibility that the evangelist finished his gospel with 10:42 and that the redactor added chs. 11–12. There is a rejection of Jesus by "the Jews" in 10:31–39.

83. Or 13:31–14:31 in the evangelist's gospel if the redactor added chs. 15–17.

signs Jesus, who has come from another world, speaks the language of this world, referring to water, bread, sight, life, etc., that persons involved in the stories misunderstand on a physical level. Such misunderstanding causes Jesus to explain further. He has not come simply to give the Samaritan woman water to slake physical thirst, but a water that springs up to eternal life (4:4–42). Jesus has not come simply to satisfy physical hunger by multiplying bread but to offer himself, the incarnate revelation, as the bread of life that will end hunger forever (6:32–35). Jesus has not come simply to give a blind man physical sight (which would put him on the same level as other people, many of whom can see no spiritual realities) but spiritual sight that enables him to recognize Jesus as the Son of Man come from God (9:1–41, especially 9:33–38).[84] The Gospel readers are drawn into these dialogues that are almost little plays or dramas, so that Jesus may offer them the same heavenly realities.[85] In my judgment he used the technique of signs to point to baptism and eucharist, so that these "sacraments" that had an important place in the life of the community were rooted in what Jesus said and did. Thus the evangelist made the gospel the vehicle of various aspects of Johannine theology.[86] In the tradition, the Paraclete-Spirit promised by Jesus would teach Jesus' followers and remind them of all that he had said.[87] If in Stage Two the BD was a major instrument of the Paraclete-Spirit in bearing witness, by producing the gospel in Stage Three the evangelist was the instrument of the Paraclete-Spirit.

Two editions? As we have seen, Boismard proposes two editions of the Gospel by the same writer (Jean IIA and IIB), one in Aramaic, one in

---

84. Jesus has not come simply to restore Lazarus to ordinary life in which he shall die again but to give eternal life whereby those who believe will never die at all (11:1–44, especially 11:25–26). Possibly chs. 11–12 were added by the redactor, but he would have been adding material similar to that used by the evangelist.

85. For more detail on the dramatic techniques employed by the evangelist, see below, Chapter Eight, pp. 287–92.

86. See Chapter Seven, below.

87. The role of the Paraclete-Spirit is developed in parallel ways in chs. 15–16 which may have been the addition of the redactor: the Paraclete would guide believers along the way of all truth, not by giving new revelation but by taking over what Jesus had said and rephrasing it to meet new situations (16:13–15). See Moloney, "The Gospel of John: A Story of Two Paracletes," in *"A Hard Saying,"* 149–66.

Greek, over thirty years apart. In the first edition of my commentary I too posited two editions[88] but went to the other end of the spectrum in terms of lack of precision. I admitted that "it is not always possible to distinguish between what belongs to the second editing of the gospel and what belongs to the final redaction." I still think it is probable that the evangelist did retouch his own work,[89] especially as an adaptation of the gospel to meet new problems. I am not convinced that there was an Aramaic first edition (Boismard);[90] but if all or part of the community moved from Palestine to Ephesus or some other site where Gentile converts may not have been familiar with certain Jewish vocabulary, the evangelist might have been responsible for the various parentheses that explain terms (e.g., 1:38, 42). Yet that step might have been the work of the redactor. Moreover, detection of what would belong to the first edition and what to the second edition is (at least as far as I am concerned) so incapable of proof that for all practical purposes the two-edition theory is not helpful in developing a coherent commentary upon the gospel as a whole.

THE REDACTOR

There is good evidence for a reworking of the Gospel by someone other than the evangelist and whom I call the redactor. I particularly wish to avoid Bultmann's terminology "Ecclesiastical Redactor," because I do not think of this figure as correcting the evangelist's gospel. The most likely supposition is that the redactor was a co-disciple of the evangelist in the following of the BD, part of the Johannine School.[91]

One of the principal contributions of the redactor to the Gospel was to preserve still available Johannine material from Stages One and Two that had not been used by the evangelist (whether or not that material was

---

88. See *John*, xxxvi. A theory of two editions by the evangelist and a final redaction by a disciple would not be extraordinary among the theories of the composition of biblical books—a very similar theory is proposed for the Book of Jeremiah.

89. As Painter, *Quest* 64, remarks, editing was inevitable "unless the author sat down and wrote the Gospel out of his head without reference to any tradition."

90. I would also part company from a theory such as that of Wilkens, who would see in the first edition only a collection of signs, and that of Parker, who posits a first edition that has no Galilean ministry. I doubt that any substantial gospel edition that is based ultimately on a historical tradition of the works and words of Jesus could have ignored the ministry in Galilee, which was so much a part of Jesus' life.

91. See below, Chapter Six, p. 199.

known by the evangelist). This material would not necessarily differ substantially in style or vocabulary from the evangelist's gospel.[92] The fact that this material was added at the end of Johannine Gospel formation does not mean that overall it was any less ancient than material that appeared in the evangelist's gospel. Thus, the age of the material is not a criterion that will always enable us to detect additions by the redactor. The awkwardness of an intrusive passage in the sequence of the present Gospel is a better criterion, but even that may be the result of the historical, theological, literary and even sociological "distance" that exists between the first-century Johannine text and the interpreter of the third millennium.[93] That some of this intrusive material represents a variant duplicate of material found elsewhere in the Gospel is another, complementary criterion and, indeed, is the reason for assuming that the final redactor was not the evangelist himself. The evangelist could have reworked his own material into a consonant whole; but the redactor, not feeling free to rewrite the Gospel as it came to him, simply inserted the duplicate discourses, often side by side with the form of the discourse that existed in the earlier edition, for example, 6:51–58 next to 6:35–50. With some discourses that had no setting, the redactor chose to add them at the end of an appropriate scene rather than to interrupt the scene, for example, 3:31–36 and 12:44–50.[94]

---

92. The evangelist's composition of his gospel meant selection, and not all of the Johannine material stemming from the evangelist's preaching would have been included. If the evangelist had preached over a number of years, he had probably phrased the tradition of Jesus' words in different ways at different times. Thus, there would have been in circulation different versions of discourses, adapted to varying needs and audiences.

93. *Editor's Note:* There are many places in James Joyce's *Ulysses* which could be judged as "intrusive," but the novel is judged on its own merits, despite a number of apparent non sequiturs, because it is a modern novel and must be read as such. A parallel criterion should be kept in mind when a contemporary reader approaches the Fourth Gospel.

94. *Editor's Note:* Contemporary readings strive harder to make sense of these texts in their present location, applying a principle from Wolfgang Iser, who insists that every reader strives "even if unconsciously, to fit everything together in a consistent pattern" (*The Implied Reader: Patterns of Communication in Prose Fiction from Bunyan to Beckett* [Baltimore: Johns Hopkins University Press, 1978], 283). On the basis of the fundamental study of John 6 by P. Borgen, *Bread from Heaven: An Exegetical*

Two of the more commonly accepted additions of Johannine material attributed to the redactor are ch. 21 (after the evangelist's gospel ending in 20:30–31) and the Prologue (a once-independent Johannine community hymn that constitutes most of 1:1–18, prefaced to the evangelist's original opening now preserved in 1:6–8 followed by 1:19).[95] Ch. 21 gives Simon Peter particular attention and assigns to him a pastoral role, and thus may represent a later era in the development of community structure, indeed one after the secession described in the Johannine epistles.[96]

Otherwise, the redactor seems to have made a large collection of Johannine material in which Jesus was portrayed as speaking to his disciples. Many think he added such a collection to the Last Supper Discourse of Jesus in chs. 15–17. That this addition was the work of the redactor and not of the evangelist seems likely from the fact that the original ending of the Last Discourse in 14:31 (which leads directly into 18:1) was not tampered with or adapted to the new insertion. Among the material thus added was 16:4–33, a variant duplicate of the discourse in ch. 14.

Much more debatable is whether the redactor was also responsible for adding the material in chs. 11 and 12 to the Gospel outline. Already in my 1966 commentary I raise the possibility that the original gospel ending of the public ministry came in 10:40–42, and I point out a historical problem caused by the presentation of the Lazarus story in 11 as the chief cause for Jesus' execution.[97] The insertion of the Lazarus motif of chs.

Study of the Conception of the Manna in the Gospel of John and the Writings of Philo (NovTSupp 10; Leiden: E. J. Brill, 1965), see my attempt to make narrative sense of 6:35–58 in F. J. Moloney, "The Function of Prolepsis in the Interpretation of John 6," in R. A. Culpepper (ed.), *The Interpretation of John 6* (BibIntS 22; Leiden: E. J. Brill, 1997), 129–48.

95. *Editor's Note:* In the light of note 91, it may be something of an overstatement for Brown to claim that his suggestions concerning redactional history of the Prologue and John 21 are "commonly accepted." I agree as regards John 21, but there is an increasing number of Johannine scholars who do not. For an annotated discussion of contemporary opinion on John 21, see Moloney, *Glory not Dishonor*, 182–92.

96. Many see parallels in the thrust of the Prologue ("the Word became flesh"), thought to have been added by the redactor, and the Christology of the epistles: "Jesus Christ come/coming in the flesh" (1 John 4:2; 2 John 7). For a full discussion of the relationship between the Johannine Gospel and letters, see BEJ, 14–35, 69–115.

97. See *John*, 414–15, 427–30. If chs. 11 and 12 represent a late addition of Johannine material, it is possible that this addition was made by the evangelist himself if he

11–12 into the account of the last days before Passover seems to have caused the redactor to shift the incident of the cleansing of the Temple, originally associated with Jesus' entry into Jerusalem, to another section of the Gospel (now in ch. 2).

Liturgical interest seems to have been a factor in shifting eucharistic material associated with Jesus' words over the bread and wine at the Last Supper from that locale to 6:51–58. In this suggestion of relocation of material, I am close to Wilkens, although I do not find compelling the motive that he attributes to such shifts; namely, to spread the theme of Passover throughout the Gospel. Rather, it is quite likely that Passover was already mentioned in 2 and 6, and that the redactor was simply shifting material from one Passover feast in Jesus' life to another.

Some of the material that the redactor added seems to be stronger in its reference to sacraments than the rest of the Gospel. *Pace* Bultmann, however, I do not believe that the redactor's purpose was to insert sacramental references in the evangelist's nonsacramental gospel, but rather to bring out more clearly the latent sacramentalism already in the gospel.[98]

A number of scholars would contend that the redactor knew one or more of the Synoptic Gospels and introduced into John some of the close parallels to the Synoptic tradition (cf. John 6:7 and Mark 6:37; John 12:3, 5 and Mark 14:3, 5).[99] I think other explanations can be offered (e.g., influence of oral tradition), so it is not necessary to posit that either the evangelist or the redactor had the Synoptic Gospels before him. But let us leave that issue to the next chapter.

Summary

THE THEORY OF THREE STAGES of Gospel formation that I have proposed solves many of the difficulties discussed in pp. 40–42. It explains why

---

did write a second edition of his gospel. However, the use of the term "the Jews" in 11–12 differs from that of the rest of the Gospel, a fact that is less difficult to reconcile if the Lazarus story had an independent history and was added by the redactor.

98. See below, Chapter Seven, pp. 229–34.

99. The Synoptic Gospels were dependent on several traditions; but I shall use the singular, "Synoptic tradition," when drawing general comparisons between these Gospels and John.

Schweizer and Ruckstuhl find a rather uniform style throughout the Gospel. The BD would have been a witness from Stage One who emerged as a major figure in shaping the community history of Stage Two, and the evangelist and redactor of Stage Three would have been disciples of the BD during Stage Two. Yet, while preserving the substantial unity of the tradition that appears in the Gospel, this theory explains the various factors that militate against unity of authorship. The redaction in Stage Three accounts for the presence of Johannine material of somewhat different style and also for the presence of duplicate discourses, of insertions that seem to interrupt, and of the seeming rearrangement of some scenes (without, however, positing elaborate displacements).

There remain many inadequacies and uncertainties in such a theory. In Stage Three, how much personal contribution did the evangelist make to what was taken over from Stage Two? How can one distinguish with any surety between the hand of the evangelist and the hand of the redactor? There are no facile answers to such questions. I would claim only to have offered a working hypothesis for understanding how the Gospel was put together. At the end of the hypothesizing, however, let me remind readers what I wrote at the beginning of this subsection before advancing my theory of composition: primary consideration in a commentary must be given to the Gospel as it now stands. I agree fully with Culpepper: "In its present form, if not in its origin, the Gospel must be approached as a unity, a literary whole." [100]

BIBLIOGRAPHY

It has not always been easy to decide which works to list here and which to list in the Bibliography of the next chapter, since some writings discuss composition largely in terms of relation to the Synoptic Gospels, e.g. Dunderberg's *Johannes*.

Backhaus, K., "Preparatio Evangelii. Die religionsgeschichtlichen Beziehungen zwischen Täufer—und Jesus Bewegung im Spiegel der sog. Semeia-Quelle des vierten Evangeliums," *TG* 81 (1991): 202–215. See

---

100. Culpepper, *Anatomy,* 49.

also *TG* 81 (1991): 279–301, in the Bibliography to Chapter Five, below.

Bauckham, R., "The Beloved Disciple as Real Author," *JSNT* 44 (1993): 21–44.

Becker, H., *Die Reden des Johannesevangeliums und der Stil der gnostischen Offenbarungsreden* (Göttingen: Vandenhoeck & Ruprecht, 1956).

Becker, J., "Wunder und Christologie," *NTS* 16 (1969–70): 130–48. See also his commentary *Johannes*, 1.29–40, and his survey articles in *TRev* in the general bibliography.

Bittner, J., *Jesu Zeichen im Johannesevangelium: Die Messias-Erkenntnis im Johannesevangelium vor ihrem jüdischen Hintergrund* (WUNT 2.26; Tübingen: Mohr/Siebeck, 1987).

Boismard, M.-É., "Saint Luc et la rédaction du quatrième évangile," *RB* 69 (1962): 185–211.

Carson, D. A., "Current Source Criticism of the Fourth Gospel: Some Methodological Questions," *JBL* 97 (1978): 411–29.

Corsani, B., *I miracoli di Gesù nel quarto vangelo. L'ipotesi della fonte dei segni* (Brescia: Paideia, 1983).

Easton, B. S., "Bultmann's RQ Source," *JBL* 65 (1946): 143–56.

Fortna, R. T., *The Fourth Gospel and Its Predecessor: From Narrative Source to Present Gospel* (Philadelphia: Fortress, 1988).

———, *The Gospel of Signs: A Reconstruction of the Narrative Source Underlying the Fourth Gospel* (SNTSMS 11: Cambridge: Cambridge University Press, 1970).

Heekerens, H.-P., *Die Zeichen-Quelle der johanneischen Redaktion. Ein Beitrag zur Entstehungsgeschichte des vierten Evangeliums* (SBS 113; Stuttgart: KBW, 1984).

Käsemann, E., "Ketzer und Zeuge, zum johanneischen Verfasserproblem," *ZTK* 48 (1951): 292–311.

Láconi, M., "La critica letteraria applicata al IV Vangelo," *Angelicum* 40 (1963): 277–312.

Lindars, B., *Behind the Fourth Gospel* (London: SPCK, 1971).

Macgregor, G. H. C., and A. Q. Morton, *The Structure of the Fourth Gospel* (Edinburgh: Oliver and Boyd, 1961).

Marguerat, D., "La 'source des signes' existe-t-elle?" in Kaestli, Poffet and Zumstein, eds., *La communauté*, 69–93.

Martyn, J. L., "Source Criticism and Religionsgeschichte in the Fourth Gospel," *Perspective* 11 (1970): 247–73.

Mayer, A., "Elijah and Elisha in John's Sign Source," *ExpTim* 99 (1987–88): 171–73.

Morton, A. Q., and J. McLeman, *The Genesis of John* (Edinburgh: Saint Andrew, 1980).

Neirynck, F., et al., *Jean et les synoptiques: Examen critique de l'exégèse de M.-É. Boismard* (BETL 49: Leuven: Leuven University Press, 1979).

———, "The Signs Source in the Fourth Gospel," *Evangelica II*, 651–77.

Noack, B., *Zur johanneischen Tradition. Beiträge zur Kritik an der literarkritischen Analyse des vierten Evangeliums* (Copenhagen: Rosenkilde, 1954).

Parker, P., "Two Editions of John," *JBL* 75 (1956): 303–14.

Robert, R., "Un examen critique de l'exégèse de M.-É. Boismard," *RThom* 83 (1983): 625–38.

Ruckstuhl, E., *Die literarische Einheit des Johannesevangeliums* (Freiburg: Paulus, 1951. New ed.; Freiburg [Switz.]: Universität, 1987).

———, "Johannine Language and Style. The Question of their Unity," in de Jonge, *L'Évangile*, 125–47.

Ruckstuhl, E. and P. Dschulnigg, *Stilkritik und Verfasserfrage im Johannesevangelium* (Freiburg [Switz.]: Universität, 1991).

Schenke, L., "Der 'Dialog Jesu mit den Juden' im Johannesevangelium: Ein Rekonstruktionsversuch," *NTS* 34 (1988): 573–603.

Schille, G., "Traditionsgut im vierten Evangelium," *TV* 12 (1981): 77–89.

Schnackenburg, R., "On the Origin of the Fourth Gospel," *Perspective* 11 (1970): 223–46. For the German, see *BZ* 14 (1970): 1–23.

Schulz, S., *Komposition und Herkunft der johanneischen Reden* (Stuttgart: Kohlhammer, 1960).

Schweizer, E., *Ego Eimi . . . Die religionsgeschichtliche Herkunft und theologische Bedeutung der johanneischen Bildreden, zugleich ein Beitrag zur Quellenfrage des vierten Evangeliums* (Göttingen: Vandenhoeck & Ruprecht, 1939).

Sinclair, S. G., *The Road and the Truth: The Editing of John's Gospel* (Vallejo, CA: Bibal, 1994).

Smith, D. M., *The Composition and Order of the Fourth Gospel: Bultmann's Literary Theory* (Cambridge: Yale University Press, 1965).

———, *Johannine Christianity*, 37–91 (see general bibliography). Three articles: "The Sources of the Gospel of John"; "The Milieu of the Johannine Miracle Source"; "The Setting and Shape of a Johannine Narrative Source."

Teeple, H. M., "Methodology in Source Analysis of the Fourth Gospel," *JBL* 81 (1962): 279–86.

———, *The Literary Origin of the Gospel of John* (Evanston, IL: Religion and Ethics Institute, 1974).

Temple, S., *The Core of the Fourth Gospel* (London: Mowbrays, 1975).

Thyen, H., "Johannes 13 und die 'Kirchliche Redaktion' des vierten Evangeliums," in *Tradition und Glaube: Das frühe Christentum in seiner Umwelt: Festgabe für Kark Georg Kuhn zum 65. Geburtstag* (eds. G. Jeremias et al; Göttingen: Vandenhoeck & Ruprecht, 1971), 343–56.

Wahlde, U. C. von, *The Earliest Version of John's Gospel: Recovering the Gospel of Signs* (Wilmington: Glazier, 1989).

Wilkens, W., *Die Entstehungsgeschichte des vierten Evangeliums* (Zollikon: Evangelischer Verlag, 1958).

———, "Evangelist und Tradition im Johannesevangelium," *TZ* 16 (1960): 81–90.

3

Johannine Tradition: Relation to the Synoptics and Historicity

◆

IN THE THEORY OF COMPOSITION that I have proposed, Stage One involves the existence of a body of material pertaining to the works and words of Jesus. How *primitive* was this material when compared to the Jesus material underlying the Synoptic Gospels? The further question of the degree to which such a primitive tradition of the Christian community was *historical,* representing the actual deeds and *ipsissima verba* of Jesus, will be taken up at the end of this discussion.

The very fact that John is classified as a Gospel presupposes that John is based on a tradition similar in character to the traditions behind the Synoptic Gospels. Even those commentators who treat the Fourth Gospel simply as a work of theology devoid of historical value must be impressed by the fact that this theology is written in a career-of-Jesus context (unlike the Johannine Epistles).[1] Paul too was a theologian, but he did not write his theology in the framework of Jesus' earthly ministry.

---

1. Indeed, some would regard the Fourth Gospel as an attempt to prevent the kerygmatic preaching of the church from being mythologized and divorced from the history of Jesus of Nazareth.

The outline of Jesus' ministry seen in the Synoptic Gospels is probably an expansion of the basic kerygmatic outline of Jesus material used by the earliest preachers. That outline is not dissimilar to the outline of the ministry in John.[2] If Mark begins with the baptism of Jesus by JBap, so does John. In the Synoptic kerygma, the baptism is followed by a long ministry in Galilee in which Jesus heals and does good; Galilean material is found in John too but more briefly, scattered (4:46–54; 6), and interspersed with Jerusalem and Samaria material. After the Galilean ministry, in both the Synoptics and John, Jesus goes to Jerusalem, where he speaks in the Temple precincts; then follow the passion, death, and resurrection. Where John differs significantly from the Synoptic outline is in the report of a much longer Jerusalem ministry, but is this an essential variation from the outline? After all, Luke too has its variations, for example, in the journey to Jerusalem, which takes some ten chapters. Despite a generally similar arrangement of material one must ask whether the activities and features peculiar to John stem from a primitive tradition, for they could conceivably represent an artificial imitation of gospel style.

To answer this question let us first evaluate the information unique to John. If what is found only in John is plausibly factual, then there are reasonable grounds for suspecting that John had its roots in a primitive tradition about Jesus. Second, I shall examine the material that is shared by John and the Synoptics to see if John draws from the Synoptic Gospels or from the traditions behind them. If John does not, then again there is reason for positing an independent, primitive tradition behind John.

The Value of the Information Found Only in John

TODAY THERE IS A GROWING TENDENCY to take seriously many of the historical, social, and geographical details peculiar to narratives found only in the Fourth Gospel.[3] Modern investigations, especially through archae-

---

2. See Dodd, "Le kérygma"; Balmforth, "Structure"; Barrett, *St John*, 43. Historical fact plausibly dictated beginning the story of Jesus with JBap and ending it with crucifixion, burial, and resurrection appearances.

3. See the works by Albright, Higgins, Leal and Stauffer, cited in the bibliography at the end of the chapter.

ology, have verified a number of details. Let me mention the following instances as the most striking:

- In ch. 4, John's references to the Samaritans, their practice of worshiping on Gerizim, and the location of Jacob's well all seem to be accurate.
- In ch. 5 the very precise information about the pool of Bethesda is accurate as to name, location, and construction.
- The theological themes brought up in relation to the Feast of Tabernacles (7–8) reflect an accurate knowledge of the festal ceremonies in the Jerusalem Temple area.
- Details about places in Jerusalem seem to be accurate, for example, the pool of Siloam (9:7), and Solomon's Portico as a shelter in wintertime (10:22–23).

From such accuracy, the Fourth Gospel seems to reflect a knowledge of Palestine as it was before its destruction in A.D. 70, when some of these landmarks perished. This does not mean that the Johannine information about Jesus has been verified, but at least the setting in which Jesus is placed is authentic.

As for the egregious blunders about Palestine once attributed to John, there is often a perfectly reasonable explanation. Theological purpose— not necessarily a naive assumption about the duration of the priestly office—guided the reference to the "high priest that year" (11:49).[4] The exaggerated role of the Pharisees, especially in the Sanhedrin (11:46–47), seems to be more a question of simplified emphasis than of an erroneous concept of their role in government. Anachronistic terminology like "the Jews" for Jesus' opponents and Jesus' use of "your Law" (8:17; 10:34) are more reflections of the apologetic tendencies of the Gospel than ignorant blunders.

Of the anachronisms once urged against John, the most serious was the abstract language the evangelist attributed to Jesus. The dualistic references to light and darkness, truth and falsehood, which are not found in the Synoptics, seemed clearly to reflect the language and thought of a later time and another place than the time and place of the ministry of Jesus. The Johannine Jesus seemed to walk and speak in the Hellenistic

---

4. *Editor's Note:* See the discussion in Moloney, *Signs and Shadows,* 173–76.

world of the second century. But we know now that the language attributed to Jesus in John was perfectly at home in the Palestine of the early first century. The DSS found at Qumran from 1947 on have given us the library of an Essene community whose span of existence covered the period from ca. 140 B.C. to A.D. 68. These documents offer the closest ideological and terminological parallels yet discovered for the dualism and the peculiar vocabulary of the Johannine Jesus.[5] The discovery does not prove that Jesus himself spoke in this abstract language, since an evangelist familiar with such language could have reinterpreted Jesus in its terminology. We must still face the problem of why Jesus speaks differently in the Synoptic Gospels. Yet at least the abstract language used by Jesus in John is no longer a conclusive argument against the Johannine use of historical tradition.

Let us turn for a moment to arrangements of the Jesus material (geographical and chronological) that are not exclusive to John, but where John's approach is noticeably different. Unlike the Synoptics, John has a ministry of baptizing by Jesus in the Jordan valley; implicitly a two- or three-year public ministry; frequent journeys to Jerusalem; clashes with the Jerusalem authorities that extend over a long period of time; a Sanhedrin decision to put Jesus to death, not on the night before he died but weeks before; Roman soldiers participating in the arrest of Jesus; a role attributed to Annas in the interrogation of Jesus; not Passover day, but the afternoon before Passover as the date of Jesus' death. A defense can be made for most of these Johannine details, and in some of them the Johannine picture is almost certainly more historical than the overall Synoptic picture.[6] For instance, passages like Luke 13:34 (several attempts to win over Jerusalem) and Mark 14:13–14 (Jesus has acquaintances in Jerusalem) are difficult to reconcile with the Synoptic outline wherein during his ministry Jesus goes only once to Jerusalem, in the last days of his life. Again, there is the well-known difficulty of reconciling the activities that the Gospels describe as taking place on Good Friday with the Synoptic dating of that day as Passover.

---

5. See below, Chapter Four, pp. 139–42.

6. *Editor's Note:* On this, see the excellent methodological remarks from MAMJ, 1.41–55, and Meier's careful use of Johannine material in his discussion of the material in his second volume, subtitled "Mentor, Message, and Miracles."

The Question of Dependence on the Synoptic Gospels

WE NOW TURN TO THE MATERIAL that John shares in common with the Synoptic Gospels. In terms of narrative this would include part of the ministry of JBap; Jesus' gathering disciples; the cleansing of the Temple (2:13–22); probably the healing of the royal official's son (4:46–54); the sequence involving the multiplication of the loaves, walking on the water, and Peter's confession (6); debates/conflicts with Jewish authorities; the anointing of Jesus and the entry into Jerusalem (12); and the general outline of Last Supper, passion, death, and resurrection. In terms of the words of Jesus, this would include many isolated sayings.

The earliest stage of theorizing about the relation of John to the Synoptics involved the supposition that the Fourth Gospel was written by John son of Zebedee who had read the Synoptic Gospels and wished to supplement their picture of Jesus' life and spirituality. Already in the nineteenth century authorship by John of Zebedee was widely challenged by critical scholars; and today the view of supplementation is almost universally abandoned,[7] for the relatively few points of direct contact between the content of John and that of the Synoptics really create more chronological and historical problems than they solve. There is nothing in John that gives any indication of how this Gospel might supplement the Synoptic Gospels.

With the ancient theory fallen into desuetude, advocates of two other views have struggled for the majority position.

---

7. H. S. Holland and W. J. Richmond, *The Fourth Gospel* (London: Murrray, 1920), argued that authorship by an apostolic eyewitness should be posited because the Fourth Gospel supplied the episodes that gave historical and theological coherence to the Synoptic Gospels. More recently, Morris, "Synoptic," also uses information from John to make better sense of the Synoptic accounts. E.g., in Mark 11:1 Jesus knows where to find an ass in a village near Jerusalem even though he has not been to Jerusalem before—one can explain that from John where he has been there several times. No! Mark intends the knowledge to be an example of mysterious prophetic prescience.

Johannine Dependence on the Synoptics or on Their Sources

In the first third of the twentieth century the majority held that John was dependent on the Synoptic Gospels.[8] Arguments were drawn on the same ordering of material in John and Mark, and a few instances of exactly the same vocabulary. Indeed, even Johannine scenes that had no parallel in the Synoptic tradition were sometimes explained as an amalgamation of Synoptic details. For instance, the story of Lazarus and his two sisters in ch. 11 was thought to be a combination of one of the Synoptic stories about the raising of a dead person, of the Lucan parable about Lazarus (see Luke 16:31), and of the Lucan story about Martha and Mary (Luke 10:38–42). Why did the fourth evangelist compose another Gospel? With supplementing out of favor, the explanation shifted to supplanting (Windisch) or surpassing the first three (most recently, see Vogler, "Johannes als Kritiker).

Although by mid-twentieth century, as we shall see below, Johannine independence had become dominant, the theory of dependence was by no means discarded. When I wrote the first edition of this commentary in 1966, I gave examples from the writings of that period. Mendner, "Zum problem," strongly insisted that John 6 was dependent on the Synoptic account of the multiplication (although for the connected scene of Jesus' walking on the water, the influence was in the opposite direction!).[9] Bailey, *Traditions*, contended that John knew Luke's Gospel, as did Parker, Osty, and Boismard.[10] Maier, "Johannes," has called attention to (some-

---

8. E.g., A. Jülicher, J. Moffatt, T. Zahn, B. H. Streeter. The primary relationship was most often detected between John and Mark; as D. M. Smith (*John among the Gospels,* 46) observes, "The discussion about John and the Synoptics becomes at bottom a discussion about John and Mark." Scholars varied in their judgment as to whether John drew on another source besides the Synoptic Gospels.

9. For Johannine dependence on Mark at least, see Lee, "St. Mark," and Barrett, *John,* 45. Other scholars would include J. Blinzler, M. E. Glasswell, D. Guthrie, W. G. Kümmel, R. H. Lightfoot. In more recent times, with different nuances, and accepting the influence of Luke, see also U. Schnelle and M. Lang.

10. In the 1970s, L. Cribbs made an interesting case for the reverse position: John did not know Luke's Gospel, but Luke knew John, as evidenced where he departed from Mark.

what distant) parallels between John and Matthew.[11] A variation of the dependence theory is found, for example, in Borgen's claim that the fourth evangelist knew the traditions behind the Synoptics rather than the Synoptic Gospels themselves. In discussing Lazarus, Martha, and Mary, J. N. Sanders posits a common source for John and Luke; and Parker argues that John and Acts are closer to each other than John and Luke and reflect a form of Jewish Christianity known and practiced in Roman-ruled Judea.[12]

In the last third of the century, the theory of dependence gained new life, particularly from the "Louvain school" of F. Neirynck, his colleagues and students.[13] Through detailed studies they showed how modern scholars could explain Johannine scenes as a reshuffling and combination of material and phrases taken over from Mark, Matthew, and Luke.[14] For the most part this new wave of scholarship resisted the compromise theory of Johannine dependence on pre-Gospel Synoptic sources; their argument was that John draws on redactional passages in the Synoptic Gospels, i.e., passages that were attributed to the Synoptic evangelists themselves rather than to their sources. I am not convinced by these scholars' arguments, and especially I do not think they have offered proof that a first-century writer would work in the manner they posit.

In a work largely independent of other scholarship, de Solages seeks to quantify with mathematical exactness the picture of John's dependence, e.g., 17.6 percent of John has Synoptic counterparts. He further breaks

---

11. Long discourses centered on Jesus as a revealer of God's will; his special care to speak to his disciples; formula citations of Scripture; frequent designation of Jesus as God's Son; messianic debates with Jewish authorities. Neirynck insists on John's dependence on Matt, and points to Boismard and Dauer as supporting that view.

12. Sanders, "Those," 332; Parker, "Kinship."

13. E.g., J. Delobel, M. Sabbe, G. van Belle. Others beyond Leuven would include R. Baum-Bodenbender, M. Hengel, K. T. Kleinknecht, N. Perrin, U. Schnelle, G. Strecker, P. Stuhlmacher, H. Thyen, M. Lang.

14. Dependence on Mark is most frequently posited, but some think of dependence on all three. The Johannine evangelist writing in the 90s would then have known all three Synoptics earlier than any other documented Christian writer. Even if one shifts the knowledge a decade later to the redactor, that is very early. Lang traces strong Markan and (not quite so strong) Lukan influence upon the formation of the Johannine passion and resurrection narratives. For a diagram depicting these influences, see Lang, *Johannes und die Synoptiker*, 349–53.

the agreements into verbatim, equivalent words and synonyms. His conclusion is that the Johannine author (the BD who had eyewitness knowledge) knew the Synoptic Gospels (Mark directly, but without copies of Matthew and Luke before him); yet did not use them as sources.[15] More complicated is the thesis of A. Dauer expounded in two books.[16] The evangelist himself did not use the Synoptic Gospels; however, he drew on a pre-Gospel source (both narrative and passion) that had been orally influenced by the Gospels of Matthew and Luke.[17]

Johannine Independence of the Synoptic Gospels or Their Widely Postulated Written Sources

Important scholarly studies from the 1920s through the 1960s turned the tide against dependence. In England, Gardner-Smith and Dodd contended that John is more easily explained as stemming from a tradition similar and parallel to but independent of the tradition that flowed into the Synoptic Gospels.[18] (Note: this is not a theory of dependence on pre-Gospel written Synoptic sources; often oral tradition is emphasized.) In America, E. R. Goodenough advocated independence. In Germany Bultmann posited sources for Jesus' deeds and discourses that are not historical and not the Synoptic Gospels,[19] and contended that even the passion

---

15. See D. M. Smith, *John among the Gospels,* 169–76; also "John and the Synoptics: de Solages and Neirynck," *Biblica* 63 (1982): 102–13; reprinted in *Johannine Christianity,* 128–44.

16. Dauer, *Passionsgeschichte; Johannes und Lukas.*

17. Neirynck, "John 4:46–54," and Sabbe, "Arrest," have criticized Dauer's thesis as an unnecessary complication since they think that the evangelist himself, not his source, drew on the Synoptics. In BDM, I disagreed with Dauer's (and others') ability to reconstruct with any exactitude a pre-Johannine passion source (which is key to his theory); and in my review of Dauer's *Passionsgeschichte* in JBL 72 (1973), 608–10, I showed how disputable was his decision as to what is redactional in Luke (the other key).

18. Gardner-Smith, *St. John;* Dodd, *Tradition.* Williams, "Tradition," argues against Dodd that one cannot separate the proposed pre-Johannine tradition from the theology of the evangelist. That objection is not valid if one supposes that the tradition was shaped within a Johannine history that reaches back to Stages One and Two explained in Chapter Two, above.

19. See Chapter Two, pp. 47–53.

narrative source, though resembling the Synoptic passion, was independent. Most of those who have continued to argue for a Johannine signs source (without Bultmann's judgment of nonhistoricity) or Johannine pre-Gospel documents have also opted for independence from the Synoptics for the pertinent section of John.[20] A preference for noncanonical and nonhistorical sources has continued in the work of J. D. Crossan, who would make John dependent on the *Gospel of Peter* and the *Secret Gospel of Mark* and of H. Koester and others, who would have John dependent on Egerton Papyrus 2. Thus, one may claim that in various ways from the mid-twentieth century on the majority of scholars held for independence—a very small majority by the end of the century because of the impact of the Louvain school.[21]

Although it is helpful to gather scholars in two groups, advocating either dependence on or independence of the Synoptic Gospels, there are problems in the classification:

- Dependence on the extant Gospel of Mark is a clear issue; dependence on "Marcan tradition" is not always clear. E.g., Glasswell speaks of the baptism of Jesus by JBap as found either in Mark or in Marcan tradition.[22] What about the likelihood that it is found in all the early Christian tradition of which we have any knowledge, as attested in Mark, Matthew, Luke, Acts, and implicitly in John? Does Marcan tradition mean tradition peculiar to Mark or tradition for which Mark is a witness, especially if we consider Mark as a witness to general apostolic tradition?[23]

------

20. With variation as to the content of the source, so R. Fortna, W. Nicol, U. C. Von Wahlde, W. Wilkens. A major exception is Boismard with his multiple-edition theory.

21. Among those who maintain independence in last half of the twentieth century, D. M. Smith's very helpful overall survey of scholarship on this subject (*John among the Gospels*) lists the following scholars (beyond those I have already mentioned): J. J. Becker, O. Cullmann, E. Käsemann, R. Kysar, J. L. Martyn, L. Morris, G. Rehm, W. Sanders, R. Schnackenburg, and S. Schulz. To these one might add Anderson, Ridderbos and Moloney.

22. Glasswell, "Relationship," 101.

23. I find Glasswell particularly confusing, e.g., ("Relationship," 112) the Gethsemane account is either traditional or Marcan. No. That Jesus was arrested on the Mt. of Olives (Gethsemane) and that he prayed to God about being delivered from death

- I am not certain where to list those who affirm independence in the main body of John, but admit that the final redactor may have seen one or more Synoptic Gospels and from them introduced into John certain Synoptic elements. Certainty that he did this and the proposed amount of the material introduced varies greatly. Thyen (in the 1970s) and Heekerens maintained that the redactor (who was so important that he should be considered the evangelist) knew Luke.[24] Dunderberg would attribute to the redactor a large body of Synoptic additions and make that a main criterion for detecting his hand.[25]
- Those who maintain independence cover a wide spectrum in how they describe what the Johannine writer(s) did draw on, running from completely fictional sources (extraneous to Johannine community history) to an independent tradition going back to Jesus.

Evaluation

Each of the scenes and sayings shared by the two Gospel traditions must be studied to see wherein John and the Synoptics are the same and wherein they differ. One must also observe whether John consistently agrees with any one of the Synoptic Gospels in material peculiar to that Gospel, or with any significant combination of the Synoptic Gospels, for example, with the material proper to Matthew and Luke. In such a study the differences are even more significant than the similarities; for if one posits Johannine dependency, one should be able to explain every difference in John as the result of a deliberate change of Synoptic material or of a misunderstanding of that material. Various motives might guide such changes; for example, better sequence or theological emphasis. At times the motives might be undetectable, e.g., Goodwin argues that the fourth

---

or removing the hour/cup just before he died (see Heb 5:7) can be traditional, while the arrangement of that in Mark may stem from that evangelist. That John has the two elements but not in the Marcan arrangement may reflect Johannine organization of the traditional material without dependence on Mark.

24. By the 1990s Thyen had come around to agree with Neirynck's position that the Johannine writer (he has given up source criticism) knew and used all three Synoptics.

25. Dunderberg, *Johannes.*

evangelist cited the OT freely from memory and that he could have done the same with the Synoptics.[26] However, any explanation of Johannine differences that must appeal as a principle to numerous capricious and inexplicable changes really removes the question from the area of scientific study.

Let me anticipate and summarize my observations and conclusions.[27] As for *similarities,* John tends to agree with Mark the most, with Luke second, and with wording or material peculiar to Matthew least of all; but over a series of scenes John does not agree in a consistent way with any one Synoptic Gospel. To posit dependence on the basis of similarities alone, one would have to suppose that the fourth evangelist knew all three Gospels and chose in an eclectic manner, now from one, now from another. Those who advocate Johannine dependence have to agree that John used Mark in a way very different from the way Matthew and Luke drew on Mark.[28] However, even this suggestion does not hold up when one examines the *dissimilarities.* In parallel scenes, most of the details peculiar to John, some of which make the story more difficult, cannot be explained as deliberate changes of the Synoptic tradition. Moreover, passages or details in the Synoptics that would have helped John's theological interests have been omitted by John. If one cannot accept the hypothesis of a careless or a capricious evangelist who gratuitously changed, added, and subtracted details, then one is forced to agree with Dodd that the evangelist drew the material for his stories from an independent tradition, similar to but not the same as the traditions represented in the Synoptic Gospels.

It is also possible that the fourth evangelist drew on one or more of the sources that seem to lie behind the Synoptic Gospels, for example, on Q

---

26. Goodwin, "How."

27. *Editor's Note.* As Brown has not changed his position on this question of the relationship between the Fourth Gospel and the Synoptics, an interested reader will find detailed analyses of relevant passages in numerous places in *John.* Some of the more important discussions are indicated below in notes 29, 31 and 34. But see my further remarks in the conclusion.

28. Windisch, *Johannes,* contended that the very freedom of John's usage of the Synoptics implied that the fourth evangelist did not consider the Synoptic Gospels authoritative. See the balanced advocacy of a Johannine use of Synoptic sources (especially Mark and Luke) that strongly affirms the uniqueness of the Johannine account in Schnelle, "Johannes und die Synoptiker."

(the source that supplied the material common to Matthew and Luke) or, in the passion, on one of the two pre-Markan sources isolated by Taylor. This is a more difficult question, since one is dealing with a reconstructed source and not with an extant work; and while there may be reasonable accuracy in reconstructing Q (since by definition it is material shared by Matthew and Luke but lacking in Mark), reconstructions of pre-Markan material are very dubious.[29] Without being absolute on the question, I come to the same solution as above, namely Johannine independence, for once again there are many differences that cannot be explained without resorting to non-Synoptic material. From the evidence available, I deem it best to accept the general solution of an independent tradition behind John.

This means that the main body of material in John was not drawn from the Synoptic Gospels or their postulated sources. However, earlier I reconstructed a long history for the composition of the Fourth Gospel;[30] it is very possible that during that history there was cross-influence from the general tradition(s) of other Christians about Jesus. Unless we are to presuppose that the Johannine community was isolated from other Christian communities (a suggestion that does not harmonize with the proposal that John was written at Ephesus or at Antioch), it is hard to believe that this community would not sooner or later have become familiar with the kind of Gospel tradition accepted by other communities, the kind of tradition that eventually found its way into the Synoptic Gospels, particularly into Mark.[31]

---

29. Also here we must face the difficulty that the Synoptic sources are only imperfectly represented in the final Gospels, and therefore a source may actually have contained material that John drew on and the Synoptics did not. To solve the Johannine differences on this principle, however, is once more to remove the solution from any real scientific control.

30. Chapter Two, pp. 62–86.

31. *Editor's Note.* This remarks adds a nuanced "newness" to Brown's earlier positions. A particularly important study in this respect is M. Labahn, *Jesus als Lebenspender. Untersuchungen zu einer Geschichte der johanneischen Tradition anhand ihrer Wundergeschichten* (BZNW 98; Berlin: de Gruyter, 1999). Depending upon the work of Walter Ong on orality, Labahn suggests that the Synoptic-like material comes into the Fourth Gospel by means of "secondary orality." This means that the fourth evangelist does not use the Synoptic texts as a "source," but is aware of these traditions which have now developed into post-Gospel orality and come to the fourth evangel-

Perhaps I can illustrate some possible instances of the complexities of cross-influence, beginning with Mark. In John 6 there are serious reasons for believing that John's narrative of the multiplication of the loaves rests on independent tradition.[32] Yet it is striking that only John and Mark (6:37) mention the sum of two hundred denarii in reference to the price of the bread needed to feed the crowd. Another arresting example is the very strange Greek expression "perfume made from real nard" which is used in John 12:3 and Mark 14:3. The sum of three hundred denarii appears only in John 12:4 and Mark 14:5 as a detail in the accounts of the anointing of Jesus. It is almost impossible to decide: do such minor parallels represent cross-influence from the Johannine tradition-bearers having knowledge of the way the story was told by other Christians, or do they flow from the fact that the story in its early (pre-Johannine and pre-Markan) form had such details and they were preserved by two independently developing ways of recounting the story?[33] One answer may fit one situation, and the other answer another situation.

The important close parallels between John and Matthew are relatively few.[34] There are, however, some interesting contacts between John and the Petrine material peculiar to Matthew (see 1:41–42; 6:68–69; 21:15–17). Moreover, one should not forget the saying phrased in Johannine style that appears in Matt 11:25–30 (Luke 10:21–22), and again we must face the possibility that all these traditions reflect independent but similar backgrounds.

In many ways, the possibility of cross-influence on John from *Luke* is the most interesting. In scenes shared by John and several Synoptics, the parallels between John and Luke are usually not impressive. Rather, it is with the peculiarly Lucan material that John has the important parallels. The following is by no means an exhaustive list (see Bailey, Cribbs, Osty,

---

ist in that form. I suspect that Brown may have been impressed by this suggestion, but would have found it unusable because of our lack of ability to trace these oral traditions with any certainty. He would most likely again suggest that it "removes the question from the area of scientific study."

32. See *John*, 235–50.

33. A modern analogy: when one has heard a long joke from two different people (who could not have heard it from each other), often most of the details will be phrased in slightly different ways, but some key words will be the same.

34. See the discussion of 13:16, 20; 15:18ff in *John*, 569–72, 693–95.

Parker, Schniewind),[35] but it does show that the parallels lie both in minute details and in the broad sweep of narrative and ideas.

- One multiplication of loaves and fish.
- Mention of figures like Lazarus; Martha and Mary; one of the Twelve named Jude or Judas (not Iscariot); the high priest Annas.
- No night trial before Caiaphas.
- Double question put to Jesus concerning his messiahship and divinity (Luke 22:67, 70; John 10:24–25, 33).
- Three "not guilty" statements by Pilate during the trial of Jesus.
- Postresurrectional appearances of Jesus in Jerusalem; the similarity here is very strong if verses like Luke 24:12 and 40 are original.
- A miraculous catch of fish (Luke 5:4–9; John 21:5–11).

How are we to evaluate such parallels?[36] Some may best be explained by assuming that the independent tradition behind John had features also found in the peculiar Lucan tradition, even though these features did not appear the same way in both traditions, e.g., John does not tell the same story concerning Martha and Mary that Luke tells. But this supposition will not explain all the parallels. For instance, in the account of the anointing of the feet in 12:1–7, John is dependent on details that come from a peculiar Lucan development of the basic narrative, and it is hard to see how the fusion of details found in both Luke and John could have happened independently.[37] On the other hand, there are incidents in Luke which may well have arisen through cross-influence from some stage of the Johannine tradition: for example, the second ending of the parable about Lazarus (Luke 16:27–31) which mentions the possibility of Lazarus's coming back from the grave. Thus, in the relations between Luke

---

35. It is interesting that the early study of parallels by Schniewind did not propose John's dependence on Luke; rather it posited a proto-Johannine account was available to both Luke and John, and shared oral tradition.

36. Boismard has given up the contention that Luke was the final redactor of the Fourth Gospel. R. Maddox, *The Purpose of Luke-Acts* (FRLANT 126; Göttingen: Vandenhock & Ruprecht, 1982), holds that John is independent of Mark; in many ways Luke is closer to John than to the other Synoptic Gospels; yet Maddox favors contact between the two traditions when they were developing in the same area (southern Judea), rather than between the finished form of both Gospels.

37. See *John*, 449–54.

and John cross-influence is possible in both directions. Since such cross-influence does not express itself in identical wording, it may well have taken place at an oral stage in the history of Gospel composition without either evangelist reading the other's gospel.[38]

To summarize: In most of the material narrated in both John and the Synoptics, I believe that the evidence does not favor Johannine dependence on the Synoptics or their sources. John drew on an independent tradition about Jesus, similar to traditions that underlie the Synoptics. The primitive Johannine tradition was closest to the pre-Markan tradition but also contained elements found in the traditions peculiar to Luke, and even to Matthew (e.g., Petrine source). In addition to the material drawn from this independent tradition, John has a few elements that seem to suggest a more direct cross-influence from the Synoptic tradition. During the oral formation of the Johannine stories and discourses (Stage Two), there very probably was some cross-influence from the emerging Lucan Gospel tradition. Although I am not convinced of this, serious scholars maintain that in the final redaction of John (Stage Three) there were a few details directly borrowed from Mark.[39] There is no evidence, however, *pace* Bultmann, that such borrowing, if it did take place, was for the purpose of making the Fourth Gospel acceptable to the church at large.

The Historical Value of John in Reconstructing Jesus' Ministry

IF CONSIDERABLE PORTIONS of its narrative were drawn from the Synoptics (or from noncanonical sources), there is very little hope that John can contribute much to our historical knowledge of Jesus.[40] That pes-

---

38. *Editor's Note:* See above, note 31, for the more developed presentation of this idea by Labahn's use of the notion of "secondary orality."

39. *Editor's Note:* It is this "cross-influence" from the Synoptic tradition, now regarded as "very probable" (at least for the unique Lukan Gospel tradition) which hints at a change of direction in Brown's approach.

40. I.e., unless one posits that the evangelist was himself an eyewitness of the ministry of Jesus or had another eyewitness source. Bacon (*The Fourth Gospel in Research and Debate*, 356–84) recognized clearly that dependence on the Synoptics by one who was not the BD supplementing those Gospels meant a loss of historical value for John.

simism has been a commonplace in early twentieth-century critical investigations of the historical Jesus. In mid-century even the "new quest" of the historical Jesus among the post-Bultmannians, especially Bornkamm and Conzelmann, neglected John. Some representatives of the "third quest," however, do consider the evidence of John.[41] That this evidence should be considered stems from the evaluation I reached above, namely, that John drew on independent and early tradition, comparable to the tradition(s) on which the Synoptics drew.

But in reopening the question of whether or not the Fourth Gospel can be a witness to the historical Jesus, one must proceed with care. Above, I posited three stages in the composition of John, with Stage Two and Stage Three each representing a step farther away from the lifetime of Jesus.[42] We cannot ignore the implications of such a development, for it sharply limits the ability of the final form of the Gospel to give a scientifically accurate portrait of the Jesus of history. Let me examine the implications in each stage of Johannine development.

Stage One

A tradition of Jesus' works and words underlies John, even as a tradition of his words and works underlies the Synoptics. These traditions offered variant narratives about what Jesus did and said, and different evaluations and memories—a variance that existed already in his lifetime. A modern awareness of how much eyewitnesses and earwitnesses vary in their accounts and understanding of what was done and said on a particular occasion should fortify us against the objection that there could have been only one perception of Jesus among his followers during his lifetime. This warns against too facile a harmonizing or judgment about what is more original.

---

41. MAMJ 2.726: Among seven miraculous healings "that have a good chance of going back to some event in the life of the historical Jesus," three are from John. Beyond the quest for the historical Jesus, most of the articles in the bibliography below (under *Historical Value*) insist on serious historical content in John.

42. See above, Chapter Two, pp. 62–86.

Stage Two

Much greater variance would have developed in this period (which in the case of John probably lasted five or six decades), catalyzed by different preachers and witnesses, different groups evangelized, different community histories. If we ask which of the variant forms of a story or a saying is the earliest, we are asking a question that admits of no simple answer. The observation that a Johannine form fits Johannine theology or a Synoptic form fits Synoptic theology does not automatically tell us that the respective form is less historical. Even within the Synoptic family, one cannot give a blanket rule as to which form of a saying is always to be preferred, e.g., the "Q" form or the Marcan form. So too in comparing John and the Synoptics, we find that sometimes the material underlying John's account seems to be more primitive than the material underlying the Synoptic account(s), for example, the story of Jesus' walking on the water in John 6:16–21. At other times, just the opposite is true. Thus, a critical judgment is necessary *for each instance.*

To speak of a Johannine narrative or saying and judge that there is early or primitive tradition underlying it would therefore mean that it goes back to the first decades of Stage Two.[43] That still allows ten to twenty or more years of development from the time of Jesus. Where possible, one should attempt to trace the origins of Johannine material back to Stage One and then to show what implications this may have for the historical ministry of Jesus. But I make no pretense that I can do that consistently. Similarly, in pointing out Synoptic parallels for Johannine stories and sayings, I have no presupposition that the Synoptic parallels are necessarily exact historical echoes of what Jesus did and said. Rather, I take for granted that there were developments within the Synoptic tradition. The purpose in presenting such Synoptic parallels is to show that John's Gospel is not so atypical as might at first seem. If Stage Two in the Johannine tradition saw dramatic, theological reshaping and weaving together of the raw material from the Jesus tradition, this same process,

---

43. One should make every effort to keep the terms primitive/early and historical distinct. In part this care derives from some of the criticism leveled against the title of Dodd's book *Historical Tradition,* and the debate over whether he had truly detected what was historical (see Carson, "Historical").

mutatis mutandis, also took place in Stage Two of the formation of the Synoptic Gospels.

At one time John the Evangelist was spoken of as *the Theologian,* (or John the Divine), almost with the implication that only in the Fourth Gospel did we have a theological view of the career of Jesus. Today we recognize that each Gospel has a theological view (and so, although consideration of the evangelist belongs in Stage Three, the fourth evangelist is one theologian among the other evangelist-theologians). Nevertheless, it is still true that the Fourth Gospel is more patently or formally theological in its presentation (and among the evangelists the fourth evangelist is the theologian par excellence). In particular, the formation of the sayings of Jesus into the Johannine discourses represented a profound theological synthesis. Seemingly, for instance, behind the final form of John 6 there lies a core of traditional material, containing not only the multiplication of the loaves but also a misunderstanding of what that scene meant and the consequent explanation of the bread by Jesus. Yet the formation of this material into the magnificent structure that we now have in John 6 represents a unique theological grasp of the ultimate implications of Jesus' deeds and words. The less-developed Synoptic accounts of the scene are not of the same theological quality or mastery. How much of this occurred in Stage Two and how much in Stage Three of Johannine formation I am not sure, but in any attempt to use John as a guide to the historical Jesus, such theological development must be taken into account. I am not suggesting that the Johannine theological insight has not been loyal to Jesus of Nazareth; rather it has often brought out implications found in a scene that came down from his lifetime.[44] But subsequent development, no matter how homogeneous, is something that is refractive when one's purpose is to establish scientifically the exact circumstances of the ministry of Jesus. And so, although I think that the Fourth Gospel reflects historical memories of Jesus, the greater extent of the theological reshaping of those memories makes Johannine material harder to use in the quest for the historical Jesus than most Synoptic material. Decisions about material found only in John are very difficult.

---

44. *Editor's Note:* For a recent thorough examination of this question, see P. N. Anderson, *The Christology of the Fourth Gospel. Its Unity and Disunity in the Light of John 6* (Valley Forge: Trinity Press International, 1997).

Stage Three

Even beyond the development that went into the formation of Johannine oral tradition is the development that took place when units of that tradition were welded into a Gospel. Selection and highlighting were required to bring about the organization now visible in John. Thus, in the evangelist's gospel there came to the fore themes that were probably quite obscure in the hustle and bustle of the actual ministry. It is quite plausible, for instance, that Jesus may have spoken publicly on the occasion of Jewish feasts and may have directed his remarks to a contrast between his own ministry and the theme of the feast. But the systematic replacement of feasts spelled out in John 5–10 is the product of much reflection by the evangelist, in an attempt to capture the significance of Jesus and his ministry.[45]

The final redaction of the Gospel placed still more obstacles to the use of John in reconstructing the ministry of Jesus. The extra Johannine material that was inserted in the Gospel narrative was not necessarily arranged in any chronological order; and indeed, according to my hypothesis, the addition of material caused the displacement of such scenes as the cleansing of the Temple. Thus, an unqualified acceptance of the present arrangement of the Gospel as truly chronological is not possible.

Let me give a chronological example of appreciating how the work of the evangelist and/or of the redactor in Stage Three complicates historical research and a desire to know exactly how things were in Stage One. John mentions at least three Passovers (2:13; 6:4; 11:55) and therefore implies at least a two-year ministry. Biographers of Jesus have used this indication to form an outline of the ministry, dividing the material found in the four Gospels into the activities of the first and second (and third) years. For instance, we may be told that the Sermon on the Mount (Matt 5–8) took place in the first year of the ministry, shortly after the Passover of John 2:13. Such a procedure is invalid. Not only does it ignore the fact that the Synoptic material itself is not chronologically ordered (e.g., the Sermon on the Mount, as it now stands, is a composite of words spoken on various occasions), but also it ignores the fact that the Gospels them-

---

45. *Editor's Note:* On the use of the expression "replacement," see my remarks in Chapter Two, p. 76, note 73. See further the more nuanced restatement of this position by Brown himself in Chapter Five, p. 161, and my further note 28 on that page.

selves give no real indications for such synchronization of Johannine and Synoptic data. The fact that neither tradition shows a systematic interest in chronology betrays itself when we seek to combine them into a consecutive picture. Even the few points of possible chronological contact between the two traditions offer difficulty. For instance, in the early part of the ministry described in John, Jesus makes several journeys into Judea and returns again to Galilee, but it is very hard to match any one of the return journeys with the Synoptic tradition of a return to Galilee after the baptism by JBap. The multiplication of the loaves found in all four Gospels might seem to offer the possibility of synchronization, but the issue is confused by the presence of *two* multiplication accounts in Mark/ Matthew. Even were there the possibility of synchronization, however, a theory of a two- or three-year ministry as a framework for dividing Jesus' activities ignores the problem created by the purpose for which the Fourth Gospel was written. Since John 20:30 specifically states that the Gospel is not a complete account of Jesus' activities, there is no way of knowing that the three Passovers mentioned were the only Passovers in that ministry. There is no real reason why one cannot postulate a four-year—or five-year—ministry. Furthermore, since the first Passover mentioned in John is intimately connected to the scene of the cleansing of the Temple, a scene that has probably been displaced, some have questioned the value of the reference to this first Passover as a chronological indication.

This chronological example has exemplified the danger of harmonizing John and the Synoptics, a by-product of trying to find history in the Gospels and a strong tendency since the time of Tatian's *Diatessaron*—a harmony of the four Gospels written ca. A.D. 170. In my judgment, when properly evaluated, the Synoptic tradition and the Johannine tradition, although at times contrary, are not contradictory in the strict sense of the word. Rather, at times they illuminate each other through comparison, as Morris, "Synoptic," has pointed out. Yet for the most part harmonization imposes on John an interest that was not that of the evangelist and does not represent proper exegesis of what he wrote.

From all these remarks it should be clear why one must be very cautious about the use of John in scientifically reconstructing the ministry of Jesus of Nazareth, even as one must be careful in so using the other Gospels. The written Gospels are distant from the modern understanding of a history or biography of Jesus. In fact, John 20:30–31 has made it clear that the author's intention was to produce a document not of history but of faith.[46] Nevertheless, lest I end on a negative note, let me reiterate my judgment that John is based on a solid tradition of the works and words of Jesus, a tradition that at times is very primitive. Indeed, I believe that often John gives us correct historical information about Jesus that no other Gospel has preserved, for example, that, like JBap, Jesus had a baptizing ministry for a period before he began his ministry of teaching; that his public ministry lasted more than a year; that he went several times to Jerusalem; that the opposition of the Jewish authorities at Jerusalem was not confined to the last days of his life; and that consideration of him in a Sanhedrin took place weeks before he was handed over to Pilate.

Historicity

This last subsection has been devoted to the issue of historicity. I find it very difficult to think of writing a commentary on a Gospel that would eschew that issue. Gospels are about Jesus; and in our time it is irresponsible never to question whether what they report had anything to do with him. After all, Christianity maintained triumphantly against pagan myths that it was a religion based on what had actually happened.[47] Yet I do not want to mislead readers; for in my understanding of the purpose of a commentary, historical issues are secondary and corollary. In my opinion, the main duty of a commentator is not to find out what happened historically, but to explain what the writer(s) intended and conveyed to the intended audience by the final Gospel narrative.[48] Even

---

46. J. N. Sanders, "Gospel," is quite right in insisting that John is deeply historical—historical in the sense in which history is concerned not only with what happened but also with the deepest meaning of what happened. See also the illuminating reflections of Hoskyns, *The Fourth Gospel*, 58–95. Mussner, *Historical*, drew upon Heidegger's insights to explain that John's perspective is that of a believing witness who sees his subject in such a way that the hidden mystery of Jesus of Nazareth becomes visible: "For John the Jesus of history and the glorified Christ are essentially identical" (90). Many reviews of Mussner, however, pointed out that more needed to be said from modern historical investigation justifying this identity.

47. That was one of the reasons for inserting in a creed that deals with creation, redemption, and sanctification the very earthly anchor of "born of the virgin Mary, suffered under Pontius Pilate."

though I think there was both an evangelist and a redactor, the duty of the commentator is not to decide what was composed by whom, or in what order it originally stood, nor whether these composers drew on a written source or an oral tradition. One should deal with the Gospel of John as it now stands, for that is the only form that we are certain has ever existed. I am perfectly aware that in ongoing church life John has fed rich theological, liturgical, and spiritual reflection, and that we have no right to exclude such hermeneutical development from the larger task of interpretation. Nevertheless, I suggest that the commentator should limit commentary to what most likely was meant by the first-century author and most likely understood by the first-century audience. That decision about limited purpose represents a firm conviction that all other subsequent reading and use of the Gospel should somehow be related to that literal sense,[49] which is already enormously rich in itself.

BIBLIOGRAPHY

JOHN AND THE SYNOPTICS

Bailey, J. A., *The Traditions Common to the Gospels of Luke and John* (NovTSup 7; Leiden: E. J. Brill, 1963).

Balmforth, H., "The Structure of the Fourth Gospel," *StEv*, 2.25–33.

Barrett, C. K., "John and the Synoptic Gospels," *ExpTim* 85 (1973–74): 228–33.

Blinzler. J., *Johannes und die Synoptiker* (SBS 5; Stuttgart: KBW, 1965).

Borgen, P. "John and the Synoptics," in *The Interrelations of the Gospels* (ed. D. L. Dungan; BETL 95: Leuven University Press, 1990), 408–58 (with response by F. Neirynck).

———, "The Independence of the Gospel of John: Some Observations," *FGFN*, 3.1816–33.

Brown, R. E., "Incidents that are Units in the Synoptic Gospels but Dispersed in St. John," *CBQ* 23 (1961): 143–60. Also in *NTE*, Ch. ix.

---

48. In BDM 1.4–13, I try to show that I am aware that discovering and expounding this "literal sense" is no easy hermeneutical task; yet it is possible.

49. Traditional Christians implicitly acknowledge this when they claim that their church and belief is apostolic, i.e., rooted in what the apostles taught and believed in the first century.

Cribbs, F. L., "St. Luke and the Johannine Tradition," *JBL* 90 (1971): 422–50.

———, "A Study of the Contacts that Exist between St. Luke and St. John," *SBLSP* 1973, 2.1–93.

———, "The Agreements that Exist between Luke and John," *SBLSP* 1979, 1.215–61.

Dauer, A., *Johannes und Lukas* (FB 50; Würzburg: Echter, 1984).

Denaux, A., ed., *John and the Synoptics* (BETL 101; Leuven: Peeters, 1992).

Dunderberg, I., *Johannes und die Synoptiker* (Helsinki: Suomalainen Tiedeakatemia, 1994).

Dunn, J. D. G., "John and the Synoptics as a Theological Question," in Culpepper and Black, eds., *Exploring*, 301–13.

Dvorak, J., "The Relationship between John and the Synoptic Gospels," *Journal of the Evangelical Theological Society* 41 (1998): 201–13.

Gardner-Smith, P., *Saint John and the Synoptic Gospels* (Cambridge: Cambridge University Press, 1938).

Gaussen, H., "The Lucan and the Johannine Writings," *JTS* 9 (1907–8): 562–68.

Glasswell, M. E., "The Relationship Between John and Mark," *JSNT* 23 (1985): 99–115.

Goodwin, C., "How Did John Treat His Sources?" *JBL* 73 (1954): 61–75.

Haenchen, E., "Johanneische Probleme," *ZTK* 56 (1959): 19–54.

Lang, M., *Johannes und die Synoptiker. Eine redaktionsgeschichtliche Analyse von Joh 18–20 vor dem markinischen und lukanischen Hintergrund* (FRLANT 192; Göttingen: Vandenhoeck & Ruprecht, 1999).

Lee, E. K., "St. Mark and the Fourth Gospel," *NTS* 3 (1956–57): 50–58.

Mendner, S., "Zum Problem 'Johannes und die Synoptiker,' " *NTS* 4 (1957–58): 282–307.

Morris, L., "Synoptic Themes Illuminated by the Fourth Gospel," *StEv*, 2.73–84.

———, "The Relationship of the Fourth Gospel to the Synoptics," *Studies*, 15–63.

Neirynck, F., *Jean et les Synoptiques. Examen critique de l'exégèse de M.-É. Boismard* (BETL 49; Leuven: Leuven University Press, 1979).

———, "John and the Synoptics [1965–1975]," in de Jonge, *L'Évangile*, 73–106.

———, "John and the Synoptics: 1975–1990," in Denaux, *John*, 3–62.

———, "John and the Synoptics in Recent Commentaries," *ETL* 74 (1998): 386–97.

Osty, E., "Les points de contact entre le récit de la passion dans saint Luc et dans saint Jean," *RSR* 39 (1951): 146–54.

Parker, P., "The Kinship of John and Acts," in CJOC, 1.187–205.

Schnelle, U., "Johannes und die Synoptiker," in FGFN, 3.1799–1814.

Schniewind, J., *Die Parallelperikopen bei Lukas und Johannes* (Hildesheim: Olms, 1958; original 1914).

Sigge, T., *Das Johannesevangelium und die Synoptiker* (NTAbh 16.2/3: Münster: Aschendorff, 1935).

Smith, D. M., *John among the Gospels: The Relationship in Twentieth-Century Research* (Minneapolis: Fortress, 1992).

———, "Historical Issues and the Problem of John and the Synoptics," in *From Jesus to John. Essays on Jesus and New Testament Christology in Honour of Marinus de Jonge* (ed. M. C. de Boer; JSNT Sup 84; Sheffield: JSOT, 1993), 252–67.

———, "John, the Synoptics, and the Canonical Approach to Exegesis," in *Tradition and Interpretation in the New Testament. Essays in Honor of E. E. Ellis* (eds. G. F. Hawthorne and others; Tübingen: J. C. B. Mohr [Paul Siebeck], 1987), 166–80.

———, "The Problem of John and the Synoptics in the Light of the Relation between Apocryphal and Canonical Gospels," in Denaux, *John*, 147–62.

Solages, B. de, *Jean et les synoptiques* (Leiden: E. J. Brill, 1979).

Thyen, H. "Johannes und die Synoptiker. Auf der Suche nach einem neuen Paradigma zur Beschreibung ihrer Beiziehungen anhand von Beobachtungen an Passions- und Östererzählungen," in Denaux, *John*, 81–107.

Wilkens, W., "Evangelist und Tradition im Johannesevangelium," *TZ* 16 (1960): 81–90.

Windisch, H., *Johannes und die Synoptiker* (Leipzig: Hinrichs, 1926).

THE HISTORICAL VALUE OF JOHN

Albright, W. F., "Recent Discoveries in Palestine and the Gospel of John," in *BNTE*, 153–71.

Barton, S., "The Believer, the Historian and the Fourth Gospel," *Theology* 96 (1993): 289–302.

Brown, R. E., "The Problem of Historicity in John," *CBQ* 24 (1962): 1–14. Also in *NTE*, Ch. ix.

Carson, D. A., "Historical Tradition in the Fourth Gospel: After Dodd, What?" *GP* 2 (1981): 83–145. See also the debate between J. S. King, "Has D. A. Carson Been Fair to C. H. Dodd?" *JSNT* 17 (1983): 97–102, and D. A. Carson, "Historical Tradition in the Fourth Gospel: A Response to J. S. King," *JSNT* 23 (1985): 73–81.

Dodd, C. H., "Le kérygma apostolique dans le quatrième évangile," *RHPR* 31 (1951): 265–74.

Higgins, A.J.B., *The Historicity of the Fourth Gospel* (London: Lutterworth, 1960).

———, "The Words of Jesus According to St. John," *BJRL* 49 (1967): 363–86.

Leal, J., "El simbolismo histórico del IV Evangelio," *EstBib* 19 (1960): 329–48. Digested in *TD* 11 (1963): 91–96.

Maier, G., "Johannes und Matthäus—Zwiespalt oder Viergestalt des Evangeliums," *GP* 2 (1981): 267–91.

Moloney, F. J. "The Fourth Gospel and the Jesus of History," *NTS* 46 (2000): 42–58.

Mussner, F., *The Historical Jesus in the Gospel of St John* (London: Burns & Oates, 1967).

Pokorný, P., "Der irdische Jesus im Johannesevangelium," *NTS* 30 (1984): 217–27.

Potter, R. D., "Topography and Archeology in the Fourth Gospel," *StEv*, 1.329–37.

Ruckstuhl, E., "Jesus und der geschichtliche Mutterboden im vierten Evangelium," in *Vom Urchristentum zu Jesus. Für Joachim Gnilka* (eds. H. Frankemölle and K. Kertelge; Freiburg: Herder, 1989), 256–86.

Sanders, J. N., "The Gospel and the Historian," *The Listener* 56 (1956): 753–57.

Stauffer, E., "Historische Elemente im Vierten Evangelium," *Homiletica en Biblica* 22 (1963): 1–7.

Thompson, M. M., "The Historical Jesus and the Johannine Christ," in Culppeper, ed., *Exploring*, 21–42.

Vogler, W., "Johannes als Kritiker der synoptischen Tradition," *Berliner Theologische Zeitschrift* 16 (1999): 41–58.

Williams, M. I., "Tradition in the Fourth Gospel: A Critique of Professor C. H. Dodd," *StEv*, 4.259–65.

4

Proposed Influences
on the Religious Thought
of the Fourth Gospel

◆

I HAVE COMMENTED on the depth of the christological perspective in the Fourth Gospel. In many ways it is a unique perspective, different from the christological outlooks (somewhat divergent among themselves) found in the Synoptic Gospels.[1] Jesus not only speaks in another manner, but also allows the majestic timelessness of his divinity to stand forth more clearly. The Johannine Jesus presents himself with the solemn "I am" formula.[2] He has come into a world of darkness as the light, into a world of falsehood and hatred as the truth; and his presence divides people into two camps as they either come to the light or turn away from it, either believing in the truth or refusing to hear. How much of John (= the evangelist or his predecessors in the Johannine tradition) has gone into

---

1. One must take care not to overstate the differences between John and the Synoptics in their portraits of Jesus. Even the most characteristically Johannine elements have some parallel in the Synoptic tradition. Yet one must still recognize a characteristic Johannine cast of thought and seek to account for it.

2. See *John*, 533–38.

this portrait of Jesus? Some will answer that because John was attuned to his subject he was able to see in Jesus more than others saw, and his genius enabled him to express it. Others will think of the portrait of Jesus as almost entirely John's creation. In any case, to some degree, perhaps indefinable, the evangelist's own outlook and insight are echoed in the Gospel. How can we explain the peculiar characteristics of John's thought? What influenced John? The three most frequently suggested influences on the evangelist are Gnosticism, Hellenistic thought, and Palestinian Judaism.

Gnosticism

THE THEORY OF GNOSTIC INFLUENCE on John was popularized by the History-of-Religions School (W. Bousset, R. Reitzenstein), so prominent in the early decades of this century. The theory had proponents in W. Bauer and Bultmann, while F. Büchsel, E. Percy, and E. Schweizer challenged it. The debate has continued, as I shall indicate below.

Gnosticism in General

The issue is unusually difficult because it is so hard to find an acceptable definition of Gnosticism.[3] It found expression in Christian and Jewish and pagan religious language. Scholars can recognize common patterns in developed Gnosticism: for example, a primordial unity in the pleroma surrounding a supreme being; intermediary beings between God and human beings; the agency of these beings in producing the evil, material world and thus producing a dualism; souls as divine sparks imprisoned in alien matter; the necessity of knowledge gained through revelation in order to free souls and lead them to light and back to their spiritual origins; the numerical limitation of the elite capable of receiving this revela-

---

3. A conference at Messina in Sicily (see the report of G. MacRae, "Gnosis in Messina," *CBQ* 28 [1966]: 322–333) tried to gain acceptance for a distinction between gnosis (knowledge of divine mysteries reserved for the elite) and gnosticism (described through the characteristics of the developed second-century gnostic systems). For a good basic discussion, see P. Perkins, in R. E. Brown, C. Osiek and P. Perkins, "Early Church," *NJBC*, 80.64–79.

tion; the saving revealer who arouses them so that they wish to leave this world. But which of these elements are essential for a movement to be truly called Gnostic?

We know that Gnosticism flourished in the second century A.D., and there are two sources for our knowledge of that period. First, in condemning Gnostics the Church Fathers (especially Irenaeus) tells us about their thought. Hostility inherent in apologetic and polemic colors that source. Second, there are works written by Gnostics. Since the writers were considered heretical, apparently only a few Gnostic writings had survived. Then in 1945 at Nag Hammadi in Egypt thirteen Coptic codices (buried ca. A.D. 400) were discovered, containing fifty-two tractates (forty-six different writings), probably stemming from one of the fourth-century monasteries associated with St. Pachomius (292–348), especially Chenoboskion. Gnostics had infiltrated those monasteries, and this seems to have been a collection of texts they had found useful and buried in face of a threatened purge.[4] Amid these writings, translated into Coptic from (second-century) Greek originals, is a spectrum of semi-Gnostic and Gnostic compositions.

One approach is, working with the two sources indicated, to compare John with Christian Gnosticism of the second century.[5] The tractate *Gospel of Truth* plausibly represents Valentinian Gnosticism; and Quispel and Barrett in their articles and Braun have compared its thought and vocabulary with that of John.[6] They find the two Gospels far apart. If there were common points of origin, a divergent development has taken place; and *GTruth* may have drawn on John.[7] Hofrichter, Janssens, J. M. Robinson, and Yamauchi have studied the *Trimorphic Protennoia* (fourth century?), especially 46.5–47.33 with three comings of a divine thought/word, a light hidden in silence who the third time comes in bodily form and is not rec-

---

4. Published by J. M. Robinson, *The Nag Hammadi Library* (3rd ed.; San Francisco: Harper & Row, 1988). See also B. Layton, *The Gnostic Scriptures* (Garden City, NY: Doubleday, 1987).

5. Highly disputable is the contention that some of the Nag Hammadi works represent early first-century Christian Gnosticism.

6. See Braun, *JT*, 1.111–21.

7. Perkins, "John's," 71, points out that *GTruth* is unusual among Gnostic systems in identifying the Son and the Word: this may be an example of Gnostic conformity to orthodox Christian expression.

ognized. I have compared John and another Nag Hammadi work, the *Gospel of Thomas*. This work is at most incipiently Gnostic, certainly not as developed toward Gnosticism as *GTruth*. Yet there is still a considerable distance between John and *Thomas*, for characteristic Johannine terms are used in *Thomas* in a manner quite different from Johannine usage. If there is any dependence of one on the other, it is quite indirect; and the direction of the dependence might be *Thomas* on Johannine tradition. The *Dialogue of the Savior* has some verbal exchanges resembling those in John, e.g, just as in John 14:8–10 Philip asks Jesus, "Show us the Father," so in *Dialogue* 132.2–19 Matthew says, "Lord, I wish to see the place of life." The Johannine Jesus responds, "Whoever has seen me has seen the Father"; the *Dialogue* Jesus responds with almost the opposite answer, "You cannot see it as long as you wear the flesh." The *Acts of John* has a picture opposite to John's "The Word became flesh": Jesus really did not take on human flesh and never really died. Thus overall, John would be out of place among the tractates found at Nag Hammadi and is not itself a typical Gnostic composition as known from the second century.

For comparison to John, however, in the first part of the twentieth century scholars reconstructed an earlier Christian (or even pre-Christian) Gnosticism[8] that would be less developed than that found in the second-century evidence. In the reconstruction, it has a dualism of light and darkness, but no speculation about the origins of darkness and evil. In the sphere of light there are supernatural beings besides God, for example, angels; but this Gnosticism posits no complicated theories of emanation. Moreover, since this Gnosticism is an offshoot of Judaism or has been influenced by Judaism, its dualism has been modified by the OT tenet of God's supremacy even over the sphere of evil. Thus, the creation of the world involved no battle between darkness and light, as in Iranian

---

8. The problem of pre-Christian Gnosticism remains difficult. The attested Gnosticism of the second century A.D. is an amalgamation of different strains of thought, certain of which are truly ancient. But were they really *joined* into Gnosticism in the pre-Christian era? Although we have evidence for Jewish and pagan Gnosticism, the figure of Christ seems greatly to have catalyzed the shaping of proto-gnostic attitudes and elements into definable bodies of Gnostic thought. See A. D. Nock, "Gnosticism," *HTR* 57 (1964): 255–79. A. H. B. Logan, *Gnostic Truth and Christian Heresy* (Peabody, MA: Hendrickson, 1996), contends that the original myth was essentially Christian.

or Zoroastrian dualism. In particular, a Gnostic redeemer myth is proposed.[9] As seen in later Gnostic documents, this myth supposes the existence of an *Urmensch,* an Original Man, a figure of light and goodness, who was torn apart and divided into small particles of light. These particles, as human souls, were seeded in a world of darkness, and it has been the task of the demons to make them forget their heavenly origins. Then God's Son is sent in corporeal form to waken these souls, liberate them from their bodies of darkness, and lead them back to their heavenly home. He does this by proclaiming the truth and by giving souls the true knowledge (*gnôsis*) that will enable them to find their way back.

Yet research on the Gnostic redeemer myth by C. Colpe (1961) and H. M. Schenke (1962) casts serious doubts on whether the ancient but heterogeneous elements that went into that myth were already joined in the pre-Christian or early Christian period. Schenke has argued that the oft-made identification of the Gnostic redeemer with "the Son of Man" is a post-Christian development. H. Koester would also see the *egô eimi* sayings in John and its picture of the Word becoming flesh as a reaction to Gnostic views rather than stemming from Gnosticism.

Gnosticism and John

What do scholars find in John that would resemble Gnostic thought?[10] Many point to the polarities of God and the world, light and darkness, truth and falsehood, above and below. Others would detect the Gnostic redeemer and heavenly revealer historicized as Jesus, a preexistent being (1:1) who became flesh (1:14) and ultimately returned to God. He was the light who came into the world (1:9; 8:12); he was the way to God (14:6). He was not of this world any more than the select ones who be-

---

9. Bultmann was very influential in such reconstruction. For his ideas on Gnosticism, see his *Primitive Christianity* (New York: Meridian, 1957), 162–71.

10. Exegetes almost universally discuss John and ancient Gnostics; but in a fascinating French article in Marchadour, *Origine*, 185–201, J. Vernette discusses the esoteric appeal of John to nineteenth- and twentieth-century gnosticizing movements. *Editor's Note:* Our present "new age" movements, and their many parallels, with their increasingly popular literature, continue to find gnostic thought appealing. See the reflections of G. Filoramo, *A History of Gnosticism* (Oxford: Blackwell, 1990), xiii–xxi.

lieve in him are of this world (17:16). Eternal life consists in knowledge (17:3; see also 8:31–32). He plans to come back and take out of this world those who believe in him, leading them to a heavenly house (14:1–3). Some would identify the Paraclete who comes when Jesus departs as another in a series of Gnostic revealers. But there are counterarguments on every one of these points, as well as other material indicating that John is not Gnostic.[11] For the moment we shall survey below the proposals of Gnostic relationship. In considering them, one should keep in mind that all the extant Gnostic works are from a date later than John, so that theories that speak of earlier Gnosticism on which John would have drawn depend on hypothetical reconstructions.

As for the range of John's relations to Gnosticism, Perkins covered the possibilities in a carefully crafted description: scholars wonder whether John's understanding of Jesus "was intended as an appropriation of or correction to the various myths of the divine savior emerging in heterodox Jewish circles which gave rise to Gnostic mythological systems. Or, if not a direct response to such developments, it has been suggested that the Johannine perspective provided the symbolic resources out of which gnosticizing Christianity might develop."[12] To cover the main possibilities we may divide theories about John's relation to Gnosticism thus:

PRE-GOSPEL RELATIONSHIP

Some propose that John's sources were Gnostic and the evangelist Christianized them (but without totally escaping Gnostic influence).[13] Bultmann claims the evangelist remodeled a Gnostic cosmological dualism into an anthropological dualism of decision.[14] The charge of circular rea-

---

11. E. g., no secret knowledge conveyed; serious historical setting of the ministry of Jesus; absence of new revelations after Jesus' lifetime. K. M. Fischer, "Der johanneische," although he thinks that John was in debate with gnostic issues, sees major differences: Gnostics would not say that God loved the world; John reports nothing about the fall of souls into a hostile world; John gives no description of the precise way Christ takes souls back into heaven.

12. Perkins, "John's," 68. See also Dubois, "Le Quatrième."

13. With variations H. Becker, Bultmann, and S. Schultz tend in this direction.

14. In his *John*, Bultmann does not describe Gnosticism. He was influenced by H. Jonas (*The Gnostic Religion* [2nd ed.; Boston: Beacon, 1963]), who took a phenomenological approach to Gnosticism, seeing it as part of a syncretistic movement in antiquity drawing its imagery from various religious traditions.

soning has been hurled against Bultmann; namely, that he presupposes that there was a Gnosticism in the background of John, and then uses John as his main source for reconstructing this Gnosticism. However, he claims that pre-Christian Gnosticism has survived in the *Odes of Solomon,* and particularly in the Mandaean literature. The Mandaeans are a baptizing sect still extant in Mesopotamia.[15] Their theology, when it appears in full bloom, is a highly syncretistic mixture of Jewish lore, Gnostic myth, and Nestorian and Syrian Christianity. Their legends tell how they fled to Babylonia under persecution from false prophets (like Jesus) and false religions (Judaism and Christianity). Their great revealer, Manda d'Hayye, whose name means "Knowledge of life," was baptized by JBap. He taught a way of salvation that would enable people to pass over to the world of light. The oldest forms of Mandaean theology available to us are to be dated to the fourth century A.D., and there is no possibility that John was influenced by this thought as we now know it. We should note, too, that there is no Mandaean work like John; nor is there a Mandaean work that exactly resembles the Revelatory Discourse Source posited by Bultmann. But Bultmann supposes that the Mandaean thought represents a later derivative of the very type of Gnosticism that he postulates in the NT era among the disciples of JBap and which served as a background for John. Hence he cites parallel symbols, thought patterns, and phrases in John and the Mandaean writings; and he looks on them as echoes of pre-Christian Gnosticism with the idea that the Gnosticism he detected there had been brought with Mandaeans from Palestine earlier. More recent research (Lady E. S. Drower; K. Rudolph[16]) makes this theory implausible. The Mandaeans may well be correct in tracing their roots to Palestine in the early pre-Christian and Christian era; and there probably was continuity between the earliest stage of their thought and the later stage known to us. But the contention is gaining ground that the Gnostic layers in Mandaean thought and writing may not be pre-Christian.

Among the Nag Hammadi tractates, F. Wisse maintains that the *Paraphrase of Shem* presents a non-Christian redeemer myth such as presupposed by Bultmann.[17] Parallels are observable between the Johannine

---

15. See Dodd, *Interpretation,* 115–30.

16. K. Rudolph, *Gnosis: The Nature and History of Gnosticism* (San Francisco: Harper & Row, 1977); "Mandaeism," *ABD,* 4.500–2; "Zum Streit."

17. "The Redeemer Figure in the Paraphrase of Shem," *NovT* 12 (1970), 130–40.

Prologue and the Sethian Gnostic tract *Trimorphic Protennoia,* which is a type of wisdom monologue. In it there were three descents of the *Protennoia,* the third time as the *Logos.* Janssens warns that while identical terms occur in the *Trimorphic Protennoia* and John, they do not have the same meaning.[18] Hofrichter suggests that a basic set of pre-Christian theological motifs visible in a preredactional reconstruction of the Prologue has been Christianized in John and undergone a Gnostic development in the Gnostic tract.[19] Schottroff points to the poem at the end of the longer version of the *Apocryphon of John*[20] that she thinks shows non-Christian roots. However, one may debate whether John and the *Apocryphon* poem are not independently derived from Hellenistic Jewish Wisdom tradition. Langbrandtner posits a pre-Gospel foundation document that had a Gnostic dualistic outlook similar to elements in the *Odes of Solomon* and some of the Nag Hammadi tractates.[21] The redactor (who for Langbrandtner is the one who should be considered the evangelist) reinterpreted the document in an anti-Gnostic way. Much more vaguely Lieu assumes that the evangelist probably knew many of the questions Gnosticism sought to answer and adopted concepts that they also adopted, even though his approach was different from theirs. H. Koester does not posit direct dependence of John on a Gnostic source but would posit a general phenomenon of "gnosis" that produced gnosticizing interpretations of religious traditions, pre-Christian, Christian, Jewish, and pagan.[22]

RELATIONSHIP ON THE GOSPEL LEVEL

Leaving aside the issue of reconstructed sources, we find a variety of views about whether the fourth evangelist and the Gospel were themselves docetic or Gnostic or anti-Gnostic.

Toward the Gnostic end of the spectrum, Käsemann classifies the evangelist as naively docetic in picturing Jesus as God striding across the

---

18. Janssens, "Trimorphic," 242.

19. Yet Hengel, *Johannine,* 113, thinks the *Protennoia* drew on John.

20. Robinson, *NHL,* 122; Layton, *Gnostic,* 50–51. A. H. B. Logan, *Gnostic,* would see this *Apocryphon* as a development beyond the Gnostic myth described in Irenaeus and thus scarcely reflective of a source for John.

21. Langbrandtner, *Weltferner.* However, the Gnosticism of the *Odes* is highly debatable.

22. Koester, "History-of-Religions," 131–32.

face of a world that was foreign to him and as one who did not really lower himself in becoming flesh.[23] The church that canonized the Fourth Gospel did not recognize the voice of one of those whom she would later condemn as heretics. Schottroff contends that John is a Gnostic work with a radically dualistic evaluation of the relationship of the redeemer to the world and a dualism of human choice for or against God.[24] John does not deny the reality of Jesus' flesh, but the world is judged unfriendly to God because it refuses to recognize Jesus' glory-salvation is for those who do not belong to the world.

The position of H. Koester is more complicated. The beginnings of Johannine tradition are not too different from that of the Synoptics.[25] Only after expulsion from the synagogue did the Johannine Christians begin to form their own cultic structures (baptism, eucharist) and develop their own form of miracle stories (syncretistic with pagan stories and a view of Jesus as a divine being on earth) and sayings of Jesus (comparable to those in the *Gospel of Thomas*). In the latter, gnosis arises for the first time, and this increases in long dialogues based on the sayings (cf. the Nag Hammadi writing *Dialogue of the Savior*, which is earlier in development than John).[26] Then the evangelist formulated "I am" sayings and introduced the Jesus-the-redeemer myth by way of answering Gnostic interpretations—contrast the *Acts of John* where Jesus was not really incarnate and did not die.

---

23. Käsemann, *Testament.* Docetism in varying degrees denies the reality of the humanity of Jesus; not all docetists were gnostic, and not all gnostics were docetist, but often the twain did meet. As part of his thesis of heterodoxy in Johannine writing, Käsemann ("Ketzer und Zeuge: Zum johanneischen Verfasserproblem," *ZTK* 48 [1951]: 292–311) contended that Diotrephes in 3 John was an orthodox leader opposing the Presbyter-writer of the letter who was a Johannine gnostic enthusiast.

24. Ruckstuhl, "Johannesevangelium," constitutes a detailed challenge to Schottroff's interpretations; Sevrin, "Jean," 254, sees a basic fault in her overly broad definition of gnosticism.

25. Koester, "History-of-Religions," 126–31.

26. H. Koester, "Gnostic Writings as Witnesses for the Development of the Sayings Tradition," in B. Layton (ed.), *The Rediscovery of Gnosticism* (2 vols.; Leiden: Brill, 1980), 1.238–61. See also Dubois, "Le quatrième," who suggests comparisons on the basis, not simply of terminology, but also of the style and construction of the discourses. The arguments for priority are extremely subtle and, in my judgment, very tenuous.

On the anti-Gnostic end of the spectrum, in antiquity Irenaeus (*Adv. Haer. 3.11.1*) reports the tradition that John wrote the Gospel to refute Cerinthus, a heretic whose views were close to Gnosticism and docetism, and the Gnostic error of the Nicolaitans. In modern times, G. Richter contends that parts of the Gospel contain a clear refutation of Gnosticism. He would attribute these to the redactor who found that, by so highly exalting Jesus, the evangelist had supplied ammunition for Gnostic interpretation.

In the middle of the spectrum is the thesis that the Gospel itself did not draw on a Gnostic background, that its approaches are not distinctively Gnostic, and it was not concerned with correcting Gnostic interpretations because that struggle came only later. In his careful study, Sevrin, "Jean," 268, sums up: "The Gnostic hypothesis appears to be superfluous in the interpretation of the Fourth gospel." Later, therefore, the Gospel's statements could be used to support either (or both) sides in the anti-Gnostic/Gnostic struggle.[27]

POST-GOSPEL RELATIONSHIP

Vouga, "Jean," 110, rightly observes that, rather than trying to resolve the question of the relation of John to gnosis on the basis of origin or development (about which we know so little), we should try the perspective of the reception of the Gospel after it was written. Let me first list the facts we know (e.g., Poffet, "Indices"). Among authors who by later standards would be considered orthodox it is difficult to show knowledge of the Fourth Gospel before A.D. 150; the Gospel is used (probably) by Justin (ca. 150), by Theophilus bishop of Antioch 170–180 in his *Apology to Autolycus* (Book Two) and by Irenaeus of Lyons in his *Adv. Haer.* just before 180.[28] Somewhat earlier, it is clear that John was known by Gnostics of

---

27. With a different tonality based on his theory that 2–3 John preceded John, G. Strecker, "Chiliasm and Docetism in the Johannine School," *Australian Biblical Review* 38 (1990): 45–61, contends that the Fourth Gospel integrated both docetic and anti-docetic material.

28. Attempts have been made to show that John was known before A.D. 150 by Clement of Rome, Ignatius of Antioch, the author of the *Shepherd of Hermas;* but their occasional use of imagery also used by John is insufficient proof. There is more agreement about Justin Martyr ca. 160: cf. *Trypho* 88.7 and John 1:20, 23; *Apology* 1.61. 4 and John 3:3–5. Pryor, "Justin," however, thinks that, although using John, Justin did not regard it as Scripture or the work of an apostle (also Dodd, *Tradition*, 13).

the Valentinian school who interpreted it in the light of their mythology. In the East (Alexandria), Theodotus (ca. 160–170) quoted it, and in the West (Rome) Ptolemy (mid-second century) commented on the Prologue and Heracleon (mid-second century) commented on the Gospel. Gnostic interest in Johannine ideas is visible in the Nag Hammadi material.[29] For instance, there is a Word (*Logos*) Christology in the *Tripartite Tractate;* and "I am" Christology in the Second *Apocalypse of James;* also in *The Thunder,* the *Perfect Mind,* and in the *Trimorphic Protennoia* (where it is joined with a docetic account of the death of Jesus). The *Acts of John* and the *Apocryphon of John* show late second-century Gnosticism expounded under a Johannine mantle. Montanus (ca. A.D. 170), who in Asia Minor led a movement of ecstatic, Spirit-filled prophecy, considered himself the embodiment of the Johannine Paraclete. In my judgment, the esoteric *Secret Gospel of Mark,* which stems from mid-second century in Alexandria, is dependent on knowledge of John.

One must theorize how that history of interpretation fits into the picture reflected in the Johannine writings. A common thesis is that after the Gospel was written at the end of the first century A.D., a large part of the Johannine community began to interpret it in an incipiently Gnostic manner: Jesus saved the world through his revelation, not through his death; people are saved through belief in his incarnation, and the way they live is not important. They are the adversaries described in 1 and 2 John who attempted to refute them by maintaining that their interpretation was not the way the Johannine tradition was understood from the beginning. These adversaries left the community, taking the Gospel along with them in their journey toward fully developed Gnosticism.[30] Pervo sees the theology of the *Acts of John* in terms of ongoing trajectories from John itself (e.g., the use of the miracles as signs, the glorified Christology), so that the gulf between the (reconstructed) opponents of 1 John and the partially Gnostic theological framework of the *Acts of John* is not so large that one has to posit the introduction of external systems of

---

29. Hengel, *Johannine,* 9, 147, contends that most of the gnostic use of John stems from the Valentinian school, whose members, at least at the beginning, sought to be Christians in the sphere of the church, so that one should not interpret gnostic usage too easily as anti-church.

30. For a full exposition of the thesis, see R. E. Brown, *Community,* 93–144; BEJ 69–115.

thought.[31] Because John was popular among the (Valentinian) Gnostics[32] and other esoteric movements, the Gospel seemingly acquired a taint of heterodoxy in the eyes of some in the "Great Church" (a term that appears in Origen, *Contra Celsum* 5.59, distinguishing the mainline church from the Gnostic conventicles).[33] Toward the end of the second century, partially through citations from 1 John,[34] Irenaeus defended the Gospel as orthodox and refuted Gnostic interpretations of it. The Muratorian Fragment attests the acceptance of John into a Western canon before A.D. 200.[35] However, the Roman presbyter Gaius (and the Alogoi) continued to be suspicious of the orthodoxy of the Johannine writings (specifically because of Montanist misuse).

Variations on this theory that places a struggle with Gnosticism after the writing of the Gospel are supported by Brown, Painter, and von Wahlde. Wide support can be found for the thesis that 1 and 2 John portray two groups of Johannine Christians (one with a tendency that would lead them, once they seceded, toward Gnosticism; and the other, represented by the epistolary writer, decidedly antignostic) and that they were reading the same Gospel differently (BEJ 69–115). In part this reflects on the issue raised on pp. 122–24 above: which group was interpreting the Gospel correctly? An evaluation of the secessionists is handicapped by having to reconstruct their views mirrorwise, but the acceptance of 1 John into the canon and the use of it by Irenaeus favor recognizing the author of 1 John as correctly analyzing the Gospel.[36]

---

31. Pervo, "Johannine," 62.

32. There is no evidence to suggest that the acquisition of John would have generated a major gnostic system (Perkins, "John's"), but it would have supplied vocabulary and theology for incorporation into such a system.

33. There were non-gnostic uses of John as well—a point insisted on by Hengel, *Johannine*, 1–23. *Epistula Apostolorum* (ca. 150), which is clearly anti-gnostic, draws on John.

34. Polycarp, Irenaeus, and Tertullian employed 1 John 4:2–3 and 2 John 7 as an argument against heretics.

35. There have been attempts to date the Fragment much later (see, for example, E. Haenchen, *The Acts of the Apostles. A Commentary* [Philadelphia: Westminster Press, 1971], 10–12), but that remains a minority view.

36. Jaschke, "Johannesevangelium," argues that Irenaeus is correct in seeing that John was not of gnostic origin. Fischer, "Der johanneische," 266, in his comparison of gnosticism to John, firmly insists that the author of 1 John understood John cor-

Extrabiblical Hellenistic Thought

IN RAISING THE QUESTION of Greek influence on John, I must make an important distinction. There was a strong Hellenistic element already present in the biblical Judaism that served as background for NT times,[37] both in Palestine and Alexandria. Therefore, if John were dependent on contemporary Judaism, Johannine thought would inevitably have reflected Hellenistic influence. I have spoken of personified Wisdom speculation: in Deuterocanonical books like Sirach and Wisdom of Solomon, this speculation has been colored by Hellenistic thought. There was strong Hellenistic influence on the Jewish groups or "sects" in Palestine. Josephus draws an analogy between the thought of the Essenes (= in part the Qumran group) and that of the neo-Pythagoreans, attributing to the Essenes an anthropology with clear Hellenistic features. Braun points out affinities between the *Hermetica* and Essene thought as it is found in Josephus and the Qumran scrolls.[38] Cullmann has attempted to draw together the Qumran Essenes, the Samaritans, and the Hellenists (Acts 6:1) under the banners of a nonconformist Judaism sharing an opposition to the Temple and a predilection for Hellenistic thought. Given these possibilities/likelihoods/certainties, I take for granted a Greek strain within Judaism that had influence on Johannine vocabulary and thought.

Yet the question I am asking here is whether there was another Hellenistic influence on John that came from outside the Bible or known Palestinian Jewish sects (Pharisees, Sadducees, Essenes)[39]—an influence through which the Gospel reinterpreted the message and portrait of Jesus. In particular, three strains of Greek thought have been offered as

---

rectly. Vouga, "Jean," in a rather idiosyncratic thesis maintains that neither the gnostics nor the Church Fathers understood John or 1 John correctly.

37. I am using the term "biblical" in the sense in which Protestant Bibles are sometimes titled as "The Complete Bible" and in the normal Roman Catholic sense, i.e., an OT including the Deuterocanonical books or Apocrypha.

38. Braun, *JT*, 2.252–76.

39. In a well-nuanced study, Borgen, "Gospel," 116–17, concludes that it is difficult to identify direct Hellenistic influence on John from outside of Judaism, but John cultivates ideas and practices that to some extent are Jewish-Christian versions of aspects and trends present in the larger Hellenistic world.

possible explanations for the peculiarities in Johannine theological expression, namely, a popular form of Greek philosophy, Philo, and the *Hermetica.* I shall discuss each in turn, but I stress that I am seeking *formative* influence on the evangelist's thought. Somewhat different problems are whether the evangelist has given the Gospel a veneer of Hellenistic phraseology in order to convert the Greek world,[40] or, no matter what the evangelist intended, how audiences with Hellenistic backgrounds would have understood him.

John and Greek Philosophy

Some older commentators on John, for example, E. A. Abbott, W. R. Inge, stressed Johannine borrowings from the schools of Greek philosophic thought, especially from Platonism or Stoicism.[41]

First I consider Platonism. In John there are contrasts between what is above and what is below (3:31), between spirit and flesh (3:6; 6:63), between eternal life and natural existence (11:25–26), between the real bread from heaven (6:32) and natural bread, between the water of eternal life (4:14) and natural water. These contrasts may be compared to a popular form of Platonism where there is a real world, invisible and eternal, contrasted with the world of appearances here below. The similarity is impressive, but popular Platonism had already infiltrated Judaism. Beside the horizontal, linear distinction between the present age in the history of Israel and the age to come after divine intervention, there was also in the Jewish thought of this period a vertical distinction between the heavenly and the earthly.[42] A contrast between spirit and flesh is not unknown in the OT (Isa 31:3), and Qumran offers a contrast between what is on the level of flesh and what is from above (1QH 10:23, 32). Even the contrast between real bread and natural bread is foreshadowed in a passage like Isa 55:1–2 where the bread of God's teaching is con-

---

40. See the discussion of the purpose of the Gospel in Chapter Five, below.

41. At the end of the twentieth century, a small group of scholars claimed that Jesus himself could be fitted into a Greek philosophical mold, e.g., an itinerant cynic preacher (see BINT, 822–23). Since that movement was skeptical of the historical value of the Synoptic Gospels (and a fortiori, of John), it really does not enter seriously into the question of special influence on John.

42. See the discussion of Johannine eschatology in Chapter Seven, below.

trasted with what is not bread. Thus, the affinities to popular Platonism that have been proposed for John are quite explicable in the light of Palestinian Judaism. Sometimes they are only seeming affinities that are explicable in terms of the OT; sometimes they are real affinities but stem from Greek thought that had already become a part of the Jewish background.

A parallel to Stoicism has been suggested by the use of *logos,* "the Word," in the Prologue, for this was a popular term in Stoic thought. My earlier treatment of this term indicated that the Johannine usage is different from that of the Stoics.[43] Moreover, the hymn that is the Prologue had its own history within Johannine circles, and it is risky to argue from terminological parallels in the Prologue to influence on the whole Gospel. Thus, there is no real reason to suppose that the Gospel was influenced by more Greek philosophy than what was already present in the general thought and speech of Palestine.

John and Philo

A dependence of John upon Philo of Alexandria has been suggested. A contemporary of Jesus, Philo represented in his work an attempt to combine Judaism and Greek thought. We have no clear evidence that Philo's work was known in early first-century Palestine; and so if the evangelist was dependent on Philo, this familiarity probably was gained outside Palestine. Those who think that John was written at Ephesus point out that according to Acts 18:24 Apollos, a Christian Jew from Alexandria, came to Ephesus (early 50s?). Apollos was eloquent and some assume that means he knew philosophy. Once again the use of *logos* in the Prologue is a key argument, for Philo employed this term. Argyle attempts to show a wider dependence of John upon Philo because some of the biblical imagery used by John (Jacob's ladder, brazen serpent, vision of Abraham) is also used by Philo, precisely in connection with the doctrine of the *logos*.[44] Perhaps I miss the point of the argument; but the very fact that, unlike Philo, John does not use this imagery in connection with "the Word" and the fact that in the total Gospel "the Word" has only a minor role would seem to weaken the case for dependency on Philo. Feuillet

---

43. See *John,* 519–20.
44. Argyle, "Philo."

contends that John's *logos* in the sense of "divine word" is very far from Philo's use of the term as a figurative expression of right reason.[45]

Wilson's cautious article on the subject is quite instructive.[46] He observes that while we know Philo's work, most of the work of his predecessors has not survived. The Philonian reflections on the *logos* are probably the culmination of a long history of such thought. Moreover, both Philo and John draw on the OT, and in the concept of *logos* they both draw on the Wisdom Literature of the OT. It is not surprising, therefore, that at times their thought develops along parallel lines. But when one comes to essential methodological procedure, Philo and John are far apart. The overwhelming philosophical coloring found in Philo does not appear in John, and the elaborate Philonic allegories have little in common with the Johannine use of Scripture. Borgen shows resemblance between the homiletic style of John and that of Philo; but again that need not be an issue of the dependence of John on Philo.[47] Dodd has said that Philo, along with Rabbinic Judaism and the *Hermetica,* remains one of our most direct sources for the background of Johannine thought.[48] But Braun states sharply: if Philo had never existed, the Fourth Gospel would most probably not have been any different from what it is.[49] Personally, I believe that the evidence points rather toward a common background shared by both Philo and John of working out biblical motifs in a partially Jewish, partially Greek world where Hellenistic thought has taken root. Also Philo's writings show us how Jews with a background in Hellenistic thought could have found sympathetic John's way of expressing Jesus' thought.

John and the Hermetica

Still other scholars who posit Hellenistic influence on John turn to a higher, philosophical religion such as that of the Hermetic literature or *Hermetica*. In Egypt, between the second and fifth centuries A.D., a body of seventeen philosophical/theological tractates, written in Greek but

---

45. Feuillet, "Les rapports," 1349.
46. Wilson, "Philo."
47. Borgen, *Bread from Heaven.*
48. Dodd, *Interpretation,* 133.
49. Braun, *JT,* 2.298.

largely independent of each other (= Corpus Hermeticum), grew up.[50] They were centered on a legendary sage of ancient Egypt believed to have been deified as the god Thoth, the thrice-greatest, who in turn was identified with the Greek god Hermes, thus Hermes Trismegistus. The thought expressed in this literature is a syncretism of (Middle) Platonic and Stoic philosophy with the religious tradition of the Near East, including Judaism. Although astrological and other pseudoscientific elements in Hermetic speculation may be dated B.C., the cosmological and moral reflections have their beginning no earlier than the late first century A.D. and were for the most part written down after the Fourth Gospel. Cast in the form of dialogues between Hermes and his sons, these writings proclaim a lofty concept of God and of human ethical obligations. The perfect human being possesses the knowledge of God, and salvation is through this revealed knowledge (see John 17:3). Elements of semi-pantheism and of Gnosticism can be found in the *Hermetica*.

In comparing these writings to John, scholars have found some very interesting parallels of thought and vocabulary (both Braun and Dodd give lists). Most would not posit direct dependence of John upon the *Hermetica,* but Dodd is impressed with the value of the *Hermetica* in interpreting John. Kilpatrick has stressed that the similarities between the two literatures should not be overemphasized.[51] Some of the theological terms that are the most important in the *Hermetica* are totally absent from John, for example, *gnôsis, mystêrion, athanasia* ("immortality"), *demiourgos* ("demiurge"). A statistical comparison of vocabulary is also interesting. There are 197 significant words in John beginning with one of the first four letters of the Greek alphabet; 189 of these appear in LXX; only 82 of them appear in the *Hermetica.*[52] Thus John is far closer to the language of the Greek OT than to that of the *Hermetica*. Braun issues another caution. Although there is no direct mention of Christianity in the

---

50. In 1945–1954 the critical edition of this corpus of writing was edited by A. D. Nock and A. J. Festugière with commentary (*Corpus Hermeticum* [4 vols.; Paris: Les Belles Lettres, 1945–54]).

51. Kilpatrick, "Religious."

52. *Editor's Note:* I wonder about the value of this comparison, if I have understood it properly. How does it fare with the next four letters of the Greek alphabet, or the next four, and so on?

Hermetica, there are indications that some of the authors of *Hermetica,* a literature later than John, knew Christianity (and John) and even wrote against it.

The common view, however, is that there is no literary dependence in either direction, but that both John and the *Hermetica* represent a similar religious milieu. In their use of terms such as "light," "life," "word," they are both dependent on a theological terminology more ancient than either of them: namely, the terminology that sprang from the combination of Oriental speculation on Wisdom and Greek abstract thought. Such a combination is already exemplified in the pre-Christian period in the deuterocanonical Book of Wisdom. That this common basis was built upon in two such different ways as we now see in the *Hermetica* and John suggests that the two literatures had little to do with each other in the formative stages. Thus, I would agree with Kilpatrick that we can evaluate the *Hermetica* on the same level as the Mandaean writings, that is, as constituting no significant part of the background of the Gospel.

Traditional Judaism

A LARGE NUMBER OF SCHOLARS are coming to agree that the principal background for Johannine thought was the traditional Judaism of the first century A.D. For want of a better term I am using "traditional" to describe a Judaism that took its main inspiration from what we call the OT (including the deuterocanonical books) without conscious adoption of large amounts of extrabiblical Hellenistic philosophy/theology. After the Babylonian exile this Judaism had undergone Persian and Greek influence and had reacted in different ways, so that it was far from monolithic.[53] Indeed, its very diversity helps to explain different aspects of Johannine thought. Specifically, let me consider the OT, Rabbinic Judaism, and the Judaism of the Qumran sectarians.

---

53. Josephus (*J. W.* 2.118–19) speaks of Pharisees, Sadducees, Essenes, and a group founded by Judas the Galilean, and to those might be added various apocalyptic and "political" strains.

John and the Old Testament

John has fewer direct OT citations than have the other Gospels. The Nestle Greek text (26th edition) indicates only 19, all from books in the Palestinian canon of the OT.[54] In the Westcott-Hort list of OT references used in the NT, 27 passages are listed for John, as compared with 70 for Mark, 109 for Luke, and 124 for Matthew. The infrequency of Johannine *testimonia* is deceptive, however, as Barrett has shown.[55] Many of the themes of the Synoptic *testimonia* have been woven into the structure of the Fourth Gospel without explicit citation of the OT. Unlike Mark 7:6, John does not cite Isa 29:13 to the effect that the hearts of the people of Israel are far from God although they honor God with their lips; yet this theme goes all through Jesus' arguments with "the Jews" in the Fourth Gospel. Also John may directly cite a section of the OT once, and yet implicitly be citing it in other Gospel passages.[56] Moreover, in terms of fulfillment or formula citations,[57] John with its seven formula references to

---

54. Actually John 6:35 is very close to Sirach 24:21. C. A. Evans, "On the," detects fifteen direct citations; Freed, *Old Testament,* counts seventeen. On the other hand, Nestle-Aland lists some two hundred allusions and parallels. This plus the occasional difficulty of discerning, when John mentions Scripture, exactly which passage he has in mind (Beutler, "Use," 148–50, lists only nine that are clear) leads many to observe that John seems more interested in the fulfillment of Scripture in general than in the fulfillment of individual passages (see 1:45; 2:22; 10:35). See below on Obermann's contribution to the idea of "fulfillment" of the Scriptures in the Fourth Gospel.

55. Barrett, "Old Testament."

56. Beutler, "Psalm 42/43," finds Ps 42:7 cited in John 12:27 (echoed in 13:21), and sees other echoes of the psalm in John 11:33–35; 14; 19:28. See Cothenet, "L'arrière-plan," 49–50.

57. I.e., citations of the Scriptures (usually of the prophets) introduced by a formula that indicates that the NT event took place in order to fulfill the OT passage being cited. See C. A. Evans, R. J. Hufmann, J. O'Rourke, B. G. Schuchard in the Bibliography. More recently, two fine studies have appeared. Both are found in the Bibliography. M. J. J. Menken, *Old Testament Quotations,* thoroughly investigates the origin of the Johannine biblical citations and makes some initial suggestions concerning their use in the Gospel. He provides an excellent bibliography. Similarly, A. Obermann, *Die christologische Erfüllung,* 409–22, especially 418–22, has investigated the origins of the Johannine citations and allusions, and has developed a convincing thesis concerning their use to point to Jesus as the christological fulfillment of Scripture, and the Gospel itself as "Scripture" (see the summary below, on pp. 137–38).

the OT is the only Gospel comparable to Matthew with its ten/fourteen; and that type of citation implies that John looked on the OT as revelation. In particular, 10:34–35 specifies that the Law/Scripture was God's word addressed to people.[58]

Of greater importance, as Braun has shown, John reflects even more clearly than the Synoptic Gospels the great currents of OT thought.[59] Jesus is presented as the Messiah, the Servant of Yahweh, the King of Israel, and the Prophet—all figures in the gallery of OT expectations. Many of the allusions to the OT are subtle, but quite real. Hanson contends that while there is no scheme of salvation history, the OT is John's essential background throughout,[60] and that far from being merely illustrative, the OT is part of the very woof and warp of John. Hoskyns has shown how Genesis influenced John, even though never explicitly cited.[61] The narrative of the first days of creation and of the first man and woman is the backbone of John 1:1–2, 10, and the theme of Jacob's vision of the ladder reaching from heaven to earth (Gen 28:10–17) is echoed in 1:47, 51. There are references to Abraham (8:31–38), Isaac (3:16), and Jacob (4:5–6, 11–12).

John mentions Moses almost twice as frequently as any other Gospel. The whole story of Moses and of the Exodus is a very dominant motif, as Glasson argues in great detail. Some scholars have even suggested that the organization of the Fourth Gospel was patterned on Exodus. J. J. Enz compares each section of John to a section of Exodus; R. H. Smith compares Jesus' signs as reported in John with Moses' signs in bringing the

---

58. John refers to *graphē* ("Scripture," almost always in the singular) and *nomos* ("Law") much more frequently than do the other Gospels. Such appeal to the OT reflects Jesus' contention that "Salvation is from the Jews" (4:22). Yet, as Dietzfelbinger, "Aspekte," stresses, there is another outlook in John in reference to "the Jews" where Jesus speaks of "your/their Law." The OT is common to both to the Johannine community and the synagogue; but unless people read the OT with Johannine christological glasses, they are not seeing or hearing God; in that sense it is "their" Law, not "ours."

59. Braun, *JT*, 2: *Les Grandes Traditions d'Israël et l'Accord des Écritures d'après le Quatrième Évangile.*

60. Hanson, *Prophetic*, 234–53. Busse, "Tempelmetaphorik," holds much the same view: Scripture for John is "the irreplaceable context of meaning for the Jesus event" (398).

61. Hoskyns, "Genesis."

plagues on Egypt.[62] Inevitably such elaborate equivalences are forced in some details, although I do agree with Smith that a very important factor in the Johannine concept of the "sign" was the use of "sign" for Moses' miracles.[63] Without overdependence on this quest for the same structural pattern in Exodus and John, one may acknowledge numerous Johannine references to the exodus story and its events: to Moses (John 1:17; 5:46, etc.), the manna (6:31–58), the water from the rock (7:38), the bronze serpent (3:14), and the Tabernacle (1:14). The speeches of Moses in Deuteronomy have often been suggested as offering a parallel in the psychology of their composition to the discourses of Jesus in John: both represent a reworking of traditional material into the format of discourse. The Johannine concept of commandment is close to the Deuteronomic concept.[64] There are also references to other events in the subsequent history of Israel (to the Judges in 10:35; to the theme of the royal shepherd in 10:1ff.). Daly-Denton has recently challenged the prevailing view that the fourth evangelist disassociates Jesus from David, claiming that David as a psalmist plays a highly significant role in the Johannine portrayal of Jesus.[65]

Half of John's explicit citations are from the prophets (five from Isaiah; two from Zechariah). Griffiths has offered that prophecy is a good OT parallel to John, for both reinterpret previous traditions with considerable originality.[66] It is to Deutero-Isaiah that we must go for the background of the Johannine usage of *egô eimi,* "I am,"[67] and for some elements of the universality attributed to Jesus' mission. The last part of Zechariah seems to lie behind John's reflections on the feast of Tabernacles and on the stream of living water (7:37–38). Vawter suggests that Ezekiel may offer background for certain features in the Johannine theology of the Son of Man and of the Paraclete.[68]

The Wisdom Literature is also important for an understanding of

---

62. Enz, "Book"; Smith, "Exodus."

63. See *John,* 527–29.

64. See, for example, A. Lacomara, "Deuteronomy and the Farewell Discourse (Jn 13:31–16:33," *CBQ* 36 (1974): 65–84.

65. Daly-Denton, *David in the Fourth Gospel.*

66. Griffiths, "Deutero-Isaiah."

67. See *John,* 532–38.

68. Vawter, "Ezekiel."

John. As in the other Gospels, so also in John, the Book of Psalms is a frequent source for *testimonia*, or passages gathered by Christians for answering their opponents. I shall maintain below that the most decisive influence on the form and style of the discourses of Jesus in the Fourth Gospel comes from the speeches of divine Wisdom in books like Proverbs, Sirach, and Wisdom of Solomon.[69]

Which form of the OT did John employ? Menken and Schuchard agree that John basically used the LXX, although Menken would posit that in two cases (12:40; 13:18) the evangelist made an independent translation from the Hebrew, and that in 19:37 he drew on a current early Christian translation from Hebrew. Boismard suggests that the pre-Gospel form of John he posits in Document C drew on the Hebrew Scriptures, whereas the form in Jean II B drew on the LXX. Some scholars have argued that at least some of the explicit citations of the OT that appear in John seem to be directly translated from the Hebrew and do not come from the LXX;[70] this would modify Goodwin's suggestion that John's variations from the LXX arise from the fact that the evangelist cited freely and from memory. Another proposal is that in passages like 3:14; 4:6, 12; 7:38, and 12:41, John may be citing the Palestinian Targums (the local Aramaic translations of Scripture) rather than the Hebrew Bible. Cothenet suggests that the exegetical work on the OT would have been carried on in the various stages of Johannine development, drawing on the varied possibilities of a text reflected in the different versions.[71] The implications for the background of the Gospel are obvious. In the original edition of this commentary I titled this section "Palestinian Judaism"; now I choose the more neutral "Traditional Judaism." John shows knowledge of Palestinian geography, festal customs, and is close to the thought of the Qumran or Dead Scroll community. All that points toward Palestine, even if there are touches that suggest a later stage among those who did not know Jewish terminology. Yet if the OT used by John was preeminently Greek, and that cannot be confined to the last stages of Gospel composition, one may doubt that early Christians used the LXX much in Palestine.[72] Some would compromise and propose a Palestinian border area in the Trans-

---

69. See Chapter Seven, below.

70. See, for example, Braun, *JT*, 2.20–21.

71. Cothenet, "L'arrière-plan," 46.

72. At Qumran some fragments of the Greek OT were found in Caves 4 and 7.

jordan or Syria where knowledge of Palestinian geography and the regular use of the LXX would be combined.

Scholars recognize that John's use of Scripture is often not literal by modern standards, and has parallels in Jewish literature of the period 200 B.C.–A.D. 300 that interpret Scripture (Qumran *pesharim*, rabbinic midrashim and targumic translations). Although some of the techniques are the same, Hanson is correct in insisting that such literature is interpreting written OT texts.[73] John's primary focus is on the Jesus tradition that it shapes and illuminates through the Scriptures. Hanson exaggerates in suggesting the introduction, on the basis of Scripture, of episodes or teaching that seem to have no other basis in history. However, Hanson is not the most extreme in this approach; in fact, he would maintain that Scripture functioned as a control on too creative an imagination.

Obermann points out that up to 12:15 (see 1:23; 6:31, 45; 10:34; 12:15) the author focuses upon the Scriptures as such, while from 12:38 till 19:36 all citations (12:38; 13:18; 15:25; 19:24, 36) are to show that something happened in order that the Scriptures "might be fulfilled." In 19:28, both elements are combined. The use of the Scripture in the first section proclaims Jesus as Lord, Temple, living bread, Son of God and king. The theme of fulfillment is introduced in 12:38, and the rest of the use of Scripture shows that what was said implicitly by Scripture becomes explicit in Jesus. For Obermann there is an external relationship between Scripture and Jesus in the gift of life, but there is also an inner, theological relationship, because Jesus is the "Word of God" become flesh. Because of the Johannine appropriation of Scripture, events in the story make the Scriptures relevant in the events of the life of Jesus (1:23; 6:31, 45; 10:34; 12:13; 13:18; 15:25); the reflection of the later community on the significance of events that took place in the life of Jesus renders the Gospel of John relevant as Scripture. John 20:31 is an indication of the

---

73. "John's Use," 358–67. He enters dialogue with the general midrash studies of R. Bloch and R. Le Déaut; with the claims of M. Black and B. Olsson that compare John to targums; and with G. Reim's refusal to recognize typology in John. Hanson is convincing that John's appeal to the serpent on the pole (3:14) and the manna (6:31–32) may be classified as typology, but he wisely rejects R. H. Smith's overuse of typology in comparing John to Exodus. Hengel, "Old Testament," speaks of a messianic, charismatic, enthusiastic interpretation of Scripture shared by much of the NT with an eschatologically oriented Judaism.

community's understanding of the Gospel as Scripture, a *graphê* that produces eternal life.[74]

Hengel insists that one cannot assign the use of the OT to a source or to the redaction, for it appears in every layer of Johannine thought.[75] Several scholars distinguish between OT passages used both in John and elsewhere in the NT—passages that one can call traditional—and ones that only John uses. Beutler observes that the evangelist depends on traditional passages mainly in the context of the passion and resurrection where he is the speaker, while in the controversies where Jesus speaks to "the Jews" there is a wider, freer, and even vaguer range of scriptural reference, as if at the period when such controversies developed in Johannine history the individual proof text no longer mattered and the whole of Scripture was at stake.[76]

John and Rabbinic Judaism

Once one moves beyond the biblical books, the documents of Jewish groups that might have influenced John become scarce. Before the middle of the twentieth century, the main comparison was with the writings of Rabbinic Judaism, i.e., the Judaism that emerged after A.D. 70, i.e., after the destruction of the Jerusalem Temple at the end of the First Jewish Revolt against Rome. None of the extant documents was written before the second century, so it is very difficult to evaluate the light they cast on the NT. No one denies that the rabbinic documents preserve elements that go back to the time of Jesus and even before. Yet the thesis that the rabbis are the continuation of the Pharisaic Judaism of Jesus' time needs considerable nuancing. The pre-70 Pharisees were in very strong contention with other Jewish groups; the post-70s rabbis, despite academic disputes, were far less contentious and served to unify Judaism. Moreover, the rabbis' application of the Law reflected the changed political and religious situation of the second century A.D. with the Temple gone and the Jews exiled from Jerusalem.

---

74. *Editor's Note:* This summary of Obermann's study is entirely my synthesis of a very large and intricately argued study. For further detail, see my review of the book in *CBQ* 60 (1998): 375-77.

75. Hengel, "Old Testament."

76. Beutler, "Use," 155-58.

Scholars like Schlatter, Strack and Billerbeck, D. Daube, and Dodd[77] have pointed out many parallels between Johannine and rabbinic thought. Concepts like that of the hidden Messiah, and speculations on the creative role of the Torah (which John attributes to "the Word") and on the nature of life in the world-to-come may contribute to understanding Johannine developments. In relation to ch. 6, Borgen has pointed out how similar the format of Jesus' Discourse on the Bread of Life is to the homiletic pattern of the rabbinic *midrashim* (or free interpretations of Scripture passages).[78] Others (E. G. B. Gärtner, *John 6 and the Jewish Passover*) have found in ch. 6 (disputable) parallels to the Jewish Passover *Haggadah* in the Seder service. Even more open to challenge is the contention of Aileen Guilding that the discourses uttered by Jesus on the occasion of great feasts are closely related to the themes of the readings assigned to be read in the synagogues at these feasts.[79] One must be aware that it is often impossible to prove that the suggested parallel reflects the thought of first-century Judaism.

John and Qumran

The discovery of the Dead Sea Scrolls (DSS) in 1947 greatly increased our knowledge of Judaism in first-century Palestine. Among the whole or very partial remains of some 800 manuscripts is the literature of the group that settled at Qumran on the northwest corner of the Dead Sea ca. 150 B.C. The fact that the Essene community at Qumran was destroyed in A.D. 68 means that with rare exception its documents antedate Christian literature.[80] For purposes of comparison to John, this gives the DSS a real advantage over the rabbinic literature, the Mandaean literature and the *Hermetica*. The best scholarly opinion and the one I shall follow

---

77. D. Daube, *The New Testament and Rabbinic Judaism* (London: Athlone Press, 1956); Dodd, *Interpretation*, 74–97.

78. Borgen, *Bread and Water.*

79. Guilding, *The Fourth Gospel and Jewish Worship.*

80. The main Qumran compositions that feature in comparisons with John are the Rule of the Community (QS) and the Damascus Document (CD). In the DSS there is no knowledge of Christianity; the direction of possible influence would have been from Qumran to John, not vice versa. Yet in the Johannine writings there are no clear quotations from a DSS or reference to Qumran history. The discussion has to concentrate on possible contacts in ideas and vocabulary.

here is that this group consisted of Essenes,[81] who were described in Josephus, Philo, and Pliny. Since both the Qumran literature and the NT are dependent on the OT, the parallels of thought and vocabulary that can be really significant for determining influence are those that are not also found in the OT.

Articles on the relation between John and Qumran (Brown, F.-M. Braun, Kuhn) have singled out modified dualism as one of the most important parallels. In the Qumran literature a prince and an angel created by God are locked in struggle to dominate humankind until the time of divine intervention. They are the prince of lights (also called the spirit of truth and the holy spirit) and the angel of darkness (the spirit of perversion). In John's thought Jesus has come into the world as the light to overcome the darkness (John 1:4–5, 9), and all must choose between light and darkness (3:19–21). The dualistic balancing of terms and the conflict may be sharper at Qumran, but see 1 John 4:6; 5:19; 2:8–11. Jesus is the truth (14:6), and after his death the struggle to overcome the evil force is carried on by the Spirit of Truth (or the Holy Spirit: 14:17, 26). All human beings are aligned in two opposing camps dominated by these two powers: children of light/darkness who do or walk in light/darkness, truth/falsehood.[82] Not only the dualism but also its terminology are shared by John and Qumran. This dualism[83] is seen in several of the Pseudepigrapha, e.g., in the *Testaments of the Twelve Patriarchs*—usually works that are in some way related to the Qumran group. O. Böcher insists that Johannine dualism is far closer to the dualism of Jewish apocalyptic and sectarian thought than it is to anything in the Hellenistic and Gnostic sources.[84]

---

81. See J. A. Fitzmyer, "The Qumran Community: Essene or Sadducean?" in *The Dead Sea Scrolls and Christian Origins* (Studies in the Dead Sea Scrolls and Related Literature; Grand Rapids: Eerdmans, 2000), 249–60. This identification would make the Essenes better documented than the Pharisees, who are only partially reflected in the rabbinic documents, and the Sadducees who are chiefly known through passing references in the NT and (hostile) rabbinic writings.

82. See John 1:6–7; 2:11; 3:21; 8:12; 12:35–36.

83. Kuhn may be right in suggesting that its ultimate roots are in Zoroastrianism where, however, it is a question of the absolute dualism of opposed, uncreated principles—a possible exception is the Zervanite form of Zoroastrianism in which the two principles are subordinate to a supreme deity.

84. *Der johanneische Dualismus im Zusammenhang des nachbiblischen Judentums* (Gütersloh: Mohn, 1965).

Another significant point shared by John and Qumran is the ideal of love of one's fellow community member (one's "brother"). While some passages in the Synoptic Gospels stress the Christian's duty to love all, John's stress is on the love of one's fellow Christian (13:34; 15:12). Qumran's concept of love as a positive command is more developed than in the OT, but always the emphasis is on the love of one's fellow sectarians, even to the extent of hating others. The relation between water and the giving of the spirit, a symbolism dear to John (3:5; 7:37–38), may also be hinted at in the Qumran literature. It is interesting but perhaps coincidental that in both the Qumranian and Johannine literature the hero of the group is remembered not by a personal name but by an honorific title (respectively, the Righteous Teacher, and the Disciple whom Jesus loved).

There are also differences. John is a Christian document, and the centrality of Jesus in Johannine thought makes it quite different from the theology of Qumran, which is centered on the Law. For instance, at Qumran there is no personal light that has come into the world. Whereas for Qumran the prince of lights and the spirit of truth are titles for the same angelic being, for John the light and the Spirit of Truth are two distinct agents of salvation. We expect such differences in any comparison between a Christian and a non-Christian literature, and it is an annoying oversimplification to think that because of these obvious differences, there can be no relation between John and Qumran. Thus, Teeple stresses that there are theological concepts and terms that are found often in the Qumran literature but not in John, and vice versa.[85] This is not greatly significant unless one is trying to show that the Qumran literature was the only and direct source of John's thought. Nor is it really significant that one can take some of the most important parallels of vocabulary between John and the Qumran scrolls and find a single or an occasional occurrence of such vocabulary elsewhere in Jewish literature. The real question is whether the other occurrences give evidence of the emphasis that is shared by John and Qumran. For instance, the OT has examples of moving from darkness to light (Isa 9:1; 42:6–7; 60:1–3), and references to light as something spiritually good; Ps 27:1 says, "The Lord is my light." But the OT does not portray a world consisting of children of light and children of darkness that is a *major factor* in the theology of Qumran and

---

85. Teeple, "Qumran."

of John. Both Qumran and John have roots in the OT; but if these two literatures have capitalized on relatively insignificant OT terms and have developed them in much the same way, then we have significant parallels.

What can be said is that for *some* features of Johannine thought and vocabulary the Qumran literature offers a closer parallel than any other contemporary or earlier non-Christian literature either in Judaism or in the Hellenistic world. And, in fact, for such features Qumran offers a better parallel than even the later, post-Johannine Mandaean or Hermetic writings. Yet there is not a single quotation in John from any known DSS, and in my judgment the parallels are not close enough to suggest a direct literary dependence of John upon the Qumran literature. Rather they suggest Johannine familiarity with the type of thought exhibited in the scrolls.[86]

Summary

IN SUM, THEN, I SUGGEST that into Johannine theological thought patterns has gone the influence of a peculiar combination of various ways of thinking that were current in Palestine during Jesus' own lifetime and after his death. The Christian preachers interpreted Jesus the Christ against the background of the OT, and the preaching behind the Fourth Gospel was no exception. However, the Fourth Gospel has done this not so much by explicit citation as by showing how OT themes were implicitly woven into Jesus' actions and words. In particular, this Gospel has gone much further than the Synoptics in interpreting Jesus in terms of the OT figure of personified Wisdom. Some of the background of Jesus' thought is to be found in the presuppositions of the Pharisaic theology of his time, as these are known to us from the later rabbinic writings.[87] Moreover, in

---

86. One must allow the possibility that this thought and vocabulary were not the exclusive property of the Qumran Essenes and were shared by other Jewish groups of which we have no record; but we cannot control that possibility.

87. The rabbinical gathering at Jamnia was taking firm shape at about the same time that John was being written; Jesus is called a rabbi more frequently in John than in any other Gospel. Thomas, "Fourth Gospel," contends that the Judaism encountered in John possesses many features that J. Neusner assigns to the pre-90 period.

John the thought of Jesus is expressed in a peculiar theological vocabulary and outlook that we now know to have been used by the important Jewish Qumran group in Palestine.

Does all this mean that after Jesus' lifetime the fourth evangelist or one of his predecessors in shaping the Johannine tradition took Jesus' simple message and reinterpreted it in terms of the OT Wisdom Literature and Qumran thought, perhaps because the evangelist himself or that predecessor was particularly familiar with such thought?[88] This would move the influence to Stage Two or Stage Three of the theory of development I have proposed.[89] Or could such elements go back to Jesus' own ministry as he was heard and interpreted by disciples familiar with such thought? This would move the influence to Stage One of Johannine development.[90] In discussing that Stage, I suggested that at the root of the Johannine tradition were Judean disciples of Jesus who had been disciples of JBap. The stretch of Judea near the Jordan where JBap bore witness was not far from the Qumran settlement, so that his disciples might well have been the corridor whereby DSS influence came into Johannine thought. There is a remote chance that JBap grew up under the influence of the Qumran Essenes, or at least knew them, and vice versa.

A nuanced answer to the questions I have posed of where in the Stages of Gospel formation to localize the distinctive Jewish influences on Johannine tradition, instead of choosing one or the other of the three Stages, might posit influence at all three. On the one hand, it is time to liberate ourselves from the assumption that Jesus' own thought and expression were always simple and always in one style, and that anything that smacks of theological sophistication must come from the (implicitly more intellectual) later evangelists. On the other hand, in the develop-

---

88. Ruckstuhl, "Jesus," 281–82, indulges in too much imagination when he proposes that BD was a member of community of Essene monks, priests, and scribes who had a residence in Jerusalem

89. See Chapter Two, pp. 62–86.

90. The absence of these elements in the Synoptic Gospels may be explained in terms of their preserving a Jesus tradition interpreted and remembered by a different group of disciples. In Greek literature the Socrates of Xenophon speaks differently from the Socrates of Plato; how much comes from Socrates, how much from Plato, and how much from Xenophon?

ment of the Johannine tradition there were people (the BD, the fourth evangelist) of theological genius who put something of themselves and their own outlook into the composition of the Gospel. The Fourth Gospel claims to be dependent on the testimony of a disciple who was particularly loved by Jesus (21:20, 24; 19:35).[91] Is this not also a claim to a certain connaturality of thought between Jesus and those responsible for the development and writing of John?

BIBLIOGRAPHY

JOHN AND GNOSTICISM

Barrett, C. K., "The Theological Vocabulary of the Fourth Gospel and of the Gospel of Truth," CINTI, 210–23.

Brown, R. E., "The Gospel of Thomas and St. John's Gospel," *NTS* 9 (1962–63): 155–77.

Dodd, *Interpretation*, 97–114.

Dubois, J.-D., "Le quatrième évangile à la lumière des recherches gnostiques actuelles," *Foi et Vie* 86 (1987): 75–87.

Fischer, K. M., "Der johanneische Christus und der gnostische Erlöser. Überlegungen auf Grund von Joh 10," in K. W. Tröger, ed., *Gnosis und Neues Testament. Studien aus Religionswissenschaft und Theologie* (Gütersloh: G. Mohn, 1973).

Fuente Adánez A. de la, "Trasfondo cultural del cuarto evangelio: sobre el ocaso del dilema judaísmo/gnosticismo," *EstBib* 56 (1998): 491–506.

Hofrichter, P., "Die konstitutive Bedeutung von Jo. 1.6f. für den gnostischen Auslegungsmythos," *Augustinianum* 23 (1983): 131–44.

———, "Gnosis und Johannesevangelium," *BK* 41 (1986): 15–21.

Janssens, Y., "The Trimorphic Protennoia and the Fourth Gospel," in *The New Testament and Gnosis: Essays in Honour of Robert McL. Wilson* (eds. A. H. B. Logan and A. J. M. Wedderburn; Edinburgh: Clark, 1983), 229–44.

Jaschke, H.-J., "Das Johannesevangelium und die Gnosis im Zeugnis des Irenäus von Lyon," *Münchener Thologische Zeitschrift* 29 (1978): 337–76.

Kaestli, J.-D., "L'exégèse valentinienne du quatrième évangile," in J.-D.

---

91. See Chapter Six, below.

Kaestli, J.-M. Poffet and J. Zumstein, eds., *La communauté johannique et son histoire* (Geneva: Labor et Fides, 1990), 323–50.

————, "Remarques sur le rapport du quatrième évangile avec la gnose et sa réception au IIe siècle," in *La communauté,* 351–56.

Koester, H., "The History-of-Religions School, Gnosis, and Gospel of John," *ST* 40 (1986): 115–36.

Langbrandtner, W., *Weltferner Gott oder Gott der Liebe. Der Ketzerstreit ub der johanneische Kirche. Eine exegetisch-religionsgeschichtliche Untersuchung mit Berücksichtigung der kotisch-gnostischen Texte aus Nag Hammadi* (Beiträge zur biblischen Exegese und Theologie 6; Frankfurt: P. Lang, 1977).

Lieu, J. M., "Gnosticism and the Gospel of John," *ExpTim* 90 (1978–79): 233–37.

Pagels, E. H., *The Johannine Gospel in Gnostic Exegesis* (SBLMS 17; Nashville: Abingdon, 1973).

Perkins, P., "Logos Christologies in the Nag Hammadi Codices," *VigChr* 35 (1981): 379–96.

————, "Johannine Traditions in *Ap. Jas.*," JBL 101 (1982): 403–14.

————, "John's Gospel and Gnostic Christologies: The Nag Hammadi Evidence," *ATR* Supplement 11 (1990): 68–76.

Pervo, R. I., "Johannine Trajectories in the *Acts of John*," *Apocrypha 3* (1992): 47–68.

Poffet, J.-M., "Indices de réception de l'évangile de Jean au IIe siècle, avant Irénée," in Kaestli, Poffet and Zumstein, eds., *La communauté,* 305–21.

Quispel G., "Het Johannesevangelie en de Gnosis," *Nederlands Theologisch Tijdschrift* 11 (1956–57): 173–203.

Robinson, J. M., "Sethians and Johannine Thought: The Trimorphic Protennoia and the Prologue of the Gospel of John," in *The Rediscovery of Gnosticism* (2 vols.; Leiden: E. J. Brill, 1980–81), 2.643–70.

Ruckstuhl, E., "Das Johannesevangelium und die Gnosis," in *Neues Testament und Geschichte. Historisches Geschehen und Deutung im Neuen Testament. Oscar Cullmann zum 70. Geburtstag* (eds. H. Baltensweiler and Bo Reicke; Tübingen: J. C. B. Mohr [Paul Siebeck], 1972), 143–56. A critique of Schottroff.

Rudolf, K., "Zum Streit um Johannes gnosticus," in *Antikes Judentum und frühes Christentum. Festschrift für Hartmut Stegemann zum 65. Geburtstag* (BZNW 97; Berlin: Walter de Gruyter, 1999), 415–27.

Schottroff, L., "Heil als innerweltliche Entweltlichung. Der gnostische Hintergrund der johanneischen Vorstellung vom Zeitpunkt der Erlösung," *NovT* 11 (1969): 294–317.

————, *Der Glaubende und die feindliche Welt. Beobachtungen zum gnostischen Dualismus und seiner Bedeutung für Paulus und das Johannesevangelium* (WMANT 37; Neukirchen: Neukirchener Verlag, 1970).

Sevrin, J.-M., "Le quatrième évangile et le gnosticisme: questions de méthode," in Kaestli, Poffet and Zumstein, eds., *La communauté,* 251–68.

Sloyan, G. S., "The Gnostic Adoption of John's Gospel and Its Canonization by the Catholic Church," *BTB* 26 (1996): 125–32.

Tröger, K.-W., "Ja oder Nein zur Welt. War der Evangelist Christ oder Gnostiker?" *Theologische Versuche* 7 (1976): 61–80.

Vouga, F., "Jean et la Gnose," in Marchadour, *Origine,* 107–25

Yamauchi, E. M., "Jewish Gnosticism? The Prologue of John, Mandaean Parallels, and the Trimorphic Protennoia," in *Studies in Gnosticism and Hellenistic Religions presented to Gilles Quispel on the Occasion of his 65th Birthday* (eds. R. van den Broek and M. J. Vermaseren; Etudes préliminaires aux religions orientales dans l'Empire romain 91; Leiden: E. J. Brill, 1981), 467–97.

JOHN AND PHILO OR HELLENISTIC THOUGHT

Argyle, A. W., "Philo and the Fourth Gospel," *ExpTim* 63 (1951–52): 385–86.

Borgen, P., *Bread from Heaven. An Exegetical Study of the Conception of Manna in the Gospel of John and the Writings of Philo* (NovTSup 10; Leiden: E. J. Brill, 1965).

————, "The Gospel of John and Hellenism: Some Observations," in Culpepper and Black, eds., *Exploring,* 98–123.

Dodd, *Interpretation,* 54–73.

Feuillet, A. "Les rapports de Philon avec S. Jean," in *DBSup* (1966): 7.1348–49.

Hagner, D. A., "The Vision of God in Philo and John," *JETS* 14 (1971): 81–93.

Meeks, W. A., "The Divine Agent and His Counterfeit in Philo and the Fourth Gospel," in *Aspects of Religious Propaganda in Judaism and Early Christianity* (ed. E. Schüssler Fiorenza; Studies in Judaism and Christianity in Antiquity 2; Indiana: Notre Dame University Press, 1976), 43–67.

Wilson, R. McL., "Philo and the Fourth Gospel," *ExpTim* 65 (1953–54): 47–49.

JOHN AND THE *HERMETICA*

Braun, F.-M., "Hermétisme et Johannisme" *RThom* 55 (1955): 22–42, 259–99.

————, "Appendices II et III," in *JT* 2.253–95.

Dodd, *Interpretation,* 10–53.

Kilpatrick, G. D., "The Religious Background of the Fourth Gospel," SFG, 36–44.

Lyman, H. E., "Hermetic Religion and the Religion of the Fourth Gospel," *JBL* 49 (1930): 265–76.

JOHN, THE OLD TESTAMENT, AND TRADITIONAL JUDAISM

Barrett, C. K., "The Old Testament in the Fourth Gospel," *JTS* 48 (1947), 155–69.

Beutler, J., "Psalm 42/43 im Johannesevangelium," *NTS* 25 (1978–79), 33–57. Reprinted in his *Studien,* 77–106.

———, "The Use of 'Scripture' in the Gospel of John," in Culpepper and Black, eds., *Exploring* 147–62. Reprinted in German in his *Studien,* 295–315.

Borgen, P., "John's Use of the Old Testament and the Problem of Sources and Traditions," *Logos,* 81–91, and *Philo,* 145–57.

Braun, *JT* 2: *Les grandes traditions d'Israël et l'accord des Écritures d'après le Quatrième Évangile.*

Busse, U., "Die Tempelmetaphorik als ein Beispiel vom implizitem Rekurs auf die biblische Tradition im Johannesevangelium," in *The Scriptures in the Gospels* (ed. C. M. Tuckett; BETL 131; Leuven Univ., 1997), 395–428.

Cimosa, M., "Giovanni e l'Antico Testamento," *Parole di Vita* 29 (1984): 359–71.

———, "La traduzione greca dei Settanta nel Vangelo di Giovanni," *BibOr* 39 (1997): 41–55.

Clark, D. K., "Signs in Wisdom and John," *CBQ* 45 (1983), 201–209.

Cothenet, É., "L'arrière-plan vétéro-testamentaire du IVe évangile," in Marchadour, *Origine,* 43–69.

Dahms, J. V., "Isaiah 55:11 and the Gospel of John," *EQ* 53 (1981): 78–88.

Daly-Denton, M., *David in the Fourth Gospel. The Johannine Reception of the Psalms* (AGAJU 47; Leiden: E. J. Brill, 2000).

———, "Shades of David in the Johannine Presentation of Jesus," *PIBA* 19 (1996): 9–47.

Davies, W. D., "Reflections on Aspects of the Jewish Background of the Gospel of John," in Culpepper and Black, eds., *Exploring,* 43–64.

Dietzfelbinger, C., "Aspekte des Alten Testaments im Johannesevangelium," in *GTRH* 3.203–18.

Dodd, *Interpretation,* 74–96.

Dutheil, J., "L'évangile de Jean et le judaïsme: le Temple et la Torah," in Marchadour, *Origine,* 71–85.

Enz, J. J., "The Book of Exodus as a Literary Type for the Gospel of John," *JBL* 76 (1957): 208–15.

Evans, C. A., "On the Quotation Formulas in the Fourth Gospel," BZ 26 (1982): 79–83.

Freed, E. D., *Old Testament Quotations in the Gospel of John* (NovT 6; Leiden: E. J. Brill, 1965).

———, "Psalm 42/43 in John's Gospel," *NTS* 29 (1983): 62–73.

Gärtner, B., *John 6 and the Jewish Passover* (ConBNT 17; Lund: Gleeruf, 1959).

Glasson, T. F., *Moses in the Fourth Gospel* (SBT 40; London: SCM, 1963).

Griffiths, D. R., "Deutero-Isaiah and the Fourth Gospel," *ExpTim* 65 (1953–54): 355–60.

Guilding, A., *The Fourth Gospel and Jewish Worship* (Oxford: Clarendon, 1960).

Hammer, R. A., "Elijah and Jesus: A Quest for Identity," *Interpretation* 19 (1970): 207–18.

Hanson, A. T., *The Prophetic Gospel. A Study of John and the Old Testament* (Edinburgh: Clark, 1991).

Hengel, M., "The Old Testament in the Fourth Gospel," in *The Gospels and the Scriptures of Israel* (eds. C. A. Evans and W. R. Stenger; JSNTSup 104; Sheffield: Sheffield Academic Press, 1994), 380–95.

Hoskyns, E. C., "Genesis 1–3 and St. John's Gospel," *JTS* 21 (1920): 210–18.

Hufmann, R. J., "The Function and Form of the Explicit Old Testament Quotations in the Gospel of John," *Lutheran Theological Review* 1 (1988–89): 31–54.

Kraus, W., "Johannes und das Alte Testament. Überlegungen zum Umgang mit der Schrift im Johannesevangelium im Horizont Biblischer Theologie," *ZNW* 88 (1997): 1–23.

Lausberg, H., *Minuscula philologica V: Jesaja 55,11 im Evangelium nach Johannes* (Göttingen: Vandenhoeck & Ruprecht, 1979).

Manns, F., "Exégèse rabbinique et exégèse johannique," *RB* 92 (1985): 525–38.

———, *L'Evangile de Jean à la Lumière du Judaïsme* (SBFLA 33; Jerusalem: Franciscan Printing Press, 1991).

Menken, M. J. J., *Old Testament Quotations in the Fourth Gospel: Studies on Textual Form* (CBET 15; Kampen: Kok Pharos, 1996).

Obermann, A., *Die christologische Erfüllung der Schrift im Johannesevangelium: Eine Untersuching zur johanneischen Hermeneutik anhand der Schriftzitate* (WUNT 2.83; Tübingen: J. C. B. Mohr [Paul Siebeck], 1996).

O'Rourke, J., "John's Fulfillment Texts," *ScEccl* 19 (1967): 433–43.

Reim, G. *Studien zum alttestamentlichen Hintergrund des Johannesevangeli-*

ums (SNTSMS 22; Cambridge Univ., 1974). Reprinted and enlarged in *Jochanan. Erweiterte Studien zum alttestamentlichen Hintergrung des Johannesevangeliums* (Erlangen: Verlag der Ev.-Luth. Mission, 1995).

Rottfuchs, W., *Die Erfüllungszitate des Matthäus-Evangeliums* (BWANT 88; Stuttgart: Kohlhammer, 1969), esp. 151–77 on John.

Schuchard, B. G., *Scripture within Scripture: The Interrelationship of Form and Function in the Explicit Old Testament Citations in the Gospel of John* (SBLDS 133; Atlanta: Scholars, 1992).

Smith, R. H., "Exodus Typology in the Fourth Gospel," *JBL* 81 (1962): 329–42.

Thomas, J. C., "The Fourth Gospel and Rabbinic Judaism," *ZNW* 82 (1991): 159–82.

Vawter, B., "Ezekiel and John," *CBQ* 26 (1964): 450–58.

Westermann, C., *The Gospel of John in the Light of the Old Testament* (Peabody, MA: Hendrickson, 1998).

Yee, G. A., *Jewish Feasts and the Gospel of John* (Wilmington: Glazier, 1989).

Young, F. W., "A Study of the Relation of Isaiah to the Fourth Gospel," *ZNW* 46 (1955): 215–33.

JOHN AND QUMRAN

Ashton, *Understanding*, 232–37.

Bauckham, R., "Qumran and the Fourth Gospel: Is There a Connection?" in *The Scrolls and the Scriptures* (eds. S. E. Porter and C. A. Evans; JSNTSup 26; Sheffield: Sheffield Academic Press, 1997), 267–79.

Baumbach, G., *Qumran und das Johannes-Evangelium* (Berlin: Evangelische Verlagsanstalt, 1958).

Böcher, O., *Der johanneische Dualismus im Zusammenhang des nachbiblischen Judentums* (Gütersloh: Mohn, 1965).

Braun, F.-M., "L'arrière-fond judaïque du quatrième évangile et la Communauté de l'Alliance," *RB* 62 (1955): 5–44.

Braun, H., *Qumran und das Neue Testament* (2 vols.; Tübingen: J. C. B. Mohr [Paul Siebeck], 1966), esp. 2.118–44. Previously *TRu* 28 (1962), esp. 192–234.

Brown, R. E., "The Qumran Scrolls and the Johannine Gospel and Epistles," *CBQ* 17 (1955): 403–19, 559–74. Reprinted in *The Scrolls and the New Testament* (ed. K. Stendahl; New York: Harper, 1957), 183–207. Also in *NTE*, Ch. VII.

Charlesworth, J. H., "A Critical Comparison of the Dualism in 1QS III.13–IV.26 and the 'Dualism' Contained in the Fourth Gospel," *NTS* 15 (1968–1969): 389–418.

————, ed., *John and Qumran* (London: Chapman, 1972); reprinted as *John and the Dead Sea Scrolls* (New York: Crossroad, 1990).

————, "The Dead Sea Scrolls and the Gospel according to John," in Culpepper and Black, eds., *Exploring*, 65–97.

————, "Reinterpreting John," *BibRev* 9 (1993): 18–25, 54.

Cullmann, O., "Das Rätsel des Johannesevangeliums im Lichte der Neuen Handschriftenfunde," in his collected *Vorträge und Aufsätze 1925–1962* (ed. K. Froelich; Tübingen: J. C. B. Mohr [Paul Siebeck], 1966), 260–91. Largely reused in his *Johannine Circle*.

Kuhn, K. G., "Johannesevangelium und Qumrantexte," *NTP*, 111–21.

Leaney, A. R. C., "John and Qumran," *StEv*, 6.296–310.

Morris, L., "The Dead Sea Scrolls and St. John's Gospel," in *Studies*, 321–57.

Painter, J., *Quest*, 35–52.

Pilgaard, A., "The Qumran Scrolls and John's Gospel," in Nissen and Pedersen, eds., *New Readings in John*, 126–42.

Teeple, H. M., "Qumran and the Origin of the Fourth Gospel," *NovT* 4 (1960): 6–25.

5

Echoes of Apologetics and the Purpose of the Gospel

COMMENTATORS ON JOHN have suggested different motives that could have prompted the writing of the Gospel, and indeed the Gospel may have had several aims.[1] If John is based on historical tradition and genuine insight, a basic reason for writing the Gospel may have been to preserve that tradition and insight. But even then the question arises of immediate aim that may have guided the choice of the material and the orientation the author gave to it.

More than any other Gospel, John betrays antagonism toward views held by other groups, e.g., toward admirers of JBap, "the Jews," and various followers of Jesus. Whitacre shows how pervasive this is.[2] Accordingly, some would propose that in whole or in part the Gospel was written with an apologetic, polemic, or missionary motif in regard to one

---

1. Schnackenburg has wisely complained that a besetting fault has been the attempt to interpret everything in the Gospel in terms of one goal, thereby failing to recognize that the various editions of the Gospel may represent the adaptation of the central message to a new need.

2. Whitacre, *Johannine Polemic.*

or all of those groups.[3] Personally I reject the thesis that the Gospel was primarily intended to refute or change the minds of the adherents of such groups. The evangelist did not envision his message being read by adherents of JBap or by synagogue authorities hostile to Jesus or even by would-be Christians who had seriously wrong estimations of Jesus. Below I shall maintain that 20:31 is truthful and accurate: "These things have been recorded so that you may have faith that Jesus is the Messiah, the Son of God, and that through this faith you may have life in his name." The Gospel was written to intensify people's faith and make it more profound. The evangelist is not opposed to bringing others to believe in Jesus, but his chief concern is strengthening those who already believe.[4] Why do they need strengthening? Because they have been challenged and attacked by those who do not accept Jesus and they have undergone traumatic expulsions from the synagogue(s). That is where the apologetics and polemics visible in the Gospel enter the picture. They reflect controversies in the community's history and serve to reinforce those who believe in Jesus that they have been and are correct despite the argumentation directed against them. The apologetics also offers believ-

---

3. Apologetic, polemic, and missionary goals are not mutually exclusive. The most virulent tract of one group of Christians against others usually wants to show how their position is wrong (apologetic), how they horrendously distort Jesus' message (polemic), and how they can be brought to the truth represented by the writer of the tract (missionary). It is another question as to whether polemics are truly effective in converting those attacked.

4. *Editor's Note:* Brown here takes a position, with which I concur, that the Gospel is written for believers, to lead them into deeper faith. Not all would agree, and it depends (to a certain extent—see below on Schnackenburg) upon a decision concerning the text of 20:31. There is a fine balance between the readings. The present subjunctive (*hina pisteuête*) and the aorist subjunctive (*hina pisteusête*) are both strongly present in the textual traditions. In support of the present subjunctive, which communicates the idea of an ever-deepening of faith, see Brown, *John,* 1056; Schnackenburg, *St John,* 3:337–338; G. D. Fee, "On the Text and Meaning of John 20:30–31," in FGFN, 3.2193–206. Schnackeburg suggests that even if the original was in the aorist tense it would not be ingressive (i.e., "come to believe"), as is claimed by those who would see the Fourth Gospel as something of a missionary tract (e.g., W. C. van Unnik, "The Purpose of St John's Gospel," StEv 1.382–411; J. A. T. Robinson, "The Purpose of St John's Gospel," NTS 6 [1959–60]: 117–31; D. A. Carson, "The Purpose of the Fourth Gospel: John 20:31 Reconsidered," JBL 106 [1987]: 639–51). The aorist would be a summons to "a new impulse in their faith" (Schnackenburg, *St John,* 338).

ers ammunition should they continue to encounter adversaries. Thus in my judgment the subdivisions on apologetics below pertain to the context out of which the Gospel developed rather than to its purpose.

Apologetic against Adherents of John the Baptist

AT THE END OF THE NINETEENTH CENTURY, W. Baldensperger, insisting that the Prologue was the key to the understanding of John, pointed out that it unfavorably contrasted JBap and Jesus. He suggested that one of the chief purposes of the Gospel was to refute the claims of the sectarians of JBap who were exalting their master at the expense of Jesus. That Baldensperger had recognized one of the Gospel's features was accepted by most of the succeeding commentaries. Bultmann even posited that the evangelist had been one of the Gnostic sectarians of JBap and that the Prologue was once a hymn in praise of JBap.[5] D. M. Smith thinks that the Johannine miracle source may have contrasted Jesus with JBap who never performed a sign (10:41).[6] More recently, however, Schnackenburg, in "Johannesjünger," and others have reacted against exaggerations in the emphasis given to the anti-Baptist apologetic motif. The following information is important in making a judgment.

The evidence about the sectarians of JBap is very limited.[7] Acts 18:24–19:7 speaks of Apollos and a group of about twelve disciples at Ephesus (the traditional site for the composition of the Fourth Gospel)—believers in Jesus who had been baptized only with JBap's baptism and did not know of the Holy Spirit. Plausibly these were followers of JBap who had maintained their identity and circulated in the Greek world. But more simply they may have been primitive disciples of Jesus who had been bap-

---

5. Although Trocmé, "Jean-Baptiste," 134, does not necessarily agree with Bultmann, he would apply 1:9–13 to JBap who prepares people to become God's children. His article surveys Johannine passages applicable to JBap.

6. Smith, "Milieu," 74–77.

7. In roughly contemporaneous studies, Backhaus, "*Jüngerkreise*," denies that there is solid evidence for a JBap school or circle, while Stowasser, *Johannes*, argues that there is. Yet even Backhaus admits that John (especially the final stage of the Gospel) portrays a conflict with a group that venerates JBap, though in fact that group had no real connection to the historical JBap.

tized (in JBap's style) with water during Jesus' ministry (John 3:23) before
the Spirit was given (7:39), for these disciples show no opposition toward
accepting full Christian initiation from Paul. Trocmé thinks that disciples
of JBap would have had a continuance in Transjordan where he had baptized (10:40), where their baptizing ministry received a theological boost
with the destruction of the visible Temple in A.D. 70.[8]

Our most important second-century source of information is the
Pseudo-Clementine writings,[9] a late third-century work drawn from earlier (probably second-century) sources.[10] The author claimed that the
sectarians of JBap maintained that their master, and not Jesus, was
the Messiah. Thus, the JBap sectarians seem to have survived well into the
Christian era and become opponents of Christianity. We cannot be sure,
however, that the first-century sectarians were already making such
claims about JBap. Indeed, the Syriac and Latin forms of *Recognitions*
1.54.8 differ significantly about calling JBap the Messiah—a difference
that may indicate a developing theology among the sectarians on this
point. At any rate, we do not have many guidelines for interpreting the
thought of the sectarians at the time when John was written.

There is no certain evidence that the early sectarians of JBap were
Gnostic, and the Pseudo-Clementines give no evidence of that. It is true
that gnosticism appears among the Mandaeans, who may well have descended from one group of the JBap sectarians,[11] but there is every suspicion that the gnosticism was a later element added through Mandaean
syncretism rather than part of the heritage from the original JBap sectarians. A better indication of a possible Gnostic element in the theology of
the sectarians of JBap is the patristic tradition that traces the origins of
Gnosticism to Samaria, where JBap was probably active.[12] The founding
fathers of Gnosticism, Simon Magus and Dositheus of Shechem, were

---

8. Trocmé, "Jean-Baptist," 149.

9. Working with an interpretation of *Sibylline Oracles* 4 and Josephus's reference
to JBap, Lichtenberger, "Täufergemeinden," maintains that a circle of JBap followers
existed in Rome at the end of the first-century A.D.

10. *Recognitions* 1.54.8; 1.60.1–11; *Homilies* 2.22. See also Ephraem's *Commentary
on the Diatessaron* 9.3, 6; 16.18.

11. In general, the Mandaean literature shows respect for JBap and mentions that
he baptized the heavenly revealer, Manda d'Hayye.

12. See the note on 3:23 in *John*, 151.

identified in patristic writings as followers of JBap. We shall discuss below the possible anti-Gnostic features in John, but whether these should also be considered as directed against the followers of JBap remains very dubious.

It is reasonable to suspect that *some* (but not necessarily all) of the negations about JBap in the Fourth Gospel were intended as refutations of claims that followers of JBap made about their master.[13] A guide may be supplied here by the direction taken by the later sectarians of JBap in the Pseudo-Clementines. Thus, apologetic motifs may be found in John 1:8–9 which states that Jesus, not JBap, was the light; in 1:30 which states that Jesus existed before JBap and is greater; in 1:20 and 3:28 which stress that JBap is not the Messiah; in 10:41 which says that JBap never worked any miracles.[14] The denial in 4:2 that Jesus himself baptized (addition of the final redactor?) refutes any claim that Jesus was a baptizer on the same level as JBap (a claim that might find support in 3:22, 26), and that idea may also lie behind 1 John 5:6 which states that Jesus did not come in water only. Perhaps the most telling line in any discussion of the relative merits of JBap and of Jesus is found in John 3:30 where JBap himself speaks of his own decreasing importance, now that Jesus, the bridegroom, has come upon the scene.

There may be other possible echoes of this apologetic, but sometimes the case is overstated. The argument from silence is very uncertain, e.g., the contention that it was as part of the apologetic against the sectarians

---

13. *Editor's Note:* I suspect that with this almost throwaway remark Brown has put his finger on the heart of the issue. The Johannine Christians did not set up a conflict between Jesus and the inferior JBap. The text will not bear that historical reconstruction. However, what is in the text probably reflects the wider problem of the difficulties some Christian communities appeared to have with the followers of John the Baptist. One of the major points of difficulty would have been the question of baptism. For an excellent study of this issue, see C. Niemand, *Die Fuschwaschungerzählung des Johannesevangeliums: Untersuchung zu ihrer Entstehung und Überlieferung in Urchristentum* (Studia Anselmiana 114; Roma: Pontificio Ateneo S. Anselmo, 1993), 320–402.

14. As for more subtle apologetics, some would see the Cana replacement of the water destined for Jewish purification (2:5) by wine as (partially) directed against the baptizing disciples of JBap. Also the "water and Spirit" of 3:5 as a replacement of JBap's "baptizing with water" (1:26); and Jesus' declaration in Samaria (a region associated with JBap) that he is the Messiah (4:25–26), a title refused by JBap (1:20).

of JBap that John does not use the title "Baptist" and gives no emphasis to JBap's ministry of preaching and baptizing such as we find described in Matt 3:1–12. John's intended readers/hearers would have known that JBap was a baptizer, and would not have noticed this silence or thought it significant—any more than a modern Christian audience notices it till some scholar points out the silence. John presents JBap primarily as a witness to Jesus, but that may be from a christological emphasis, rather than from any apologetic interest. Also, although a case can be made for at least an indirect relationship between JBap and Qumran, it is quite improbable that John has sprinkled Jesus' speech with Qumran echoes in order to win over the sectarians of JBap.[15]

Apologetic against JBap sectarians has left traces on only a few passages, and it is impossible to interpret the whole Gospel against the background of sectarian theology. After all, the Fourth Gospel gives a place of honor to JBap himself. It is true that John does not record the saying found in Matt 11:11 and Luke 7:28 in which Jesus identifies JBap as the greatest among those born of women. Nevertheless, for John the role of JBap was very important: like Jesus he was sent by God (1:6); his exalted task was to reveal Jesus to Israel (1:31; 3:29); he possessed a very full revelation, lacking in the Synoptics, about the identity of Jesus as the Lamb of God, the preexistent, God's chosen one, and the bridegroom of Israel (1:29–34; 3:39). JBap was one of the major witnesses to Jesus, to be ranked alongside the Scriptures and miracles (5:31–40). Thus, the view of JBap in the Fourth Gospel is no less complimentary than that of the Synoptics.[16] The cautions uttered against exaggerating the role of JBap and placing him on the level of Jesus may have arisen in Johannine history out of conflict with the sectarians of JBap, but in the final Gospel they are not addressed to such sectarians. They have a christological function of deepening the faith of John's Christian readers by showing how Jesus is

---

15. JBap lived at the same time and in the same region of Judea as the Qumran sectarians, and his thought and vocabulary have many Qumran affinities.

16. *Editor's Note:* A further crucial element in evaluating the evangelist's understanding of JBap is his description of him as "sent from God" (*aspestalmenos para theou*) in 1:6. Apart from this description of JBap, Jesus is the only "sent one" in the entire Gospel. For further cautions on the understanding of the Gospel as an anti-Baptist apologetic, see F. J. Moloney, "The Fourth Gospel and the Jesus of History," *NTS* 46 (2000): 49.

the unique light of the world even in the presence of JBap "the lamp, set aflame and burning bright" (5:35).

Apologetic against Jews

UNDER THIS HEADING I shall discuss hostility manifested by John toward Jews who refused to believe in Jesus and Jews who did believe in Jesus but refused to do so publicly.

Apologetic against "the Jews" Who Refused to Believe in Jesus

Since Jesus lived in Palestine, addressed himself primarily to the people of Israel, and tried to bring them to believe that the kingdom of God was present in his own ministry, we naturally expect to find this element preserved in the Gospels either in the form of missionary appeal to Israel or in terms of an apologetic to answer the Jewish rejection of Jesus. For instance, in a Gospel that contains historical tradition we would expect to find some memory of Jesus' struggle with the Pharisees.[17] The issue here, however, is the generalization and translation of that into a terminology whereby his adversaries are "the Jews," to an extent that at times one gets the impression that he and his followers are not Jews. There is only one instance of that in the Synoptic tradition, namely the reference to "Jews" in Matt 28:15; whereas in John the generalization of the adversaries as "the Jews" is extremely frequent.[18] Moreover, it is marked by intense hos-

---

17. Matthew expands the picture of hostility to the Pharisees by drawing on Christian relationships that existed after Jesus' historical ministry. Also Matt 27:25 generalizes when he has *all* the people ask for Jesus to be crucified by saying, "His blood on us and on our children" (see BDM, 831–38).

18. In the three Synoptic Gospels *Ioudaios* occurs a total of 16 times, of which 12 involve the title "King of the Jews." Three others (Mark 7:3; Luke 7:3; 23:51) are neutral descriptions, presumably to clarify the description for Gentile readers. *Ioudaios* occurs 71 times in John and 79 times in Acts. (The latter statistic suggests that its Christian usage belongs to the postresurrectional period.) Von Wahlde, "Johannine," 41, estimates about 38 to 40 of the Johannine uses are hostile. In general, the level of hostility increases as one moves progressively through the Gospel episodes (see Culpepper, "Gospel," 276–80). Not many will be convinced by the attempt of O'Neill, "The Jews," to attribute the majority of references to later copyists—thus not part of the original text of John.

tility: "the Jews" (occasionally mixed in with Pharisees) do not really believe in Moses (5:46–47); they judge by human standards, not honestly (7:24; 8:15); they do not keep the Law and seek to kill Jesus (7:19); they will surely die in their sins (8:24); they act sinfully and are the slaves of sin (8:34); they are the devil's children, not Abraham's (8:41, 44); they do not belong to God (8:47); they are liars (8:55); they are the spiritually blind who claim to see and so their guilt remains (9:41).

The analysis of the designation "the Jews" (see below) will show a variety of connotations. Sometimes it is ethnic (Jews distinct from other peoples); sometimes it may be geographical (Judean Jews as distinct from Jews elsewhere); sometimes it may be neutrally informative (Jewish); but many times it seems to be a generalized reference to those who are hostile to Jesus and his followers and whom he attacks bitterly. Therefore, an analysis of "the Jews" raises the issue of whether Jesus or John was anti-Jewish.[19] Let me make this analysis on two levels, distinguishing between usage in the 20s (Jesus' lifetime) and usage after A.D. 70 (when the Gospel was written).[20]

---

19. Some commentators persist in discussing under the title of anti-Semitism, but that is anachronistic, and causes confusion. As Jewish writers like Hannah Arendt and Shaye Cohen have clearly pointed out, "anti-Semitism" reflects racial theories about the Jews that have flourished in the last two centuries. Even "anti-Judaism" has to be confined, for the issue in John has none of the tones of pagan Gentile dislike for Jews attested in the period 200 B.C. to A.D. 100, e.g., purification rules (no pork), odd Sabbath behavior, mutilating their bodies in circumcision, impiously not appreciating the honor paid to the gods. On this, see P. Schäfer, *Judeophilia: Attitudes Toward the Jews in the Ancient World* (Cambridge MA; Harvard University Press, 1997). *Editor's Note:* See now the comprehensive discussion of this question by R. Bieringer, D. Pollefeyt and F. Vandecasteele-Vanneuville, "Wrestling with Johannine Anti-Judaism: A Hermeneutical Framewortk for the Analysis of the Current Debate," in *Anti-Judaism and the Fourth Gospel. Papers of the Leuven Colloquium, 2000* (eds. R. Bieringer, D. Pollefeyt and F. Vandecasteele-Vanneuville; Assen: van Gorcum, 2001), 3–44. See also the essays in that volume by J. D. G. Dunne (pp. 47–67), R. A. Culpepper (pp. 68–91), S. Motyer (pp. 92–109) and J. Lieu (pp. 126–43). These essays are collected under the heading, "Anti-Judaism in the Fourth Gospel. General Approaches," and the subheading, "Exegetical Approaches."

20. I am skipping the intermediate period of the development of the community's life when orally (and perhaps) in nonpreserved writing the Johannine tradition was significantly shaped. In his excellent study, Grelot, *Les Juifs*, traces the development

THE LEVEL OF JESUS' LIFETIME

Was Jesus anti-Jewish? This may seem like a silly question, since Jesus himself was a Jew; but sometimes a change of religious or spiritual outlook can make one turn against one's maternal religion.[21] I deem the Synoptic Gospel evidence undeniable that Jesus had religious disputes with other Jews, e.g., over issues of Law observance with Pharisees, and of Temple practices with priestly authorities. The history of Judaism in the last centuries before the Roman destruction of the Temple in A.D. 70 shows almost constant conflict among groups, Pharisees, Sadducees, and Essenes, even to the point of killing one another;[22] but since all were Jews, one would not speak of an "anti-Jewish" attitude. Nor to my knowledge did one of these groups call their opponents "the Jews." Thus Jesus as depicted in the Synoptic Gospels was certainly not anti-Jewish, even if sometimes he may have been anti-Pharisee or anti-Sadducee.

Some of the Johannine uses of "Jews" are not implausible on this level, e.g., the ethnic and geographical uses to be described below. Jesus could have told a Samaritan that salvation is from the Jews; in response to Jesus, Pilate could have asked, "Am I a Jew?"; not inappropriate would be the comment that Jesus traveled in Galilee and not in Judea because the Jews (= Judeans?) were looking for a chance to kill him (7:1). But clearly implausible is John's usage of "the Jews" in so many hostile instances, whether by the Johannine writer in descriptions, or more rarely by Jesus himself. Can one conceive Jesus the Jew saying to his Jewish disciples, "As I told the Jews, so now I tell you too" (13:33)? Addressing the Pharisees, he surely would not have said in reference to the Jewish Scriptures, "In *your* own Law it is stated" (8:17); or have asked, "Is it not written in *your*

---

of terminology through this period as well. I shall refer to events that happened during that period, but I am primarily interested in anti-Judaism as related to the purpose of the final document.

21. I am not interested here in historical fact (Did Jesus say these things?) but in historical possibility/plausibility (Could/would Jesus have spoken this way?). Moreover the issue must be kept precise, not "Is it plausible that Jesus had Jewish enemies?" but "Is it plausible that he would have spoken of them as 'the Jews'?"

22. See L. T. Johnson, "The New Testament's Anti-Jewish Slander and the Conventions of Ancient Polemic," *JBL* 108 (1989): 419–41.

[= 'the Jews'] own Law?" (10:34).[23] Because of this historical judgment, some would eliminate "Jews" from the translation of John. Although their goal is good (preventing modern readers from developing a hostile attitude toward Jews), I disagree strongly with this solution. One is not translating a Greek Gospel written in Jesus' lifetime, but a Gospel written some six decades later. Therefore for those interested in the literal sense of the Gospel, the starting issue must be what the Johannine writer meant and what he wrote, not what Jesus meant during his lifetime.

THE LEVEL OF THE WRITTEN GOSPEL

The mind of the writer(s) toward Judaism must be diagnosed from what is described.[24] Certainly there is no hostility toward much of the religious heritage from Judaism. "No work of the NT is more profoundly Jewish than the Gospel of John."[25] The Jewish Scriptures testify on behalf of Jesus (5:39). Abraham rejoiced at the prospect of seeing Jesus' day (8:56). The Prologue (1:17) describes the Law as a gift through Moses, who wrote about Jesus (5:46). Jesus is the Messiah, the expected king of the House of David.[26] JBap came that Jesus might be revealed to *Israel* (1:31); Jesus is hailed as the King of Israel (1:49; cf. 18:33–37); and Pilate testifies to his being the King of the Jews (19:19–22). John identifies Jesus with a number of figures featured in OT and Jewish apocalyptic expectations: the Servant of God;[27] the apocalyptic lamb (1:29); the Holy One of God (6:69). A

---

23. See "their Law" in 15:25 which has to refer to "the Jews." That such language belongs to a later period after Jesus' lifetime one may see from the comparable Matt 23:34 where Jesus predicts to the Pharisees a *future* scourging in "your synagogues" of those whom he sends. One does not solve this issue by contending that Jesus is objecting not to the Law but to his opponents' interpretation of the Law. To be precise, he is depicted as objecting to their overlooking what is in the Law. Moreover, he could scarcely be referring to an interpretation when he says "written in your own Law."

24. In this discussion, I am not concerned with distinguishing between the evangelist and the redactor in the use of *Ioudaios*, although in fact there may have been a difference. I am concerned with the final Gospel and use "John" to describe the compound writer(s) of it.

25. Grelot, *Les Juifs*, 187.

26. John uses the Greek form of this title (*christos*) more frequently than does any other Gospel and is the only Gospel to employ the transliterated form *messias* (1:41; 4:25).

27. See *John*, 58–65.

glance at the Outline of the First Book of the Gospel (see Chapter Nine) shows the importance given to the theme of Jesus' replacement or reinterpretation of Jewish institutions like ritual purification, the Temple, and worship in Jerusalem (chs. 2–4) and of Jewish feasts like the Sabbath, Passover, Tabernacles, and Dedication (chs. 5–10)—a replacement that does not deny the meaningfulness of the institutions and feasts but finds this meaning fulfilled and reinterpreted in Jesus.[28] The Johannine Jesus bestows a high encomium on Nathanael by calling him a genuine Israelite. To explain the alienation from Judaism that we shall see below, Hickling and others would appeal to stages in the development of Johannine community history: an earlier period emphasizing that Jesus fits into the expectations of Israel, and a later period where claims are made for Jesus that are hard to reconcile with a Jewish outlook.[29] Be that as it may, the final Gospel gives a picture both of continuity and discontinuity.[30]

The anti-Jewish issue rests chiefly on how John refers to "the Jews."[31] Let me now discuss that in detail under several headings, for "the Jews" does not always have the same meaning.

Ethnic usage. Those of Jewish birth as distinct from other ethnic groups. In areas of mixed population, "Jews" was a standard way of alluding to Jewish people, and this is a normal usage in the Pauline writings and Acts. In John *Ioudaios* refers to Jews as different from Samaritans (4:9, 22) or from Romans (18:35); it characterizes Jewish burial customs for an audience that might not be familiar with them. Related to the latter is its narrative use in the context of the Roman trial of Jesus to keep the dialogue partner distinct from Pilate, i.e., the locals who were outside the

---

28. *Editor's Note:* See below, Chapter Nine. This more muted description of what Brown had earlier simply described as "replacement" corresponds better to my concerns, expressed above, in Chapter Two, p. 67, n. 63.

29. Hickling, "Attitudes."

30. See Vouga, "Antijudaismus."

31. Unless it is significant, I shall not attempt consistently in this discussion to distinguish the rare Johannine singular (4 times: *Ioudaios*) from the plural (67 times: *Ioudaioi*). *Editor's Note:* For well-documented recent discussion of the use of "the Jews" in the Fourth Gospel, from a number of perspectives, see the essays of J. Beutler (pp. 229–38), H. J. de Jonge (pp. 239–59, M. C. de Boer (pp. 260–80), R. F. Collins (pp. 281–300), P. J. Tomson (pp. 301–40), A. Reinhartz (pp. 341–56), and C. K. Barrett (pp. 401–17), in Bieringer et al. (eds.), *Anti-Judaism and the Fourth Gospel*.

praetorium (18:31, 36, 38; 19:7, 20, 31). Similarly, 18:12 distinguishes the attendants or police of the Jews from the (implicitly Roman) cohort and tribune. The title "the King of the Jews," as the charge against Jesus, may have this neutral meaning, making precise Jesus' claimed realm. Some would interpret "feast of the Jews" (5:1; 6:4; 7:2; cf. 2:13; 11:55) in the same way, but more likely the distinction there has a religious connotation: their feast not (any longer) ours.

Geographical usage. Judeans. Politically, at the time of Jesus' public ministry the Roman province of Judea, of which Pilate was prefect and which included Idumea and Samaria, was distinct from the tetrarchy of Herod Antipas, which included Galilee and Perea (in the Transjordan). Politically at the end of the century when John was written, Judea would have included all Palestine. Yet, since John 4:3 distinguishes between Judea and Samaria, and since nowhere does John mention Herod or emphasize the extent of Pilate's jurisdiction when writing of Judea (4:47, 54; 7:1, 3; 11:7), the author was probably thinking primarily of geographical territory, rather than of political division. The Johannine Jesus goes several times from Galilee to Judea, so it is not implausible that at times John might wish to distinguish between Judeans and Galileans, and *Ioudaios* can refer to an inhabitant of Judea (cf. "the Judean region" of Mark 1:5). Lowe would argue for a massive geographical use of *Ioudaioi* in John, e.g., "feasts of the Judeans" keeps these feasts distinct from those of other religious groups, like the Samaritans; "King of the Jews" means "King of Judea"; Judeans go to mourn Lazarus in ch. 11; the people of Jerusalem are designated Judeans in ch. 7; similarly the authorities opposed to Jesus in Jerusalem are called "Judeans," etc.[32] Grelot takes pains to show that such an interpretation is implausible.[33] I would agree emphatically, for there are serious objections to any dominant geographical thesis. When Jesus asks "the Jews" in 10:34, "Is it not written in your own Law?" John is referring not to Judeans specifically but to the Scriptures shared by all Jews. Why in the totally Jewish religious context of the Gospel narrative

---

32. Lowe, "Who?" Also Cuming, "Jews"; Pietrantonio, "Los 'Ioudaioi' "; Meeks "Am I"; and those who, without the kind of research exhibited by Lowe, suggest translating *Ioudaioi* as Judeans since it is not religiously offensive.

33. Also rejected by Thyen, Wengst, Smiga, and ultimately by Ashton, even though Ashton follows Meeks in thinking of Jesus as a Judean.

would John need to keep distinguishing feasts of Judea or the Judeans as distinct from feasts of the Samaritans or other religions?[34] Why, since we are told they came from Jerusalem, would those who sent priests and Levites to question John have to be identified as Judeans (1:19)? Why would water at Cana in Galilee be identified as "for the purification of the Judeans"? Why is Jesus speaking to Judeans in a Galilean (Capernaum) synagogue and how do they know his family who live at Nazareth (6:41, 42, 52, 59)? Why would the parents of the blind man who apparently live in Judea be afraid of the Judeans? And, above all, why for readers who plausibly lived outside Palestine would the final Johannine writer want to portray an immense hostility to Judeans of whom they would have little experience? Overall I would judge that 7:1; 11:8, 54 are possible examples of the meaning Judeans, but there is no indisputable instance.

Role usage. Jewish (largely Jerusalem) *authorities,* including Temple chief priests (10 times in John), Pharisees (19 times), and Sanhedrin members.[35] Linguistically "Jewish authorities" is not a normal or automatically recognizable meaning of *Ioudaios,* so that the supporting argumentation has rather to draw on comparative Synoptic evidence and plausible history. The first three Gospels attribute to a Sanhedrin with priests, scribes, and elders (wealthy aristocrats?) an important role in deciding against Jesus, handing him over to the Romans, and persuading Pilate to sentence him to crucifixion.[36] John 18–19 attributes these roles to "the Jews." By way of internal proof, John 18:3 speaks of attendants/police from the chief priests and the Pharisees and 18:12 speaks of the same people as "attendants of the Jews." In 1:19 we hear of the Jews sending emissaries to JBap, and one interpretation of 1:24 has John speaking of the emissaries as having been sent by the Pharisees. In 8:13 alongside 8:22 and in

---

34. I am not denying that in certain historical writing such a distinction occurs, but is that the significance in John taken as a narrative about Jesus and his rejection by his own (1:11)? A suggestion that he has taken over a customary description and repeated it a half dozen times without thinking of how it would be read in relation to what Jesus has accomplished does no justice to the kind of sensibility shown in 2:19–22.

35. As in the previous note, this translation removes religious offense—the motive of many of its advocates.

36. In BDM 1.372–97, I argued for the historical plausibility of much of this picture.

9:15–16 alongside 9:18, the Pharisees seem to be interchangeable with the Jews; similarly the chief priests (and Temple) police are interchangeable with the Jews in 19:6 and 7. In 2:18, 20, it is plausible that "the Jews" who challenged Jesus about his behavior in the Temple would be Temple authorities, and that "the Jews" who challenged him about his Sabbath behavior in 5:10, 16 would have been Pharisees. Since the authorities at Jerusalem would have had the greatest ability to bring about Jesus' death, they may plausibly be meant in the passages where "the Jews" seek to kill Jesus (5:18; 7:1; see also 20:19).

Despite these observations, however, one must ask why John would use the designation "the Jews," which in itself has no implication of "authorities," if he was thinking only of the authorities.[37] In part, one could argue that the generalizing term was substituted because by the time John was written precision about different types of authorities had lost relevance. The Synoptic scene has a richer palette of Herodians, elders, tax collectors, scribes, poor, and rich property holders, all of whom are missing from John. Only the chief priests and the Pharisees remain in John—the chief priests because their role in the Sanhedrin and the Jerusalem opposition to Jesus was too essential a part of the story to be forgotten, and the Pharisees because they are precisely that Jewish sect whose mind-set survived the calamity of 70 and influenced Rabbinic Judaism.[38] But if the more varied Jewish situation of Jesus' time no longer was significant when John was

---

37. I did not wrestle with this issue sufficiently in my first edition, and the flood of writing on the subject since that time has caused me to be more careful. Moreover, although how and when the designation "the Jews" appears may reflect editorial and redactional differences, one must consider the impact of the usage in the Gospel as it now stands. Ashton, "Identity," 41, comments that the first appearance of *Ioudaioi* in the Gospel (1:19) is a relatively late editorial insertion and from the interpreter's point of view not very important. But from a narrative point of view it is very important: from the start "the Jews" are antagonistic and JBap does not seem to be a Jew.

38. Also absent from John are Jesus' attacks on the Pharisees for hypocrisy or for their moral and social behavior and disputes about how to interpret the Law. Although in 9:28 the disciples of Jesus are contrasted to the disciples of Moses, John does not treat the Law as either a problem for Christians or as an enemy; it belongs to "the Jews" (8:17; 10:34; 15:25), for it has been superseded by the great act of divine covenant love in Jesus Christ (1:17). Thus the whole critique of "the Jews" and occasionally the Pharisees centers on their refusal to believe in Jesus as the unique Son of

written, one can still ask why John chose such an ambiguous term as "Jews" that in itself does not distinguish Jesus the Jew from his opponents, instead of consistently employing "the authorities" (*archontes*) which this Gospel uses four times elsewhere (3:1; 7:26, 48; 12:42; also Luke 23:13; 24:20). Moreover, this interpretation of "the Jews" as authorities does not do justice to the many passages where opponents of Jesus are called *Ioudaioi* and there is no suggestion that authorities are meant and nothing that would make hearers/readers think of authorities. Indeed in 7:35 "the Jews" seem to be distinct from the chief priests and Pharisees of 7:32 who apparently are in another place. A general group of Jewish people or crowds seems to be meant in 6:41, 52; 7:15; 8:22, 31, 48, 52, 57; 10:19, 24, 33; 11:8, 54; 13:33; 18:20,[39] and the attempted stoning by "the Jews" seems to be mob action (8:59; 10:31). To translate some instances of *Ioudaioi* as

---

God. The Judaism of the time in which the Gospel was written was the end of Pharisaic Judaism and the beginning of Rabbinic Judaism; the conflict with Christians, where it occurred, was christological. Christians did not feel themselves obligated by rabbinic interpretations of the Law. Even the Johannine emphasis on Jesus as a rabbi (7 times compared to 4 in Mark, 0 in Luke, and a title forbidden in Matt) may reflect polemics, contrasting Jesus with the emerging rabbis of the Jewish assembly at Jamnia in the last quarter of the first century.

39. Not an exhaustive list. Von Wahlde, "Johannine 'Jews,'" 39–40, gives a detailed chart of scholarly positions about which texts apply to authorities and which to people. Von Wahlde's own position that "there seems to be almost no evidence for seeing them [the Jews] as common people" is overstated (he has to admit that 6:41, 52 constitutes an exception) and reflects his theory (which has not had much acceptance) that one can distinguish editions of the Gospel and stages of community development according to whether John uses Pharisees or Jews for the authorities—terms that stem from different writers. When he comes to a relatively clear text that refers to people like 7:35, von Wahlde, "Johannine 'Jews,'" 45, resorts to the theory that the sequence of texts is artificial. I contend that the primary issue is what John means to hearers/readers in the present sequence, the only one given to us. *Editor's Note:* Since that time, see the fine article, U. C. von Wahlde, " 'The Jews' in the Gospel of John: Fifteen years of Research (1983–98)," *ETL* 86 (2000): 30–55. After a masterly survey of the literature, focusing particularly on the way newer methods of reading the NT text have influenced the question, von Wahlde concludes (in a way similar to Brown [see the following]): "I do think that scholarship has shown that *hoi Ioudaioi* was intended to represent the authoritative position of the traditional Judaism, the position which rejected Jesus. While this is not a new position, I would now feel comfortable saying that such a statement is justified by the text" (p. 53).

"the Jewish authorities" and other instances as "Jewish people" or "the Jewish crowd" is unwarranted to clarify texts that John has left vague and cloaks the fact that by calling them both "the Jews," John deliberately joins them together in their hostility to Jesus.

Religious usage. Those of Jewish birth who refused to believe in Jesus, spurned arguments proposed to support his divine identity, and were hostile to him and his followers (in the Johannine community) even to the point of killing. My remarks at the end of the preceding paragraph point to this as the most plausible sense for *a large number* of Johannine passages, including those where in the story-flow the agents described are explicitly or implicitly authorities, or implicitly, ordinary people.[40] Grelot correctly contends that even though much of the conflict takes place in Judea and the participants would be inhabitants of Jerusalem, whether they are an anonymous crowd, or pilgrims, or authorities makes little difference; John lumps them together as "Jews."[41] They have in common a religious rejection of Jesus as God's unique Son.[42] Given the charge that the Jews expelled from the synagogue those who confessed Jesus as the Messiah, the Johannine Christians who had undergone such expulsion may have attributed a touch of this meaning to the "feast of the Jews" and "the Passover of the Jews," feasts employed in the Gospel as occasions for recounting hostility to Jesus. The tonality may be "feasts no longer ours

---

40. Perhaps here I come close to Ashton's distinction ("Identity," 57), followed by Smiga (*Pain*, 157–70) between "sense" and "referents" with the latter being close to my "agents." See also von Wahlde, "Fifteen Years," 45–46, 53–54.

41. Grelot, *Les Juifs*, 189.

42. Cook, "Gospel," and Culpepper, "Gospel," recognize in different ways that John's negative use of "the Jews" is based on theology or Christology. De Jonge, "Conflict," 353, observes: "Belief stands over against belief, one view of God's intentions over against another." *Timewise*, I have pointed out that John made a connection between those who acted thus in Jesus' time and those who were acting thus when the Gospel was written. There is no evidence that John thought about Jews of the future. *Placewise*, John refers to Jews who encountered Jesus or his disciples who preached about him [17:20]. There is no evidence that John thought about Jews scattered elsewhere who had never heard of Jesus and who by the time of the Gospel could still have been some 90 percent or more of the Jews of the first century. Thus hostile application of John to Jews throughout the many centuries since the Gospel was written cannot claim justification in the intent of the Johannine writers.

but celebrated by those who expelled us." A number of observations must accompany accepting this as the dominant meaning intended by John.

Ioudaioi rendered as "the Jews" without substitutions (Judeans, Judaists) or explanatory, ameliorating additions (Jewish authorities) best catches the import of the designation on John's intended readers. The audience of the finalized work probably lived in the Diaspora where there would not have been Temple authorities or Jerusalem crowds or many people from Judea. They would hear it in reference to the Jews they knew at the end of the century in their own area. And they would connect any hostility they encountered from those Jews with the hostility manifested toward Jesus in John's account. As de Jonge observes, "the Jews" are representative of those who in Johannine experience observe Jewish customs and regulations and respond negatively to Jesus.[43] Ashton states, "So it is not just the Pharisees that attract his [the evangelist's] ire and resentment: it is the Jewish people as a whole who are made the symbol of the human shadow."[44] Uncomfortable as that may make modern readers because of the horrible history of anti-Jewish persecution in subsequent centuries, it is what John meant. If he describes "the Jews" as wanting to put Jesus to death, he has Jesus predict that the synagogue Jews will put his followers to death. In other words, for John the hostile "Jews" of the evangelist's time are the heirs of the hostile Jewish authorities and crowds in Jesus' time.

In order to alert hearers/readers to John's peculiar understanding and that he is not thinking of all those who in the first century were Jews by birth, in commenting on hostile passages I have written "the Jews" with quotation marks. I would maintain strongly that, although the designation "the Jews" should not be eliminated if one wishes to understand John's mentality;[45] it should be carefully explained. Kysar contends that

---

43. de Jonge, "Conflict," 352.

44. Ashton, "Identity," 65.

45. However well-meaning, the attempt to remove indications that Jesus was in sharp conflict with some of his own people and their authorities (and a corresponding attempt to blame his death virtually entirely on the Romans) has the effect of distancing him from any prophetic parallel in Israelite history. Prophets are called by God to bring God's own people to be what they should be. The Israelite prophets are rejected by their own, not by outsiders, for what message would they exemplify if their main enemy were external?

while the Gospel is not anti-Jewish it can nurture anti-Judaism.[46] Cook, in a sensitive article, is uncomfortably correct in pointing out that John may give the impression that God is anti-Jewish.[47] Today, therefore, in proclaiming John preachers must be careful to caution hearers that John's passages cannot be used to justify any ongoing hostility to Jewish people, any more than one should appeal for justification in our times to the genocidal cleansings of Palestine described in the OT as God's instructions for Israel at the time of Joshua's conquest (Lev 27:28–29; Josh 6:21; 8:22; 10:38–39). Regarding the Bible as sacred does not mean that everything described therein is laudable.

In some passages those described as (the) Jews are open to Jesus and even come to believe in him, e.g., 11:19, 31, 33, 36, 45; 12:9, 11. Scholars who think there were several editions of the evangelist's composition or that there was a redactor who added to the evangelist's composition will tend to attribute this favorable usage to a different stage of editing from the hostile usage of "the Jews,"[48] or to different bodies of Johannine material. Be that as it may, readers/hearers of the final document hear side-by-side hostile and favorable descriptions of "the Jews" and thus get a sense that Jewish reaction to Jesus was not one-sided.[49] This should be remembered in reflecting on the impact of the usage described in the preceding observation.

If the Johannine writers and many of the Johannine Christians were of Jewish birth, their generalizing use of "the Jews" for those hostile to Jesus indicates deep alienation from their ancestral people. (As I have indicated, the Johannine Jesus is portrayed as sharing this alienation, so that

---

46. Kysar, "John's."

47. Cook, "Gospel," 270.

48. The favorable usage of "the Jews" in chs. 11–12 constitutes one of the arguments for regarding those chapters as having been added after the evangelist's original composition. *Editor's Note:* For a more literary-theological interpretation, rejecting resort to later redaction, and insisting that "the Jews" are still presented in a negative fashion in chs. 11–12, see F. J. Moloney, "The Faith of Martha and Mary. A Narrative Approach to John 11:17–40," *Biblica* 75 (1994): 471–93.

49. An impression also communicated by Matthew (1:19; 2:3–4, 20: Law-observant believing Joseph vs. hostile Herod, the chief priests, and scribes who sought the life of the child) and Luke (1:5–6; 2:25, 36; 4:29: faithful, receptive Jews like Zechariah, Elizabeth, Simeon, Anna vs. hostile Nazareth townspeople who seek to kill him).

at times he speaks as if he himself were not a "Jew.") Being expelled from synagogues and using "Jews" as a designation for others may have had the civil effect that the Roman tolerance of Jewish religious observance no longer applied to them, and that could have left them open to Roman investigation and persecution such as that experienced under Pliny in Asia Minor ca. A.D. 110. That is one way to explain the charge that those who put Jesus' followers out of the synagogue were putting them to death (16:2). As a variant of this thesis, Wengst and Locher hold that the Jews were a dominant group in the Northern Transjordan where the Gospel was composed and had positions wherein they could persecute Christians.

Although they recognize hostility between the Johannine Jesus and "the Jews," some scholars (e.g., Vouga) question whether one may appropriately call this "anti-Jewish." They contend that we are hearing a dispute between one group of Jews and another and therefore "anti-Jewish" is no more appropriate here than it would be if applied to hostility between the Qumran Essenes and the Jerusalem high-priestly family. I agree that in its *beginnings* the hostility between Johannine Christians and Jews who did not believe in Jesus may have been comparable to other inter-Jewish hostilities. Yet the situation changed. I know of no evidence that in their various intramural hostilities the Pharisees, the Essenes, and the Sadducees ever said to the other, "You are no longer Jews" or spoke of their enemies as "the Jews." In its later stage the Johannine community seems to have regarded expulsion from the synagogue as meaning that they no longer could look on themselves as Jews. Thus John can be described as anti-Jewish in a qualified sense when through Jesus' words it attacks those whom it calls "the Jews," from whom the (Johannine) disciples of Jesus differ religiously, not necessarily ethnically or geographically. And even the religious difference is narrowly restricted: The Johannine Christians and "the Jews" do not differ in venerating the Scriptures and the Jewish religious heritage but in their estimation of Jesus.[50]

---

50. *Editor's Note:* As Ashton, *Understanding*, 151, points out, one must "recognize in these hot-tempered exchanges the type of family row in which the participants face one another across the room of a house that all have shared and all call home." See further, J. H. Charlesworth, "The Gospel of John: Exclusivism Caused by a Social Setting Different from That of Jesus (John 11:54 and 14:6," in Bieringer et al. (eds.), 479–513.

We saw that only rarely in the author's intent does the designation "Jews" have an ethnic sense, viz., when on the lips of a Samaritan or a Roman it distinguishes the speaker's background from that of Jesus. Yet on the part of John's non-Jewish hearers/readers there may have been a wider ethnic understanding of "the Jews" used hostilely in the Gospel. If the Jewish Johannine Christians, when they heard about "the Jews" as hostile to Jesus, thought of their former coreligionists who had expelled them, Samaritan and Greco-Roman Johannine Christians would have thought of that other, alien people whom often they had not liked even before they heard about Christ. In particular, a generalized hostile use of "the Jews" would have come naturally to the lips of Samaritans, since there was no love between them and the Jews of Palestine (4:9). In fact, when they came to believe in Jesus, they may have catalyzed the hostile use of "the Jews" among their Johannine Christian fellows.

A number of scholars (Bultmann, Porsch, Pratscher) would in whole or in large part equate "the Jews" in its negative usage with "the world," at least in passages where they are portrayed hostilely.[51] There is certainly some parallelism in the reaction to God's plan. God loved the world and sent the divine Son to save the world by giving witness to the truth, only to encounter rejection and opposition led by the Prince of this world, so that "the whole world lies in the grasp of the Evil One" (1 John 5:19). That is not unlike the Johannine view of Jesus' relation to "the Jews," e.g.: "To his own he came; yet his own people did not accept him" (John 1:11), and "The devil is the father you belong to" (8:44). Yet "the world" is a wider concept than "the Jews."[52] (The attitude toward it may stem from the experience of Johannine preachers when they shifted from debate

---

51. Sometimes this theory stems from positing a gnostic element in the origins or direction of the Gospel, for in a gnostic view the main obstacle to salvific revelation is not rejection by any one ethnic group, but the general failure of human beings to recognize embedded in their flesh a spiritual spark that belongs to another world. Other times the theory arises from the desire, laudable in its intent but inaccurate in its solution, to deny that John singled out the Jews as a particular object of enmity.

52. In the flow of the Prologue (1:10–11) "to his own he came" is a specification of "He was in the world." Some favor equating "the Jews" with the world because they think that makes the Gospel less anti-Jewish. Yet Townsend, "Gospel," 79, observes, "Using 'the Jews' to denote, not only the Jewish opponents of Jesus, but the whole sinful world is scarcely pro-Jewish. In such a case 'the Jews' have become the epitome for what is evil!"

with their fellow Jews to proclaiming Jesus among the Gentiles [in a new area?] and found a similar history of acceptance and rejection.)[53] The Jews were Jesus' "own" (*idioi*) people; he does not belong to the world (17:16). That gives to rejection by "the Jews," to which the Gospel gives more attention than rejection by the world, a greater incomprehensibility and poignancy. De Jonge, "Conflict," 345, comments pungently that the Jews in John are not representative of humankind in general: "When the author of the Fourth Gospel pictures the Jews as adversaries and enemies of Christ, he means what he says." Ashton quotes N. Dahl approvingly: "It is, however, equally important that the *Jews* are those who represent the world."[54]

I have contended that a good part of the relations between Jesus and "the Jews" described in the Gospel (although related to conflicts that did arise between Jesus and Pharisees and Temple authorities in the late 20s) goes beyond what actually happened during Jesus' lifetime. Rather, to a considerable degree the description reflects what happened to the Johannine Christians in their interactions with synagogue authorities. For example, they faced charges that they were making Jesus equal to God and thus were introducing another God alongside the God of Israel (see 5:16–18); they were put on trial before the authorities and other opponents in the synagogue; they marshaled arguments from the Scriptures and the Jesus tradition to answer the authorities; they were expelled from synagogues and reacted in alienated hostility toward their former coreligionists (ch. 9). Despite that community history the Gospel gives us a *literary* presentation of the disputes with "the Jews" and makes those disputes the occasion of expounding a Christology for believers. John does

---

53. Note that the Paraclete Spirit who comes after Jesus struggles with the world (14:17; 16:8–11), not with "the Jews." Indeed in chs. 14–16 of the Last Discourse which foresees the time after Jesus' departure the term *Ioudaioi* does not occur. Thus it is not unwarranted to posit that, in the self-understanding inherent in Johannine community history, rejection by "the world" may for the most part have come later than rejection by "the Jews." *Editor's Note:* See further, J. Zumstein, "The Farewell Discourses (John 13:1–16:33) and the Problem of Anti-Judaism," in Bieringer, (ed.), *Anti-Judaism in the Fourth Gospel,* 461–78. Zumstein concludes: "While the Johannine school reflects on the traditions of the narratives that it transmits, the question of Israel is no longer at the center of its concern—or constitutes no longer—the polemic front in relation to which it constructs the Christian identity" (p. 478).

54. Ashton, "Identity," 68.

not give an objective, dispassionate history of all the factors that entered the picture, especially on the part of the synagogue authorities.[55] From the synagogue viewpoint the treatment of the Johannine Christians may have looked very different.[56] The Gospel portrayal has been colored by Johannine dualism where there is only light and darkness, truth and falsehood, so that opponents are painted as blind and false. Surely there were sincere religious synagogue leaders who genuinely thought that what was said about Jesus was blasphemous (10:31–36) and thought they were acting against him and his followers out of conscience (as 16:2 surprisingly admits).

Apologetic against Jews Who Did Not Confess Publicly Their Belief in Jesus

By the time John was completed (ca. 90–110) the era of large Christian missionary inroads into Judaism has passed.[57] Jesus had been preached to Jews both in Palestine and the Diaspora, and decisions had been made for or against Jesus. For the most part, the Jews who had accepted Jesus were now simply Christians and part of the church. If one agrees that the hostile attitude toward "the Jews" described above reflects pre-Gospel struggles, that is quite different from claiming that the purpose of the Gospel

---

55. Porsch, "Ihr habt," contends that there is an element of projection on the part of the Johannine community, but that does not mean that John has created a "pseudo-Judaism," as Caron, "Exploring," suggests. See the same defect in Caron, *Qui sont?*.

56. I have spoken of expulsion from the synagogue because that is the way John describes it. It would not be surprising if the synagogue authorities looked on that as secession—voluntary to the extent that if the offenders had modified their divine claims about Jesus they could have remained affiliated with the synagogue. Most contemporary Johannine scholars would accept that expulsion from the synagogue(s) was part of the Johannine experience. It cannot but be the experience that generated 9:22; 12:42 and 16:2. However, they increasingly insist that this expulsion may have been a very local experience, and should not be linked to the insertion of the *Birkat ha-mînîm* into the Jewish prayer, the Eighteen Benedictions (the *Shemoneh 'Esreh*), a thesis classically developed by Martyn, *History and Theology*. See P. W. van der Horst, "The Birkat ha minim in Recent Research," *ExpTim* 105 (1994–95): 363–68.

57. See Chapter Six, below.

was to convert such "Jews," or that it was a missionary document to Diaspora Jews.[58] There is no indication that the Johannine writers thought that "the Jews" hostile to Jesus would read the Gospel or be preached to from it. Moreover, the violence of the language in ch. 8, comparing the Jews to the devil's brood, is scarcely designed to convert the synagogue. Rather John echoes apologetics; indeed, some of the discussions between the Johannine Jesus and "the Jews" anticipate the classic apologetic that Justin addressed to Trypho in the mid-second century. If the Gospel entered into any continued dealings with "the Jews" in the evangelist's time, it would have been one of countering Jewish propaganda rather than of persuading Jews with a hope of mass conversions.

Yet there may have been a hope to reach and persuade one group of Jews. Having been expelled from the synagogues for what they regarded as the courage to stand up to the authorities and confess Jesus, the Johannine Christians could not help being critical of those who lacked that courage—those who believed in Jesus but did not confess it publicly. It is not implausible that in the 80s and 90s such Jewish crypto-Christians were undergoing a crisis as to whether to stay on as part of synagogue Judaism or openly to join one of the developing churches or communities. Anachronistically, on several occasions in his story of Jesus, John refers to such people. In 9:22, John implies that the parents who knew that Jesus had cured their son believed that Jesus was the Messiah, but were afraid to acknowledge that because they would have been expelled from the synagogue. In 12:42–43, John states that many, even among the authorities, believed in him; yet because of the Pharisees, they refused to admit it, or they would have been put out of the synagogue. This reference is accompanied with biting scorn: "They preferred human praise to the glory of God." Believers are warned in 16:2 that they are going to be put out of

---

58. As proposed by Bornhäuser, *Johannesevangelium*, J.A.T. Robinson, "Destination," and van Unnik, "Purpose," but denied by Schnackenburg, "Messiasfrage," and de Jonge. "Conflict." Cribbs, "Reassessment," would date the Gospel to the 50s or early 60s, and thinks that in part it is addressed to convince Jews that Jesus is the Messiah. More plausibly, in my judgment, that represents an early stage in Johannine community formation, not the stage of the written Gospel. Van Unnik may well be right in arguing that the formula "Jesus is the Messiah" of 20:31 took shape in missionary preaching to Jews in synagogues (Acts 17:2–3; 18:5, 28; Justin, *Trypho* 46.1; 47.1), but John's addition of "the Son of God" shifts the force of the formula to accentuate Jesus' life-giving authority on the basis of his relationship with God.

the synagogues. John 9:33–34 glamorizes the man born blind who confessed before "the Jews" that Jesus was from God, and because of that was thrown out. Nicodemus cautiously first came to Jesus at night (3:2); and although he spoke against unjust behavior toward Jesus by the Sanhedrin authorities (7:50–52), apparently he never told them he had dialogued with Jesus whom he acknowledged as a man sent by God. Yet once Jesus had been lifted up on the cross, along with Joseph from Arimathea (another secret disciple who hitherto had feared the Jews), Nicodemus came forward publicly to honor Jesus with a costly burial (19:38–42).

Was at least a partial goal of the Gospel to persuade such Jewish crypto-Christians to confess Jesus publicly, even if they would have to leave the synagogue? Favoring an affirmative answer is the strong sense of Jesus' mission in John, for in the same manner believers were sent with a missionary goal (20:21). Possibly, as believers in Jesus, the crypto-Christians might have been willing to read John—a gesture very unlikely on the part of the disbelieving "Jews." The crypto-Christians should not have been unduly offended by the Gospel's harsh attacks on "the Jews," for it was precisely "the Jews" hostile to Jesus who were making it dangerous in the synagogue(s) for Jews with Christian leanings. The man born blind, Joseph of Arimathea, and Nicodemus can be seen as heroes held up to be imitated by crypto-Christians.[59] The Gospel's strong emphasis on Jesus as "the Messiah, the Son of God" (20:31) should have strengthened their faith in this crucial confession which had become the testing stone for their being removed from the synagogues. The theme of Jesus' replacement or reinterpretation of Jewish institutions and feasts could have been an encouragement to them, for they would have to leave such practices behind if they withdrew from the synagogues. On the other side of picture, by condemning the crypto-Christians for loving human praise John makes no effort to understand sympathetically plausible better motives. Although the man born blind is held up as a hero for the Johannine Christians, was he also representative of the sarcasm with which the Johannine Christians answered synagogue authorities (9:27, 30)? The Jewish Christians who hesitated to go public may have observed that such effrontery was not likely to bring about understanding and acceptance and may have decided to avoid confrontation till a later, more opportune period. Weighing this evidence, I would allow at least a likeli-

---

59. See Allen, "Jewish."

hood that an appeal to the Jewish crypto-Christians was a minor purpose of the Gospel.

Apologetic against or Rivalry with Other Adherents of Jesus

THERE IS BOTH EXTERNAL AND INTERNAL evidence about this aspect of Johannine thought.

External Evidence about Apologetic against Heretics

A tradition going back to the second century and Irenaeus (*Adv. Haer.* 3.11:1; SC 34.179–80) says that the Gospel of John was written against Cerinthus, a heretic of Asia Minor with Gnostic leanings. Our very limited knowledge of Cerinthus comes not from his own writings but from adversarial descriptions by church writers. The heresiologists writing many years later supply an ever more damning accumulation of accusations against him.[60] Irenaeus (1.26:1; PL 7:686) says that Cerinthus considered *Jesus* to be the son of Joseph, while *Christ* was a celestial aeon who descended on Jesus in the form of a dove for a while at the time of his baptism and left him before his death. If this is a correct picture of Cerinthus's doctrine, there is little in the Gospel designed to refute such a theory. The real refutation of this type of thought comes in 1 John with its strong insistence that Jesus is the Christ come in the flesh. The human Jesus cannot be severed from his being the Christ (4:2–3). Perhaps all that Irenaeus's information tells us is that in the Johannine literature there was an attack on Cerinthus. It may be that Cerinthus also held that the world was created by a demiurge rather than by God. In this case, John 1:3 would be significant, for it insists that all creation was effected by the Word of God. But this is scarcely a major emphasis in the Gospel.

---

60. See BEJ, 766–71. He is sometime pictured as a Jewish Christian who accepted only the humanity of Jesus and sometimes as a Gnostic akin to Simon Magus. In the latter more plausible case, a tradition that Cerinthus wrote John might represent a garbled way of reporting that Cerinthian thought represented a development of the interpretation of John by the secessionists described in 1 John who seem to have moved toward Gnosticism.

Jerome (*In Matt. Prolog.*; PL 26:19) mentions that the Gospel was directed to Ebion along with Cerinthus. Ebion was probably not a real person but an eponymous hero of the Ebionites, a Jewish Christian group.[61] The thought that the Fourth Gospel was written to confute Christians like the Ebionites, who had not abandoned their Jewish practices, is somewhat akin to the proposal made above that it was written in part as an address to the Jewish Christians in the synagogues. The Ebionites had features of theological thought, e.g, dualism, that are also found at Qumran.[62] The fourth evangelist may have chosen language like that of Qumran to appeal to groups who shared similar language and thought. In summary, while certain features that appear in later Ebionite theology correspond to features in John, so that the Gospel might be usefully read by those with incipient Ebionite tendencies, nevertheless there is little evidence that the Gospel was directed to the Ebionites specifically.

It has also been suggested that the Fourth Gospel was directed against docetism. Docetism was not so much a heresy by itself as it was an attitude found in a number of heresies. Its central contention (with different nuances) was that Jesus Christ did not truly come in the flesh, for his flesh was only an appearance—he only seemed to be a man. Some of the remarks of Ignatius of Antioch, ca. 110, seem to be directed against such an error, so this heretical thought may well have been in circulation when John was written. Wilkens's theory of various editions of the Gospel posits an increasing polemic against docetism in the later editions of the Gospel.[63] Certainly there are passages in John that may have an antidocetic thrust. "The Word became flesh" (1:14) springs to mind immediately. The scene in 19:34 would be shattering to the docetic cause, for the realism of the blood and water pouring from Jesus' side (underlined by the editorial parenthesis in the next verse which claims eyewitness verifi-

---

61. Irenaeus first mentions Ebion in the same passage where he mentions Cerinthus (*Adv. Haer.* 1.26.2; PL 7.686). Perhaps this is why Jerome assumes that the Gospel was also directed to Ebion. Victorinus of Pettau, ca. 300, joins the Gnostic Valentinus to Ebion and Cerinthus as another target against whom the Gospel was supposedly directed (*In Apoc.* 11:1; CSEL 49.97).

62. See J. A. Fitzmyer, "The Qumrân Scrolls, the Ebionites and Their Literature," *TS* 16 (1955): 335–72.

63. See above, Chapter Two.

cation) militates against any theory that he was a phantasm.[64] Docetists seem to have neglected the eucharist, denying that it was the flesh of Jesus (Ignatius, *Smyrnaeans* 7.1). Therefore, the eucharistic realism of John 6:51–58 may also have been antidocetic in tendency. The difficulty is that all these passages are perfectly understandable even without the antidocetic interpretation. A prudent judgment would be that an antidocetic motif is possible in the Gospel, but it has no great prominence.[65] By contrast, 1 John offers more verses capable of antidocetic interpretation than does the much longer Gospel.

Not one of the suggestions that John was written against early Christian heretics is without difficulty. More likely they represent the way the Gospel could be used by church theologians who designated these figures as heretics and wrote against them.

Internal Evidence about Other Followers of Jesus, Some of Them Inadequate

John is the only Gospel that shows an awareness that there are other followers of Jesus who are not united with those who are the main concern in the Gospel,[66] and its attitude toward them runs from a critique reflecting rivalry to harsh apologetics. Because the BD emerges in the Gospel as the closest disciple to Jesus, one suspects that the Johannine Christians who identified him as their hero thought they were closer to what Jesus wanted than were others. Nevertheless, among those others John paints a more favorable attitude toward Peter, who might be a hero for non-Johannine Christians, than toward disciples whom it condemns for inad-

---

64. However, 19:34 might have had a totally different theological goal (sacramentalism, fulfillment of 7:38–39).

65. If it exists, its best attestation is found in passages that belong to the latest stage of Gospel composition, probably to the redaction. *Editor's Note:* The issue has been comprehensively studied, suggesting that Brown is too confident in this conclusion. U. Schnelle, *Antidocetic Christology in the Gospel of John: An Investigation of the Place of the Fourth Gospel in the Johannine School* (Minneapolis: Fortress Press, 1992). Schnelle concludes, convincingly, that "the Fourth Gospel (appears to be), *in some essential ways*, a reaction to docetic christology" (p. 228). Stress mine.

66. The man who on his own exorcizes by using Jesus' name in Mark 9:38–41 and Luke 9:49–50 is not parallel. A closer period is supplied in Acts 19:1–7 at Ephesus ca. A.D. 54 where one group of Jesus' followers did not know about the Holy Spirit.

equate faith. The second group is my main interest under the present heading, but they stand out in better relief if I describe two groups of non-Johannine followers of Jesus in the Gospel.[67] I shall begin with the group treated favorably. Let me alert readers that I am reading between the lines of the Gospel, and my analysis is far from certain.

Christians of the larger church who looked on Peter as the most representative apostolic figure. In 10:16, Jesus says that he has other sheep who are not of this fold but whom he wishes to be one with those who are already in it (10:16). The prayer that they may be one in 17:21–22 pertains to those who believe in Jesus through the word of those disciples who are already with him, so that John is thinking about the Christian situation after Jesus' lifetime. Who are those other sheep who belong to Jesus? The BD is consistently counterpoised to Simon Peter, and over and over again he is closer to Jesus than Peter and more perceptive in his faith. There is no doubt that Simon Peter is a true follower of Jesus: he is called by Andrew among the first disciples, and Jesus made the gesture of giving him a new name (1:40–42). When some disciples left Jesus, Peter stayed faithful as the spokesman of the Twelve, confessing that Jesus is God's Holy One who has the words of eternal life. Peter is the most frequently named among Jesus' "own" at the Last Supper (13:1, 6, 24, 36). The Johannine writings do not use the terms "apostle" and "disciple" as the key category. If those scholars are correct who think that the BD was not one of the Twelve, the contrast between that disciple and Peter may represent the difference between the Johannine community and the churches that prided themselves in having been founded by the preaching of the apostles, among whom Peter was remembered by many as the most prominent (Eph 2:20; Matt 16:18; 1 Pet 5:1–2). In John's estimation, they shared a true faith in Jesus, but the perception of the Johannine group (represented by the BD) was deeper,[68] so that it was closer to Jesus. There

---

67. See Brown, *Community,* 73–91.

68. Andrew, Peter, and Philip confess Jesus in 1:35–49, but Jesus says in 50–51 that they will see greater things. One of the Twelve, Thomas, makes the highest profession of faith in the Gospel: "My Lord and my God" (20:28); yet that profession comes only after he has seen the risen Jesus, while the BD believed without seeing the risen Jesus. Matt is a Gospel that portrays a church founded upon Peter; the highest Christology in Matt is Peter's confession of Jesus as "the Messiah, the son of the living God" (16:16), but there is no suggestion of the type of preexistence that one finds in John.

may have been another difference in that the "apostolic" churches had developed an articulated church structure with human shepherds caring for the flock, while for most of their history the Johannine Christians had argued that Jesus was the only shepherd necessary (10:1–3, 7–8). There is no indication that John expected Christians of the larger church to read the Gospel; rather the Gospel seems concerned that the Johannine Christian understand Jesus' hope for unity with those other Christians and Jesus' prayer for that unity.

Christians of inadequate faith. Distinct from the Twelve in the Gospel story are those disciples of Jesus who broke away and would not follow when he spoke of giving his flesh to eat and his blood to drink (6:60–66).[69] John 6:64 regards this as refusing to believe, and in contrast to them Simon Peter confesses Jesus as God's Holy One. Are these similar to the Jews who had believed Jesus but become hostile when he makes divine claims about himself (8:31ff.)? Are they similar to the brothers of Jesus in 7:3–5 who urge Jesus to go to Judea to perform his miracles there instead of in obscurity? The sources of the *Pseudo-Clementine* writings offer evidence from mid-second century that Christians of a low Christology, who said they differed from the synagogue only in believing in Jesus as the Messiah, held up James the brother of the Lord as their hero. Ignatius of Antioch, who wrote a decade or two after the Johannine evangelist, criticized Jewish Christians particularly in *Magnesians* and *Ephesians*. C. K. Barrett sums up Ignatius's charges against them, "They reverenced Jesus as a teacher, but perhaps were not prepared to allow his person to upset the unity of the Godhead. . . . They adopted the sacred meal . . . and thought of it in terms of fellowship rather than as a sacrament on Ignatian lines."[70] Thus it is possible that in situating in his story of Jesus an apologetic critique of disciples who could not believe in Jesus as the bread from heaven and as existing before Abraham was inadequate, John may be criticizing Jewish Christians at the turn of the century

---

69. They had been following Jesus publicly, and so they are not the same as the crypto-Christians in the synagogue.

70. "Jews and Judaizers in the Epistles of Ignatius," in *Jews, Greeks, and Christians. Religious Cultures in Late Antiquity Essays in Honour of William David Davies* (eds. R. Hamerton-Kelly and R. Scroggs; SJLA 21; Leiden: E. J. Brill, 1976), 220–44, esp. 242.

who shared these inadequacies. In John's judgment such people did not believe; and seemingly he would have had no hope of their conversion. Indeed, his description of such Jewish believers in 8:31ff. places them on the same plane as Jews who did not believe in Jesus.

Purpose: Encouragement to Believing Christians, Gentile and Jew

OF ALL THE GOSPELS John is the most articulate about its purpose: "These things have been recorded so that you may have faith that Jesus is the Messiah, the Son of God, and that through this faith you may have life in his name" (20:31). Thus whatever conflicts in the past history of the community may have shaped the tradition, whatever was the varied and disunited situation among Christian communities reflected in the Gospel, the evangelist was not writing primarily to them or even about them. He was writing about Jesus Christ to those whom he considered sympathetic believers. How wide was the spectrum of these believers? Who were the "you" in "that you may have faith that Jesus is the Messiah, the Son of God"?

Were the "you" Jews or Gentiles? J. A. T. Robinson and Van Unnik maintain that John shows little interest in the Gentiles. The contention that believing that Jesus was the Messiah would not have meaning for Gentiles is very weak.[71] Christian preachers carried over to the Gentiles much Jewish religious terminology. Gentiles who became interested in the message about Jesus would soon have to learn some OT background and have to learn what "Messiah" meant.[72] The parentheses scattered throughout the Gospel explaining Semitic terms (including the transliterated *Messias*) envision readers not initially familiar with Jewish vocabulary, and passages like 7:35 and 12:20–23 hint that Jesus' message will have a future among "the Greeks."[73] However, even if Gentiles would have

---

71. As Schnackenburg, "Messiasfrage," emphasizes, there is no doubt that the second title, "Son of God," would appeal to a Gentile religious background where the gods had sons.

72. A good example is Paul's argument from the OT addressed to the Gentile converts in Galatia.

73. The role of 12:20 in the plan of the Gospel marking the coming of the hour and Jesus' evaluation of his ministry to the Jews (12:37–41) cannot be explained un-

been among John's "you," in another sense John was not interested in Gentiles as distinct from Jews, or in Jews as distinct from Gentiles or Samaritans, because all ethnic categories had lost significance.[74] Natural parents can beget only flesh; to be a child of God one must be begotten/born of water and Spirit, and that is open to all who believe (3:5–6). When "his own [people]" rejected him, Jesus empowered all those who did accept him to become God's children (1:11–12). As part of John's universalism, we are told that Jesus comes into the world as a light for *everyone* (1:9). Jesus takes away the sins of the world (1:29); and he was sent that the *world* might be saved though him (3:17). Jesus was to die not only for the Jewish nation, but also to gather together the dispersed children of God and make them one (11:51–52). When he is lifted up on the cross and in resurrection/ascension, he draws *all* to himself (12:32).

Did "you" include "the world"? Can there have been a Johannine missionary effort to persuade what the Gospel calls "the world"? Despite generalizing negative statements about "the world" and even "the whole world," was there in Johannine thought hope for a portion of the world? Did each generation of humankind experience what is described in 3:16–21, namely, that out of love God has sent the Son into the world and people have the opportunity of making a choice for light and darkness according to their own deeds? Jesus is the Lamb of God who takes away the sin of the world (1:29), the Savior of the world (4:42), the bread from heaven that gives life to the world (6:33), the light of the world (8:12; 9:5; 12:46). In Johannine expectation is the access of the world closed with the judgment of the world that took place in the defeat of the Prince of this world by the lifting up of Jesus (12:31–32)? Accordingly, would the only solution for those who believe in Jesus be to have nothing to do with this world which hates them (15:19; 17:14), a world in which there is suffering (16:13)? That is not so clear. Although the Paraclete Spirit treats the world as an adversary, Jesus speaks of his followers being sent into the

---

less "Greeks" means Gentiles. Many would see a relationship between John's account of the conversion of a Samaritan village (4:39–42) and the mission of the Hellenists to Samaria (Acts 8:4–8). It is interesting that Acts 11:19–21 gives the impression that the Hellenists were the first to preach Jesus Christ to the Greeks.

74. Even if John would never deny that salvation is from the Jews, the time has come when the argument over the proper place of worship that distinguished Samaritans from Jews has been resolved by worship in Spirit and truth (4:21–23).

world even as he was sent (17:18). Jesus is concerned that the world recognize that he loves the Father (14:31), that God sent Jesus (17:21), and
that Jesus loves those who believe in him (17:22). Thus some type of continued proclamation to the world seems envisioned.[75] G. W. MacRae suggested that John consciously incorporated into the Gospel different
attitudes, symbols, traditions, etc., in order that it might reach out to as
many religious backgrounds and experiences as possible, and his work
would have had appeal in the universalizing and transcendent Hellenistic
religious world.[76]

Were *"you"* those who already believed or those who were to come to belief? Does "that you may have faith" in 20:31 mean "that you may continue to have faith" or "that you may get faith"? The textual evidence and
scholars are divided on which form of the Greek verb to read: the present
subjunctive ("keep believing") or the aorist subjunctive (possibly: "make
an act of faith"). Can both views be true?[77]

Certainly the Gospel was written in good part to deepen the faith of
believers so that they could understand that what they had gained by
way of God's life more than made up for what had been lost in their former religious adhesion.[78] The evangelist speaks to those who accepted
Jesus, thereby becoming God's children, begotten not by human intervention but by God (1:12–13), in order to make them appreciate the life
they had been given. Some of the decisive theological emphases in the
Gospel are directed to crises within the believing community,[79] rather

---

75. One must always consider the context within which the Johannine use of the
expression *ho kosmos* (the world) appears. It has a number of possible meanings. For
a nuanced treatment, see N. H. Cassem, "A Grammatical and Contextual Inventory
of the Use of *kosmos* in the Johannine Corpus with some Implications for a Johannine Cosmic Theology," *NTS* 19 (1972–73): 81–91.

76. "The Fourth Gospel and *Religionsgeschichte,*" *CBQ* 32 (1970): 13–24.

77. *Editor's Note:* See above, note 4.

78. Von Wahlde, "Literary," claims that, with the goal of preventing Jewish Christians from apostatizing, John presents the rejection of Jesus in debates with "the
Jews" as groundless. I do not detect any warnings against going back.

79. See below, Chapter Seven. R. A. Culpepper, "Synthesis and Schism in the Johannine Community and the Southern Baptist Convention," *PRS* 13 (1986): 1–20,
points out all the factors in community history that have contributed to the Johannine synthesis, but thinks that the danger of dissolution prompted the writing of the
Gospel.

than to the conversion of nonbelievers. If the Gospel stresses realized eschatology, it is to lead believers to realize that they already possesses eternal life, that they are already children of God, and have already undergone judgment successfully by choosing light rather than darkness. If the Gospel has a sacramental tone, it roots baptism and the eucharist in what Jesus said and did in his ministry and gives the believer a sense of contact with the earthly Jesus. If the evangelist brings forward the Spirit as Paraclete, his purpose is to reassure the believer that with the passing of the eyewitness generation the connection with Jesus is not lost because the Paraclete is a continuation of Jesus' presence in the Christian. Thus the theological emphases of the Gospel enable believers to appreciate existentially what this Jesus in whom they believe means in terms of life. Bultmann has not done Johannine studies a disservice in pointing out some of the existential qualities of the Fourth Gospel. Much more than Bultmann, however, I would stress that the evangelist rooted this existential goal in a picture of Jesus that had not only historic but also historical value.

As for bringing people to faith, there is not much evidence that the Gospel was a missionary document in the ordinary sense of offering a text to be read to or by nonbelievers. Yet John manifests a conviction that if the faith of believers is intense, thereby others will gain knowledge about Jesus. In that sense those who possess the Paraclete become witnesses to Jesus (15:26–27). When believers share Jesus' glory by becoming one with God and Jesus, the world will come to know that God sent Jesus as a manifestation of love (17:22–23). Thus John's primary purpose of deepening the faith of believers has a secondary goal of thereby bringing others to make an act of faith.

BIBLIOGRAPHY

RELATIONS TO JBAP SECTARIANS

Backhaus, K. "Täuferkreise als Gegenspieler jenseits des Textes. Erwägungen zu einer kritieriologischen Verlegenheit am Beispiel der Joh-Forschung," *TG* 81 (1991): 279–301.

———, *Die "Jüngerkreise" des Taufer Johannes* (Paderborn:Schöningh, 1991).

Bacon, B., "New and Old in Jesus' Relation to John," *JBL* 48 (1929): 40–81.

Baldensperger, W., *Der Prolog des vierten Evangeliums. Sein polemisch-apologetsischer Zweck* (Tübingen: J. C. B. Mohr [Paul Siebeck], 1898).

Dobbeler, S. von, *Das Gericht und das Erbarmen Gottes. Die Botschaft Johannes des Täufers und ihre Rezeption bei den Johannesjüngern* (BBB 70; Frankfurt: Athenäum, 1988).

Lichtenberger, H., "Täufergemeinden und frühchristliche Täuferpolemik im letzten Drittel des 1. Jahrhunderts," *ZTK* 84 (1987): 36–57.

Schnackenburg, R., "Das vierte Evangelium und die Johannesjünger," *Historisches Jahrbuch* 77 (1958): 21–38.

Stowasser, M., *Johannes der Täufer im Vierten Evangelium* (Östereichisches Biblische Studien 12; Klosterneuburg: Österreichisches Katholisches Bibelwerk, 1992).

Trocmé, E., "Jean-Baptiste dans le Quatrième Évangile," *RHPR* 60 (1980): 129–51.

Whitacre, R. A., *Johannine Polemic. The Role of Tradition and Theology* (SBLDS 67; Chico: Scholars Press, 1982).

RELATIONS TO "THE JEWS," TO SECRET BELIEVERS IN SYNAGOGUES, AND TO OTHER CHRISTIANS

An exhaustive and up-to-date bibliography can be found in R. Bieringer, D. Pollefeyt and F. Vandecasteele-Vanneuville (eds.), *Anti-Judaism and the Fourth Gospel. Papers of the Leuven Colloquium, 2000* (Assen: van Gorcum, 2001), 549–70. The whole volume provides a valuable and multifaceted approach to this question: exegetical, hermeneutical, theological and ecumenical.

Allen, E. L., "The Jewish Christian Church in the Fourth Gospel," *JBL* 74 (1955): 88–92.

Ashton, J., "The Identity and Function of the *Ioudaioi* in the Fourth Gospel," *NovT* 27 (1985): 40–75.

Barrett, C. K., *The Gospel of John and Judaism* (London: SPCK, 1975).

Beutler, J., "Die 'Juden' und der Tod Jesu im Johannesevangeliun," *Studien*, 59–76.

Boer, M. C. de, "L'Évangile de Jean et le Christianisme Juif (Nazoréen)," in *Le déchirement Juifs et Chrétiens au premier siècle* (ed. D. Marguerat; Geneva: Labor et Fides, 1996), 179–202.

Bornhäuser, K., *Das Johannesevangelium, eine Missionsschrift für Israel* (Gütersloh: Bertelsmann, 1928).

Botha, F. J., "The Jews in the Fourth Gospel," *Theologia Evangelica* 2 (1969): 40–45.

Bowman, J., *The Fourth Gospel and the Jews* (Pittsburgh: Pickwick, 1975).

Broer, I., "Die Juden im Johannesevangelium," *Diakonia* 14 (1983): 333–41.

Caron, G., "Exploring a Religious Dimension: The Johannine Jews," *SRSR* 24 (1995): 159–71.

———, *Qui sont les Juifs de l'évangile de Jean?* (Recherches 35; Québec: Bellarmin, 1997).

Carroll, K. L., "The Fourth Gospel and the Exclusion of Christians from the Synagogues," *BJRL* 40 (1957–58): 19–32.

Cook, M. J., "The Gospel of John and the Jews," *RExp* 84 (1987): 259–71.

Cribbs, F. L., "A Reassessment of the Date of Origin of the Fourth Gospel," *JBL* 89 (1970): 38–55.

Culpepper, R. A., "The Gospel of John and the Jews," *RExp* 84 (1987): 273–88.

Cuming, G. J., "The Jews in the Fourth Gospel," *ExpTim* 60 (1948–49): 290–92.

Epp, E. J., "Anti-Semitism and the Popularity of the Fourth Gospel in Christianity," *Central Conference of American Rabbis Journal* 22 (1975): 35–57.

Ferrando, M. A., "Los judíos en el Evangelio según Juan," *Teología e Vida* 40 (1999): 255–67.

Florival, E., "Les siens ne l'ont pas reçu. Regard évangélique sur la question juive," *NRT* 89 (1967): 43–66.

Fuller, R. H., "The 'Jews' in the Fourth Gospel," *Dialog* 16 (1977): 31–37.

Geyser, A. S., "Israel in the Fourth Gospel," *Neotestamentica* 20 (1986): 13–20.

Grässer, E., "Die Antijüdische Polemik im Johannesevangelium," *NTS* 11 (1964–65): 74–90.

Granskou, D., "Anti-Judaism in the Passion Accounts of the Fourth Gospel," in *Anti-Judaism in Early Christianity; Vol. I: Paul and the Gospels*, (ed. P. Richardson; Waterloo, Ontario: Canadian Corporation for Studies in Religion, and Wilfrid Laurier University, 1986), 201–16.

Grelot, P., *Les Juifs dans l'Évangile selon Jean. Enquête historique et réflexion théologique* (CahRB 34; Paris: Gabalda, 1995).

Harrington, D. J., " 'The Jews' in John's Gospel," *BibTod* 27 (1989): 203–9.

Hickling, C. J. A., "Attitudes to Judaism in the Fourth Gospel," in de Jonge, *Évangile*, 347–54.

Jocz, J., "Die Juden im Johannesevangelium," *Judaica* 9 (1953): 129–42.

Jonge, M. de, "The Conflict between Jesus and the Jews and the Radical Christology of the Fourth Gospel," *PRS* 20 (1993): 341–55.

Kaufman, P. S., "Anti-Semitism in the New Testament: The Witness of the Beloved Disciple," *Worship* 63 (1989): 386–401.

Kysar, R., "John's Anti-Jewish Polemic," *BibRev* 9 (1993): 26–27.

Lea, T. D., "Who Killed the Lord? A Defense against the Charge of Anti-Semitism in John's Gospel," *Criswell Theological Review* 7 (1994): 103–23.

Leibig, J. E., "John and 'the Jews': Theological Antisemitism in the Fourth Gospel," *Journal of Ecumenical Studies* 20 (1983): 209–34.

Leistner, R., *Antijudaismus im Johannesevangelium? Darstellung des Problems in der neueren Auslegungsgeschichte und Untersuchung der Leidens-geschichte* (Theologie und Wirklichkeit 3; Bern: Lang, 1974).

Locher, C., "Die Johannes-Christen und 'die Juden'," *Orientierung* 48 (1984): 223–26.

Lowe, M., "Who Were the *IOUDAIOI?*" *NovT* 18 (1976): 101–30.

Lutgert, W., "Die Juden im Johannesevangelium," in *Neutestamentliche Studien für Georg Henrici* (Leipzig: J. C. Heinrich, 1914), 147–54.

Manns, F., "L'évangile de Jean, réponse chrétienne aux décisions de Jabne," *SBFLA* 30 (1980): 47–92; 32 (1982): 85–108.

Meeks, W. A., " 'Am I a Jew,' Johannine Christianity and Judaism," in CJOC, 1.163–86.

Moloney, F. J., "Israel, the People and the Jews in the Fourth Gospel," in *Israel und seine Heilstraditionen im Vierten Evangelium* (eds. A. Strotmann, M. Labahn and K. Scholtissek; Paderborn: Schöningh, 2002). In press.

———, " 'The Jews' in the Fourth Gospel: Another Perspective," *Pacifica* 15 (2002): 17–37.

O'Neill, J. C., "*The Jews* in the Fourth Gospel," *IBS* 18 (1996): 58–74.

Painter, J., "The Church and Israel in the Gospel of John: A Response," *NTS* 25 (1978–79): 103–112.

Pancaro, S., "The Relationship of the Christ to Israel in the Gospel of St John," *NTS* 21 (1974–75): 396–405.

Pereyra, R., "El significado de *IOUDAIOI* en el Evangelio de Juan," *Teologika* 3 (1988): 116–36.

Pietrantonio, R., "Los 'ioudaioi' en el evangelio de Juan," *Revista Bíblica* 47 (1985): 27–41.

Porsch, F., " 'Ihr habt den Teufel zum Vater' (Joh 8,44). Antijudaismus im Johannesevangelium?" *BK* 44 (1989): 50–57.

Pratscher, W., "Die Juden im Johannesevangelium," *Bibel und Liturgie* 59 (1986): 177–85.

Rensberger, D., "Anto-Judaism and the Gospel of John," in *Anti-Judaism and the Gospels* (ed. W. Farmer; Harrisburg PA; Trinity Press International, 1999), 120–57.

Rissi, M., " 'Die Juden' im Johannesevangelium," *ANRW* 2.26/3 (1996): 2099–2141.

Schnackenburg, R., "Die Messiasfrage im Johannesevangelium," *NTAuf,* 240–64.

Schnelle, U., "Die Juden im Johannesevangelium," in *Gedenkt an das Wort. Festschrift für Werner Vogler zum 65. Geburtstag* (eds. C. Kähler, M. Böhm and C. Böttrick; Leipzig: Evangelische Verlagsanstalt, 1999), 217–30.

Scholtissek, K., "Antijudaismus im Johannesevangelium? Ein Gesprächsbeitrag," in *"Nun steht aber diese Sache im Evangelium . . . ?" Zur Frage nach den Anfängen des christlichen Antijudaismus* (ed. R. Kampling; Paderborn: Schöningh, 1999), 151–81.

Shepherd, M., Jr., "The Jews in the Fourth Gospel: Another Level of Meaning," *ATR* Suppl. 3 (1974): 95–112.

Smiga, G. M., *Pain and Polemic. Anti-Judaism in the Gospels* (New York: Paulist, 1992): 134–73.

Thyen, H., " 'Das Heil kommt von der Juden,' " in *KGB,* 163–84.

Townsend, J. T., "The Gospel of John and the Jews: The Story of a Religious Divorce," in A. Davies, ed., *Antisemitism and the Foundations of Christianity* (New York: Paulist Press, 1979).

Watson, A., *Jesus and the Jews: The Pharisaic Tradition in John* (Athens GA: University of Georgia Press, 1995).

Valle, C. A., "Los Judios en el Evangelio de Juan," *Cuadernos de Teologia* 13 (1964): 31–48.

Vouga, F., "Antijudaismus im Johannesevangelium?" *TG* 83 (1993): 81–89.

Wahlde, U. C. von, "The Terms for Religious Authorities in the Fourth Gospel," *JBL* 98 (1979): 231–53.

——, "The Johannine 'Jews': A Critical Survey," *NTS* 28 (1982): 33–60.

——, " 'The Jews' in the Gospel of John: Fifteen Years of Research," *ETL* 86 (2000): 30–55.

THE PURPOSE OF THE FOURTH GOSPEL

Bowker, J. W., "The Origin and Purpose of St. John's Gospel," *NTS* 11 (1964–65): 398–408.

Freed, E. D., "Did John Write His Gospel Partly to Win Samaritan Converts?" *NovT* 12 (1970): 241–56.

Jonge, M. de, *Jesus,* 97–102.

MacRae, G. W., "The Fourth Gospel and *Religionsgeschichte,*" *CBQ* 32 (1970): 13–24.

Minear, P. S., "The Audience of the Fourth Evangelist," *Interpretation* 31 (1977): 339–54.

Robinson, J. A. T., "The Destination and Purpose of St. John's Gospel," *NTS* 6 (1959–60): 117-31. Also in *TNTS,* 107–25.

Smith, T. C., "The Secondary Purpose of the Fourth Gospel," *RExp* 50 (1953), 69–86.

Stanley, D. M., "The Purpose of the Fourth Evangelist," in *Trinification of the World. A Festschrift in Honour of Frederick E. Crowe in Celebration of His 60th Birthday* (eds T. A. Dunne and J.-M. Laporte; Toronto: Regis College Press, 1978), 259–78.

Thomas, W. H. G., "The Purpose of the Fourth Gospel," *BSac* 125 (1968): 254–62.

Unnik, W. C. van, "The Purpose of St. John's Gospel" *StEv*, 1.382–411.

Wind, A., "Destination and Purpose of the Gospel of John," *NovT* 14 (1972): 26–69.

6

The Author, the Place,

and the Date

◆

THESE TOPICS ARE RELATED since a decision about the author can point us to where that author functioned and hence where and when he wrote.

The Author

THE FOLLOWING DISCUSSION contains some complexities, so it may help from the start for me to state that my principal concern is *the identity of the person who was responsible for composing the body of the Gospel,* the person whom I called the evangelist in the Third Stage of my understanding of the development of the Gospel.[1]

Although I used the accepted title for this topic, the concept of "author" needs clarification. In modern terminology "author" and "writer" are most often synonymous. When they are not, it is customary to identify the literary collaborator ("ghost writer") as well as the main author. Antiquity did not share this fine sense of proper credits, and frequently the men or women whose names were attached to biblical books never

---

1. See above, Chapter Two, pp. 79–82.

set pen to papyrus. Therefore, in considering biblical books, many times we have to distinguish between the *author* whose ideas the book expresses and the *writer.* Writers ran the gamut from recording secretaries who slavishly copied down the author's dictation to highly independent collaborators who, working from a sketch of the author's ideas, gave their own literary style to the final work. Even if we confine authorship to responsibility for the basic ideas that appear in a book, the principles that determine the attribution of authorship in the Bible are fairly broad. If a particular author was surrounded by a group of disciples who carried on his thought even after his death, their works could be attributed to him as author, as seemingly happened in the case of the post-Pauline literature (e.g., Eph, 1–2 Tim, Titus). The Book of Isaiah was the work of at least three principal contributors, and its composition covered a period of over 200 years. Yet it is not simply a miscellaneous anthology, for it has similarities of theme and style which reflect a *school* of thought and which, in the broad biblical sense of authorship, justify the attribution of the book to Isaiah. Wider afield is the custom in antiquity to attribute literature to an author in the sense of the *authority* behind that style of literature. Solomon was spoken of as the author of the Wisdom Literature (Prov, Eccl, Wisdom of Solomon) because his court offered an atmosphere in which wisdom literature could develop, and thus he served as the patron of the wisdom writers. In a similar way David was spoken of as author of the Psalms, and Moses as author of the Pentateuch, though parts of these works were composed many hundreds of years after the traditional author's death. Modern scholars dispute whether any of the Pentateuchal writing goes back to the time of Moses. But even if one ignores historical criticism, Moses scarcely wrote the account of his own death at the end of Deuteronomy (Deut 34:1–12). Accordingly when we see ancient statements about the person responsible for the Fourth Gospel, we have to be careful about what we are being told, lest we make those testimonies say more than they were meant to say.

Special problems affect an investigation of the Fourth Gospel. First, the issue of the identity of the Beloved Disciple (henceforth in this chapter the BD) and the issue of the author tend be run together. A figure called "the disciple whom Jesus loved" appears in six Gospel passages and under a less specific description in three more. We are told in 21:24 that "this disciple wrote these things." In the most ancient references to the Gospel, John (presumably, but not always specifically, the son of Zebedee) was identified as both the BD and author of the Gospel. Leaving aside for the moment the ancient attribution, and drawing on current critical investigation, these distinctions may be made. If John of Zebedee was the author of the Gospel, he was almost surely also the BD. However, if he was the BD, he was not necessarily the author of the Gospel. And he might have been neither.[2] I have addressed the question of the role and the identity of the BD elsewhere.[3] My conclusion is that he was a minor disciple whose name we cannot know but who was idealized because he lived through and embodied the Johannine community's development in the knowledge and love of Jesus.[4] Lest it seem overly skeptical or even impious to doubt the late second-century attribution, let me point out that Gospel attributions to Matthew, Mark, and Luke have also been challenged in modern scholarship, with the first of the three most dubious. My concern here, however, is authorship. No matter who the BD was personally, was the author (i.e., the writer) the BD? If not, who was he?

The problem of author and writer has been translated into modern literary criticism of John in terms of the relationship between the BD and the narrator.[5] The implied author, he says, is one who knows Jesus intimately, shares his theological perspective, and can interpret reliably, that is, "his witness is true," and 21:24 characterizes the implied author as the BD. John's separation of the narrator (who in my judgment would have the role of the writer) from the implied author came as a result of idealizing the BD and the comment of an editor.[6]

---

2. Dodd is most insistent that the Fourth Gospel contains independent historical tradition (which could logically have stemmed from an eyewitness), and yet he denies authorship by John of Zebedee.

3. Brown, *The Community*, 31–34.

4. Such an identification does not necessarily exclude his authorship of the Gospel. Cullmann, *Johannine*, thinks that we cannot know the name of the BD but he was the evangelist.

5. See Culpepper, *Anatomy*, 47–48.

6. *Editor's Note:* Brown here uses the language of contemporary narrative criticism rather loosely. Neither "implied author" nor "narrator" should be identified with historical "writers," even in the broadest sense of this term. See the Excursus, "Narrative Approaches to the Fourth Gospel," in Chapter One, pp. 30–39, above. See also F. J. Moloney, "Narrative Criticism of the Gospels," in *"A Hard Saying,"* 85–105.

Second, most scholars posit the contributions of both an evangelist and a redactor. To complicate matters, a few attribute so much activity to the redactor that he becomes the main composing agent. That is not the majority view, and so our concern here is the author in the sense of the principal writer, i.e., the evangelist. In this view, the redactor has made additions of material not included by the evangelist but has not changed radically the theological view of the evangelist. Practically no one would theorize that the redactor was the BD if the evangelist was not, and so we can specify further the questions at the end of the last paragraph. *Was the evangelist the BD? If not, who was he?* And to avoid any confusion, I shall refer to the writer, rather than the author. The BD might be the authority behind the Johannine tradition (and in that broad sense the author of the community's tradition) without being the writer of the Gospel.

Was the Evangelist the Beloved Disciple?

THE MOST PERTINENT GOSPEL PASSAGES

Only two passages in the Gospel are devoted to the identity of the writer of the Gospel:

19:35: When one of the soldiers stabs at the side of the dead, crucified Jesus with a lance and immediately blood and water flow out, we are told, "This testimony has been given by an eyewitness, and his testimony is true. He is telling what he knows to be true that you too may have faith." This eyewitness is very plausibly the BD of 19:26–27; so one may interpret this text to mean that the BD is the authority behind the Johannine tradition. Yet the passage is a parenthesis, perhaps added to the evangelist's account. Therefore, we cannot be certain that the evangelist himself attributed the Gospel tradition to an eyewitness disciple.[7] But certainly at some stage of the Gospel, such an attribution was prevalent in Johannine circles.

21:24: The Gospel writer (redactor?) tells us that this disciple (the BD) is "the witness for these things; it is he who wrote these things; and his

---

7. Some have deemed it an attempt to clothe an anonymous work with the mantle of apostolic authority, but an attribution without a personal name does not seem specific enough for that purpose. In any case I would maintain that before any concession is made, the first task is to see if the attribution can be taken at face value.

testimony, we know, is true."[8] What does "he wrote these things" mean? The surface meaning of the passage is that the BD is the evangelist; he wrote the Gospel. *What brings me and others not to accept that literal meaning is the difficulty of reconciling the body of the Gospel with writing by an eyewitness of Jesus' ministry.*[9] I reject the suggestions that the redactor who wrote this misunderstood the "he is telling" of 19:34 or changed the meaning of that verse in order to give greater status to the Gospel by making the BD the evangelist.[10] Here let me list some observations about the passage made by those who do not think the BD wrote the Gospel: (1) It cannot mean that the BD wrote everything in the Gospel, for it is immediately preceded (21:22–23) by a probable indication that the BD was dead when chap. 21 was written. (2) The statement distinguishes the disciple from a "we" who are the spokespeople in ch. 21. John normally phrases comments of the narrator in the third person (e.g., 19:24b, 35), so the "we" is important. It is not like the "we" of the Prologue (1:14, 16) which is a community "we"; but an authorial "we" similar to that in 1 John 1:1–4—a group that had something to do with the composition of the work.[11] (3) "Wrote" has to be understood in a general, not a literal

---

8. "These things" might refer only to the events in ch. 21; but since this is surely a reference to the same eyewitness as in 19:35, it may be that the disciple in question is proposed as the source for the whole Gospel narrative.

9. Barrett, *John*, 125, says this conclusion must be drawn: the Gospel was drawn up, edited, and published by persons who had no personal historical contacts with Jesus, certainly not by an apostle.

10. See *John*, 1124–25, 1127–29.

11. This need not mean that a group wrote the epistle, but that the writer (the "I" of "I write" in 2:12–13) considers himself functioning as part of the "we." Quoting A. G. van Aarde and using the language of narrative criticism, Kurz, "Beloved," 103, says that the BD in 21:24 is a narrator who carries the real author's values. (*Editor's Note:* Kurz's use of narrative critical terms is again somewhat loose. See my remarks above in note 6, and the references there). Much ancient evidence does not attribute to John son of Zebedee the undivided authorship of the Gospel. Clement of Alexandria (EH 6.14.7) says that John was encouraged by his companions. The Muratorian Fragment (ca. 170) also speaks of the instigation of John's fellow disciples and bishops, and reports that John related "all things in his own name, aided by the *revision* of all." A third-century (?) Latin Preface to John found in the Codex Toletanus speaks of Papias's writing the Gospel at John's dictation. The Latin Preface to the Vulgate of

sense. For instance, it could be causative: "He brought about the writing of these things," even as in 19:19 the affirmation that Pilate "wrote" a notice and placed it on the cross means that he had a notice written and placed. This would imply that the BD and his recollections stand behind the Gospel and enabled its writing—a meaning that agrees with the import of "telling what he knows to be true" of 19:35. I judge this interpretation as possible. If another was the actual evangelist who put the Gospel into its effective dramatic shape and thus literally wrote it, this interpretation of 21:24 still preserves the essential import of making the final contribution of the BD the essential witness enshrined in the Gospel through which Jesus who has gone to God still speaks to people. In this Gospel the writing enabled by the BD has remained until Jesus comes back. But that brings us to the question whether another actually wrote the final text.

WAS THE GOSPEL WRITTEN BY AN EYEWITNESS OF JESUS' MINISTRY?

This is clearly a speculative issue, but the answer should not be falsified by pointing out that there is tradition in the Gospel that could stem from an eyewitness. That fact might tell us that the BD was an eyewitness, not necessarily that he wrote the Gospel. Let me list factors that I think make a negative answer probable, without claiming any more than that.

- Certainly the BD was not the redactor responsible for ch. 21. As I pointed out above when I discussed 21:24, the statement distinguishes the BD from a "we" who are the spokespeople in ch. 21, and previously 21:22–23 indicates that the BD was probably dead when ch. 21 was written.
- Could the "we" of "his testimony, we know, is true" in 21:24 (at the very end of the Gospel) be guarantors of more than ch. 21? Could they be guaranteeing the whole Gospel, in which case they would be distinct from the BD whose testimony we hear in 19:35 and who is mentioned elsewhere? Indeed, it seems more appropriate that oth-

---

John speaks of John's calling together his disciples in Ephesus before he died. There is a fourth-century tradition that Marcion was the scribe of John; and in the fifth-century *Acts of John* (different from Leucian *Acts*) Prochorus, a disciple of John, claims to have been the scribe to whom John dictated the Gospel at Patmos. These legends probably constitute an ancient interpretation of the "we."

ers are describing a figure in the third person as "the disciple whom Jesus loved," rather than that he is describing himself in this indirect and laudatory way.[12] I find most unpersuasive Bauckham's contention that if the author spoke of himself as "I," it would be too obtrusive of the authorial presence—the author/writer of 1 John did not think it too obtrusive to speak of himself as "I" in 2:12–14.[13]

- This idea of a "we" of authorship finds support in 1 John. A "we" appears in a guaranteeing and writing role in 1 John 1:1–4: "As we have seen and testify and we proclaim to you . . . we are writing this." The style of 1 John is remarkably like that of the Gospel; yet there is no reference to the BD in 1 John. There is a good chance that 2 and 3 John were written by the same person who wrote 1 John, and in both the sender identifies himself as "the Presbyter." It seems unlikely that this is another self-designation of the BD.
- It is generally agreed that the Synoptic Gospels were not written by eyewitnesses. When one compares material in John to roughly parallel material in the Synoptics, sometimes John seems to have older (and, at times, more historically likely) material; other times, and probably more frequently, the Synoptics have material of that quality. If John were written by an eyewitness and the Synoptics were not, one would expect more consistency in the antiquity and reliability of the Johannine tradition.[14]

The solution that seems to do the most justice to the Gospel evidence is that the BD was the eyewitness who was responsible for the basic testi-

---

12. This is not a matter simply of the third person. Kügler, *Der Jünger*, 407, speaks of a historiographical rule at this period that an author speaks of himself in the third person when he is a figure in the narrative.

13. See Bauckham, "Beloved," 44.

14. To offer an example, many think that the anointing of Jesus' feet (12:1–7) represents an amalgamation of diverse details from two independent stories, in one of which a woman anointed Jesus' head and in the other of which a sinful woman wept and her tears fell on his feet. If so, is it likely that an eyewitness who had seen what happened wrote down such a mixed account? Those scholars who think John drew on the Synoptics should have even greater reason to doubt that John was written by an eyewitness. (One of the better arguments that Matt was not written by an eyewitness is the dependence of Matt on Mark, a Gospel that even in antiquity was recognized as not having been written by an eyewitness).

mony/witness that was incorporated into the Fourth Gospel. But others were responsible for composing the written Gospel and redacting it.[15]

The Evangelist as Part of a Johannine School

A common solution today is to propose the existence of a Johannine school of tradition bearers and writers, disciples of the BD. They were not eyewitnesses themselves; but imbued with the spirit of the BD and under his guidance and encouragement, they had preached and developed his reminiscences even further, according to the needs of the community to which they ministered. Since the Gospel seems to imply that the BD lived longer than most of the other eyewitnesses, we need not suppose that the source of the historical tradition was closed off at the beginning of the continued preaching. The preachers could return to their master and share in more of his insights into the ministry of Jesus. In part, this may explain the fact that some of the Johannine stories show greater polish and development than do other stories. They so identified themselves with the BD's testimony that they proclaimed "what we have heard, what we have seen with our own eyes, what we looked at and felt with our own eyes" (1 John 1:1–4).

Let me clarify how I understand "school" in this proposal. Culpepper studied the term as it was employed for other groups in antiquity (Pythagoreans, Plato's Academy, Aristotle's Lyceum).[16] While what is envisioned for John meets some of the characteristics of those schools, we need not think of anything like formally trained disciples.[17] Culpepper

---

15. Some would find a partial parallel to the Johannine situation in the Gospel according to Mark. Ancient comments (probably oversimplified) posit that Peter was the eyewitness source of Mark's tradition. (That may be a way of remembering that behind Mark was a standard apostolic preaching for whom Peter could stand as a representative.) But the written Gospel was attributed to an evangelist, Mark, who was not an eyewitness.

16. Culpepper, *The Johannine School.*

17. Hengel's dismissal of the hypothesis of a school of writers (*Johannine,* 25, 81) in part envisions an overly formal definition where there would have been a series of heads. (*Editor's Note:* Brown makes regular reference to Hengel's *Johannine.* A more detailed and richly documented study of the same issues may be found in Hengel, *Die Johanneische Frage.* Brown acknowledges this in the bibliography, and thus I have retained Brown's references to the briefer work in English. Interested readers may

would extend the term "school" to the whole of the Johannine community. I agree that there is a communality in the Johannine notion of discipleship: every community member is a disciple, and the BD is a model for them all. Also the Gospel tradition was developed in the context of that community and in dialogue with the experiences of the community members, e.g., in contact with Samaritans, in expulsion from the synagogue(s), etc. Nevertheless, the community was not the author of the Gospel. I envision "school" in a much more restricted sense of a special group (all of them disciples of the BD) who preached to the community, helped to vocalize what their experiences meant in terms of salvifically understanding Jesus, and then committed this to writing as a guide to other believers (especially Johannine) for encountering Jesus and receiving life in his name.[18]

We do not know the names of individuals in this Johannine school;[19] they were content to see themselves in communion with each other, speaking as "we." Yet three are detectable by their work:

The evangelist. He stands out among all the other members of the school in terms of dramatic genius and profound theological insight. Already before writing, it was probably this disciple of the BD who gave shape to the stories and discourses now found in the Fourth Gospel. From the results, we would have to judge that he was a remarkably gifted thinker who

---

like to consult the larger German volume for more detail.) The positing of a Johannine school of three or four writers, all of them disciples of the BD, is no more fantastic than positing a post-Pauline school of four or five disciples (whose names are not known to us) to account for 2 Thess, Col, Eph, and the Pastorals (perhaps with a different writer for 2 Tim).

18. Somewhat similarly but more formally K. Stendahl, *The School of St. Matthew* (2nd ed.; Philadelphia: Fortress, 1968), posited a school of learned interpreters behind Matthew because of the learned way choices had been made as to which text or version of an OT passage best matched what the Gospel was describing in Jesus' words or deeds. I see no need to posit special scholarly linguistic learning in the Johannine school.

19. An exception is often made for the evangelist whom some identify as Presbyter John mentioned by Papias. The theory is that confused memory of this explains why the Gospel was attributed to John son of Zebedee, who by further confusion was identified as the BD. Since we know nothing about Presbyter John, however, that identification is of little help.

selected the parts of the tradition that would best serve to bring others to appreciate who Jesus really was, namely, the unique Son of God who had the Father's own life and could give it to all who believe. Much of that tradition had been shaped into legal form in debates with the synagogue authorities who had put community members on trial, but the evangelist turned such material into a positive teaching that gave believers reassurance, especially in terms of the rich Jewish liturgical and festal heritage from which they had now been excluded.[20] Above all, he was a stunning dramatist shaping scenes of encounter with Jesus in which various figures exemplify different faith reactions. He acknowledged his debt to the BD, the great eyewitness ("his testimony is true") who had lived and grown through much of the community experience and who served as a model in his closeness to Jesus. In fact, the evangelist's sense of authority, so evident in the Gospel, stems in part from his claim to rely on valid witness. But there was another source for the evangelist's authority. In the community's understanding, the BD had been moved and guided by the Paraclete Spirit to bear witness, and the evangelist also understood himself as the embodiment of the Paraclete's continued activity when he wrote his account of Jesus in such a way that Jesus could continue to speak to Christians long after going to the Father.

The writer of the Epistles.[21] The gospel the Johannine Christians had received from the evangelist had been misunderstood by some members of the Johannine community who did not know many of the Johannine presuppositions not included by the evangelist in his written work. The evangelist had taken for granted that Jesus was truly human and that Jesus had demanded a moral life—there had been no fights with the synagogue authorities over such issues and there was no need to emphasize

---

20. In the decades that passed from what happened in Jesus' time to the writing of the basic Johannine Gospel, tradition about Jesus was simplified, amplified, organized, dramatized, and theologically developed. Often it will not be possible to theorize responsibly how much of that was the work of the BD and how much the work of the evangelist. One can detect, however, certain skills apparent in the finished Gospel.

21. There could have been several epistolary writers if the Presbyter of 2 and 3 John was not the author of 1 John. I remind readers that in this context I use lowercase "gospel" for the writing of the evangelist, and uppercase "Gospel" to describe the completed work that has come down to us from the redactor.

them—but some who read the gospel as their only guide interpreted it to mean that Jesus' humanity was not important, nor the way he lived on earth. They thought that the only important issue was to believe that he had come from God. The epistolary writer insisted on the importance of the coming of Christ in the flesh and walking (living) as Jesus had walked. He saw himself as a presbyter or elder who knew what the message had been from the beginning. The division over the gospel was so sharp that the community had split; but since there was no rigorous authority structure in the community, the epistolary writer could only appeal to what was known from the beginning and the necessity of testing which Spirit belongs to God. This was not enough to correct the false interpreters of the Gospel and their teaching; so, as exemplified by Diotrephes in 3 John, some began to seek the possibility of exercising more authority in the churches of the community.[22]

The redactor. He completed the Gospel by adding Johannine material, some of it ancient, that had not been included by the evangelist. He so respected the work of the evangelist that he did not rearrange it but made additions at the end of sections. For instance, he did not dismantle the evangelist's original ending in 20:30–31, but appended a new chapter and concluded it with a second ending in 21:24–25. Much of the time he simply complemented the evangelist's thought, but particularly in 21:15–17 he recognized the need for human pastoral authority that divisions made urgent. Perhaps he did his work in a new area to which much of the community had moved (from the Palestine region to Ephesus?). That brings us to a discussion of locale.

The Place of Composition

THE EARLY TRADITIONS about the composition of John mention Ephesus,[23] but other candidates have emerged from examination of the internal evidence of the Gospel itself and the way it was used in antiquity. Many scholars think of a movement of the community during the period

---

22. For a fuller development of these issues, see BEJ, 69–115.

23. Irenaeus, *Adv. Haer.* 3.1.1: "John the disciple of the Lord who also had leaned upon his breast, published a Gospel during his stay at Ephesus in Asia."

of the formation of the Gospel tradition (Stage Two in my theory of composition) or between the work of the evangelist and that of the redactor. That could mean two different sites in the history of the Gospel. I am primarily concerned here with the most likely place of final composition (by the redactor). Let me first list some factors that need to be taken into account, and then consider the proposed candidates.

Since much geography is involved, a few general words need to be said. Even more than scenes in the other Gospels, scenes in John are carefully localized. Kundsin perceptively pointed out that this is not accidental, for in many instances the story takes on the coloring of the place.[24] These places are firmly rooted on the soil of Palestine. Yet, as Scobie points out, geographical information (often peculiar to John) needs to be evaluated carefully: some of it can be verified, some cannot.[25] The latter situation leaves open the possibility that the unverifiable locales may be fictive, introduced for theological or symbolic import. Where it can be verified, does such knowledge tell us about where historically Jesus (or JBap) was active? And/or does it tell us about Johannine community life, e.g., where its components came from or lived. Kundsin thought of many of the sites mentioned in John as Johannine Christian community or cult centers. And/or does it tell us about the theological interests of the evangelist, and thus help to locate the final writing of the Gospel? These possibilities need to be kept in mind in evaluating the factors listed below.

Factors That Need to Be Considered

1. The Gospel gives evidence of detailed knowledge of Jerusalem and Palestine. Indeed, John never describes Jesus going outside the confines of Palestine (contrast Mark 7:24, 31). Sites that seem to be described accurately include Sychar/Shechem and the nearby sacred mountain (Gerizim) in Samaria; the pool of Bethesda,[26] the fountain of Siloam, Solomon's portico, and Kidron in Jerusalem. There are other sites that of-

---

24. Kundsin, *Topologische,* 50.

25. Scobie, "Johannine," 77–78.

26. Some of these places are so tightly connected to the story-flow that they can scarcely have been added as decoration to a story that once lacked them.

fer problems: Bethany across the Jordan, Aenon near Salim,[27] Ephraim in the desert region. Yet Schwank points out that there is no place designation that is surely false.[28]

2. The Gospel gives evidence of knowledge of Jewish feasts, including Jerusalem ceremonies, e.g., the water and light ceremonies of the Feast of Tabernacles, and the sacrificing of lambs for Passover in the Temple.

3. Much of the action in the Gospel takes place in Jerusalem/Judea rather than in Galilee as in the Synoptics.[29]

4. The first followers of Jesus are portrayed as disciples of JBap, and there are traditions about JBap not known in other Gospels, e.g., Aenon near Salim (in Samaria?). Yet there are disciples of JBap who are envious of Jesus, so the Gospel takes care to indicate that Jesus is greater than JBap.

5. The Johannine tradition knows of the conversion of Samaritans.

6. "The Jews" are of major importance in the Gospel; the synagogue and its leaders disapprove of the followers of Jesus because they proclaim openly the divinity of Jesus. Those who confess Jesus have been expelled from the synagogue.

7. The Scripture passages used in the Gospel are most often from the Greek Bible (the LXX), including the deuterocanonical Sirach, although occasionally there is evidence of use of the Hebrew or of another Greek tradition.

8. Some basic transliterated Hebrew/Aramaic words ("Rabbi," "Messiah") are translated into Greek for the sake of the readers.

9. There are references to the Greeks (Gentiles) as if they are part of

---

27. Although these two sites are unverifiable, they are involved in JBap stories. There is good reason to think that John has some valid tradition about JBap. (*Editor's Note:* For this position, the discussion, and further bibliography, see F. J. Moloney, "The Fourth Gospel and the Jesus of History," *NTS* 46 [2000]: 45–52.) The fact that John does stop to call attention to the symbolic meaning of Siloam (a place we know existed) cautions us about assuming unmentioned geographical symbolism for such sites.

28. Schwank, "Ortskenntnisse," 439.

29. Meeks and others have argued that for John Judea is the native country of Jesus. I judge that quite wrong. See my comment on 4:44 in *John*, 187–88. Nor is it accurate to say that Judea is a place of disbelief and Galilee a place of belief. Disbelief is found in Galilee in 4:48; 6:41–42, 52; 7:3–5; belief is found in Judea in 7:31; 8:30; 11:27, 42, 45; 12:11.

Jesus' future ministry. Those among the Gentiles who reject Jesus may be part of the "world."[30]

10. There are a variety of other followers of Jesus, with some of whom there is hope of unity, but others of whom are looked on as having left Jesus because they could not accept his divine claims.

11. In 1–2 John, there are references to those who have gone out from the community and broken the *koinônia;* they did not accept the importance of Jesus come in the flesh and of a moral life ("walking as he walked"). They seem to have been moving in a Gnostic direction. There is in the Epistles and perhaps in the Gospel what many deem to be an anti-Gnostic apologetic.

12. Apostles are not mentioned in the Gospel or the Epistles; there is not much evidence of church structure (presbyters, teachers). In 3 John the author shows hostility to Diotrephes who likes first place in a church.

The question that now needs to be asked is, Which of the following suggestions best fits that evidence?[31]

Possible Candidates for Locale of Composition

Alexandria has had a certain following at least as a strong possibility (Brownlee, J. N. Sanders [for a while], Martyn). The wide circulation of John in Egypt, as attested by the papyri, is a factor here. However, caution is demanded, for a major reason why there are Egyptian papyri of any work is that the climate of Egypt was more favorable than that of the other Christian centers for the survival of papyri. The fact that Alexandria was the home of Philo, of the authors of the Hermetic Corpus, and of the Gnostic Valentinus has had some importance in the thinking of scholars who maintain that the Gospel was influenced by one or the other of those schools of thought.[32]

---

30. Martyn, "Gentile," challenges this, but see my discussion of 12:20 in *John*, 470.

31. I shall not treat those only rarely proposed. E.g., Kemper, "Zur literarischen," detects parallels with Seneca's tragedies and on that basis proposes that John was written before A.D. 66 by a Jewish writer in Rome. In my judgment the ethos of the Roman church (see BMAR) would have been quite un-Johannine, as the later opposition to the Gospel by Gaius, a Roman presbyter, suggests.

32. *Editor's Note:* See, however, the recent suggest of Frenschowski (*"ta baïa"*), that there are sufficient indications within the Gospel (especially the use of an Egyptian loanword ([*ta baïa*]) to claim that it was written in Egypt.

Antioch or Syria is another candidate, and one upheld by W. Bauer, Burney, and H. Koester. The possibility that Ignatius of Antioch draws on John is an important factor here. Whether or not there is direct literary dependence, the fact that there are similarities in Ignatius's theology to Johannine themes is enough to raise the question of whether they come from the same region. There is evidence of a tradition among Latin writers that Ignatius was a disciple of John (paraphrases by Rufinus of Eusebius, EH 3.36.1–2 [GCS 9¹.275] and by Jerome of Eusebius *Chronicle* [GCS 47.193–4]). For Syriac evidence of the same tradition in the fourth through sixth centuries, see Burney, *Aramaic,* 130. Others draw an argument from the relations between the moral teaching in 1 John and that in Matt, since the latter is generally thought to have been a Gospel from Syria. The lack of close parallels between John itself and Matthew, however, renders this argument dubious. Another argument is that the BD of John is consistently counterpoised to Peter, and Peter was an authority for the church of Antioch (as seen in Matt; also in the aftermath of the dispute with Paul in Gal 2:11–14). Still another argument is based on resemblances between John and the *Odes of Solomon,* a Syrian work. The basic document that lies behind the Pseudo-Clementine writings (which offers evidence of the continuance of disciples of JBap) and the Leucian *Acts of John* seem to have been composed in Syria. Also those who think there was Gnostic influence on Johannine origins often favor Syria because they trace Gnostic thought to that area. In general, however, whatever is valid in these arguments can be explained if some Johannine thought made its way to Syria. The evidence for Syria as the place of composition is not compelling, but recently it has attracted a large number of adherents.

Northern Transjordan has been proposed by some (Cullmann, Klauck, Reim, Wengst) as an area where the kind of Judaism witnessed at Jamnia would have direct influence. The areas of Gaulanitis, Batanea, and Trachonitis were under the control of the Jewish king Agrippa II until his death in A.D. 100 or slightly earlier. This was a region where there would have been both Jews and Gentiles (Josephus, *J. W.* 3.56–57), but Jews would have had power since Agrippa II showed respect for the Jewish Law. Gaulanitis is immediately across the Jordan, so JBap's name and following still may have been important there. Batanea was settled with pious Jews (*Ant.* 17.26) and Wengst points to a connection between the academy at Jamnia and Jews in Bathyra, a city in this area.[33] Manns, who discusses religious scholarship in the area, also points to the importance of Bathyra.[34] There is a tradition that Christians fled to Pella, just south of Gaulanitis, before the fall of Jerusalem. If Johannine Christians were part of that or an earlier exodus,[35] they could have brought with them from Judea an independent Jesus tradition marked by an accurate memory about Palestinian geography and Jewish customs. If the conflicts with the synagogue had not already taken place, they could have occurred here. The somewhat isolated character of this area would have enabled the Johannine community to develop its own peculiarities, but would there have been the contact with other Christians implied in John? Even though the evidence is not very persuasive,[36] one cannot exclude this area as a site for the final steps in the formation of the Johannine tradition and even for the written work of the evangelist. The suggestion could be combined with the theory of another site for the final redaction of the Gospel and the Epistles.

Ephesus still remains the primary contender. It is supported by the almost unanimous voice of the ancient witnesses. However, at times the witnesses are supposing that the evangelist (whom they do not distinguish from a redactor) was John the son of Zebedee whom they also assume was the "John" of Rev 1:1, 4, 9, a prophet on the island of Patmos, some sixty-five miles southwest of Ephesus. Today very few think that the Gospel and Revelation were written by same person; and although there

---

33. Wengst, *Bedrängte*, 89.

34. Manns, "Le Galilée," 56.

35. John 10:40 speaks of Jesus going back across the Jordan to the place where John had been baptizing earlier. Reim, "Nordreich," has detected an echo of the Northern Kingdom theology in John, e.g., Jacob at Bethel scene (1:47, 51); Shechem (4:5); Prophet-like-Moses emphasized over David. John 1:43 reports that Philip was from Bethsaida (in Gaulanitis), and Reim would place the community not far from there. On recent debates over the flight from Pella, see the summary of V. Balabanski, *Eschatology in the Making. Mark, Matthew and the Didache* (SNTSMS 97; Cambridge: Cambridge University Press, 1997), 101–05.

36. Hengel, *Johannine*, 115, is blunt: there is not the slightest hint in John that it was written in northern Transjordan; it is primarily interested in Jerusalem and Judea. Some would find a context here for John's use of the LXX, but others deny that Greek was spoken by Jews except in a few cities of the northern Transjordan. Reim, "Zur Lokalisierung," 73–74, who thinks John used the Aramaic Targums, points to the context of Aramaic-speaking synagogues in this area.

are parallels between the two works, they are not close enough to demand the same place of composition. John's anti-synagogue motif in the Gospel makes sense in the Ephesus region; there were major colonies of Jews in the major cities of Asia Minor; and Rev 2:9 and 3:9 attest bitter Christian anti-synagogue polemics.[37] Yet Matt 6:2; 10:17; 23:34 also attest anti-synagogue polemics, presumably in the Antioch area. More helpful is the argument that there is in the Gospel a polemic against the disciples of JBap, and the NT mentions disciples baptized with JBap's baptism at only one place outside the Palestine area, namely Ephesus (Acts 19:1–7). If there are parallels between John and the Qumran scrolls, is it an accident that Qumran parallels are most visible in Colossians and Ephesians, epistles supposedly addressed to the Ephesus region? Samaritan synagogue inscriptions have been found on the island of Delos, ca. 150 miles from Ephesus. Incipient antidocetic and anti-Gnostic polemic would also have been at home on the Ephesus scene. Cerinthus is associated with Ephesus, and Rev 2:6 mentions the Nicolaitans. Philip, one of the Twelve, who is mentioned twelve times in John, is supposed to have been buried at nearby Hierapolis.[38] Polycarp of Smyrna, also nearby, in his *Epistle to the Philippians* 7:1 (140 or earlier) is the first witness to show knowledge of 1 John.[39] A variety of Christians would have been present in the Ephesus area, stemming from Paul and Apollos (Acts 18:24–28), and some would have been opposed to others whom they regarded as false teachers (20:29–30).[40] The post-Pauline tradition attests to a presbyteral structure there (1 Tim 1:3; 3:1–6; also Acts 20:17), even as Ignatius (*Eph.* 4:1) attests to the development of the pattern of one bishop. Thus Johannine

---

37. Some argue that Ephesus is an implausible site for the writing of John because the promulgation of the *Birkat ha-mînîm* at Jamnia would have taken a long time to be put into effect at such a distant place. However, as we have seen, that *Birkat* may have had nothing to do with John.

38. EH 3.31.3—although that tradition may confuse the apostle Philip with Philip the evangelist, one of the Hellenists (Acts 6:5; 8:5; 21:8).

39. Yet his failure to cite John is a problem, as is the failure of Ignatius in his *Ephesians*. There are echoes of symbolism used by John, but no clear indication of knowledge of the Gospel.

40. H. Koester, "Ephesos," and R. Schnackenburg, "Ephesus," relate the long history of Christianity at Ephesus, drawing on Acts; Gal, Phil, Phlm, 1 Cor (from Ephesus), later 1–2 Timothy; Ephesians (?); Rev 2:1–7; Ignatius, *Ephesians*. Koester would add Rom 16 which he thinks, wrongly in my judgment, was directed to Ephesus.

Christians who had not developed this structure might be forced to decide about which pattern of shepherding was the most effective against error.

The question of the exact locale of the Gospel's final writing is not extremely important, for the Gospel's appeal to believers in 20:30–31 transcends place and perhaps even time.[41] Yet in my judgment the Ephesus region fits the internal evidence of John best of all the proposals, and is the only site that has ancient attestation. If one looks at the numbered factors above, one could trace Johannine beginnings visible in 1, 2, and part of 3 during the ministry of Jesus to Jerusalem and Judea;[42] an important portion of the formation of the Johannine tradition (Stage Two) visible in 3 (partially), 4, 5, 6, 7, 8 (partially) to a Greek-speaking area near Palestine,[43] and final redaction (second part of Stage Three) to Ephesus. It makes the best sense when it is combined with an earlier stage of formation/composition in a Greek-speaking area in or near Palestine from which a major part of the Johannine community was driven out or moved to Ephesus.

The Date of the Written Gospel

IT SHOULD BE STRESSED that here I am not concerned with Stages One and Two of Gospel formation, involving the shaping of the tradition behind the written Gospel, but with Stage Three, the work of the evangelist and the redactor.[44] Although I have suggested an interval between the contribution of those two figures, my primary concern is dating the final redacted Gospel, including ch. 21. From that Stage (Three B) of formation comes the only form of the Gospel we have; all that preceded it is hypothetical.

---

41. The locale colors elements in the Gospel's presentation (lack of emphasis on structure, equality of disciples) but not its goal of relating people to Jesus.

42. See above, Chapter Two, pp. 64–66.

43. Some would also place the writing by the evangelist (first part of Stage Three) there; others would place it at Ephesus with the redaction. For me, that is an insoluble issue.

44. See above, Chapter Two, pp. 79–86.

The Latest Plausible Date

The range for the dating of John has been greatly narrowed in the last thirty years. Most scholars today regard as impossibly high the dates once suggested by H. Delafosse (A.D. 170) and A. Loisy (150–160—his opinion in 1936), B. W. Bacon (150), and E. Hirsch (140).[45] The general opinion fixes 100–110 as the latest plausible date for the written composition of John. Let us discuss some of the factors that have helped to determine this *terminus ante quem.*

The classic argument used to support a very late dating for John was the development of theology. F. C. Baur put the Synoptics, Paul, and John into the framework of Hegelian thesis, antithesis, and synthesis, with John representing a period that had gone far beyond Pauline theology. Although Baur still has his admirers (e.g., Mary Andrews), the theory of linear development of NT theology has been successfully refuted. If we remember that Paul's writings antedated the Synoptic Gospels, a developed Christology becomes a precarious chronometer, as Goodenough has pointed out. The view that Johannine sacramentalism, e.g., 6:51–58, is too developed to have been formulated in the first century reflects antiquated ideas about the origins of sacramental thought in the church. Another example of the argument from the development of theology was the claim that the Fourth Gospel must be late because it is by the same author as the Johannine Epistles, and the latter are late because they reflect church presbyteral organization. However, the common authorship of the Gospel and the Epistles is widely called into doubt, and it is far from certain that "the Presbyter" of 2 John 1 and 3 John 1 refers to a presbyter as envisioned in Titus and 1 Tim. Thus, it may be said that, while most scholars still think of John as the latest of the four Gospels, it is very difficult to fix the date of the Gospel on the basis of a theory of theological development. There is nothing in the theology of John that would clearly rule out final composition in the first century.

Another argument used to demonstrate the necessity of dating John in the late second century was the claim that there is no evidence of the use of John by early second-century writers. It is quite clear that in the last part of the 2nd century, ca. 170 and later, the Fourth Gospel was known

---

45. Yet as late as 1992, W. Schmithals was proposing 160–180.

to Tatian, Melito of Sardis, Theophilus of Antioch, Irenaeus, and others.[46] There is evidence that it was known somewhat earlier to the Montanists, in the Quartodeciman discussions (celebrating Easter on the feast of Passover), and among the Gnostics.[47] As for the period before 150, on the one hand, a close examination of the earlier writers has led Sanders, Barrett, and Poffet to maintain that there is no satisfactory proof for their use of the Gospel. On the other hand, Braun affirms that John was accepted in orthodox circles in Egypt, Rome, Syria, and Asia Minor from the early years of the second century. He points to Ignatius of Antioch, ca. 110, even though Ignatius does not cite the Gospel *ad litteram*. Maurer's full-scale treatment of Ignatius comes to the same conclusion, but that is still a minority view.[48] Tarelli and Boismard believe that Clement of Rome, A.D. 96, used the Fourth Gospel, but this is very difficult to establish. The evidence at most seems to show that Clement had a knowledge of theological thought and vocabulary similar to that found in John. Thus, on the issue of the use of John before A.D. 150 there remains much difference of opinion. An objective evaluation would seem to indicate that on the one hand the argument for the late dating of John because the Gospel was not used in the early second century has lost whatever probative

---

46. Dodd, Romanides, and Braun agree that Justin Martyr, ca. 160, knew the Fourth Gospel, but Strecker, "Eine Evangelienharmonie," 307, remains uncertain. Although they agree that Justin drew on John, Dodd and Pryor doubt that he knew the Gospel was by an apostle, while Davey thinks he did.

47. Beyond differentiating between a Gnostic use of John and a Gnostic origin of John, we would now recognize that the origins of Gnosticism are too complex to be dated precisely. Most of the Gnostic treatises found at Nag Hammadi stand at a much greater distance from the primitive gospel message than does John. See Chapter Two, pp. 40–42. As for noncanonical evidence, there is debate whether the mid-second-century (?) Jewish-Christian author of the source of Pseudo-Clementine *Recognitions* drew on John or both drew independently on similar tradition (Martyn, "Clementine"). Similarly Charlesworth/Culpepper, "Odes," 320, and Hengel, *Johannine*, 143–44, disagree whether the undisputed parallels between the *Odes of Solomon* and John stem from independent origin or John's dependence on *Odes*.

48. *JT*, 1: *Jean le Théologien et son Évangile dans l'Église ancienne*. Suggested Ignatian echoes of John: *Ephesians* 5:2, "the bread of God" = John 6:33; *Romans* 7:2, "water living and speaking in me, saying from within to me" = John 4:10; 7:38; *Philadelphians* 9:1, "the gate of the Father" = John 10:7.

force it may have had. On the other hand, there is no conclusive argument for a precise dating of the Gospel drawn from the supposed use of it by Clement or by Ignatius. Even if Ignatius did know Johannine tradition, how can we be sure that his knowledge derived from the Gospel itself rather than from a pre-Gospel stage of composition or tradition John shared with others?

The thesis that John was dependent on the Synoptic Gospels has favored a late dating, especially if Matthew and Luke are dated in the 80s. No other Christian author indisputably knew all three Synoptics in the first century. Yet this dependency is marginally not the majority opinion among scholars.[49] The opposite view which posits an independent tradition behind John tends to lower the dating of the Fourth Gospel. If there is in John a correct tradition of Palestinian places, situations, and customs, it seems logical to maintain that the tradition took shape before the destruction of 70 or, at least, shortly after 70 when there was still a witness who could remember the Palestinian scene as it was.[50] It is unlikely that one could return to Palestine in the 80s and compose such a tradition about Jesus on the basis of untapped local memories, for the Roman ravaging of the land and the exile of the Christian community in the 60s constituted a formidable barrier to the continuity of tradition. Accordingly, the subsequent stages of Gospel composition cannot be prolonged much beyond 100—such a tradition would not have survived far into the second century before taking final written form.

The most conclusive argument against the late dating of John has been the discovery of several second-century papyri texts of John. In 1935 C. H. Roberts published Rylands Papyrus 457 (p^{52}), an Egyptian codex fragment of John 18:31–33, 37–38. The dating of this papyrus to 135–50 has been widely accepted.[51] More recently, two substantial late second-

---

49. See above, Chapter Three, pp. 94–104.

50. Thomas, "Fourth Gospel," argues that John is concerned with many issues that J. Neusner assigns to pre-90 Judaism.

51. K. and B. Aland, *The Text of the New Testament. An Introduction to the Critical Editions and to the Theory and Practice of Modern Textual Criticism* (Grand Rapids: Eerdmans, 1987), 99, date the papyrus ca. 125. It must be kept in mind that a date assigned to papyri usually involves an approximation of fifty years, twenty-five on either side.

century or early third-century (175–225) witnesses to the Fourth Gospel have been published as Bodmer Papyri II and XV (P⁶⁶, P⁷⁵).[52] Another Egyptian witness to John is Papyrus Egerton 2, a composite work from ca. 150 which some think draws on both John and the Synoptics. Similar date and provenance may be assigned to *The Secret Gospel of Mark* that seems to incorporate into Mark a passage influenced by John. It is significant that Egerton 2 and *Secret Mark* and Tatian's *Diatessaron* (harmony of the four Gospels, ca. 175) give to John an equal status with the Synoptic Gospels. That is not likely if John had just been composed.

Thus, John circulated in many copies in Egypt in the period 140–200. The theory that John was composed in Egypt has had little support. If, as is generally supposed, it was composed in Asia Minor (or Syria) we must allow time for it to have reached Egypt and to have passed into common circulation there. Moreover, the Bodmer Papyri reflect partially different textual traditions of the Gospel, that is, P⁶⁶ is close to the text we later find in Codex Sinaiticus, while P⁷⁵ is almost the same as the text of Codex Vaticanus. The development of such variation must have required time.

To sum up, the positive arguments seem to point to 100–110 as the latest plausible date for the writing of the Gospel.[53]

The Earliest Plausible Date

In some ways the *terminus post quem* is more difficult to establish than the *terminus ante quem*. Again I shall mention the factors that bear on this question, with the reminder that the primary concern is the final written form of the Gospel.

In discussions in several chapters above, I pointed out that certain aspects of the tradition behind the Fourth Gospel were most likely formed before 70, and that several decades probably elapsed between the forma-

---

52. P⁹⁰ is dated to the second century and contains 18:36–19:1; 19:2–7. Ironically John, which is normally dated the last of the canonical Gospels to be completed, is represented on twenty-three of about one hundred papyri which are in general the oldest preserved NT mss. (second through eighth centuries). Hengel, *Johannine*, 6, says that of the roughly twenty Gospel papyri of the time before the early 300s, John comes first with eleven.

53. Barrett, *John* 128, thinks of 140 as an extreme limit, with 100 "probably very near the truth."

tion of this tradition (Stage Two) and the final redaction of the Gospel (end of Stage Three). The traditions that underlie the Synoptic Gospels are usually dated to the period between 40 and 60. Some would wish to date the tradition underlying John later; but, as I have insisted, no overall judgment can be passed that the basic core of pre-Johannine tradition is more developed than pre-Synoptic tradition. In stories and sayings shared by the two traditions, a judgment has to be made in each instance, and sometimes that judgment favors the antiquity of John. Thus, I would be willing to assign the same date to the tradition behind John that is assigned to the Synoptic sources, and to date Stage Two of the composition of the Gospel to the period before 70.[54]

Nevertheless, even with the Synoptic Gospels, there was a lapse of time between the formation of the collections of tradition behind the Gospels and the actual writing of the Gospels. For instance, Matthew and Luke are often dated between 75 and 90. According to my hypothesis that there was both an evangelist and the redactor, I think it possible that the Johannine *evangelist* composed the body of the Fourth Gospel ca. 90,[55] thus toward the end of the period assigned for Matthew and Luke.

I have advised against recklessly fixing the date of NT works on the basis of the comparative development of their theologies. Yet, when confined to a single form of literature, this method has a certain validity. If one compares the four Gospels in order to decide in general which is the most primitive and which the most developed, I believe on the whole that the precritical judgment that John is the most theologically developed and the latest of the Gospels is essentially sound. In my opinion, Matthew is the latest of the Synoptic Gospels and offers John the most rivalry in theological development.[56]

---

54. In my judgment, many authors who argue for a pre-70 date for the written Gospel offer a number of arguments that prove only the existence of Johannine tradition before 70 (see Turner, "Date").

55. Although I think it possible that the evangelist reedited his gospel, I have acknowledged my inability to detect what might belong to the first edition and what to the second edition. Similarly it would be useless for me to speculate about the time interval between the two editions.

56. *Editor's Note:* This is a surprising statement. Contemporary Gospel study highlights the theological originality of all three Synoptic Gospels, including the most primitive, Mark.

However, others, for example, Goodenough, have used comparative theology to argue for a very early date for John. For instance, John does not report the institution of the eucharist at the Last Supper, and therefore it is claimed that John represents a period before the Pauline account of the institution came to dominance. (The assumption that the account of the institution stems from Paul and not from the earliest tradition is highly questionable.) This fails to recognize that John 6:51–58 may well enshrine the *adapted* Johannine account of the institution, moved here from the account of the Last Supper. Another argument from silence is that John, like Mark and Paul, is ignorant of Jesus' birth at Bethlehem,[57] and so is earlier than Matthew or Luke. Beyond the likelihood that some Christian areas did not know the tradition of birth at Bethlehem well into the second century, John's interest in what preceded the baptism of Jesus did not concern the human origins of Jesus but his preexistence. If the final Johannine writer chose to preface the Gospel with a community hymn to Jesus as the Word, this does not mean that he was ignorant of all infancy information. Quite plausibly, he is simply reflecting the local usage in Asia Minor where people sang "hymns to Christ as to a God," while Matt and Luke are reflecting the mentality of Palestine where popular traditions of the birth of Jesus were preserved. Cribbs, "Reassessment," draws attention to parallels with Mark (frequency of the personal name "Jesus"; addressing Jesus as "rabbi") to argue for dating John to the late 50s or early 60s; but such usage at most dates the formative stage of the tradition, not the final writing. The same may be said for the heavy OT and Jewish influence apparent in John to which Cribbs appeals.[58]

The argument used by J. A. T. Robinson to date virtually the whole NT early, the absence of a clear reference to the destruction of Jerusalem, is less applicable to a Gospel than to the other writings, for the evangelist is not grossly anachronistic in what he places on Jesus' lips. In judging the attempts to argue for an early date from comparative theology, I find no

---

57. However, there is at least a possibility that in John 7:42 the observation about Jesus' birth is left unanswered, not because of the ignorance of the evangelist, but as an instance of Johannine irony, an irony that implies that the evangelist did know the true story of the birth of Jesus.

58. See Chapter Four, pp. 133–44.

theology in John that would demand a date before 70 for the final *written* form of the Gospel.[59]

In the post-70 period, many have found a reasonably precise indication for the *terminus post quem* for the dating of John in the theme of excommunication from the synagogues (9:22; 12:42; 16:20) which, as we have seen, plays an important role in the Gospel.[60] They have related it to the formulation of the twelfth blessing or benediction in the *Shemoneh 'Esreh* (Eighteen Benedictions) which involves a curse on deviants, *Birkat ha-mînim*. It has been contended that the expansion of the benediction to specify Christians was the work of Samuel the Small in the time of Rabban Gamaliel II (the Younger) ca. A.D. 85.[61] However, the dating is now being called into doubt, as well as the idea that it functioned as a universal Jewish decree against Christians. More likely, local synagogues at different times in different places no longer tolerated the presence of Christians, and the specification in the *Birkat* may have come at the end of the process rather than enabling it.[62] Without appealing to that blessing, however, one may still argue that the situation in John where many of the opponents of Jesus' ministry in the Synoptic Gospels have disappeared and only the Temple authorities and the Pharisees are specifically mentioned fits well into the 80s with the emergence of Rabbinic Judaism at Jamnia after fall of Jerusalem.[63] Justin's *Dialogue against Trypho,* ca.

---

59. *Editor's Note:* On Robinson's thesis, see also Moloney, "The Fourth Gospel's," although my remarks on the separation between the Johannine community and the local synagogue(s) should be modified in the light of the following, and in agreement with Painter's assessment in note 63.

60. See Chapter Five, pp. 166–75.

61. *bBerakot,* 28b; Martyn, *History,* 53–62.

62. *Editor's Note:* Among many, see the important studies of R. Kimelman, "*Birkat Ha-Minim* and the Lack of Evidence for an Anti-Christian Jewish Prayer in Late Antiquity," in *Jewish and Christian Self-Definition* (ed. E. P. Sanders; 2 vols.; Philadelphia: Fortress, 1981), 2.226–44; W. Horbury, "The Benediction of the *Minim* and Early Jewish-Christian Controversy," *JTS* 33 (1982): 19–62. See the survey of the discussion in van der Horst, "The Birkat ha-minim."

63. Painter, *Quest,* 77, puts it well: "It makes no sense to defend the *birkat hamminim* hypothesis as if the understanding of Jn depends upon it. Rather the case depends on the recognition that the Johannine believers were excluded for their profession of faith, whatever the circumstances in which it occurred."

160, represents an accumulation of the Jewish-Christian polemic that had developed throughout the second century. It often seems to stand in direct continuity with the polemic against the synagogue in John, and this offers another reason for not dating the final form of John too early in the first century.

There is symbolic but relatively clear witness in 21:18–19 to the fact that Peter had died by crucifixion, an event that took place in the mid-60s. Moreover, if the BD is a historical figure, as I believe to be the case, then, seemingly at an interval after Peter's death, a long-lived eyewitness of the ministry of Jesus passed away—an eyewitness who was intimately connected with the Fourth Gospel.[64] Indeed, the tone of crisis in the chapter would seem to indicate that this disciple's death marks the end of an era in the Johannine community and the close of the period of the eyewitnesses. Once again a date much earlier than 80 makes all of this implausible, and a date in the 90s seems more likely.[65]

The basic theological problems of the Gospel, as I understand them, suggest a date after 70.[66] The realized eschatology that dominates the Gospel takes away emphasis on a parousia coming soon, as anticipated in Paul's letters. Similarly, the doctrine of the Paraclete as the continued presence of Jesus plausibly responds to the passing of the eyewitness period and the severance of the human links with Jesus of Nazareth.[67] The sacramentalism of the Gospel, aimed at rooting the sacraments in the ministry of Jesus, seems directed to an age where the relationship between church life and the historical life of Jesus has grown dim.[68]

In sum, then, I find that the span of time during which the final form of

---

64. The discussion in 21:22–23 is really intelligible only in these terms; for why would there arise a problem about this disciple's dying before the return of Jesus if the disciple were alive and healthy? The intricate attempt to reason around the more obvious interpretation of Jesus' statement is a patently desperate attempt to justify what is a fait accompli.

65. Discussion in de Jonge, "Beloved," 113. Another NT work that is concerned with this problem of the passing of the apostolic generation, namely 2 Peter (3:3–4), is generally considered by critics, Protestant and Catholic, to be one of the latest of the NT works (ca. 130).

66. See below, Chapter Seven.

67. See *John*, 1135–44.

68. See Moloney, "When Is John Talking about Sacraments?" in *"A Hard Saying,"* 109–30.

the Fourth Gospel may have been written is, at its outermost limits, A.D. 75 to 110, but the convergence of probabilities points strongly to a date between 90 and 110. In my treatment of the Johannine Epistles I suggested that the evangelist might have written his gospel ca. A.D. 90, and another Johannine writer may have written 1–2 John ca. 100, to be followed shortly by 3 John.[69] The redactor would then have completed the Johannine writing by finishing the Gospel no later than 110. Thus the period from the beginning of the developing tradition in Stage Two of Gospel composition to the end of the writing in Stage Three may have lasted as long as seven decades. (That should be remembered as a caution against dating Johannine ideas to the moment of the final writing.) The testimony given ca. 180 by Irenaeus (Eusebius, EH 3.23.1–4), our most important early witness to the Fourth Gospel, says that John, the disciple associated with the Gospel, lived on at Ephesus into the reign of Trajan (98–117). One may suspect that the identity of the author is a simplification and still think that the dating was reasonably accurate for the final Gospel.

BIBLIOGRAPHY

AUTHORSHIP

Andrews, M. E., "The Authorship and Significance of the Gospel of John," *JBL* 64 (1945): 183–92.

Boismard, M.-E., *Le martyre de Jean l'apôtre* (CahRB 35; Paris: Gabalda, 1996).

Cullmann, O. *The Johannine Circle: Its Place in Judaism, among the disciples of Jesus and in early Christianity: A Study in the Origin of the Gospel of John* (Philadelphia: Westminster, 1976).

Culpepper, R. A., *The Johannine School: An Evaluation of the Johannine School Hypothesis Based on an Investigation of the nature of Ancient Schools* (SBLDS 26; Missoula, MT: Scholars, 1975).

Eckhardt, K. A., *Der Tod des Johannes* (Berlin: De Gruyter, 1961).

Hengel, M., *The Johannine Question* (Philadelphia: Trinity, 1989).

———, *Die johanneische Frage. Ein Lösungsversuch mit einem Beitrag zur Apokalypse von Jörg Frey* (WUNT 67; Tübingen: J. C. B. Mohr [Paul Siebeck], 1993).

---

69. BEJ, 100–103.

Kügler, J., *Der Jünger, den Jesus Liebte: Literarische, theologische und historische Untersuchungen zu einer Schlüsselgestalt johanneischer Theologie und Geschichte* (Stuttgarter Biblische Beiträge 16; Stuttgart: Katholisches Bibelwerk, 1988).

Kurz, W., "The Beloved Disciple and Implied Readers," *BTB* 19 (1989): 100–107.

Nunn, H. P. V., *The Authorship of the Fourth Gospel* (Oxford: Blackwell, 1952).

Rese, M., "Das Selbstbezeugnis des Johannesevangeliums über seinen Verfasser," *ETL* 72 (1996): 75–111.

Ruckstuhl, E., "Zur Antithese Idiolekt—Sociolekt im johanneischen Schrifttum," *SNTU* 12 (1987): 141–81.

Schüssler Fiorenza, E. "The Quest for the Johannine School: The Apocalypse and the Fourth Gospel," *NTS* 23 (1976–77): 402–27.

Wenham, D., "The Enigma of the Fourth Gospel: Another Look," *Tyndale Bulletin* 48 (1997): 149–78.

PLACE

This includes treatments of the geographical knowledge exhibited in John, for that is often looked on as a key to where the tradition or the Gospel took shape.

Brownlee, W. H., "Whence the Gospel According to John," in Charlesworth, *John*, 166–94.

Díez Merino, L., " 'Galilea' en el IV Evangelio," *EstBib* 31 (1972): 247–73.

Fortna, R. T., "Theological Use of Locale in the Fourth Gospel," *ATR* Supp. 3 (1974): 58–95.

Frenschkowski, M., "*Ta baïa tôn phoinikôn* (Joh 12,13) und andere Indizien für einen ägyptischen Ursprung des Johannesevangeliums," *ZNW* 91 (2000): 212–229.

Kemper, F., "Zur literarischen Gestalt des Johannesevangeliums," *TZ* 43 (1987): 249–64.

Koester, H., "Ephesos in Early Christian Literature," in *Ephesos Metropolis of Asia* (H. Koester, ed.; Harvard Theological Studies 41; Valley Forge, PA: Trinity, 1995), 119–40.

Krieger, N., "Fiktive Orte der Johannestaufe," *ZNW* 45 (1954): 121–23.

Kundsin, K., *Topologische Überlieferungsstoffe im Johannes-Evangelium* (FRLANT 22; Göttingen: Vandenhoeck & Ruprecht, 1925).

Manns, F., "La Galilée dans le quatrième Évangile," *Antonianum* 72 (1997): 351–64.

Matsunaga, K., "The Galileans in the Fourth Gospel," *AJBI* 2 (1976): 139–58.

Meeks, W. A., "Galilee and Judea in the Fourth Gospel," *JBL* 85 (1966): 159–69.

Reim, G., "Zur Lokalisierung der johanneischen Gemeinde," *BZ* 32 (1988): 72–86.

———, "Nordreich-Südreich. Der vierte Evangelist als Vertreter christlicher Nordreichstheologie," *BZ* 36 (1992): 235–40.

Rodríguez-Ruiz, M., "El lugar de composición del cuarto Evangelio. Exposición y valoración de las diversas opiniones," *EstBib* 57 (1999): 613–41.

Sanders, J. N., "St. John on Patmos," *NTS* 9 (1962–63): 75–85.

Schnackenburg, R., "Ephesus: Entwicklung einer Gemeinde von Paulus zu Johannes," *BZ* 35 (1991): 41–64.

Schwank, B., "Ortskenntnisse im Vierten Evangelium?" *ErbAuf* 57 (1981): 427–42.

Scobie, C. H. H., "Johannine Geography," *SRSR* 11 (1982): 77–84.

Tilborg, S. van, *Reading John in Ephesus* (NovTSup 83; Leiden: E. J. Brill, 1996).

Wengst, K., *Bedrängte*, 77–96.

DATE

These sources include relevant discussions of the *Birkat ha-mînîm*.

Berger, K., *Im Anfang war Johannes: Datierung und Theologie des vierten Evangeliums* (Stuttgart: Quell, 1997).

Cribbs, F. L., "A Reassessment of the Date of Origin and the Destination of the Gospel of John," *JBL* 89 (1970): 38–55.

Goodenough, E. R., "John a Primitive Gospel," *JBL* 64 (1945): 145–82.

Grelot, P., "Problèmes critiques du IVᵉ Évangile," *RB* 94 (1987): 519–73. A response to J. A. T. Robinson's early dating.

Horst, P. W. van der, "The Birkat ha-minim in Recent Research," *ExpTim* (105 (1994–95): 363–68.

Joubert, S. J., "A Bone of Contention in Recent Scholarship: The 'Birkat ha-Minim' and the Separation of Church and Synagogue in the First Century AD," *Neotestamentica* 27 (1993): 351–63.

Kemper, F., "Zur literarische Gestalt des Johannesevangeliums," *TZ* 43 (1987): 249–64.

Moloney, F. J., "The Fourth Gospel's Presentation of Jesus as 'the Christ' and J. A. T. Robinson's Redating," *DR* 95 (1977): 239–53.

Robinson, J. A. T., *Redating the New Testament* (London: SCM, 1976), 254–311.

———, *The Priority of John* (ed. J. F. Coakley; London: SCM Press, 1985).

Thomas, J. C., "The Fourth Gospel and Rabbinic Judaism," *ZNW* 83 (1991): 159–82.

Turner, G. A., "The Date and Purpose of the Gospel of John," *BETS* 6 (1963): 82–85.

JOHN AND SECOND-CENTURY WRITERS

Bauckham, R., "Papias and Polycrates on the Origin of the Fourth Gospel," *JTS* 44 (1993): 24–69.

Bellinzoni, A. J., *The Sayings of Jesus in the Writings of Justin Martyr* (NovTSup 17; Leiden: E. J. Brill, 1967).

Boismard, M.-É., "Clement de Rome et l'Évangile de Jean," *RB* 55 (1948): 376–87.

Charlesworth, J. H., and R. A. Culpepper, "The Odes of Solomon and the Gospel of John," *CBQ* 35 (1973): 298–322. See also in Charlesworth, *John,* 107–36.

Davey, D. M., "Justin Martyr and the Fourth Gospel," *Scripture* 17 (1965): 117–22.

Dubois, J.-D., "La posterité du quatrième évangile au deuxième siècle," *LumVie* 29 (1980): 31–48.

Martyn, J. L., "Clementine Recognitions 1,33–71, Jewish Christianity and the Fourth Gospel," in *God's Christ and His People. Studies in Honour of Nils Alstrup Dahl* (J. Jervell and W. A. Meeks, eds.; Oslo: Universitets-forlaget, 1977), 265–95. Revised and reprinted in his *Gospel,* as "Persecution and Martyrdom," pp. 54–89. See also the reprint of that part of the text of the Pseudo-Clementines in "The Pseudo-Clementine Recognitions Book One, Chapters 33–71," on pp. 122–47 of *Soshel.*

Maurer, Christian, *Ignatius von Antiochien und das Johannesevangelium* (Zürich: Zwingli, 1949).

Pervo, R. I., "Johannine Trajectories in the *Acts of John,*" *Apocrypha* 3 (1992): 47–68.

Pryor, J. W., "Justin Martyr and the Fourth Gospel," *Second Century* 9 (1992): 153–69.

Reuss, J., *Johannes Kommentare aus der Griechischen Kirche* (TU 89; Berlin: Akademie Verlag, 1966).

Romanides, J. S., "Justin Martyr and the Fourth Gospel," *Greek Orthodox Theological Review* 4 (1958–59): 115–34.

Sanders, J. N., *The Fourth Gospel in the Early Church* (Cambridge: Cambridge University Press, 1943).

Smith, Jr., J. D., *Gaius and the Controversy over the Johannine Literature* (Yale University Doctoral Dissertation; Ann Arbor, MI: University Microfilms International, 1979).

Strecker, G., "Eine Evangelienharmonie bei Justin und Pseudoklemens?" *NTS* 24 (1977–78): 297–316.

Tarelli, C. C., "Clement of Rome and the Fourth Gospel," *JTS* 48 (1947): 208–9.

Wiles, M. F., *The Spiritual Gospel. The Interpretation of the Fourth Gospel in the Early Church* (Cambridge: Cambridge University Press, 1960).

7

Crucial Questions in
Johannine Theology

◆

IN THE FIRST EDITION (1955) of his great commentary on John, C. K. Barrett dared to call the fourth evangelist "perhaps the greatest theologian in all the history of the Church."[1] A quarter-century later (1978), with greater caution, in the second edition he rephrased "perhaps, after Paul."[2] Yet something may be said for the exuberance of the more youthful insight; for Paul was recognized as *ho apostolos* ("the apostle"), while it was John who was hailed as *ho theologos* ("the theologian" or more quaintly "the divine," stemming from those gracious days when theologians were called divines). This Introduction does not give scope for an exhaustive treatment of Johannine theology but a brief examination of certain disputed questions in Johannine theology adds to what has already been said concerning one's whole outlook on the purpose and composition of the Gospel.

---

1. Barrett, *St John* (1955), 114.
2. Barrett, *St John* (1978), 114.

Ecclesiology

IN THE EXCURSUS on Johannine Community history, theories of the history of that community were discussed;[3] but here there is a different concern: whether there is a theology of church in John.[4] For Bultmann, the evangelist was a converted Gnostic and one of the basic sources of the Gospel was Gnostic; therefore the Fourth Gospel cannot be expected to show a real sense of tradition, church order, salvation history, or the sacraments.[5] This approach would see the Johannine church as a collection of individuals joined by personal faith to Jesus, rather than the people of God descended from Israel (4:23). It would detect no stress in John on the organic unity of the church. Schweizer does not share Bultmann's Gnostic preoccupations, but his conclusions about Johannine ecclesiology are not very different.[6] Käsemann sees the Johannine community as a heretical group opposed to the concept of ecclesiastical life and church order in the mainstream church.[7] Similarly, those who regard the Johannine community as a sect do not tend to find a theology of church in John.[8] On the other hand, for Barrett the fourth evangelist is more aware than any other evangelist of the existence of the church.[9] Cullmann vigorously challenges Bultmann's contention that John has lost the perspective of salvation history.[10]

Methodological Considerations

The argument from silence (i.e., an argument based on significant omission) plays an important role in the minimal views of Johannine ecclesiology. A tacit principle seems to be that what John does not mention

---

3. See above Chapter Two, pp. 69–75.

4. For a discussion of approaches, see O'Grady, "Individualism," and "Johannine."

5. Bultmann, *Theology,* 2.8–9, 91.

6. See Schweizer, "Concept."

7. Käsemann, *Testimony,* 76.

8. See, for example, Meeks, "The Man from Heaven"; Petersen, *The Sociology.*

9. Barrett, *St John,* 92.

10. "L'évangile johannique et l'histoire du salut," *NTS* 11 (1964–65): 111–22. Also his *Salvation in History* (New York: Harper & Row, 1967), 268–91.

John rejects, or at least considers of minimal importance. Such a presupposition is not without its dangers.[11]

As a first example of the problematic argument from silence, I mention the claim that many ecclesial terms are not found in John. D'Aragon observes that we do not find in John descriptions of the Christian community as "church," or as "people of God," or as "body of Christ." There is no imagery of the community as a building. Other ecclesial terms occur seldom, e.g., "bride" (3:29) and "kingdom of God" (3:3, 5).[12] But how is such silence to be evaluated? The terms cited are NT ecclesial terms; but, with the exception of "kingdom of God," they are not really *Gospel* terms.[13] A tacit assumption seems to be that if John were interested in the church, John would be just as free as the Pauline Epistles in the use of later ecclesial vocabulary. However, if John was dependent on a historical or, at least, early tradition of the words of Jesus, then there were limits imposed on the vocabulary used in the Gospel. Certainly, Johannine thought represents a development and an expansion beyond what Jesus had taught during his ministry, but the format of a Gospel may have made it imperative to express this development in a way that was reasonably faithful to the vocabulary of Jesus. We cannot expect to find the evangelist placing flagrant anachronisms on the lips of Jesus—for example, to find the Johannine Jesus talking about his body that is the church. Moreover, John has extended treatments in ch. 10 of the flock of believers (including the idea that there are other sheep who are not of this fold) and in ch. 15 of the vine and the branches—imagery showing a strong concept of collectivity or community. Flock and vine are OT images for Israel, and offer reason to think that God is calling a people in Jesus Christ. Entrance to that people, however, is through faith not through natural birth, so there is a Johannine emphasis on the obligation of indi-

---

11. In querying the minimalist results of the argument from silence, I do not mean to favor the maximalist alternative: one should attribute to John's view of the church anything found in other NT ecclesiology that is not denied. That also has many dangers.

12. D'Aragon, "Le caractère."

13. How would the Synoptic Gospels fare if this criterion of ecclesiology were applied to them? In those three Gospels, the term "church" in the strict sense occurs only in Matt 16:18 (see Matt 18:17). In Mark, in only one passage (2:19–20) is there any use of the imagery of the bride/bridegroom to describe the relation of Jesus to his disciples, and Mark does not use the concept of the "people of God."

vidual belief. Those who believe will be one with one another and with Jesus and the Father (17:21, 23).[14]

The second methodological consideration about the argument from silence concerns comparisons made between John and the other Gospels. It is noted that John fails to record some of the ecclesial expressions and scenes recorded in the Synoptic Gospels. For instance, Schweizer says of John: "He does not mention either the election (Mark 3:13 ff.) or the sending forth of the disciples (Mark 6:7 ff.)."[15] As we shall see below, other scholars characterize John as nonsacramentalist because the Fourth Gospel omits the scenes pertaining to the eucharist and baptism found in the Synoptics. Yet the selection of scenes to be reported in Gospels was very much determined by the respective purpose of the evangelist, and it is not to be expected that all the Gospels would express their ecclesiology in the same way. Does John really ignore the election and sending forth of the disciples? True, John gives no list of the Twelve and has no scene by the Sea of Galilee where the disciples are called to leave their fishing and follow Jesus. But is not the scene in 1:35–50 the Johannine equivalent of the election of disciples? This election is presupposed in 6:70; 13:18; and 15:16, as is the existence of the Twelve in 6:67, 70; 20:24. A mission of the disciples is reflected in 4:38; 15:16; 17:18; 20:21, and is acted out in 21:1–11.[16] Similarly, it would not be true to state that John had no sense of a covenant with a new people of God because John failed to record the words of Jesus about the blood of the covenant (Mark 14:24). The covenant theme appears in another form in John 20:17, "I am ascending . . . to my God and your God." This saying adapts to the new Christian situation the covenant formula of Lev 26:12 and Exod 6:7: "I will be your God."

Third, at times the argument from silence can be turned around; for it may be that certain things are not mentioned in John, not because they

---

14. Also 1 John 1:3. Rossé, *Spirituality,* is an effective corrective of interpretations that neglect John's strong emphasis on community.

15. Schweizer, "Concept," 237.

16. Although I think ch. 21 was added to the Gospel by a later hand, I do not think that the fishing scene of 21:1–11 (which implies an evangelizing ministry by the disciples) was a later outlook in the Johannine tradition. Rather, the later outlook is inherent in John 21:15–17 where Simon Peter, previously a missionary, is assigned pastoral care—plausibly the community acceptance of structured shepherding.

did not exist in Johannine community life but because the evangelist would modify elements in them. If the Gospel was written to show the Christians that their life in the church was rooted in Jesus' own ministry, then, quite logically, we may suspect that the evangelist was presupposing the existence of ecclesiastical community. If the evangelist stressed the individual's union with Jesus, this need not have been because the evangelist was opposed to the church and the sacraments, but perhaps because he was opposed to the formalism that is the inevitable danger of established institutions and practices. There is no way of knowing with certitude whether there were figures called apostles, prophets, and teachers in the Johannine community.[17] But by constantly stressing disciples (78 times) John shows that priority is not to be placed on roles (or offices) toward or over others but on relationship to Jesus and receiving life from him. There is no overt attack or disparagement of ecclesiastical institutions in John (with the possible exception of 10:1 if that is aimed at Christian shepherds);[18] his ecclesiology is marked by what he emphasizes, and from that one may deduce a stress on meaningfulness. His may not have been a disdain of the church institution but a fear that the church would gradually come to be thought of as an entity independent of Jesus. Thus, one must be extremely careful in inferring the evangelist's motive or adversarial attitude from his silence.

In particular, Bultmann's approach to the Gospel leaves itself open to methodological objections on the question of ecclesiology (and of the sacraments). Bultmann recognizes that in the Gospel as it now stands there are clear references to the sacraments and to salvation history, but he regards these as the additions of the Ecclesiastical Redactor who imposed

---

17. The leading triad in 1 Cor 13:28. John never mentions apostles. Is that because by the time the Gospel was written "apostles" had taken on the aura of foundational figures supporting structured authority? (In their place John had the Beloved *Disciple*.) In 1 John the author speaks of false prophets (4:1) and tells believers, "You have no need for anyone to teach you" (2:27).

18. *Editor's Note:* There are very few contemporary Johannine scholars today who would take that position. John 10:1 is widely regarded as intimately linked to 9:39–41, and thus, 10:1 (and 10:1–6) is aimed at "the Pharisees" of v. 40. See Moloney, *John,* 290–91, 308–309, and especially J. Beutler and R. T. Fortna, eds., *The Shepherd Discourse of John 10 and Its Context* (SNTSMS 67; Cambridge: Cambridge University Press, 1991). See especially pp. 6–17 for the contribution by U. Busse, "Open Questions on John 10."

ecclesiology on the original Gospel. Sometimes there are solid reasons drawn from literary criticism for attributing such passages to the final redaction of the Gospel; but in other instances passages (e.g., 19:34) are often attributed to the redactor precisely because they are sacramental—a circular reasoning. Moreover, as I have insisted, the concept of the redactor as one who corrects the evangelist's theology is far from proved. If we think of the redactor as a disciple of the BD and thus a fellow disciple of the evangelist, then the ecclesiology of scenes added by the redactor may be a clarification and amplification of the evangelist's own outlook or an adaptation to a new situation.

This leads to a final methodological observation. Just as Acts is used along with the Gospel of Luke in a study of Lucan theology, so also must the other works of the Johannine school, the Epistles, be consulted before generalizing about the Johannine view of the church.[19] Feuillet and Schnackenburg have done this in their studies; and their interpretation of Johannine ecclesiology is, in my opinion, more satisfactory than that of scholars who seem to posit a necessary opposition among these Johannine works, even though they have so much in common by way of style, ideology, and terminology. The limitations imposed on a Gospel by its format and purpose warn us that a Gospel will necessarily be an incomplete index to its author's thoughts. Quite often the Johannine Epistles, especially 1 John with its stress on what was from the beginning, should be able to help us fill in points in Johannine theology on which the Gospel has been silent. Recourse to other Johannine works is in many instances far less risky than speculative reconstructions based on what the evangelist did *not* say.

---

19. In my first edition, I appealed also to Revelation. Subsequent reflection has convinced me that this is methodologically unwise. The detectable relationships between John and Revelation are limited, and one should not extend them to other areas for which we have no proof.

Disputed Points in Johannine Ecclesiology [20]

THE QUESTION OF CHURCH/COMMUNITY.

Does the stress in John on an individual relationship with Jesus obviate a concept of community that is essential to ecclesiology? For instance, it has been claimed that the fourth evangelist took the vineyard, the OT symbol for the nation of Israel, and adapted it to the figure of a vine representing Jesus and branches representing believers who remain in Jesus. Not collectivity but dependence on Jesus is now the thrust of the symbol. However, the symbolism of the vine and the branches is not that simple. The symbol does not lose its collectivity when it is employed to stress individual relationship to Jesus. The LXX in Ps 80:14–15 had already identified the vine with the "son of man," so the identification of the vine as Jesus may have had roots in an older tradition.[21] The fact that in Dan 7:13 a "son of man" is a human figure representing the whole of God's people warns us against too facilely cataloging the Johannine use of the vine and the branches as exclusively individualistic. A symbol need not lose its collective force when it is expanded to stress individual relationship to Jesus.

Above I have stressed that there was no sharp distinction between community and personal union with Jesus. The foundation of community is the response of individuals to Jesus as the revealer of God and the unique way to God, but those individuals form a unity. It is interesting that at Qumran, for instance, the word *yahad*, "oneness," which is the

---

20. The question of whether or not John has lost the perspective of salvation history will be treated under eschatology. But I may say here that there should be some qualification of the claim made by Schweizer, "Concept," 240, that John does not picture the church as a people based on an act of God in history. For John, no Christian life is possible without the death, resurrection, and ascension of Jesus; for that salvific act of God in history is the source of the Spirit, which is the principle of the Christian life. John may not use the term "people" to describe those whose Christian status is dependent on this act of God; but John 1:11 does speak of a new "his own" replacing the old "his own," i.e., God's people who preceded Jesus. There are also other Johannine ways of indicating unity among believers. *Editor's Note:* I would further claim that this use of *ta idia* within the context of the death of Jesus, "the hour" and the handing over of Mother to Disciples and vice versa in 19:25b–27, continues the Johannine theology of the foundation of a new community. See Moloney, *John,* 503–04.

21. See *John,* 669–74.

name for the community, emphasizes the unity of the members. A very important factor in this unity was the acceptance of a particular interpretation of the Law. Mutatis mutandis, the same idea would be applicable to the Christian community and the adherence of the members to Jesus. One of the lessons of the symbol of the vine and the branches is that if one is to remain as a branch on the vine, one must remain in the love of Jesus (15:9). Yet this love must be expressed in love for one's fellow believer (15:12). No Gospel stresses more than John that Christian love is a love of fellow disciples, and thus a love within the Christian community. There is strong emphasis in 17:22–23 that those who are given by the Father to Jesus must be brought to completion as one.

Nor is the vine the only metaphor in the Gospel relevant to the Johannine concept of community.[22] There is also the imagery of the flock and the sheepfold in ch. 10. Some have objected that in this parable "fold" or "sheep herd" is mentioned only once (10:16). But running throughout is the imagery of the flock that is also symbolic of community, and again oneness with the shepherd is stressed. It is true that in the Fourth Gospel there is no stress on blood continuity with Israel, a problem that bothered Paul. For John the true Israelite is Nathanael (1:47) who believes in Jesus. True Israelites are not born of carnal lineage (1:13) but begotten of water and Spirit (3:5); they are children of God because they are believers (1:12). But thereby they have the obligation to attract others who will believe.[23] These believers are knit into community through faith in Jesus and their love for one another, and they are gathered from the whole world into one (11:52). In the larger body of Johannine literature, 1 John 2:19 describes Antichrists as those who have cut themselves off from the community.[24]

---

22. One may debate whether the comparisons whereby Jesus is the new representative of God going beyond Moses (1:17; 5:45–46; 6:31–32; 7:22–23) imply that the Johannine Jesus would look on those who believe in him as the *people* of God (11:51–52).

23. See the pattern of drawing others in 1:40–49; also 4:39–42; 17:20; symbolism of 21:9–11; and the missionary brothers who are "coworkers with the truth" in 3 John 5–8.

24. Rev 19:6–8 and 21:2 use the imagery of the bride of Christ (also John 3:29); and Rev 21:3 refers to the people of God, implicitly presenting the Christians as the heirs to Israel of old. *Editor's Note:* See my later reservations on Brown's inconsistency regarding the use of Revelation for the explanation of matters concerning the Fourth Gospel. This footnote, left out of respect for the original author, indicates the unfinished nature of the manuscript.

THE QUESTION OF CHURCH ORDER

The Johannine figure of the vine is often contrasted with the Pauline ecclesial imagery of the body. While both figures portray Jesus as the source of life, there is no emphasis in John's symbol on the different functions of the various members of the community. For John what is important is that all members are united to Jesus, and there is no emphasis that some branches are the channels through which life passes from Jesus to others. By an argument from silence, this might imply that there is no sense of church order in John.[25] My cautions above about the argument from silence apply here. From the symbolism of the vine and the branches, all that one may conclude is that the evangelist wishes to stress union with Jesus. Such an emphasis fits the purpose of the Gospel.

Better information comes from combining John and the Johannine Epistles. If one thinks of figures titled apostles, prophets, and teachers (1 Cor 12:29; Acts 13:1; Eph 3:5), one has good evidence that this was not the the structure in the Johannine church. None of these Johannine writings refers to people titled apostles (although the Twelve are known); and the one use of *apostolos* (13:16) reflects on the function of being sent as a messenger, applicable to any disciple. The only prophets mentioned are false prophets (1 John 4:1), and 1 John 2:27 states, "You have no need for anyone to teach you." Authority was centered in Jesus (John 13:14) and his Paraclete replacement (16:13). However, that Paraclete has produced a "Johannine School" of writers and witness-bearers (15:26–27; 21:24; 1 John 1:2–4) that had an authoritative role in transmitting the tradition. The Presbyter of 2–3 John does not hesitate to give directives, even if he is not always listened to (3 John 9). If more formal structure developed late in Johannine community history, the redactor of John 21:15–17 found a way to combine it successfully with Johannine ideals.

THE QUESTION OF THE KINGDOM OF GOD

The omission in John of the formula *basileia tou theou*, "kingdom of God [or of heaven]," except for 3:3, 5, is a difficult problem, although not so formidable an obstacle to Johannine ecclesiology as it might first seem.

---

25. Schweizer, "Concept," 237, says of the Johannine picture of the church: "It has no priests or officials. There is no longer any diversity of spiritual gifts. . . . There is no church order at all."

The Synoptic emphasis on the *basileia* making itself felt in Jesus' activity seems to have become in John an emphasis on Jesus who is *basileus* ("king") and who reigns. John refers to Jesus as king fifteen times, almost double the number of times that this reference occurs in any of the other Gospels. Moreover, the parables that the Synoptics associate with the *basileia* seem to give way in John to figurative speech centered about the person of Jesus. If the Synoptic *basileia* is like leaven working in a mass of dough, the Johannine Jesus is the bread of life. If there is a Synoptic parable of the shepherd and the lost sheep, the Johannine Jesus is the model shepherd. If the Synoptics record a parable where the *basileia* is like the vineyard that shall be handed over to others (Matt 21:43), the Johannine Jesus is the vine.

This change of emphasis means that in John there is less apparent reference to collectivity than there is in the Synoptic concept of *basileia*. But we must not exaggerate. If the Johannine Jesus is "the King of Israel" (1:49), he has an Israel of believers to rule over; if Jesus is the shepherd, he has a flock that has to be gathered; if Jesus is the vine, there are branches on the vine. Moreover, in comparing the symbolism of the Synoptics and of John on this point, we must have a precise understanding of what is meant in the Synoptic Gospels by *basileia tou theou*. Most often the primary stress in this phrase is on God's reign or rule, and not on realm or kingdom—something active is meant, not something static; not a place or institution, but the exercise of God's power over people's lives. Thus, the *basileia tou theou* is not simply the church, and the rarity of the phrase in John does not necessarily reflect a lack of appreciation for community. In stressing the reign/role of Jesus as *basileus* and in applying the parabolic language to Jesus himself (rather than to "the reign of God"), John brings out more clearly than do the Synoptics the role of Jesus in the *basileia tou theou*. Such a clarification is quite understandable in terms of the purpose of the Gospel.

Sacramentalism

IN MY ORIGINAL COMMENTARY, I listed a group of Johannine scholars, both Protestant (Cullmann, Corell) and Roman Catholic (Bouyer, Vawter, Niewalda, Stanley), who find many references to the sacraments in John. In general, the British commentaries by Hoskyns, Lightfoot, and

Barrett also showed themselves decidedly favorable to Johannine sacramentalism.[26] One would now have to add Becker, Boismard-Lamouille, Lindars, Schnackenburg, Schneider, Schulz, Moloney, to those favorable to the recognition of sacraments. In general, John's theology of a divine Word who comes from a heavenly world and expresses himself in the language of this world is a highly sacramental approach if sacraments are understood as external signs that give God's grace. Beyond that these scholars tend to see symbolic references to baptism in Johannine passages that mention water, and to the eucharist in Johannine passages dealing with meals, bread, wine, and vine.[27] An even broader range of sacramental reference has been proposed by Roman Catholic writers, for example, to matrimony at Cana, and to anointing of the sick in the scene of the anointing of the feet (12:1–8). In 1962, I listed twenty-five proposed sacramental references in John![28] Almost all these proposed sacramental references are by way of symbolism. Why the evangelist presented the sacraments through symbolism has been explained through this principle: the recognition that OT prophecy had a fulfillment in the NT created a Christian sensitivity to typology; therefore, it was intelligible to present Jesus' words and actions as prophetic types of the church's sacraments. To that, one may add the fact that John treats Jesus' miracles as "signs" through which one must see Jesus' christological import—an outlook that would facilitate further representative possibilities as signs pointing to sacraments. Cullmann stresses that baptism and the eucharist were familiar to the early Christian communities, and that therefore symbolic references to them would be easily recognized. By associating baptism and the eucharist with Jesus' own words and actions, John would be once more trying to show the roots of church life in Jesus himself.

Another group of Johannine scholars sees no references to the sacraments in John. For some of these, the original Gospel was even antisacramental. Among those who take a minimal view of Johannine

---

26. Barrett, *St John*, 82, comments: ". . . there is more sacramental teaching in John than in the other Gospels."

27. For an example of this type of approach, see the interesting study of X. Léon-Dufour, "Towards a Symbolic Reading of the Fourth Gospel," *NTS* 27 (1980–81): 439–56.

28. Brown, "Sacramentary," 205–6.

sacramentality one may list Bultmann, Haenchen, Lohse, and Schweizer,[29] noting however that their views vary widely. In general, they base their case on the lack of overt references to baptism and the eucharist in John which narrates neither the eucharistic action of Jesus at the Last Supper nor an explicit baptismal command like Matt 28:19. Moreover, some would insist that in centering salvation on personal acceptance of Jesus as the one sent by God, John has created a theological atmosphere that would obviate material intermediaries like the sacraments. The emphasis in John is on word, not on sacrament. We have already seen Bultmann's attribution to the Ecclesiastical Redactor of what he considers the three clear sacramental references in the Gospel. As for the symbolic references to the sacraments, these scholars of the nonsacramentalist school would simply regard the uncovering of much of this symbolism as eisegesis.

How is one to judge such radically opposed views? Sacramentalism is no longer the most divisive point of Johannine theology. I would now judge that most scholars recognize some form of sacramentalism. Let me begin with the more explicit Johannine references to the sacraments, those relegated by Bultmann to the Ecclesiastical Redactor. There are good reasons for thinking that 6:51–58 were added to ch. 6.[30] By not considering the literary arguments for such a view, some sacramentalist interpreters of John have weakened their case. But even if a more explicit reference to a sacrament, like 6:51–58, is an addition, was this addition designed to correct the evangelist's theology or to make his thought more explicit? H. Koester is perfectly correct, for instance, in insisting that there was already a cultic and sacramental element present in ch. 6, even without vv. 51–58.[31] Therefore, the recognition that some of the explicit

---

29. In 1956, Bornkamm was attributing 6:51c–58 to an ecclesiastical redactor; in 1971 he considered it an integral part of ch. 6.

30. See *John*, 281–94.

31. Koester, "Geschichte," 62–63. *Editor's Note:* It is surprising that Brown, who acknowledges this study elsewhere, makes no mention of Peder Borgen's groundbreaking study, *Bread from Heaven*. Borgen has shown that 6:51–58 are an integral part of a typical homiletic midrash, based on the (difficult) citation from the OT in 6:31: "He gave them bread from heaven to eat." Vv. 51–58 exegete the second half of the OT citation "to eat." For a recent attempt to read John 6 as a literary unity, see F. J. Moloney, "The Function of Prolepsis in the Interpretation of John 6," in *The Interpretation of John 6* (ed. R. A. Culpepper; BibIntS 22; Leiden: E. J. Brill, 1997), 129–48.

sacramental references belong to the final redaction does not mean that the original Gospel was nonsacramental or anti-sacramental. It may be a question of seeing different degrees of sacramentality in the work of the evangelist and that of the final redactor.

Turning to the implicit, symbolic Johannine references to the sacraments, I would judge that many of the sacramentalist interpreters have not used truly scientific criteria in determining the presence of sacramental symbols. Their guiding principle seems to be that since a passage can be understood sacramentally, it was intended sacramentally. Not only Bultmann, but more conservative scholars like Michaelis and Schnackenburg have detected the danger of eisegesis here. For some of the sacramental references proposed by Cullmann and Niewalda, there is no evidence in the context that the evangelist so intended the passage. Faced with this difficulty, Niewalda has thrown aside as impractical the search for internal indications of the author's sacramental intent. He falls back on external evidence, namely, an indication in the early centuries that a passage of John was understood as a symbolic reference to a sacrament. For this purpose he consults the patristic writings, the liturgy, catacomb art, etc.

In my article "Sacramentary," I presented a detailed exposition of what I regarded as solid criteria for accepting symbolic sacramental references in John. In brief, I would accept the external evidence proposed by Niewalda as a *negative* criterion. If there is no evidence in the early church that a passage of John was understood sacramentally, then one should be suspicious of modern attempts to introduce a sacramental interpretation. Behind this is a fundamental supposition that the evangelist intended his implicit references to the sacraments to be understood, and that some trace of that understanding would probably have survived in the early Christian use of the Gospel. The sacraments of baptism and the eucharist were popular themes among Christian writers and artists, and it is unlikely that they would have overlooked a Gospel passage that was generally understood to be a sacramental reference.

However, external evidence alone is insufficient as a *positive* criterion of sacramental reference. Many of the early Christian writers were not exegeting the Gospel but employing it freely as a catechetical tool. Therefore, even though they may use a Johannine story, like that of the healing in ch. 5, as an illustration of Christian baptism, this is not a sufficient guarantee that the evangelist so intended the story. Often a considerable period of time separates the Gospel from the pertinent liturgical, literary, and artistic reference that would find a sacramental use for a passage of the Gospel. In that time, a symbolism may have developed that was not part of the original Gospel.

And so, in addition to the negative check supplied by external evidence, we must have a positive indication within the text itself that the evangelist intended a reference to the sacraments. In determining what constitutes a positive indication, exegetes will disagree. Michaelis, for instance, in rejecting virtually all of Cullmann's examples, seems to demand from the evangelist the type of indication that we might expect from a twentieth-century writer. This is to be overcritical, for the symbolism taken for granted in the first century may not seem at all obvious to a modern mind much less attuned to symbolism. Who would have dared to see in the lifting up of the bronze serpent on the pole a symbol of the crucified Jesus if the evangelist himself had not indicated this (3:14)? From the symbols identified in the Johannine tradition itself (see also 21:18–19), it is obvious that the evangelist's mentality was not at all the same as our modern mentality.[32]

Thus, the necessary criterion for recognizing symbolic references to the sacraments is found in the combination of internal, textual indication and external, early Christian allusion. This criterion is not foolproof, but it does reduce considerably the dangers of eisegesis, while not exposing the Gospel to a minimalist exegesis. Using this criterion of combined evidence, I would find that, in addition to the more explicit references to the sacraments (some of which may come from the final redactor), there is in the very substance of the Gospel a broad sacramental interest; and in this respect John is quite in harmony with the church at large.

What then of the omission in John of sacramental passages found in the Synoptics? The absence of the scene often thought to represent the institution of baptism (Matt 28:19) is not really a problem, since that scene is not found in Mark or Luke either.[33] The omission of the eu-

---

32. Examples of what I would regard as adequate positive indication that the evangelist intended a sacramental reference can be found in the commentary upon John 9 and 13:1–11 in *John*, 380–82 (John 9), 558–62 (John 13:1–11).

33. It should be noted that the classical theologians are not in agreement that the scene describes the institution of baptism. There are some, for example, Estius, who would associate the institution with the Nicodemus scene found only in John. In any case this is a post-NT problem.

charistic scene at the Last Supper is more difficult; but echoes of the Johannine form of this scene have been incorporated into 6:51–58.[34] When one compares John's treatment of baptism and the eucharist with similar material in the Synoptics, this Gospel does not associate these sacraments with a single, all-important saying of Jesus uttered at the end of his life as part of his departing instructions to his disciples. The Johannine references to these two sacraments, both the more explicit references and those that are symbolic, are scattered in scenes throughout the ministry. This seems to fit in with the Gospel's intention to show how the institutions of the Christian life are rooted in what Jesus said and did during his life.

Moreover, among the four Gospels it is to John most of all that we owe the deep Christian understanding of the purpose of baptism and the eucharist. It is John who tells us that through baptismal water God begets children unto himself and pours forth upon them his Spirit (3:5; 7:37–39). Thus baptism becomes a source of eternal life (4:13–14), and the eucharist is the necessary food of that life (6:57). Finally, in a dramatic scene (19:34), John shows symbolically that both of these sacraments, baptismal water and eucharistic blood, have the source of their existence and power in the death of Jesus. This Johannine sacramentalism is neither merely antidocetic nor peripheral, but reflects the essential connection between the sacramental way of receiving life within the church at the end of the first century and the way in which life was offered to those who heard Jesus in Palestine. If symbolism is used, it is because only through symbolism could the evangelist teach his sacramental theology and still remain faithful to the literary form of Gospel in which he was writing. He could not interpolate sacramental theology into the Gospel story by anachronistic and extraneous additions, but he could show the sacramental undertones of the words and works of Jesus that were already part of the Gospel tradition.

Eschatology

As we shall see, eschatology touches on many topics in Johannine thought (e.g., life, faith, Son of Man, Paraclete/Spirit, judgment, union

---

34. See *John*, 272–80, 284–90.

with God, the hour, parousia, the Prince of this world),[35] so there is an enormous body of literature dealing with this topic both in the NT and in John. Almost every point about eschatology is disputed, including its definition; and the problem is so complicated that here I can touch lightly only the ramifications of the problem in John. By way of background, the OT offers a picture of an initial paradise from which humanity has fallen, and a God who does not abandon creation but intervenes (especially in the patriarchs and the history of Israel) to bring people closer to him. There developed a hope/expectation that in a later or final period God would intervene definitively and bring about an idyllic situation (almost duplicating paradise), with a diversity as to whether the fulfillment of that expectation would take place on the present earth or would involve bliss in heaven above or a recreated earth. The adherents of Jesus recognized in him and especially in his resurrection that divine intervention; however, since no visible idyllic situation resulted, they believed that Jesus had enabled them (as individuals and/or as a community) to participate in eschatological bliss in heaven above and/or that it would come at the end of time. Accordingly we can conveniently approach Johannine eschatology under two headings.

The "Vertical" and the "Horizontal" View of God's Salvific Action

To use spatial terminology, we may characterize the dominant biblical view of salvation as "horizontal," for while God acts from above, God acts in and through the sequence of history. From the time of creation God has guided the world with its population inexorably forward to a climax, a climax that is often seen in terms of divine intervention in the linear course of history. Thus, salvation lies either in history or as a climax to history. Counterpoised to this is a "vertical" view that sees two worlds coexistent, one heavenly, one earthly; and the earthly world is but a shadow of the heavenly—not primarily a world to come but a world above that already exists. Earthly existence is fallen existence, and history is a prolongation of the meaningless. Salvation is made possible through escape

---

35. Frey's exhaustive *Die johanneische Eschatologie* surveys a century of virtually the whole of Johannine research. The root meaning of eschatology involves the "last things" in human experience. Cook, "Eschatology," 87, finds in John 34 references to death, 26 to heaven, 21 to judgment, 18 to eternal life, and four to Christ's return.

to the heavenly world, and this can occur only when someone or something comes down from the heavenly world to set people free from earthly existence. This latter view is often identified (too easily) as Gnostic. Toward which of these views of history and salvation (which I have simplified) does the Fourth Gospel incline?

In many ways, John betrays a vertical approach to salvation, catalyzed by the incarnation. The Son of Man has come down from heaven (3:13), the Word has become flesh (1:14), with the purpose of offering salvation. The culmination of his career is when he is lifted up toward heaven in death and resurrection to draw all to himself (12:32). There is a constant contrast in John between two worlds: one above, the other below (3:3, 31; 8:23), a contrast that is not merely spatial but qualitative; a sphere that belongs to Spirit, and a sphere that belongs to flesh (3:6; 6:63). Jesus brings the life of the other world, "eternal life," to the people of this world, and death has no power over this life (11:25). Jesus' gifts are "real" gifts, that is, heavenly gifts: the real water of life, as contrasted with ordinary water (4:10–14); the real bread of life, as contrasted with perishable bread (6:27); he is the real light that has come into the world (3:19). These characteristics betraying an atemporal and vertical approach to salvation have constituted one of Bultmann's main arguments for advancing the hypothesis of Gnostic influence on John,[36] and Dodd's stress on Platonic similarities.

But there is also much of the horizontal approach to salvation in John. The Prologue, which describes the descent of the Word into human flesh, does not deny a salvation history that began with creation;[37] it recognizes that "the Law was a gift through Moses" (1:17). If the coming of Jesus represents the era of the dominance of Spirit over flesh so that all can

---

36. As we saw in Chapter Four, above, there are variations as to whether an earlier stage/edition was Gnostic and was corrected by the evangelist, or the latter was Gnostic.

37. Even though, as most have recognized, the overall salvation-history approach to John of Cullmann, applied to eschatology by Ricca (see also Corell) with past, present, and future does not do justice to the dominant Johannine stress on realized eschatology. The OT period is seen almost exclusively in relationship to Jesus, supporting John's own witness to Jesus. There is no sharp division in John between the ministry of Jesus and the period of the church as there is in Luke. The Spirit is handed over to the BD by the dying Jesus on the cross, and the Paraclete/Spirit is the continued presence of Jesus after he has gone to the Father.

worship God in Spirit, Israel's history has been the preparation for this climactic era: "Salvation is from the Jews" (4:21–23). The whole of the Scriptures that record salvation history points to Jesus (5:39). The "hour" of which we hear so much in John (2:4; 8:20; 12:23, etc.), the hour of Jesus' passion, death, resurrection, and ascension, is the culminating hour in the long history of God's dealings, bringing "the Scripture to its complete fulfillment" (19:28). Jewish customs, feasts, and religious institutions also find their fulfillment in Jesus.[38] Nor does the story stop with this hour. John's problem is not whether there will be an ongoing community, but how it can be related to Jesus. John presupposes missionary activity (4:35–38), a conflict of Christians with the world (16:8; 17:14), an influx of those who will come to believe through the preaching of the word (17:20), and a gathering of them into a flock to be shepherded (11:52; 10:16; 21:15–17). The last chapter of John, probably the contribution of the redactor, has the risen Jesus speak of coming again (21:22).[39]

Thus, the Johannine view of salvation is both vertical and horizontal. The dominant vertical aspect expresses the uniqueness of the divine intervention in Jesus; the horizontal aspect establishes a relationship between this intervention and what has gone before and what follows. This is why a Gnostic interpretation of the Fourth Gospel cannot do justice to

---

38. *Editor's Note:* Brown's use of the expression "fulfillment" here better reflects the Johannine approach to the institutions of Israel. They are not "replaced" by the Johannine Christology, as Brown claims elsewhere, and as I have noted each time. Interestingly, as I have remarked in my Introduction, here is one of the places where Brown's own redaction of his own text (the one author) shows that conflicting (or at least) different interpretations can creep in as a long text evolves over a period of time.

39. The Book of Revelation, which has some relation to the Johannine writings, is concerned with a salvation that is to come at the end of history. Revelation and John betray different emphases on this question, and one should not interpret John's eschatology through that of Revelation; but one should also be wary about assuming that their positions are contradictory. *Editor's Note:* In the light of the previous note, in the present (unfinished) state of his script, Brown's use of Revelation to draw literary and theological conclusions about the Gospel of John was also inconsistent, showing a blend of his confident use of Revelation in 1966–70, and his acceptance of current scholarship, judging against a close relationship in 1998. I have generally left Brown's text untouched, and indicated difficulties by means of a note. See my further remarks in the Conclusion.

its full teaching. The blending of the vertical and the horizontal has been said (often too facilely) to represent a blending of the Hellenistic and the Hebrew approaches to salvation, but such a blending occurred long before the Fourth Gospel was written. For instance, it was already present in the deuterocanonical Book of Wisdom. Dodd has shown that early rabbinic thought reflects two different aspects of the "future life." [40] One borders on the horizontal, for it posits two ages in which the life of the age to come replaces the life of the present age; the other borders on the vertical, for its posits a life beyond the grave, differing from the life of people upon this earth. Christian theology has made a similar synthesis of the vertical and the horizontal in positing immortality of the soul as well as the final resurrection of the dead.

Realized Eschatology and Future Eschatology

Let us look at eschatology under another modality.[41] In the Synoptic Jesus' preaching about the *basileia tou theou* and in his attitude toward his own ministry, there is clearly an eschatological outlook, for he presents himself as in some way having introduced the definitive moment in human existence. But in what precise way?

On the one hand, advocates of final or apocalyptic eschatology (e.g., A. Schweitzer) maintain that in speaking of the coming of the *basileia,* Jesus was speaking of that dramatic intervention of God that would bring history to a conclusion. He would have taken over this expectation from the Jewish apocalypticism of the last centuries B.C. In this interpretation, Jesus expected the final divine intervention in his own ministry or in the immediate future so that it would come about through his death. When

---

40. Dodd, *Interpretation,* 144–46.

41. Other terms for "realized" eschatology are inaugurated, proleptic, and fulfilled. Occasionally Johannine realized eschatology has been called mysticism and seen as exclusively individualistic—rather it represents a basic understanding of what God has done in Christ for all. From the viewpoint of Jesus' ministry there are various ways in which eschatology can be future or not yet complete, e.g., passages can refer to what will happen in the life of the disciples after crucifixion/resurrection or to what will happen at the end of time (traditional eschatology). When the latter is accompanied by vivid features (battles, angels, demons, dramatic appearance on clouds, wrathful judgment on God's enemies), it flows over into apocalyptic.

his hopes were disappointed and the *basileia* did not come, the church eventually solved the problem by projecting the final coming of Jesus into the distant future. On the other hand, advocates of realized eschatology (e.g., C. H. Dodd) maintain that Jesus proclaimed the presence of the *basileia* within his own ministry, but without the apocalyptic trimmings usually associated with the event. His presence among people was the one and only coming of God. But his followers were the heirs of an apocalyptic tradition that spoke of a coming in might and majesty, so they could not believe that all had been realized in Jesus' ministry. To satisfy their expectations they projected a second, more glorious coming in the future— at first, in the near future; then, in the distant future.

Between those extreme views of Gospel eschatology there is a whole range of intermediate views. A view, once common, is now losing popularity, namely, that the *basileia tou theou* established as the result of Jesus' ministry was the church. Perhaps the most widely accepted intermediate view is that the eschatological reign of God was present and operative in the ministry of Jesus, but in a provisional way. The establishment or realization of the *basileia* is yet to come, and the church is oriented toward that future *basileia*.

In many ways, John is the best NT example of realized eschatology. God has been revealed in Jesus in a definitive form. If one points to OT passages that seem to imply a coming of God in glory, the Prologue (1:14) answers, "We have seen his glory." If one asks where is the judgment that marks God's final intervention, John 3:19 answers, "Now the judgment is this: the light has come into the world." In a figurative way, Matt 25:31–46 describes the apocalyptic Son of Man coming in glory and sitting on the throne of judgment to separate the good and the bad. But for John the presence of Jesus in the world as the light separates people into those who are walking in darkness, hating the light, and those who come to the light. All through the Gospel, Jesus provokes self-judgment as people line up for or against him; truly his coming is a *crisis* in the root sense of that word, where it reflects the Greek *krisis* or "judgment." Those who refuse to believe are already condemned (3:18), while those who have faith do not come under condemnation (5:24). Even the reward is realized. For the Synoptics, "eternal life" is something that one receives at the final judgment or in a future age (Mark 10:30; Matt 18:8–9), but for John it is a present possibility: "The one who hears my words and has faith in Him who sent me *possesses* eternal life ... he has passed from death to life" (5:24). For Luke (6:35; 20:36) divine sonship is a reward of the future life; for John (1:12) it is a gift granted here on earth.

A few passages have the peculiar combination: "an hour is coming and is now" (4:23; 5:25; see 16:32). That cannot simply be regarded as an awkward correction of future eschatology to present eschatology. More plausibly, it reflects a Johannine liking for joined contraries, e.g., believers may die or never die at all (11:25–26); God has been glorified and will be glorified (12:28; 13:31).

There are more passages in John that seem to reflect a purely future element in their eschatology. We may distinguish between those that are simply futuristic and those that are apocalyptic. For instance, one prominent futuristic element is the wide-ranging gift of life that comes after Jesus' resurrection. When Jesus speaks of a present opportunity to receive life, we should realize that, whatever may have been offered in Jesus' earthly lifetime, in the intention of the evangelist Jesus is speaking through the pages of the Gospel to a postresurrectional Christian audience. These Christians have the chance to obtain life through faith in Jesus, through baptism (3:5), and through the eucharistic food (6:54) that is a future gift from the viewpoint of the public ministry (6:27, 51). The life-giving factor is the Spirit (6:63; 7:38–39), and that Spirit is active for believers only after Jesus is glorified by being lifted up to the Father (7:39; 16:7; 19:30; 20:22). It is after the resurrection that Thomas sets an example by confessing Jesus as Lord and God (20:28), the full understanding of what Jesus means when he says, "I AM" (8:28). There is another futuristic element in Jesus' attitude toward what happens after a person's death. Although Jesus insists that "eternal life" is offered here below, he recognizes that physical death will still intervene (11:25). This death cannot destroy eternal life, but there must be an aspect of completeness to eternal life after death that is lacking in those who have yet to pass through physical death. Another indication of future reward is the statement that Jesus passes through death and resurrection so that he may prepare dwelling places in his Father's house to which he will bring those who believe in him (14:2–3). If people see the glory of Jesus on this earth, there is a future vision of glory to be granted when they shall join Jesus in the Father's presence (17:24; see 1 John 3:2).

Most scholars recognize the futuristic elements mentioned thus far, even if sometimes they reinterpret them according to a theory of totally realized eschatology. A major problem concerns apocalyptic elements in the eschatology of John. Is there to be a second coming, a resurrection of the dead at the end of time, and a final judgment? There are clear passages that speak in this manner (5:28–29; 6:39–40, 44, 54; 12:48). How are these passages to be treated and reconciled with what we have seen of realized eschatology? For Bultmann, they are the additions of the Ecclesiastical Redactor, adapting Johannine theology to the theology of the church at large. That this is not a satisfactory view even on purely literary grounds has often been remarked, for some of the passages do not seem to be additions.[42] On the other hand, even if one believes that there is a strain of apocalyptic eschatology in genuine Johannine thought, there is little doubt that Van Hartingsveld's attempt to refute Bultmann by putting the emphasis in John on future eschatology swings the pendulum too much in the opposite direction.[43] Stauffer has suggested that the evangelist is a reformer in the sense that by his emphasis on realized eschatology and the hidden Messiah he is stripping off the vulgar apocalyptic elements that have entered Christian thought since the death of Jesus. His view is not far from Dodd's contention that Johannine realized eschatology is close to Jesus' original thought. Boismard, however, thinks that the passages dealing with final apocalyptic are the earlier passages in the development of Johannine thought, and those dealing with realized eschatology represent later insight.[44]

Without attempting to discuss all the suggestions, I shall first offer a hypothesis about the development of NT eschatology, and then comment on Johannine present and future eschatology.

---

42. See Smith, *Composition*, 230–32.

43. van Hartingsveld, *Eschatologie*. Sometimes the stress on future eschatology is tied in with the dubious theory that the Gospel of John was an evangelical ruse designed to convert Jews who would have been familiar with such eschatology as seen in Jewish apocalyptic (e.g., J. A. T. Robinson, van Unnik). The newness of this promise of "life now" was developed to attract Jewish converts.

44. From a different viewpoint, Strecker dates 2 John early and disputably finds in v. 7 an attack on those who deny that Jesus Christ is coming (i.e., is to come) in the flesh. He posits an early chiliastic (millennialist) stage of Johannine thought.

A WORKABLE HYPOTHESIS ABOUT THE GENERAL
DEVELOPMENT OF NT ESCHATOLOGY

Within Jesus' own message there was a tension between realized and final eschatology. In his ministry, the reign of God was becoming manifest among people: Jesus spoke about the revelation and definitive realization. Yet, as heir of an apocalyptic tradition, Jesus also spoke of a final manifestation of divine power yet to come—as "Our Father . . . may your kingdom come" indicates, the kingdom was in God's control. The obscurity of the Gospel references would indicate that, even though the overall impression is of "soonness," Jesus had no clear teaching on how or precisely when this final manifestation would take place. There are some statements that seem to refer to its coming in the very near future (Mark 9:1; 13:30; Matt 10:23; 26:64); others seem to suppose a lapse of time (Luke 17:22) and no fixed date (Mark 13:32–33). It is a dubious procedure to excise one or the other group of statements in order to reconstruct a consistent eschatological view held by Jesus.[45] The recognition that there were both realized and final elements in Jesus' own eschatology means that in the subsequent developments seen below, the NT writers were not creating ex nihilo theories of realized or of final eschatology, but were applying to a particular situation one or the other strain already present in Jesus' thought. It may be added that there were strains of both types of eschatology in the Judaism contemporary with Jesus. The *War Scroll* (1QM) shows Qumran's expectations of final divine intervention. Yet at the same time the sectarians believed that they already shared in God's heavenly gifts, were delivered from judgment, and enjoyed the companionship of the angels.[46]

Ambivalence about eschatology is a mark of early Christian thought. Acts 2:17ff. portrays Peter as proclaiming that the last day has arrived in the resurrection of Jesus and the outpouring of the Spirit. From that one might judge that the first emphasis in eschatological expectation seems to have been that all things were accomplished by and in Jesus Christ and

---

45. That Jesus may have said different things at different times is very plausible. J. T. Sanders, "The Criterion of Coherence," *NTS* 44 (1998): 1–25, points out that saying things that are apparently contradictory would have enhanced Jesus' charismatic authority.

46. See J. Licht, "The Doctrine of the Thanksgiving Scroll," *IEJ* 6 (1956): 12–13, 97.

that only a short interim would be granted by God to allow the eschato-logical proclamation to be made to people. The rejection of this procla-mation by many would have brought to the fore another strain of Jesus' tradition that spoke of a coming of the Son of Man in judgment on the wicked, a picture that was naturally colored by apocalyptic elements from the preachers' own background. The gradual passing of the years raised more acutely the problem of how soon this coming would take place, a problem that caused anguish in the Pauline correspondence with the Thessalonians and Corinthians.

The destruction of Jerusalem in 70 was a watershed in the develop-ment of NT eschatological thought. One can deduce from passages like Luke 21:20 and Rev 4–9 that some theologians saw the destruction of Je-rusalem as the (partial) fulfillment of Jesus' words describing the coming of the Son of Man in wrath to punish the wicked. But what of the glori-ous establishment of the *basileia?* Some seem to have kept their hopes of an immediate parousia alive as long as there was a representative of the apostolic generation still among them. The reactions to the passing of this last tangible sign of immediate parousia are found in the cynicism that is the target of 2 Pet 3:4 and the disappointment that is the target of John 21:22–23. Others turned toward a more positive answer.[47] Leaving aside the question of when Jesus would return, they emphasized what the Christians had already received in Jesus Christ. There need be no exces-sive worry about final judgment, for the reaction of people to Jesus in faith or in disbelief was already a judgment. There need be no excessive longing for the blessings that the parousia would bring, for divine son-ship and eternal life, the two greatest gifts, were already in the possession of Christians through faith in Jesus and through baptism and the eu-charist. For those who died in Jesus there was no indefinite agony of wait-ing till the last day and the resurrection of the dead, for after death there was a continuation of the eternal life that they already possessed[48]—a

---

47. Ephesians and 1 Peter may both have been written after A.D. 70. Eph 1:13 ex-claims, "God has delivered us from the dominion of darkness and transferred us to the kingdom of His beloved Son" (echoing realized eschatology) while 1 Pet 4:7 could still proclaim, "The end of all things is at hand."

48. To some this makes a final resurrection of the dead otiose. Yet, as Ricca points out, that future resurrection, while it would not give eternal life, would ensure its reality.

continuation that death could not affect and a continuation that constituted even closer union with Jesus and his Father. From time to time persecution and trial would revive the passionate yearning for the
immediate return of Jesus and divine deliverance. We see this in Revelation 12–22 where Roman persecution acts as a catalyst for apocalyptic
hopes. But the ordinary Christian teaching was more and more phrased
in terms of realized eschatology. This combination of a dominant realized eschatology with admixtures of apocalyptic expectation has continued as a standard Christian outlook even until the present day.

Many other factors would have to be taken into account in evaluating
the theory just described and applying it to John. For instance, the destruction of Jerusalem may have had less significance for emphasizing future eschatology than some local event that touched the Johannine
community more directly, e.g., ejection from the synagogues, the death
of the BD.[49]

INTERPRETING JOHN'S PRESENT AND FUTURE ESCHATOLOGY

De Jonge in several articles has pointed out that, despite its peculiar emphases, Johannine eschatology has significant similarities to Synoptic eschatology. Yet, even if eschatological concepts were derived from the OT
and from the Jesus tradition, there could have been extraneous influences
in the Christian development of them. As I have mentioned, some would
trace the heavy emphasis on realized eschatology to Gnosticism. Yet
the theory of Gnostic influence is very disputed, and one can appeal
to strains of realized eschatology in Jewish Wisdom Literature and at
Qumran.[50]

If one posits a long development in the composition of the Fourth
Gospel from the stage of historical tradition about Jesus until the stage of

---

49. So Stimpfle, *Blinde*. Much more dubious is the suggestion that a catalytic factor was Johannine rejection of the theology of the larger church (of Peter), considered to be false believers (despite 6:68; 21:19!).

50. One must distinguish between factors that may have caused preference for an
eschatological emphasis in Johannine development, e.g, expulsion from the synagogue and the isolation that resulted, and the elevation of those factors to creative
original causes of the eschatology and the accompanying Christology. This distinction reflects an appreciation that the basic Christology and eschatology may ultimately have come from Jesus.

final redaction, a priori one may expect to find in John traces of the swinging to-and-fro of eschatological expectation in the first century. Undoubtedly such varying emphasis would have been related to developments in Johannine Community history; but given scholarly disputes about that history, it is perilous to relate exactly a particular type of eschatology to a particular stage in that history. Moreover, the witness of the Johannine Epistles would also have to be brought into the picture. Although most scholars date them to after the Gospel, and they put greater emphasis on the final eschatology (I John 2:28; 3:2–23; 4:17), 1 John seems to be recalling what was held from the beginning, so that final eschatology may have been early.

Bultmann, Dodd, and Blank are correct in insisting that the main emphasis in the Gospel is on realized eschatology.[51] One of the purposes of the Gospel was to teach Christians what a gift they had received in Jesus who was the source and basis of their life. The Gospel very clearly regards the coming of Jesus as an eschatological event that marked the change of the aeons. If the Gospel begins with "In the beginning," it is because the coming of Jesus will be presented as a new and definitive creation. Jesus' breathing on the disciples in 20:22 as he communicates to them the life-giving Spirit is like God's breathing on the dust in the original creation of the human being (Gen 2:7), but now through Jesus' Spirit God has recreated people as his own children (1:12–13).

The passages in John that treat of apocalyptic eschatology may represent (with development) a remembrance that this theme was found in Jesus' own preaching. They would have come to the fore at a period in the development of Johannine thought when final eschatology was an important motif. Was this an early period as Boismard thinks, or a late period as Bultmann and Schmithals think, or even both? It may be impossible to answer that question, but the following observations are pertinent.

The final eschatology passages are often doublets of other passages where the same words of Jesus are interpreted in terms of realized eschatology; for example, compare 5:26–30 (apocalyptic) with 5:19–25 (real-

---

51. In part this may be related to the date when the Gospel proper was written: in the period after the fall of Jerusalem when hopes of an immediate parousia quickly faded. Bultmann relates the emphasis on realized eschatology to the existential thrust of the evangelist as he uses motifs taken over from Gnosticism for his own goal.

ized). In such instances, Bultmann would attribute the addition of the passage with final eschatology to the redactor, added in an attempt to make the Gospel more orthodox and acceptable to the larger church. That interpretation is not a necessary part of the redactional approach. The redactor may have been trying to make the Gospel as complete a collection of Johannine tradition as possible, including material pertaining to final eschatology that was not included in the evangelist's edition. What was added to the Gospel was not necessarily late material; moreover "the larger church" position on eschatology was not so uniform that such additions would have been required.[52]

While some final eschatology passages could have been later additions to the evangelist's work, that solution is overly artificial when applied to all passages. In my original Commentary, I was attracted by the logic that the same person would scarcely have combined the two eschatologies as John's Gospel does, but now I recognize that this needs to be queried. Differing from Bultmann, Stählin maintained that Johannine eschatology expressed its truth only in contradictory sentences.[53] Indeed, even in the hypothesis of later addition, a final redactor did not deem it illogical to set the two eschatologies side by side.[54] Moreover, the reading audience to which the Gospel is directed (20:30–31) can scarcely have been expected to read the eschatological statements through the light of different stages in community history or different writers. Therefore a perspective must be sought from and in which the *diverse* eschatology of John as it now stands makes sense—a perspective involving some form of complementarity rather than correction.[55]

---

52. See, for example, V. Balabanski, *Eschatology in the Making. Mark, Matthew and the Didache* (SNTSMS 97; Cambridge: Cambridge University Press, 1997).

53. Stählin, "Zur Problem."

54. Many would find a double eschatology in the writings of Ignatius of Antioch (see *Trallians* 9:2; *Ephesians* 11:1; *Polycarp* 3:1) writing shortly after the fourth evangelist, but there again Bultmann would explain away the future references as irrelevant.

55. Some would identify the Lazarus story as a reinterpretation or anticipation of the parousia, but that would be true only for those who thought of the parousia as a resuscitation of the dead to ordinary (even if enduring) life. Kysar, "Eschatology," would posit that two types of eschatology were placed side by side in order to show that future statements should be interpreted in a present way. This posits overly complicated pedagogy. Why not omit the future statements since the statements involv-

One does not know the context in which the Gospel was read/ heard, and it is possible that cult supplied the perspective (Aune) for combining present and future eschatology, since cult is a present anticipation of future participation with God. Unfortunately we have little hard evidence in the Johannine writings about cult,[56] but Aune suggests that cult is not mentioned because it is presupposed. With or without a cultic setting the readers are to read not only Jesus' promises for the future but also his words and signs during the ministry as addressed to them.

The perspective for the present/future combination may have been supplied by Johannine thought and/or style of presentation.[57] It is probably too simple to say that the ministry of Jesus was looked on as a first stage followed by the second stage of postresurrectional experience that completed it. Was the whole account of the ministry written from the postresurrectional stance (Bornkamm, Hoegen-Rohls)? Or is it more accurate to speak of a form of compenetration,[58] e.g., already in Jesus' ministry the dead come forth from the tombs, but only after this death and glorification comes the Spirit (7:39)? How does the Paraclete as the pres-

---

ing present eschatology already included reinterpreted future concepts (judgment, eternal life, coming of Jesus from heaven)? 1 John shows that a futuristic understanding of eschatology was part of the Johannine picture. De Jonge, "Christology," 3.1852, is right when he contends that the Johannine community, joined to Jesus in faith, still awaited a moment when they would be taken out of this world to see the glory that the Father had given to the Son before the creation of the world (17:24).

56. Highly speculative is Aune's appeal (*Cultic,* 47) to John 1:51 as the kind of event that the Johannine community experienced pneumatically in community worship. In support of Aune, however, see Moloney, "The Fourth Gospel: A Story of Two Paracletes," in *"A Hard Saying,"* 149–66, see especially pp. 157–60.

57. Aune, *Cultic,* 56–57, argues against the tendency to make the evangelist "an exceedingly creative theologian who consciously altered or transformed the traditional and dominantly futuristic Christian eschatology for one or more reasons." I agree that Johannine eschatology is not simply the product of sophisticated theological reflection but mainly the articulation of community spirituality. In this articulation I would see the evangelist, under the influence of his (and his community's) Christology, capitalizing on the realized-eschatology strain in early Christian thought, not to refute other eschatology but to make people grasp more fully God's gift of life.

58. Bultmann contends that for the evangelist Easter (resurrection), Pentecost (gift of the Spirit), and the parousia are one and the same. I would modify that claim, however, by contending that in transferring to the incarnation many aspects of the parousia, the evangelist still preserved an interest in the second coming of Christ.

ence of Jesus after Jesus' return to the Father fit into this issue? Is the sorrow of those at the Last Supper facing Jesus' departure and absence shared by postresurrectional believers who, despite the gift of the Paraclete, still must wait to join Jesus in the presence of the Father?[59] Is such compenetration made more intelligible when we consider John's approach to signs?[60] One way or another in the Johannine narrative there is a blending of horizons: the ministry of Jesus and his dealings therein with his disciples; the time of the community where the Paraclete dwells in each believer; the ultimate joining of believers with Jesus and the Father in the heavenly realm above.[61]

In that narrative with its blended horizons, eschatology would be only one of several intermingled factors. For instance, one cannot appreciate John's eschatology without factoring in John's Christology.[62] Ricca rightly states, "The Johannine Christology is completely centered and comprehended in the person of the pre-existent, incarnate, crucified, resurrected Christ living in heaven and represented on earth by his alter ego, the Spirit."[63] That Christology affected individual believers and their relation to one another as branches on the vine, thus bringing ecclesiology into the picture.

---

59. In more narrative and reader-response criticism (see Chapter One, Excursus: "Narrative Approaches to the Fourth Gospel," pp. 30–39.) the Gospel is a stratagem by which the author attempts to guide the response of the implied readers (who mirror the original readers). Despite the revelation given by Jesus and interpreted by the Paraclete, there would still be open questions for the Johannine community as to the fate of the world in God's plan. Thus even though there are future eschatological promises, they are for the sake of present believers. *Editor's Note:* Another question that would have inevitably arisen (as it did already in the Pauline communities [see 1 Thess 4:13–5:11]) was the question of the physical death of the members of the community. There may even have been the need to explain the experience of violent death (see 16:2).

60. On the Johannine "Signs," see *John*, 525–32.

61. The "last day" of horizontal eschatology would be the final step in vertical eschatology.

62. As de Jonge, "Christology," (*Editor's addition:* And an ever-increasing number of contemporary Johannine scholars [see Bibliography] reminds us, the Johannine Christology cannot be appreciated independently of John's theology, i.e., the relationship of Jesus to the Father).

63. Ricca, *Eschatologie*, 85.

Christology

THERE CAN BE NO DOUBT about the importance of Christology in Johannine thought. The evangelist is clear: "These (signs) have been recorded so that you may have faith that Jesus is the Messiah, the Son of God, and that through this faith you may have life in his name." Modern commentators have recognized that by speaking of Christology as the center or heartbeat of John's thought, to the point where Christology is spoken of as *the* gospel message. Nevertheless a number of comments are necessary.

Theocentrism

The Gospel is focused on Jesus for several reasons: it is he who has brought God's life, and he became the object of synagogue rejection. Nevertheless, there is a presupposition that Jesus leads believers *to God;* Jesus is supremely important because whoever has seen him has seen the Father (14:9), and the Father and he are one (10:30). Even though others may see Jesus as arrogantly making himself God (10:33) and equal to God (5:18), he says "the Father is greater than I" (14:31). There is no sense in which the Johannine Jesus replaces the God of Israel who has traditionally been confessed as one: "Eternal life consists in this: that they know you, the one true God, and Jesus Christ, the one whom you sent" (17:3). The last warning in 1 John (5:21) is, "Guard yourselves against idols." Jesus is angry at people in the Temple precincts because people are turning *his Father's* house into a market place. The themes of the feasts of Israel are reinterpreted to relate to Jesus, but the worship of God involved in those feasts is preserved. Thus Johannine Christology never replaces theology.[64]

---

64. In Barrett's *Essays,* see "Christocentric or Theocentric," 1–18; " 'The Father Is Greater Than I,' " 19–36. On p. 8, he says concisely, "Jesus is central; yet he is not final." See also F. J. Moloney, "Telling God's Story: The Fourth Gospel," in *The Forgotten God: The God of Jesus Christ in New Testament Theology: Essays in Honor of Paul J. Achtemeier on the Occasion of His Seventy-fifth Birthday* (eds. A. A. Das and F. J. Matera; Louisville: Westminster John Knox Press, 2002), 107–22.

Conflicting statements

Part of the difficulty in analyzing Johannine Christology (or even the broader theology) is that the Gospel contains statements that seem to have opposing views:

- See the preceding paragraph for statements of equality and subordination in relation to the Father. That begins already in 1:1 where the Word is both in God's presence (toward God) and is God.
- See the previous subsection for statements of realized and final eschatology.
- There are statements that seem to indicate predestination of those who come to Jesus (10:3, 26; 17:6) and statements that indicate choice (3:19–21).[65] A particular instance of this is seen in the implications of the varied patterns, "Everyone who has or has not been begotten from God does or does not . . ." (3:3, 5; 1 John 3:9; 5:4a, 18), and "Everyone who does or does not . . . has or has not been begotten by God" (1:12–13; 1 John 2:29; 4:7; 5:1).
- There are statements where Jesus offers eternal life to those he encounters during his public ministry (4:10; 5:24) and statements where life will be given after he is lifted up (3:14–15).
- There are statements capable of being read as Gnostic Christology (17:16: Jesus does not belong to this world) and others that would cause trouble for Gnostics (1:14: The Word became flesh).

How can these be explained? Several different solutions have been proposed. A number of scholars think the statements are irreconcilable, and attribute one set of statements to an earlier stage of Johannine writing and another set to a later stage. For instance, to the putative source vs. the evangelist, or to the evangelist vs. the redactor. Even then, there is not agreement in how to read the evangelist. Bultmann, for instance, thinks the source was Gnostic, but the evangelist corrected the material in a

---

65. Trumbower, *Born*, joins the Valentinian Gnostic Heracleon, and A. Hilgenfeld (1849 commentary) in arguing (143–44) that John is a protognostic whose thought is that "The believers could consider themselves before the savior's arrival a special group set apart by their origin from God," although that is not the interpretation of the vast majority of ancient or modern scholars.

non-Gnostic way by stressing the authentic human existence of Jesus. There was a demythologizing of the miracles to signs, and no literal understanding of having come down from heaven. Käsemann, however, would see the evangelist as naively docetic, so that he pictures Jesus as a god marching triumphantly across the world and working miracles as a manifestation of divine power.

Other scholars question the irreconcilability of the statements and warn against exaggerating the apparent import. They would insist that, since the conflicting statements appear in the same document, they did not seem contradictory to the Johannine writer(s) and that their different thrust shows the complexity of Johannine thought.[66]

Still other scholars would combine these views. There is some truth in the first approach, for there may well have been a different thrust in Johannine thought in the three different Stages discussed above.[67] Yet statements reflecting these differences could be joined because they are not truly irreconcilable. The later Stage was not primarily correcting the earlier but complementing it. Thus the second view is correct in appreciating the complexity of the final thought expressed in the Gospel. My own position is harmonious with this combined approach.

Words and Motifs as Keys

Scholars have chosen various designations, portrayals, and titles as a key to Johannine Christology:

- Jesus as the divine Logos (Word) become flesh.
- The Father's sending of Jesus into this world, especially with mission of revealing the Father.
- Jesus as God's only Son—a theme often combined with the preceding.
- Jesus as the descending/ascending Son of Man.
- The special use of "I am," which may be the name that the Father has given to Jesus.

---

66. *Editor's Note:* This position would be particularly applicable to a narrative critical approach to the Gospel.

67. See Chapter Two, pp. 62–86.

- A portrayal of Jesus heavily influenced by the OT picture of personified Wisdom, especially in the books written in the Hellenistic period (Sirach, Wisdom).
- Jesus as the prophet-like-Moses and/or the prophet of the endtime.
- Jesus and the Paraclete/Spirit functioning sequentially.
- A portrayal of Jesus influenced by Samaritan thought.

It is very difficult to rank these suggestions according to importance, especially if one is proposed as *the* key. Some may be more frequent than others; but they seem to be woven together by the evangelist into a larger picture. In a well-reasoned book, Loader describes a central structure of Johannine Christology that catches many of the motifs in a complementary manner:

> The Father sends and authorises the Son, who knows the Father, comes from the Father, makes the Father known, brings light and life and truth, completes his Father's work, returns to the Father, exalted, glorified, ascended, sends the disciples and sends the Spirit to enable greater understanding, to equip for mission, and to build up the community of faith.[68]

A number of these motifs have been comprehensively covered in my earlier commentary.[69] It may be useful to have special treatments of the Johannine use of Son of Man and Wisdom motifs, two issues that have been covered comprehensively since the publication of the Introduction to my 1966–70 Commentary.

Son of Man

THIS TITLE OF JESUS, although puzzling, is very important. O. Cullmann states, "It embraces the total work of Jesus as does almost no other idea."[70]

---

68. Loader, *Christology,* 225.

69. See, for example *John,* 519–24 (on Jesus as *logos*) and 532–38 (on Jesus' use of *Egô Eimi*).

70. *The Christology of the New Testament* (London: SCM, 1959), 137. *Editor's Note:* Cullmann's remark, however, pertains to the use of the expression in the Synoptic tradition. The claim should not really be made for the Fourth Gospel, where

By way of statistics, "[the] Son of Man" appears some eighty times in the Gospels, in all but two of which (Mark 2:10; John 12:34) as a self-designation by Jesus.[71] Outside the Gospels the phrase occurs only four times. If the use of this title did not come from Jesus, why was it so massively retrojected, being placed on Jesus' lips on a scale far outdistancing the retrojection of "the Messiah," "the Son of God," and "the Lord"? And if this title was first fashioned by the early church, why has it left almost no traces in non-Gospel NT literature, something not true of the other titles? Yet there are curious features about the title: no person addresses Jesus by this title, and Jesus never explains its meaning. When the question comes up as to who Jesus is, "the Son of Man" is never suggested by others as an identification of him.

We do not know how it became a title. In the Synoptics there are three groups of Son of Man sayings: (1) those that refer to the earthly activity of the Son of Man (eating, dwelling, saving the lost); (2) those that refer to the suffering of the Son of Man; (3) those that refer to the future glory and parousia of the Son of Man in judgment. Some would attribute only the last to the historical Jesus. The usual Gospel phrase *ho huios tou anthrôpou* (with two definite articles) is unknown in secular Greek and makes as little sense in Greek as "the son of the man" would make as a title in English conversation.[72] As for its use in the Synoptic Gospels, most trace it terminologically to Semitic origins.[73] The divine voice that speaks

---

"Son/Son of God" are the determining christological expressions. See, for example, the careful and deliberate use of "Son of God," modifying "the Christ," in 20:31. Johannine readers are not simply asked to continue in their belief that Jesus is the Christ, but the Christ insofar as he is, above all, the Son of God.

71. It has been estimated that these constitute some 51 sayings; in the Synoptic tradition 14 are in Mark, 10 in Q.

72. Burkett, *Son* 45–50, proposes the unusual translation, "the son of the Man," and relates it to Prov 30:1–4, where the Man says ("to Ithiel" in the usually corrected MT), "Who has ascended to heaven and descended?"—see John 3:13. The thesis that Jesus was identifying himself as the obscure Ithiel, the son (LXX) of the Man who speaks there, dependent as it is on a very disputable reading, will not get much following. For a recent restatement of this position, see Burkett, *Son of Man*, 66–67.

73. One of the problems is the dating of the evidence invoked for Semitic parallels. In particular Semitists sharply disagree on whether post-NT Aramaic rabbinic documents can be invoked in translating the Aramaic for "son of man," *bar nasha*, as "I," or "I and no other," or "a man like me" (yes: G. Vermes, "The Use of *br nsh/br nsh'* in

to Ezekiel addresses him over ninety times as "son of man" (= "O human being"), a term that highlights the contrast between the heavenly message and the mortal recipient. More pertinently, in the Aramaic of Dan 7:13 "one like a son of man" (contrasted to the beasts used as symbols of the pagan powers) enters the discussion—a human being who is a symbol of Israel and given dominion, glory, and kingdom (*basileia*). There is a long debate whether this passage may have prompted the development of a title,[74] especially since it is one of the few sections of the OT that features the kingdom of God, another motif associated with Jesus. Similarly debated is whether there could be influence from the Son of Man passages in the "Parables" (Similitudes) of *I Enoch* (37–71) where a preexistent figure who seems also to be called the Messiah is seated on a throne of glory. Although this section is missing from the copies of *I Enoch* found among the DSS, there is reason to think it was in existence in the early first century A.D.[75] Thus many think there was a Jewish concept of the Son of Man on which Jesus drew. Others deny that and appeal to a background in Gnosticism with its portrayal of a revealer who comes to enlighten the chosen ones or to what was purportedly a widespread notion in the ancient Near East of a preexistent primal man (sometimes royal) living in heaven who comes to earth at the end of time.[76] This debate is interesting

---

Jewish Aramaic," in M. Black, *An Aramaic Approach to the Gospels and Acts* [Oxford: Clarendon Press, 1967], 310–28; no: J. A. Fitzmyer, "Another View of the 'Son of Man' Debate," *JSNT* 4 [1979]: 56–68). Also debated is whether the term implies association with others or even serves as a corporate figure.

74. Tied in with that is the issue whether the title in the Gospels covers Jesus' associates as well as himself, and/or describes a corporate figure. Pamment, "Son," thinks "the Son of Man" highlights Jesus' representative humanity with attributes that all should exemplify.

75. This is an important remark in terms of tracing a "background" to Jesus' possible use, and then the early Church's use of "the Son of Man." See M. Casey, *Son of Man. The Influence and Interpretation of Daniel 7* (London: SPCK, 1979), 99–112, for agreement on the dating, but the rejection of any messianic significance for the use of the expression "son of man" in the Similitudes.

76. The evidence for this posited background is slim. For a more detailed discussion, see BDM 1.506–15. Schnackenburg, "Son" 538–41 studies such proposals and contends that John did not derive the "Son of Man" from Gnosticism or from an archetypal primordial man myth.

but inconclusive. Moreover, the answer does not necessarily cover John's use of "the Son of Man."[77]

There are thirteen Son-of-Man passages in John, all but one in the Book of Signs.[78] There are parallels with the Synoptic usage, so that Higgins, Maddox, Schnackenburg, and Moloney, among others, posit that many of the Johannine and Synoptic sayings came from a similar type of tradition and developed in a similar manner.[79] Yet there are different aspects that make John's use of "the Son of Man" special. The Johannine sayings overlap the three Synoptic groups; they lack strong apocalyptic trappings,[80] the element of realized eschatology dominates; and only in John does the Son of Man descend.[81] That descent means that during his ministry he can offer life to those who believe in him (6:27, 53), a partial similarity to Synoptic group 1. Probably too 1:51, which has the angels of God ascending and descending upon the Son of Man, refers to the union of the Son of Man with heaven during his earthly existence. Three of the

---

77. *Editor's Note:* This is an important consideration. Did John receive the notion of "the Son of Man" from a non-Christian or a Christian tradition? For a recent survey of the history of the Son-of-Man debate, see Burkett, *Son of Man.*

78. 1:51; 3:13,14; 5:27; 6:27, 53, 54, 62; 8:28; 9:35; 12:23, 34; 13:31. Although Jesus speaks often of his return in the Last Discourse [13–17], he does not use "the Son of Man" in such references. Smalley, "Johannine," thinks the Johannine Son-of-Man sayings might be earlier than the Synoptic ones; Borsch, *Son,* 258, thinks "most, if not all, of John's Son of Man logia bears signs of being more primitive than the evangelist's overall Christology."

79. Burkett, *Son,* claimed that his understanding of the Johannine Son of Man (see above, note 72) could go back to the historical Jesus, and also explain the use of the expression in the Synoptic tradition. He has since abandoned this view. See *Son of Man,* 67.

80. Rhea, *Johannine,* argues against any apocalyptic elements; but 5:28–29 foresees a judging role for the Son of Man in the final resurrection of the dead, and 1:51 has angels ascending and descending on the Son of Man. For Rhea, the Johannine Son-of-Man portrait reinterprets the way in which Jesus is the Messiah (see 12:34) and the prophet.

81. See 3:13; 6:62 (the latter implies that he descended; also it speaks of seeing the Son of Man ascending [cf. Dan 7:13]; Synoptic sayings speak of seeing the Son of Man at God's right hand or coming on the clouds of heaven.) Sidebottom, "Ascent," makes the point that although *I Enoch* 48:2–6 portrays the Son of Man as preexistent in heaven, it does not speak of his descent.

Johannine Son-of-Man passages concern his being "lifted up" (3:14; 8:28; 12:34), an expression that refers both to the crucifixion and to the return to the Father's presence in heaven—thus passages that touch on Synoptic groups 2 and 3.[82] Similarly, John 3:13 states that no one has gone up into heaven except the one who came down from heaven, and 12:23; 13:31–32 speak of the glorification of the Son of Man in relation to his death and resurrection. The power to pass judgment that has been given by God to Jesus "because he is Son of Man" (5:27; only time in the Gospels there is no definite article before either noun) is probably exercised both during Jesus' life on earth and after his ascension at the end of time (see 5:28–29).[83] Twice in John's account (9:35–36; 12:34) people are not fazed by Jesus' references to the Son of Man (as if they were familiar with the title) but want to know who he is. This would give the impression of an existing Jewish concept. Particularly important is John 9:35 where, in what may be an echo of the Johannine baptismal confession, the man born blind is asked, "Do you believe in the Son of Man?"

That last passage raises the issue of the relation of the Son of Man designation to the frequently used "Son" (twenty times in John, eighteen of which are in the Book of Signs or first half of the Gospel) and "Son of God" (eight times, six of which are in the Book of Signs),[84] for in other

---

82. *Editor's Note:* Brown's reading of the Greek *hypsothênai dei* as reference to Jesus' return to the Father does not fully acknowledge the double meaning involved in the expression. It does not mean "return to the Father" (as it does in Phil 2:9), but that Jesus is simultaneously physically "lifted up" on a stake (as was the serpent in 3:14) and in the moment of crucifixion is also "exalted." It says nothing about departing for the Father, as the parallel with the serpent in 3:14 makes clear. The serpent was also "lifted up," but did not ascend! The parallel must be maintained: "just as . . . so also."

83. *Editor's Note:* I sense a sleight of hand here. The reference to "Son of Man" in 5:27 is clearly dependent upon Dan 7:13 (see Moloney, *Son of Man*, 80–82). The sayings in vv. 28–29 on future judgment are determined by the dominant theme of 5:19–30: the relationship between the Father and the Son (see esp. vv. 19–20, 22–23, 30).

84. John 3:14–16 relates closely "Son" and "the Son of Man"; 1:49, 51 relates "the Son of God" and "the Son of Man." *Editor's Note:* This brief note says nothing about context, and thus says little but implies much. In 1:49, Nathanael's use of "the son of God" (see his use of "Rabbi" and "King of Israel") is a limited confession of faith, but "the Son of Man" in 1:51 is on the lips of Jesus, and thus a *correction* of Nathanael's

churches the latter functioned creedally (Rom 1:3–4). Moloney, *Son of Man*, would argue that "Son of God" is used by John to describe Jesus' relationship with the Father before, during, and after his incarnation, while "Son of Man" is limited to the earthly career of Jesus (and perhaps, one might add, to his relation to human beings). Moloney would also contend that "Son of Man" corrected any attempt to picture Jesus, on the one hand, simply as a traditional Jewish Messiah,[85] and, on the other hand, as a second God. Others do not see so sharp a distinction between Son of Man and Son of God in terms of divine origin.[86] Significantly, in 1:51 Jesus uses "the Son of Man" as a deepening improvement of the titles given him by his disciples throughout the chapter (Messiah, the one described in the Mosaic Law and the prophets, Son of God, King of Israel), but none of those titles is repudiated.

A great deal of discussion has been centered on whether the preexistent and descending/ascending aspect of the Johannine Son of Man[87] can

---

confession in 1:49 (see 1:50). Similarly, the two appearances of "the Son of Man" in 3:13–14 point to the unique revelation of God that will take place on the cross, while 3:16 speaks of the Father *sending* the Son. "The Son of Man" is never *sent by the Father* in the Fourth Gospel. These are intended distinctions, and should be respected.

85. Martyn, *History* 129–51, also sees the Son-of-Man portrayal as modifying an earlier picture of Jesus as the Mosaic Prophet-Messiah; the Paraclete continues and makes effective Jesus' presence as the Son of Man binding together heaven and earth. Coppens would see the stratum of the Son-of-Man passages, which have a unity, as a later level than the main emphasis of the Gospel on Son and Son of God and correcting a nationalistic understanding of the Davidic Messiah.

86. The two are identified with only a modal difference in S. Kim, *The 'Son of Man' as the Son of God* (WUNT 30; Tübingen: J. C. B. Mohr [Paul Siebeck], 1983). See also Burkett, *Son*.

87. Moloney's attempt to deny that the Son of Man preexists or postexists has little following and requires implausible readings of 3:13 and 6:62. *Editor's Note:* Far too much is made of the "movement" of the Son of Man in John. However, I do not deny the descent of the Son of Man. That is clearly in the text. But the issue of a pre- and postexistent Son of Man is more subtle. I claim (whatever the weakness of my exegesis of 3:13 and 6:62 in 1976), that the title "the Son of Man" is never used in a way that parallels the preexistent or postexistent Son, in much the same way as John would never speak of the preexistent or postexistent "Jesus of Nazareth." For John, as *logos* and Son of God, Jesus, the Son of Man, preexisted and postexisted. But the names "Jesus of Nazareth" and "Son of Man" are not used to speak of those aspects. The Son of Man is certainly above (3:13) and returns to the Father (6:62), but only

be derived from the Jewish apocalyptic background—a question that needs to be answered even if one thinks (as I do) that John shares background with some of the Synoptic usage and that usage drew on Jewish apocalyptic. Higgins speaks of a Synoptic Son of Man overlapped by a non-Synoptic Son of Man.[88] The appeal to an Oriental Gnostic myth reconstructed from later Mandaean and Manichaean texts (Bultmann), or to a primal Man prototype (Cullmann) or to a royal man myth (Borsch) has more following here than it has for the Synoptic imagery, but both the lateness of the sources and the difficulty of explaining how such diverse sources gave rise to a unified notion remain a formidable obstacle. Appeals to a Hellenistic heavenly man invoke Philo (commenting on Gen 1:26) and the Hermetic tract *Poimandres*.[89] But the Philonic "man" is a Platonic ideal that does not really descend into this world, while *Poimandres'* man does not antedate creation and is not a redeemer.

Those who opt for a biblical background for the Johannine descent motif frequently suggest two OT possibilities (either or both of which can be combined with a more general ambience for non-Johannine features of the Son of Man in Jewish apocalyptic). Borgen is a particularly strong proponent of a parallelism with the descent of Moses from the presence of God on Sinai with divine revelation embodied in the Law, and indeed from the very beginning John 1:17 tells us of the centrality of the Moses/Jesus comparison. That really does not cover the preexistence motif. The other proposed OT background is the career of personified divine Wisdom. These points are shared by the Johannine Son of Man

---

insofar as Jesus of Nazareth, the Son of Man, is to be identified with "the Son (of God)" and the *logos*. For example, the Johannine Jesus never says: "Father, glorify the Son of Man with the glory which he had before the world was made" (see 17:5)! As far as my "following" is concerned, see the important contributions of Hare, *The Son of Man Tradition*, 79–111, and Lindars, *Jesus Son of Man*, 145–57. Lindars comments on p. 218 n. 1: "The conclusions reached in the present chapter agree largely with those of Moloney."

88. Higgins, *Jesus*. Complicated and idiosyncratic is the proposal by Bühner, *Der Gesandte:* Jesus, a human prophet with vision of a divine call, ascended into heaven and was transformed into the Son of Man (3:1) and descends as an angel (with Dan 7:13 interpreted to refer to an angel).

89. See Dodd, *Interpretation*, 43–44; A. J. M. Wedderburn, "Philo's 'Heavenly Man,' " *NovT* 15 (1973): 301–26. Also C. H. Talbert, "The Myth of a Descending-Ascending Redeemer in Mediterranean Antiquity," *NTS* 22 (1975–76): 418–40.

and Wisdom: preexistence with God, coming from heaven into this world, communication of revelation or divine knowledge, offer of spiritual food, producing division or self-judgment when some people accept and others refuse.[90] Some think that the Son-of-Man and Wisdom motifs were joined in pre-Christian Judaism (F.-M. Braun, Moeller) or in Christian tradition prior to John (Schnackenburg, Maddox, Moloney); others think John made the union (Dion, Meeks), at times invoking an identification of the Word with Wisdom. As a caution, however, one should note with M. Scott that no Johannine writing mentions Wisdom (Sophia—perhaps because Jesus is male?) and that the exact vocabulary for descend/ascend is not applied in the OT to Wisdom (whence the complementary appeal to Moses and Sinai). Beyond its relationship to the Son-of-Man portrayal, however, Wisdom is so frequently invoked in discussions of Johannine theology that it deserves a special subsection.

Wisdom Motifs

THE FOURTH GOSPEL STANDS APART from the other Gospels in its presentation of Jesus as incarnate revelation descended from on high, indeed from another world, to offer people light and truth. In discourses of quasi-poetic solemnity, Jesus proclaims himself with the famous "I am" formula, and his divine and celestial origins are apparent both in what he says and in the way he says it. Otherworldliness is visible in the way that he can treat with majestic disdain the plots against him and the attempts to arrest him. In his own words, he is "in the world but not of it." In drawing this portrait of Jesus, plausibly John has capitalized on an identification of Jesus with personified divine Wisdom as described in the OT. Just as NT writers found in Jesus the anti-type of elements in the historical books of the OT (e.g., of the Exodus, Moses, David) and the fulfillment of the words of the prophets, so also the fourth evangelist saw in Jesus the culmination of a tradition that runs through the Wisdom Literature of the OT.

---

90. Many of the features of the later Gnostic pictures of a descending revealer and of the Philonic and *Poimandres* portrayals are found in the certainly pre-Christian OT picture of Wisdom, which may in fact be one of their sources. See G. W. MacRae, "The Jewish Background of the Gnostic Sophia Myth," *NovT* 12 (1970), 86–101.

The Wisdom Literature covers a wide spectrum of material and is one of the most cosmopolitan sections of the OT, sharing much in common with the writings of sages in Egypt, Sumer, and Babylon. This ecumenism of the wisdom movement showed itself in a later period in the openness of the biblical sages to Hellenistic influence, for it was in works like Ecclesiastes and the Wisdom of Solomon that Greek philosophic thought and vocabulary made their greatest inroads into the Bible. Almost half the deuterocanonical literature, preserved in the canon of Alexandria, is of a sapiential character. The blend of Oriental mysticism and mythology with Greek philosophy, found in the Wisdom Literature, had an influence that continued even after the biblical period, and traces of it can be found in Egyptian Gnosticism and Hermeticism.

In the NT, James represents a Christian wisdom book, illustrating that part of sapiential writing dealing with practical ethics.[91] Some of the more mystical trends in wisdom thought had ramifications in Colossians and Ephesians. The Gospel of John, supposedly from the same section of the world as that addressed in these two epistles, also betrays this influence. The concept of the "Word" or *logos* finds some of its background in the Wisdom Literature,[92] but here I shall be more concerned with the Johannine portrait of Jesus.

References to personified divine Wisdom (a female figure, since the Hebrew word for wisdom, *hokmâ*, and the Greek word *sophia* are feminine) are scattered widely in the OT;[93] but our chief sources here will be

---

91. See BINT, 740.

92. See *John*, 519–24.

93. Willett, *Wisdom* 43–48, debates whether the better description of the portrayal of Wisdom is hypostatization or personification. Hypostatizing depicts as an independent being an attribute that otherwise would be thought of as the action or characteristic of another, especially God, and Willett rejects it as applicable to biblical Wisdom which is not a being independent of God. Personification involves representing in personal terms something, especially an attribute, that is not a person. In the various biblical pictures of Wisdom, she personifies God's orderliness in creation, God's revelation (especially the Law) and working in the world, God's invitation to closeness. *Editor's Note:* I add here a clarification from David Noel Freedman, communicated to me in his editing of my text: "For the Hebrew Bible, Lady Wisdom is described in two ways. She is fully personified, i.e., as someone in association with God, and reflecting a polytheistic background in which goddesses played major roles in mythology. At the same time, the word itself is an attribute of God, part of his

the poems dedicated to Wisdom, e.g., Job 28; Prov 1–9; Baruch 3:9–4:4; Sirach 1; 4:11–19; 6:18–31; 14:20–15:10; 24; Wisdom 6–10.[94] According to these descriptions, Wisdom came forth from the mouth of the Most High (Sirach 24:3) and existed with God from the beginning even before there was an earth (Prov 8:22–23; Sirach 24:9; Wisdom 6:22)—so also the Johannine Jesus is the Word who was in the beginning (1:1) and was with the Father before the world existed (17:5). Wisdom is said to be a pure emanation of the glory of the Almighty (Wisdom 7:25), and those who hold her fast inherit glory (Sirach 4:13)—so also Jesus had glory with the Father before the world was created and then manifests the Father's glory to human beings (1:14; 8:50; 11:4; 17:5, 22, 24). Wisdom is said to be a reflection of the everlasting light of God (Wisdom 7:26); and in lighting up the path for people (Sirach 1:29), she is to be preferred to any natural light (Wisdom 7:10, 29)—in Johannine thought God is light (1 John 1:5); and Jesus who comes forth from God is the light of the world (John 1:4–5; 8:12; 9:5).

Wisdom is described as having descended from heaven to dwell with human beings (Prov 8:31; Sirach 24:8; Baruch 3:37; Wisdom 9:10; James 3:15)—so also Jesus is the Son of Man who has descended from heaven to earth (John 1:14; 3:31; 6:38; 16:28). In particular, John 3:13 is very close to Baruch 3:29 and Wisdom 9:16–17.[95] Wisdom worked signs to deliver a

---

makeup, and the instrument by which he plans and executes his program. The short answer to the question would be 'both,' but a longer answer might be 'neither,' on the grounds that such terms do not really apply to the religion of the Hebrew Bible."

94. Willett, *Wisdom*, 238–43, raises the issue of whether the Johannine School (which for him is the Johannine community) particularly studied OT Wisdom literature.

95. *Editor's Note:* Interestingly, Brown claims a parallel between Wisdom who comes down from heaven and the Son of Man who also descended, but none of the texts cited in parentheses refer to "the Son of Man." They refer to the *logos* or the Son of the Father. The only text (indeed with a close relationship to the Wisdom tradition) that speaks of the descent of the Son of Man is 3:13. Maybe this is an anomaly, and calls for special attention. Particularly helpful is P. Borgen, "Some Jewish Exegetical Traditions as Background for Son of Man Sayings in John Gospel (3:14–14 and context)," in de Jonge, ed.; *L'Évangile,* 243–58. On the uncalled-for fascination that scholars have with the descending and ascending Son of Man (for which there is only one text [3:13], once you exclude the "lifting up" as referring to the cross), see Moloney, *Son of Man,* 240.

holy people and guided them along a marvelous way (Wisdom 10:15–17), while Jesus worked signs and constituted the way (John 14:6). The ultimate return of Wisdom to heaven (*I Enoch* 42:2) offers a parallel to Jesus' return to his Father.[96]

The function of Wisdom is to teach people about the things that are above (Job 11:6–7; Wisdom 9:16–18), to utter truth (Prov 8:7; Wisdom 6:22), to give instructions as to what pleases God and how to do God's will (Wisdom 8:4; 9:9–10), and thus to lead people to life (Prov 4:13; 8:32–35; Sirach 4:12; Baruch 4:1) and immortality (Wisdom 6:18–19). This is precisely the function of Jesus, the revealer portrayed in numerous passages in John. In accomplishing her task, Wisdom speaks in the first person in long discourses addressed to her hearers (Prov 8:3–36; Sirach 24)—so also Jesus takes his stand and addresses people with his discourses, often beginning with "I am." For the instruction that she offers, Wisdom uses symbols like food (bread) and drink (water, wine); and she invites people to eat and drink (Prov 9:2–5; Sirach 24:19–21; Isa 55:1–3 [God offering his instruction])—so also Jesus uses these symbols for his revelation (6:35, 51ff.; 4:13–14).

Wisdom is not satisfied simply to offer her gifts to those who come; she roams the streets seeking people and crying out to them (Prov 1:20–21; 8:1–4; Wisdom 6:16)—so also the Johannine Jesus walks along, encountering those who will follow him (1:36–38, 43), searching out people (5:14; 9:35), and crying out his invitation in public places (7:28, 37; 12:44). One of the most important tasks that Wisdom undertakes is to instruct disciples (Wisdom 6:17–19) who are her children (Prov 8:32–33; Sirach 4:11; 6:18)—so also in John those disciples who are gathered around Jesus are called his little children (13:33). Wisdom tests her disciples and forms them (Sirach 6:20–26) until they love her (Prov 8:17; Sirach 4:12; Wisdom 6:17–18), and they become friends of God (Wisdom 7:14, 27)—so also Jesus purifies and sanctifies his disciples with his word and truth (15:3; 17:17) and tests them (6:67) until he can call them his beloved friends (15:15, 16:27). On the other hand, there are those who reject Wisdom (Prov 1:24–25; Baruch 3:12; *I Enoch* 42:2)—so also we see in John many who will not listen when Jesus offers them the truth (8:46; 10:25). For those who reject Wisdom, death is inevitable; truth is unat-

---

96. Ziener, "Weisheitsbuch," and Clark, "Signs," relate the signs in John to the signs in Wisdom 11–19, although the exact correspondence requires great imagination.

tainable; and their pleasure in the things of life is transitory.[97] Thus the coming of Wisdom provokes a division: some seek and find (Prov 8:17; Sirach 6:27; Wisdom 6:12); others do not seek and when they change their minds, it will be too late (Prov 1:28). The same language in John describes the effect of Jesus upon people (7:34; 8:21; 13:33).

Besides these comparisons between the career of Wisdom and the ministry of the Johannine Jesus, another parallel to Wisdom may be found in the Spirit-Paraclete who teaches people to understand what Jesus told them.[98] Also the postresurrectional inhabitation of Jesus within those who believe in him (14:23) may be compared to Wisdom's power to penetrate people (Wisdom 7:24, 27).

This short treatment should help to support the contention that the Wisdom Literature offers better parallels for the Johannine picture of Jesus than do the later Gnostic, Mandaean, or Hermetic passages sometimes suggested.[99] However, John has noticeably modified details of the presentation of Wisdom by introducing a much sharper historical perspective than is found in the OT poems. Wisdom was a poetic personification; Jesus was a living historical figure. If Jesus was incarnate Wisdom, the incarnation occurred at a particular place and time, once and for all. Demythologizing the Wisdom concept by incorporating it into salvation history is not totally new, for one encounters the same tendency in the very late Wisdom Literature. Sirach 24:23 and Baruch 4:1 would identify Wisdom with the Law given on Sinai, and Wisdom 10 illustrates the activity of Wisdom in the lives of the patriarchs from Adam to Moses. It is interesting to note that John's references to the OT are largely to figures like Abraham, Moses, and Isaiah who have given testimony to Jesus and foreseen his days, and thus have been witnesses of divine wisdom (5:46; 8:56; 12:41). John carries this further by seeing in Jesus the supreme example of divine Wisdom active in history, and indeed divine Wisdom itself.

---

97. Bruns, "Some," has pointed out that the bleak outlook caused by the bankruptcy of human wisdom in Ecclesiastes is not unlike that envisaged in John 6:63, where it is said that the flesh is useless and only the Spirit can give life.

98. See *John*, 1135–44.

99. What John shares in common with these latter bodies of literature often represents a common but independently received heritage from the Jewish Wisdom Literature.

Is the presentation of Jesus as divine Wisdom a peculiarly Johannine development, or can it be traced back into the early tradition known by the other Gospels? In them, Jesus manifested certain characteristics of the wisdom teacher.[100] The Marcan Jesus was addressed as "Teacher." He gathered disciples; he answered questions about the Law; he spoke in proverbs and parables. Matthew and Luke generalize sayings of Jesus once directed to a particular situation and make them wisdom sayings with a universal application.[101] Scholars differ as to how much of this sapiential character was found in "Q" (the source common to Matthew and Luke), but the fact that "Q" has at least some wisdom features means that the sapiential emphasis goes back to a relatively early stage in the formation of the Gospel tradition. However, one must note that in general the sapiential strain in the Synoptic tradition does not develop in exactly the same way that it develops in John. In the Synoptics, Jesus' teaching shows a certain continuity with the ethical and moral teachings of the sages of the Wisdom Literature; in John, Jesus is personified Wisdom.

However, there are a few passages in the Synoptics that are much closer to the sapiential strain in John. In Luke 21:15, Jesus promises to give his disciples wisdom that will enable them to speak. In Luke 11:49, a saying is attributed to "the Wisdom of God," which Matt 23:34 attributes to Jesus himself. The enigmatic saying, "Wisdom is justified by [all] her children [or deeds]," is found in both Matt 11:19 and Luke 7:35 in a context that might lead the reader to identify Jesus as the "Wisdom" of the saying. In another "Q" passage (Luke 11:31; Matt 12:42) Jesus is exalted over the wisdom of Solomon. In Mark 10:24 Jesus addresses his disciples as "Children," a form of address that, as we saw above, both personified Wisdom and the Johannine Jesus employ. The theme of Jesus coming to call people is found in all three Synoptics (Mark 2:17 and par.). In Luke 6:47 (but not in Matt 7:24) Jesus refers to: "Everyone who *comes to me* and bears my words"—a saying in the style of personified Wisdom and typical of the Johannine Jesus (5:40; 6:35, 45).

The most important passage in the Synoptic Gospels reflecting the

---

100. See A. Feuillet, "Jésus et la sagesse divine. Le 'logion Johannique' et l'Ancien Testament," *RB* 62 (1955), 179–84.

101. For examples, see W. D. Davies, *The Setting of the Sermon on the Mount* (Cambridge: Cambridge University Press, 1966), 457–60.

theme of personified Wisdom is the "Johannine logion" (Matt 11:25–27; Luke 10:21–22), a "Q" saying:

> I thank you, Father, Lord of heaven and earth, because you have hidden these things from the wise and foolish and revealed them to babes—yes Father, for so was it pleasing to you. All things have been given over to me by my Father; and no one knows (who is) the Son except the Father, nor does anyone know the Father except the Son and anyone to whom the Son chooses to reveal Him.

Davies suggests that the original emphasis in this revelation may have been more eschatological than sapiential.[102] Nevertheless, we have here a saying of a markedly Johannine type that goes back to early tradition. The saying that follows it in Matt 11:28–30, wherein Jesus invites people to come to him to find rest, closely echoes the appeals of Wisdom in Sirach 24:19 and 51:23–27.

The Synoptic evidence is not overwhelming, but there is enough of it to make one suspect that the identification of Jesus with personified Wisdom was not the original creation of the Fourth Gospel. Probably here, as with other Johannine themes like "the hour," and the "I am" sayings, John has capitalized on and developed a theme that was already in the primitive tradition.

Summary

BY WAY OF EVALUATION, then, how are we to estimate the place of Johannine theology in the spectrum of NT theology? Little credence can be given to the older view that placed the Synoptics, Paul, and John in a Hegelian sequence of thesis, antithesis, and synthesis. In reaction to such artificially smooth sequences, the more recent tendency has been to treat Johannine theology as if it stood out of sequence—either in the sense that the evangelist stood so far apart from orthodox Christian thought that his work needed censorship in order to be accepted, or in the sense that he was an unconscious prophet of an existential approach to Jesus who cut through the externalism of church and sacraments and placed

---

102. Davies, *Setting,* 207.

each Christian in a direct "I-thou" relationship to Jesus. Still another suggestion is that John represents thought that circulated in a "backwater" community, cut off from the church at large.

Personally, I find no major difficulty in fitting John into the mainstream of Christian thought; it is another facet of the manifold understanding of Jesus. John's theology is not the same as that of Paul, or that of James, or that of any of the Synoptic writers. Although the writers of all these works shared an essential unity in faith that made them Christians, they also exhibited a notable diversity in theological approach and emphasis.[103] Such diversity is well illustrated in the various NT treatments of the problems just discussed: ecclesiology, sacraments, and eschatology. It can also be claimed, in my opinion, for the Johannine Son of Man.[104] I am not convinced that any NT writer regarded the church, the sacraments, the parousia, much less its Christology, as irrelevant. But the writers expressed very differently the relevance of these topics, and this expression was greatly guided by factors of time, place, and individual understanding. Through comparison we can find traces of development and sequence, but there is no all-embracing linear development in NT thought. Recognizing this makes more understandable the place of highly individual theological thought like John's.

That John has much in common with other NT works has been emphasized in comparative articles. Besides the studies of John and the Synoptics mentioned in Chapter Three, there have been examinations of similarities between Johannine and Pauline thought, despite the very different articulation.[105] The Prologue, a seemingly unique Johannine hymn, has definite parallels with the Pauline hymns in Colossians and Philippians.[106] C. Spicq's exhaustive commentary on Hebrews devotes a very in-

---

103. See my "Unity and Diversity in New Testament Theology," *NovT* 6 (1963): 298–308.

104. *Editor's Note:* This sentence is my addition to Brown's text.

105. E.g., A. Fridrichsen, in *The Root of the Vine* (New York: Philosophical Library, 1953), 37–62, P. Benoit, "Paulinisme et Johannisme," *NTS* 9 (1962–63): 193–207 (summarized in English in *TD* 13 [1965]: 135–41), and J. Becker, "Geisterfahrung und Christologie—ein Vergleich zwischen Paulus und Johannes," in *Antikes Judentum und frühes Christentum. Festschrift für Hartmut Stegermann zum 65. Geburtstag* (BZNW 97; Berlin: Walter de Gruyter, 1999), 428–42. See also U. Schnelle, "Johannes als Geisttheologe," *NovT* 40 (1998): 17–31.

106. See *John*, 23–36.

teresting study to some sixteen parallels in thought between John and that epistle.[107] A long list of parallels between John and the Catholic Epistles, especially 1 Peter, could also be drawn up. The honor paid to the fourth evangelist by acknowledging him as *"the* theologian" (or even as "the divine") is justified, but that does not mean that he was as solitary or as out-of-step as some would have us believe.

BIBLIOGRAPHY

JOHANNINE THEOLOGY IN GENERAL

Beasley-Murray, G., *Gospel of Life: Theology in the Fourth Gospel* (Peabody, MA: Hendrickson, 1991).

Braun, F.-M., *Jean le Théologien*.

Cook, W. R., *The Theology of John* (Chicago: Moody, 1979).

Crehan, J. H., *The Theology of St. John* (London: Darton, Longman, & Todd, 1965).

Culpepper, R. A., "The Theology of the Gospel of John," *RExp* 85 (1988): 417–32.

Dunn, J. D. G., "Let John Be John: A Gospel for Its Time," in *Das Evangelium und die Evangelien*, (ed. P. Stuhlmacher; WUNT 28; Tübingen: Mohr/Siebeck, 1983), 309–39.

Fenton, J. C., "Towards an Understanding of John," *StEv* 4.28–37.

Giblet, J., "Développements dans la théologie johannique," in de Jonge, *Évangile*, 45–72.

Grossouw, W., *Revelation and Redemption* (Westminster: Newman, 1955).

Grundmann, W., *Zeugnis und Gestalt des Johannes—Evangeliums* (Stuttgart: Calwer, 1961).

Harrington, D., *John's Thought and Theology* (Wilmington: Glazier, 1990).

Howard, W. F., *Christianity According to St. John* (London: Duckworth, 1943).

Klaiber, W., "Die Aufgabe einer theologischen Interpretation des 4. Evangeliums," *ZTK* 82 (1985): 300–24.

Lee, E. K., *The Religious Thought of St. John* (London: SPCK, 1971).

Morris, L., *Jesus is the Christ. Studies in the Theology of John* (Grand Rapids: Eerdmans, 1989).

---

107. *L'Épître aux Hébreux* (2 vols.; EB; Paris: Gabalda, 1952), 1.109–38. On 1.134 Spicq remarks that Hebrews seems to represent a link between the theological elaborations of Paul and John.

Painter, J., *John: Witness and Theologian* (London: SPCK, 1975).

Panimolle, S. A., *L'evangelista Giovanni. Pensiero e opera letteraria del quarto evangelista* (Rome: Borla, 1985).

Price, J. L., "The Search for the Theology of the Fourth Evangelist," *Journal of the American Academy of Religion* 35 (1967): 3–15.

Smith, D. M., *The Theology of the Gospel of John* (Cambridge: Cambridge University Press, 1995).

Summers, R., *Behold the Lamb. An Exposition of the Theological Themes in the Gospel of John* (Nashville: Broadman, 1979).

Taylor, M. J., ed., *A Companion to John. Readings in Johannine Theology* (New York: Alba House, 1977).

Vawter, B., "Some Recent Developments in Johannine Theology," *BTB* 1 (1971): 30–58.

SPECIFIC TOPICS IN JOHANNINE THEOLOGY

Appold, M. L., *The Oneness Motif in the Fourth Gospel. Motif Analyses and Exegetical Probe into the Theology of John* (WUNT 2.1; Tübingen: J. C. B. Mohr [Paul Siebeck], 1976).

Beutler, J., *Martyria: Traditionsgeschichtliche Untersuchungen zum Zeugnis-thema bei Johannes* (Frankfurt: Knecht, 1972).

Butterworth, R., "John and the Law," *Bellarmine Commentary* 3 (1962): 50–59.

Howard-Brook, W., *Becoming Children of God—John's Gospel and Radical Discipleship* (Maryknoll: Orbis, 1995).

Lachowski, J., *The Concept of Redemption according to the Gospel of John* (Rome: Angelicum, 1958).

Lazure, N., *Les valeurs morales de la théologie johannique* (EB; Paris: Gabalda, 1955).

Meeks, W. A., "The Ethics of the Fourth Evangelist," CBEGJ, 318–26.

Pancaro, S., *The Law in the Fourth Gospel* (NovTSup 42; Leiden: Brill, 1975).

Payeur, A., "Johannine Soteriology," *Bellarmine Commentary* 3 (1962): 42–49.

Rodriguez Ruiz, M., *Der Missionsgedanke des Johannesevangeliums* (FB 55; Würzburg: Echter, 1987).

Samuel, S. J., "The Johannine Perspective on Mission in Christ's Praxis," *Bangalore Theological Forum* 20 (1989): 8–16.

Trites, A. A., *The New Testament Concept of Witness* (SNTSMS 31; Cambridge Univ, 1977), esp. pp. 128–53, 222–30.

ECCLESIOLOGY

Bussche, H. van den, "L'Église dans le quatrième Évangile," *Aux origines de l'Église* (Recherches Bibliques 7; Louvain: Desclée de Brouwer, 1965), 65–85.

Dahl, N. A., "The Johannine Church and History," *CINTI*, 124–42.

D'Aragon, J.-L., "Le caractère distinctif de l'Église johannique," in *L'Église dans la Bible* (Paris: Desclée de Brouwer, 1962), 53–66.

Edanad, A., "Johannine Vision of Covenant Community," *Jeevadhara* 11 (1981): 127–40.

———, "Johannine Theology of the Church," *Jeevadhara* 15 (1985): 136–47.

Ferreira, J., *Johannine Ecclesiology* (JSNTSup 160; Sheffield: Sheffield Academic Press, 1998).

Feuillet, A., "Le temps de l'Église d'après le quatriéme évangile et l'Apocalypse," *MD* 65 (1961): 60–79. Summarized in English in *TD* 11 (1963): 3–9.

Giesebrecht, H., "The Evangelist John's Conception of the Church as Delineated in His Gospel," *EQ* 58 (1986): 101–19

Haacker, K., "Jesus und die Kirche nach Johannes," *TZ* 29 (1973): 179–201.

Infante, R., "Lo sposo e la sposa. Contributo per l'ecclesiologia del Quarto Vangelo," *Rassegna di Teologia* 37 (1996): 451–81.

Klauck, H. J., "Gemeinde ohne Amt? Erfahrungen mit der Kirche in den johanneischen Schriften," *BZ* 29 (1985): 193–220.

Le Fort, P., *Les structures de l'Église militante selon S. Jean* (Geneva: Labor et Fides, 1970).

Marrow, S. B., "Johannine Ecclesiology," *CS* 37 (1998): 27–46.

Meeks, W., "The Man from Heaven in Johannine Sectarianism," *JBL* 91 (1972): 44–72.

O'Grady, J. F., "Individualism and Johannine Ecclesiology," *BTB* 5 (1975): 227–61.

———, "Johannine Ecclesiology: A Critical Evaluation," *BTB* 7 (1977): 36–44.

Painter, J., "The Church and Israel in the Gospel of John," *NTS* 25 (1978–79): 103–12.

Pancaro, S., " 'People of God' in St. John's Gospel," *NTS* 16 (1969–70): 114–29.

———, "The Relationship of the Church to Israel in the Gospel of St. John," *NTS* 21 (1974–75): 396–405.

Pastor Piñeiro, F. A., "Comunidad y ministerio en el evangelio joaneo," *EstEccl* 50 (1975): 323–56.

———, *La eclesiología juánea según E. Schweizer* (Analecta Gregoriana 168; Rome: Gregorian University Press, 1968).

Petersen, N. R. *The Gospel of John and the Sociology of Light. Language and Characterization in the Fourth Gospel* (Valley Forge: Trinity Press International, 1993).

Rossé, G., *A Spirituality of Communion in the Writings of John* (Hyde Park, NY: New City Press, 1998).

Schelkle, K. H., "Kirche im Johannesevangelium," *Theologische Quartalschrift* 156 (1976): 277–83.

Schnackenburg, R., *The Church in the New Testament* (New York: Herder and Herder, 1965), esp. 103–17. Reprinted in Taylor (ed.), *Companion,* 247–56.

Schnelle, U., "Johanneische Ekklesiologie," *NTS* 37 (1991): 37–50.

Schweizer, E., "The Concept of the Church in the Gospel and Epistles of St. John," in *New Testament Essays in Memory of T. W. Manson* (ed. A. J. B. Higgins; Manchester: Manchester University Press, 1959), 230–45.

Via, D. O., "Darkness, Christ, and the Church in the Fourth Gospel," *ScotJT* 14 (1961): 172–93.

ROLE OF WOMEN IN JOHN

Brown, R. E., "Roles of Women in the Fourth Gospel," *TS* 36 (1975): 688–99. Also available in *Community,* 183–98.

Conway, C. M., *Men and Women in the Fourth Gospel: Gender and Johannine Characterization* (SBLDS 167; Atlanta: Scholars Press, 1999).

Fehribach, A., *The Women in the Life of the Bridegroom. A Feminist Histori-cal-Literary Analysis of the Female Characters in the Fourth Gospel* (Collegeville: The Liturgical Press, 1998).

Grassi, J. A., "Women's Leadership Roles in John's Gospel," *BibTod* 35 (1997): 312–17.

Nortjé, S. J., "The Role of Women in the Fourth Gospel," *Neotestamentica* 20 (1986): 21–28.

Schneiders, S. M., "Apostleship of Women in John's Gospel," *Catholic Charis-matic* 1 (1977): 16–20.

————, "Women in the Fourth Gospel and the Roles of Women in the Con-temporary Church," *BTB* 12 (1982): 35–45.

Seim, T. K., "Roles of Women in the Gospel of John," in *Aspects on the Johan-nine Literature. Papers presented at a Conference of Scandinavian New Testament Exegetes at Uppsala, June 16–19, 1986* (eds. L. Hartman and B. Olsson; ConBNT 18; Stockholm: Alqvist & Wiksell Interna-tional, 1987), 56–73.

SACRAMENTALISM

Aune, D. E., "The Phenomenon of Early Christian 'Anti-Sacramentalism,'" in *Studies in New Testament and Early Christian Literature,* ed. D. E. Aune (A. P. Wikgren Festschrift; NovTSup 33; Leiden: Brill, 1972), 194–214.

Braun, F.-M., "Le baptême d'après le quatrième évangile," *RThom* 48 (1948): 347–93.

Brown, R. E., "The Johannine Sacramentary Reconsidered," *TS* 23 (1962): 183–206. Also in *NTE*, ch. 4.

Bultmann, R., *Theology of the New Testament* (2 vols.; New York: Scribner, 1955), 2.3–14.

Clavier, H., "Le problème du rite et du mythe dans le quatrième évangile," *RHPR* 31 (1951): 275–92.

Cosgrove, C. H., "The Place Where Jesus Is: Allusions to Baptism and the Eucharist in the Fourth Gospel," *NTS* 35 (1989): 522–39.

Craig, C., "Sacramental Interest in the Fourth Gospel," *JBL* 58 (1939): 31–41.

Cullmann, O., *ECW*.

García-Moreno, A., "Teología sacramentaria en el IV evangelio," *Salmanticensis* 42 (1995): 5–27.

Klos, H., *Die Sakramente im Johannesevangelium* (SBS 46; Stuttgart: KBW, 1970).

Köster, H., "Geschichte und Kultus im Johannesevangelium und bei Ignatius von Antiochien," *ZTK* 54 (1957): 56–69.

Lindars, B., "Word and Sacrament in the Fourth Gospel," *ScotJT* 29 (1976): 49–63.

Lohse, E., "Wort und Sakrament im Johannesevangelium," *NTS* 7 (1960–61): 110–25.

Matsunaga, K., "Is John's Gospel Anti-Sacramental?" *NTS* 27 (1980–81): 516–24.

Moloney, F. J., "When is John Talking about Sacraments," in *"A Hard Saying,"* 109–30.

Michaelis, W., *Die Sakramente im Johannesevangelium* (Bern: BEG, 1946).

Niewalda, P., *Sakramentssymbolik im Johannesevangelium* (Limburg: Lahn, 1958).

Paschal, R. W., Jr., "Sacramental Symbolism and Physical Imagery in the Gospel of John," *Tyndale Bulletin* 32 (1981): 151–76.

Randellini, L., "La Chiesa e i sacramenti nel ciclo giovanneo," in *La dignità dell'uomo,* (ed. B. Mariani; Rome: Antonianum, 1979), 229–43.

Schnackenburg, R., "Die Sakramente im Johannesevangelium," *SacPag* 2.235–54.

Schneiders, S. M., "Symbolism and the Sacramental Principle in the Fourth Gospel," in Tragan (ed.), *Segni* 221–35. (See below, under Tragan).

Smalley, S., "Liturgy and Sacrament in the Fourth Gospel," *Evangelical Quarterly* 29 (1957): 159–70.

Tragan, P.-R., ed., *Segni e sacramenti nel Vangelo di Giovanni* (Studia Anselmiana 66; Rome: S. Anselmo, 1977).

————, *Fede e sacramenti negli scritti giovannei* (Studia Anselmiana 90; Rome: S. Anselmo, 1985).

Vawter, B., "The Johannine Sacramentary," *TS* 17 (1956): 151–66.

ESCHATOLOGY

Aune, D. E., *The Cultic Setting of Realized Eschatology in Early Christianity* (NovTSup 28; Leiden: Brill, 1972), esp. pp. 45–135.

Blank, J., *Krisis: Untersuchungen zur johanneischen Christologie und Eschatologie* (Freiburg: Lambertus, 1964).

Boismard, M.-É., "L'évolution du thème eschatologique dans les traditions johanniques," *RB* 68 (1961): 507–24.

————, "Deux exemples d'évolution 'régressive'," *LumVie* 29 (1980): 65–74.

Bultmann, R., "Die Eschatologie des Johannesevangeliums," in *Glauben und Verstehen I* (Tübingen: J. C. B. Mohr [Paul Siebeck], 1961), 134–52.

Cadman, W. H., *The Open Heaven* (ed. G. B. Caird; New York: Herder and Herder, 1969).

Cook, W. R., "Eschatology in John's Gospel," *CTR* 3 1988): 79–99.

Corell, A., *Consummatum Est: Eschatology and Church in the Gospel of St. John* (London: SPCK, 1958).

Frey, J., *Die johanneische Eschatologie.* Band 1, *Ihre Probleme im Spiegel der Forschung seit Reimarus;* Band 2, *Das johanneische Zeitverständnis;* Band 3, *Die eschatologische Verkündigung in den johanneischen Texten* (WUNT 96, 110, 117; Tübingen: Mohr/Siebeck, 1997, 1998, 1999).

Grech, P., "L'escatologia degli scritti Giovannei (Quarto vangelo e lettere)," *Annali di storia dell'esegesi* 16 (1999): 117–32.

Hartingsveld, L. van, *Die Eschatologie des Johannesevangeliums. Ein Auseinandersetzung mit Rudolf Bultmann* (Assen: van Gorcum, 1962).

Hoegen-Rohls, C. *Der nachösterliche Johannes. Die Abschiedsreden als hermeneutischer Schlüssel zum vierten Evangelium* (WUNT 2.84; Tübingen: J. C. B. Mohr [Paul Siebeck], 1996).

Jonge, M. de, "Eschatology and Ethics in the Fourth Gospel," *Jesus,* 169–91.

————, "The Radical Eschatology of the Fourth Gospel and the Eschatology of the Synoptics," in Denaux, *John,* 481–87.

————, "Christology and Theology in the Context of Early Christian Eschatology, Particularly in the Fourth Gospel," FGFN 3.1835–53.

Kysar, R., "The Eschatology of the Fourth Gospel. A Correction of Bultmann's Redactional Hypothesis," *Perspective* 13 (1972): 22–33.

Niederwimmer, K., "Zur Eschatologie im Corpus Johanneum," *NovT* 39 (1997): 105–16.

Preisker, H., "Das Evangelium des Johannes als Teil eines apokalyptischen Doppelwerks," *Theologische Blätter* 15 (1936): 185–92.

———, "Judische Apokalyptik und hellenistischer Synkretismus im Johannesevangelium," *TLZ* 77 (1952): 673–78.

Ricca, P., *Die Eschatologie des Vierten Evangeliums* (Zurich: Gotthelf, 1966).

Stählin, G., "Zur Problem der johanneischen Eschatologie," *ZNW* 33 (1934): 225–59.

Stauffer, E., *"Agnostos Christos:* Joh. ii. 24 und die Eschatologie des vierten Evangeliums," BNTE, 281–99.

Stimpfle, A., *Blinde sehen. Die Eschatologie im traditionsgeschichtlichen Prozess des Johannesevangeliums* (BZNW 57; Berlin: de Gruyter, 1990).

Wolfzorn, E. E., "Realized Eschatology: An Exposition of Charles H. Dodd's Thesis," *ETL* 38 (1962): 44–70.

CHRISTOLOGY

Anderson, P. N., "The Cognitive Origins of John's Unitive and Disunitive Christology," *HBT* 17 (1995): 1–24.

———, *The Christology of the Fourth Gospel* (Valley Forge: Trinity, 1996).

Boismard, M.-É., *Moses or Jesus: An Essay in Johannine Christology* (Minneapolis: Fortress, 1993).

Birger, O., *"Deus semper maior?:* On God in the Johannine Writings," in Nissen and Pedersen, eds., *New Readings in John*, 143–71.

Brown, R. E., "The Kerygma of the Gospel According to John: The Johannine View of Jesus," *Interpretation* 21 (1967): 387–400.

Davey, J. E., *The Jesus of St. John* (London: Lutterworth, 1958).

Dupont, J., *Essais sur la Christologie de saint Jean. Le Christ, Parole, Lumière et Vie, La Gloire du Christ* (Bruges: Editions de l'Abbaye de Saint-André, 1951).

Ellis, E. E., "Background and Christology of John's Gospel: Selected Motifs," *Southwestern Journal of Theology* 31 (1988): 24–31.

Fortna, R. T., "Christology in the Fourth Gospel: Redaction-Critical Perspectives," *NTS* 21 (1974–75): 489–504.

Grob, F., *Faire l'oeuvre de Dieu. Christologie et éthique* (Paris: Presses Universitaires, 1986).

Grundmann, W. *Der Zeuge der Wahrheit. Grundzüge der Christologie des Johannesevangliums* (ed. W. Wiefel; Berlin: Evangelische Verlaganstalt, 1985).

Hartman, L., "Johannine Jesus-Belief and Monotheism," in HOAJL, 85–99.

Kohler, H., *Kreuz und Menschwerdung im Johannesevangelium* (ATANT 72; Zurich: Theologischer Verlag, 1987).

Kügler, J., *Der andere König. Religionsgeschichtliche Perspektiven auf die Christologie des Johannesevangeliums* (SBS 178; Stuttgart: KBW, 1999).

Larsson, T., *God in the Fourth Gospel. A Hermeneutical Study of the History of Interpretations* (ConBNT 35; Stockholm: Almqvist & Wiksell, 2001).

Lemcio, E. E., "Father and Son in the Synoptics and John: A Canonical Reading," in *The New Testament as Canon* (eds. R. W. Wall and E. E. Lemcio; Sheffield: Sheffield Academic Press, 1992), 78–108.

Loader, W., *The Christology of the Fourth Gospel* (BBET 23; 2nd. ed.; Frankfurt: Lang, 1992).

Mealand, D. L., "The Christology of the Fourth Gospel," *ScotJT* 31 (1978): 449–67.

Menken, M.J.J., "The Christology of the Fourth Gospel. A Survey of Recent Research," FJJ, 292–320.

Miranda, J. P., *"Der Vater, der mich gesandt hat"* (2nd ed.; Frankfurt: Lang, 1976).

———, *Die Sendung Jesu im vierten Evangelium* (SBS 87; Stuttgart: KBW, 1977).

Moloney, F. J., "God So Loved the World: The Jesus of John's Gospel," in *"A Hard Saying,"* 167–80.

———, "Telling God's Story: The Fourth Gospel," in *The Forgotten God: The God of Jesus Christ in New Testament Theology: Essays in Honor of Paul J. Achtemeier on the Occasion of his Seventy-fifth Birthday* (eds. A. A. Das and F. J. Matera; Louisville: Westminster John Knox Press, 2002), 107–22.

———, "The Fourth Gospel's Presentation of Jesus as 'the Christ,' and J. A. T. Robinson's *Redating*," *DR* 95 (1977): 239–53.

———, "The Johannine Son of God," *Salesianum* 38 (1976): 71–86.

Nicholson, G. C., *Death as Departure. The Johannine Descent-Ascent Schema* (SBLDS 63; Chico, CA: Scholars, 1983).

Penna, R., "Lessico di rivelazione e cristologia nel Quarto Vangelo," *Vivens Homo* 8 (1997): 141–68.

Reinhartz, A., ed., *God the Father in the Gospel of John* (Semeia 85; Atlanta: Scholars Press, 1999).

Sabugal, S., *Christos. Investigacion exegética sobre la cristologia joannea* (Barcelona: Herder, 1972).

———, "Una contribución a la cristologia joannea," *Augustinum* 12 (1972): 565–72.

Schlosser, J., "Les *logia* johanniques relatifs au Père," *RevSR* 69 (1995): 87–104.

Schnackenburg, R., "Synoptische und johanneische Christologie—ein Vergleich," FGFN, 3.1723–50.

Schneider, H., " 'The Word Was Made Flesh': An Analysis of the Theology of Revelation in the Fourth Gospel," *CBQ* 31 (1969): 344–56.

Schnelle, U., *Antidocetic Christology in the Gospel of John. An Investigation of the Place of the Fourth Gospel in the Johannine School* (Minneapolis: Fortress, 1992).

Scroggs, R., *Christology in John and Paul* (Philadelphia: Fortress, 1988).

Thompson, M. M., *The Humanity of Jesus in the Fourth Gospel* (Philadelphia: Fortress, 1988). Reprinted as *The Incarnate Word* (Peabody, MA: Hendrickson, 1993).

Thüsing, W., *Die Erhöhung und Verherrlichung Jesu im Johannesevangelium* (2nd ed.; Münster: Aschendorff, 1970).

Trumbower, J. A., *Born from Above. The Anthropology of the Gospel of John* (Tübingen: J. C. B. Mohr [Paul Siebeck], 1992).

Weder, H., *"Deus incarnatus:* On the Hermeutics of Christology in the Johannine Writings," CBEGJ, 327–45.

SON OF MAN

Borgen, P., "Some Jewish Exegetical Traditions as Background for the Son of Man Sayings in John's Gospel (3,13–14 and Context)," in de Jonge, *L'Évangile,* 243–58.

Borsch, F., *The Son of Man in Myth and History* (Philadelphia: Westminster), 257–313.

Bühner, J.-A., *Der Gesandte und sein Weg im 4 Evangelium* (WUNT 2.2; Tübingen: J. C. B. Mohr [Paul Siebeck], 1977), esp. pp. 374–99, 422–29.

Burkett, D., *The Son of the Man in the Gospel of John* (JSNTSup 56; Sheffield: JSOT Press, 1991).

———, *The Son of Man Debate. A History and Evaluation* (SNTSMS 107; Cambridge: Cambridge University Press, 1999).

Coppens, J., "Le Fils de l'homme dans l'évangile johannique," *ETL* 52 (1976): 28–81.

———, "Le logia johannique du Fils de l'homme," in de Jonge, *L'Évangile,* 311–15.

Dion, H.-M., "Quelques traits originaux de la conception johannique du Fils de l'Homme," *ScEccl* 19 (1967): 49–65.

Fernández Ramos, F., "El hijo del hombre en el cuarto evangelio," *Studium Legionense* 40 (1999): 45–92.

Freed, E., "The Son of Man in the Fourth Gospel," *JBL* 1986 (1967): 402–9.

Ham, C., "The Title 'Son of Man' in the Gospel of John," *Stone Campbell Journal* 1 (1998): 67–84.

Hare, D. R. A., *The Son of Man Tradition* (Minneapolis: Fortress Press, 1990), 79–111.

Higgins, A. J. B., *Jesus and the Son of Man* (Philadelphia: Fortress, 1964), 153–84.

Kinniburgh, E., "The Johannine 'Son of Man,' " *StEv* 4.64–71.

Lindars, B., "The Son of Man in the Johannine Christology," in *Christ and Spirit in the New Testament: Studies in Honour of Charles Francis Digby Moule,* (eds. B. Lindars and S. S. Smalley; Cambridge: Cambridge University Press, 1973), 43–60.

———, *Jesus Son of Man. A fresh examination of the Son of Man sayings in the Gospels* (London: SPCK, 1983), 145–57.

Maddox, R., "The Function of the Son of Man in the Gospel of John," in *Reconciliation and Hope. Essays on Atonement and Eschatology Presented to Leon Lamb Morris on His 60th Birthday* (ed. R. Banks; Grand Rapids: Eerdmans, 1974), 186–204.

Moloney, F. J., *The Johannine Son of Man* (2nd ed; Rome: Libreria Ateneo Salesiano, 1978).

———, "The Johannine Son of Man," *BTB* 6 (1976): 179–89.

———, "A Johannine Son of Man Discussion?" *Salesianum* 39 (1977): 93–102.

———, "The End of the Son of Man?" *DR* 98 (1980): 280–90.

Painter, J., "The Enigmatic Johannine Son of Man," FGFN 3.1869–87.

Pamment, M., "The Son of Man in the Fourth Gospel," *JTS* 36 (1985): 56–66.

Pazdan, M. M., *The Son of Man. A Metaphor for Jesus in the Fourth Gospel* (Collegeville: The Liturgical Press, 1991).

Preiss, T., "Le fils de l'homme dans le IVᵉ Évangile," *Études Théologiques et Religieuses* 28 (1953): 7–61.

Rhea, R., *The Johannine Son of Man* (ATANT 76; Zurich: Theologischer Verlag, 1990).

Roth, W., "Jesus as the Son of Man: The Scriptural Identity of a Johannine Image," in *The Living Text. Essays in Honor of Ernest W. Saunders* (eds. D. W. Groh and R. Jewett; Lanham: University of America Press, 1985), 11–26.

Ruckstuhl, E., "Die johanneische Menschensohnsforschung," in *Theologische Berichte I,* (eds. J. Pfammatter and F. Furger; Zurich: Benzinger, 1972), 171–284.

———, "Abstieg und Erhöhung der johanneischen Menschensohns," in *Jesus der Menschensohn. Festschrift für Anton Vögtle* (eds. R. Pesch and R. Schnackenburg; Freiburg: Herder, 1975), 314–41.

Sasse, M., *Der Menschensohn im Evangelium nach Johannes* (TANZ 35; Tübingen/Basel: A. Francke Verlag, 2000).

Schnackenburg, R., "Der Menschensohn im Johannes-evangelium," *NTS* 11 (1964–65), 123–37.

Schulz, S., *Untersuchungen zur Menschensohn-Christologie im Johannesevangelium* (Göttingen: Vandenhoeck & Ruprecht, 1957).

Sidebottom, E. M., "The Ascent and Descent of the Son of Man in the Gospel of John," *ATR* 2 (1957): 115–22.

———, "The Son of Man as Man in the Fourth Gospel," *ExpTim* 68 (1956–57): 231–35, 280–83.

Smalley, S. S., "The Johannine Son of Man Sayings," *NTS* 15 (1968–69): 278–301.

WISDOM MOTIFS

Braun, F.-M., "Saint Jean, la Sagesse et l'histoire," *NTP*, 123–33. See also *JT* 2.115–50.

Bruns, J. E., "Some Reflections on Coheleth and John," *CBQ* 25 (1963): 414–16.

Clark, D. K., "Signs in Wisdom and John," *CBQ* 45 (1983): 201–9.

Manns, F., "La sagesse nourricière dans l'"Évangile de Jean," *BibOr* 39 (1997): 207–234.

Moeller, H. R., "Wisdom Motifs and John's Gospel," *BETS* 6 (1963): 92–100.

Sandelin, K.-G., "The Johannine Writings within the Setting of Their Cultural History," HOAJL, 9–26.

Scott, M., *Sophia and the Johannine Jesus* (JSNTSup 71; Sheffield: JSOT Press, 1992).

Willett, M. E., *Wisdom Christology in the Fourth Gospel* (Ann Arbor: University Microfilms, 1985).

Ziener, G., "Weisheitsbuch und Johannesevangelium," *Bib* 38 (1957): 396–418; 39 (1958): 37–60.

8

The Language, Text, and Format of the Gospel: Some Considerations on Style

◆

The Original Language of the Gospel

IT IS MOST PROBABLE that Jesus' ordinary conversation and preaching was in Aramaic, although he may have known how to read Hebrew and understood it in the synagogue. The fact that the DSS are largely in Hebrew means that, longer than was formerly thought, Hebrew was preferred as a sacred and a literary language and that spoken Hebrew remained in use among the educated of Judea. But this evidence really does little to prove that a Galilean prophet like Jesus would speak to the people in Hebrew. The few times his words are transcribed from Semitic into Greek in the Gospels, the language reflected is Aramaic, not Hebrew.[1]

---

1. Mark 5:41; 7:34; 14:36; 15:34; John 1:42 (Kêphas). Although some scholars have claimed that Jesus spoke Greek, a more probable scenario is that he might have known some conversational Greek phrases that were part of ordinary life in Galilean towns. There is not the slightest evidence that he preached in Greek.

Jesus' Aramaic background naturally had an effect on the quality of the Greek in which Jesus' words were preserved. Moreover, there was further Semitic influence on this Greek, for the early preachers who proclaimed the tradition of Jesus' words and deeds in the Greek world were also Semites for whom Greek was, at most, a secondary language. Perhaps, too, the first language of the four evangelists was not in all cases Greek. Still another factor was that the Christian message in the Greek world was first preached in the Diaspora synagogues and consequently was phrased in the religious vocabulary of Greek-speaking Judaism—a Greek that was influenced by the Semitized style of the LXX, the Greek OT. Therefore, from all these channels Aramaisms, Hebraisms, and Semitisms (i.e., constructions abnormal in Greek, but normal in Aramaic, in Hebrew, or in both these Semitic languages) made their way into the Gospels. It must be clear that the presence of such features is not sufficient to prove that a Gospel was first written in one of the two languages; at most it *may* show that certain sayings once existed in Aramaic or Hebrew.

Is it possible that the Fourth Gospel was originally written in Aramaic in whole or in part, and what would indicate this? The possibility can scarcely be denied, for it does seem that some gospel material was written in Aramaic. For instance, Papias reports that "Matthew arranged in order the sayings [*logia*] in the Hebrew [= Aramaic?] language" (EH 3.39.16). A gospel "written in Hebrew letters" was known as late as Jerome's time.[2] Among the modern scholars who have suggested that, in whole or in part, John was first written in Aramaic are Burney, Torrey, Burrows, Macgregor, Black, and Boismard; and we remember that Bultmann supposes an Aramaic original for the Revelatory Discourse Source. The following arguments have been proposed:

- The presence of Aramaisms, but not Hebraisms—Torrey considers this conclusive, but Burney does not.
- The presence of mistranslations, that is, the confused state of a Greek passage is thought to have resulted from an error in rendering into Greek an obscure Aramaic phrase, and the true sense of the passage is apparent only with retroversion into Aramaic—Burney depends heavily on this.

---

2. This *Gospel of the Nazoreans* seems to have existed in Aramaic—was it a retroversion of Matthew from Greek?

- The existence of Greek manuscript variants that may represent two different possible translations into Greek of the Aramaic original— Black and Boismard have brought forward numerous examples.
- The fact that some of John's OT citations seem to be drawn directly from the Hebrew (Burney) or from the Targums (Boismard).[3]
- The possibility of retroverting the "poetry" of the discourses or of the Prologue into good Aramaic poetry (Burney)—we remember that Bultmann suggested the parallel of the *Odes of Solomon,* which are in Syriac (a later form of Aramaic).

These arguments are not of equal value. I have already called attention to the insufficiency of (a) as a proof. The mistranslations mentioned in (b) are more persuasive, but there is always an element of subjectivity in deciding that the Greek makes no sense as it now stands. With (d) we have always to face the possibility that the evangelist was really citing the Greek OT, but freely and from memory. Moreover, even if the citation of the OT was drawn directly from the Hebrew or even from the Targums, that may simply reflect Jesus' own usage or the later choice of the most apposite translation without proving that the Gospel was written in Aramaic. Moreover, considerable uncertainty taints the appeal to Targums for interpreting John.[4] Thus, no one argument is sufficient, and it is more a question of convergence of probabilities. The difficulty of the problem is indicated by the ever-increasing caution of the proponents of an Ara-

---

3. Targums (or Targumim) are Aramaic translations (some literal, some very free) of the OT; presumably they would have been used in the Galilean synagogues where people no longer spoke Hebrew. Almost all preserved Targums date from after A.D. 100, but the discovery of a Targum of Job in Cave 11 of Qumran proves they existed in the pre-Christian era. A distinction is made between earlier Palestinian Targums and later Babylonian ones. Those cited in reference to John include: Targum Neofiti: a Palestinian Aramaic translation with readings from the second century A.D. and later. Targum Pseudo-Jonathan: a Palestinian or Babylonian Aramaic translation of the Prophets edited around the fifth century A.D. but containing readings that may go back to the second century A.D. The same may be said for Targum Onqelos: a Babylonian Aramaic translation of the Pentateuch. The dating and utility of Targums for NT research are highly disputed. See R. Le Déaut, "Targumic Literature and New Testament Interpretation," *BTB* 4 (1974): 243–89; S. A. Kaufman, "On Methodology in the Study of the Targums and their Chronology," *JSNT* 23 (1985): 117–24.

4. See above, note 3.

maic original. Burney was more cautious than Torrey; and Black and Boismard are more cautious still than Burney.

Personally, I agree with the majority of scholars who do not find adequate evidence that a complete edition of the Gospel according to John ever existed in Aramaic. It is possible that bits of the historical tradition underlying John were not only spoken but also written in Aramaic. Yet even this possibility lies beyond proof. If there are genuine mistranslations into Greek,[5] these may have arisen in the oral transmission and translation of items of historical material before the first stage of the written Gospel. If early alternate Greek translations found their way into different manuscript traditions of the Fourth Gospel, this would be a strong argument for an Aramaic original of the Gospel; but those are not easy to distinguish from variants representing scribal freedom or improvements in copying Greek.

The Greek Text of the Gospel

APPROXIMATELY 3,000 MANUSCRIPTS OF THE GREEK NT (part or whole) have been preserved, copied between the second and seventeenth centuries, plus over 2,200 lectionary manuscripts containing sections (pericopes) of the NT arranged for reading in church liturgies from the seventh century on. These witnesses to the text of the NT do not agree among themselves in myriad ways, but relatively few of the differences are significant.[6] No autograph or original manuscript of a NT book has been preserved; the differences came in the course of copying the original. Not all the differences stemmed from mistakes by copyists;[7]

---

5. Again, however, do we have the ability to distinguish mistranslations from awkward Greek expressions?

6. Some are. The main theologically significant variant in the Johannine corpus is the so-called "Johannine comma," an addition to 1 John 5:7–8, articulating a trinitarian faith in Father, Word and Holy Spirit. The text is universally recognized as a scribal addition. For a full discussion, see BEJ, 775–87.

7. Copyists' mistakes occurred through both the eye (misreading and carelessly copying from a text) and the ear (misunderstanding a person who was dictating the text aloud). One should allow too for a misreading by the person who was dictating to the copyists.

some arose from deliberate changes. Copyists, at times, felt impelled to improve the Greek of what they received, to modernize the spelling, to supplement with explanatory phrases, to harmonize Gospels, favor a particular theological slant,[8] and even to omit something that seemed dubious. One might think that the oldest preserved copies of the Greek NT (part or whole) would be the best guide to the originals; but that is not necessarily so. For instance, a sixth-century MS might be the only remaining exemplar of a much earlier, now lost copy that was closer to the autograph than an extant second- or fourth-century copy.

Given the variety of Greek manuscript readings of John, determining the one that is most plausibly original is difficult. As with most of the other NT works, the basic Greek text of John is determined by a comparison of the great codices of the fourth and fifth century: Vaticanus (designated B), Sinaiticus (S), and the Greco-Latin Codex Bezae (D). In general, Vaticanus represents an "Eastern" textual tradition popular in Egypt, particularly at Alexandria, while Bezae represents a "Western" textual tradition, also found in the early translations into Latin (OL) and Syriac (OS).[9] While elsewhere Sinaiticus is close to Vaticanus, for the first eight chapters of John the original hand produced a text closer to Bezae. Alexandrinus (A) is nowadays given little credibility. However, dating from the fifth and sixth centuries, it is an early witness, and occasionally has superior readings. Importantly, it is not an exemplar or the Textus Receptus, the once universally used Greek text developed by Erasmus and published in 1516. It still continues to influence modern text critics.

One must evaluate the different readings of these and other Greek textual witnesses, plus the evidence of the early versions in Latin, Syriac, Coptic, and Ethiopic. The citations of John in the early Church Fathers are also important. Worthy of attention are recent papyri discoveries that affect the text of John, for these are of major importance. We now have more papyri copies of John (twenty-two—eleven dated before 300) than

---

8. Mees, "Erhöhung," points out christological bias even in the papyri.

9. In several articles, Ehrman has argued that Heracleon, the early Gnostic commentator on John who wrote in Rome ca. 170, had available a "Western" text, different from that used by Origen, an Alexandrian, a half-century later.

of any other NT book.[10] Two Greek papyri from the Bodmer collection published between 1956 and 1961 are the most remarkable because of their antiquity (probably just before and after A.D. 200 respectively). The Gospel of John is preserved as a book, except for some minor damage round the edges. From the first folio there were 52 leaves (26 double leaves to John 14) preserved in their entirety, with the remainder of the book more or less fragmentary.[11] They are major textual witnesses for the Gospel some 150 years older than the great codices mentioned above. It is quite clear that P[75] (Bodmer XV) agrees more closely with Codex Vaticanus than with any other manuscript. P[66] (Bodmer XIV), however, has a text that stands somewhere between Vaticanus and Sinaiticus, slightly closer to the latter. When these two papyri agree, they constitute very strong evidence, but must be rejected when the laws of textual criticism seem to point to another reading found in a later witness as the more original. After all, the very fact that P[66] and P[75] do not always agree means that even by A.D. 200 many copyists' changes and mistakes had already crept into the copies of the Gospel text.

Another development worthy of note in the textual study of John has been the work of M.-É. Boismard, who spent decades seeking to establish readings more primitive than those preserved in any of the Greek witnesses. As his chief tools he used the early versions, the citations found in the Church Fathers, and *the Diatessaron* of Tatian.[12] The patristic readings, for example, those of John Chrysostom, are often significantly shorter than the readings found in the codices, and brevity is frequently a sign of a more original reading.[13] Boismard's *Un évangile pré-johannique*

---

10. Comfort, "Greek," studies the impact of the papyri readings on the widely used 26th ed. of the Nestle-Aland *Novum Testamentum Graece* (1979), which in general follows Codex Vaticanus.

11. K. Aland and B. Aland, *The Text of the New Testament*, 87. On the papyri in general, see pp. 83–102.

12. A harmony of the Gospels written about 175, probably in Greek, but preserved only in later commentaries and translated harmonies.

13. *Editor's Note:* I am leaving this affirmation as it came to me in Brown's script. However, in his editorial notes to me, David Noel Freedman modifies it as follows: "While this may be true in some cases, the reverse may be true in others. Accidental omission is a leading cause of scribal error in transmission. At least (one) should balance this known fact against the supposed tendency to expand on the part of scribes.

is a massive ongoing effort to distinguish and reconstruct beneath Chrysostom's homilies an older commentary, probably by his teacher, Diodorus of Tarsus (died before 394). Although Chrysostom the homilist drew on a Greek text similar to those known in the codices, the commentator used an archaic Greek text; and Boismard theorizes that the two texts represent different translations from the same Aramaic original. J. N. Birdsall argues that the divergent patristic text reconstructed by Boismard may still have been available in Photius's time (ninth century). Boismard's contentions had considerable influence on the French translation of John in SB, but where his readings are entirely dependent on the versions and the patristic citations, and have no support in the Greek manuscript witnesses, I am hesitant to accept them. The Fathers often cited freely and presented a short form of a passage because they were interested only in what was pertinent; they often adapted for theological purposes; and so they have their limitations as guides to the exact wording of the passages of Scripture.

Even with the use of all the latest evidence and the application of the rules of textual criticism, scholars will disagree on the original Greek readings of some disputed passages.

The Poetic Format of the Gospel Discourses

THAT THE JOHANNINE PROSE of the discourses of Jesus is uniquely solemn has been recognized by many. Some have suggested that this prose is quasi-poetic and should be printed in poetic format. This would offer one more point of similarity between the Johannine Jesus and personified Wisdom, for Wisdom speaks in poetry. What would be the basis for considering the Johannine discourses as quasi-poetic?

The fundamental principle in OT poetry is parallelism, and occasionally parallelism appears in the words of Jesus as reported by John. Synonymous parallelism, where the second line repeats the idea of the first, is exemplified in John 3:11; 4:36; 6:35, 55; 7:34; 13:16. Antithetic parallelism, where the second line says the same thing as the first, but the first

---

I have yet to see a proven case of deliberate expansion on the part of a scribe, while there are thousands of cases of inadvertent omission. . . . Albright's parting words on the subject were "losses not glosses."

says it positively and the second says it negatively, is found in 3:18; 8:35; 9:39. There is an interesting example in 3:20 and 21 where one whole verse is balanced against another. Synthetic parallelism, where the sense flows on from one line to another, is well illustrated in 8:44. A particular form of this, "staircase" parallelism, where one line picks up the last principal word of the preceding line, is found in the Prologue and in 6:37; 8:32; 13:20: 14:21. The presence of parallelism, however, while frequent in John, is not the dominant characteristic of the discourses.[14]

Rhyme is not very frequent in Semitic poetry, but it does occur. Burney retroverted John 10:1–5 into Aramaic and shows a pattern of rhyme.[15] Not only is the retroversion quite speculative, but also there are relatively few sections of the Gospel that lend themselves to a pattern of rhyme, even when retroverted.

If the discourses of Jesus in John are to be printed in poetic format, the basis of the quasi-poetic style lies in rhythm. Some would propose a rhythm of accentual beats. To some extent at least such delineation of ictus is calculated on a hypothetical Aramaic original. For instance, Burney has found lines of four beats each in 14:1–10; lines of three beats in 3:11 and 4:36; and the sorrowful *Qinah* meter of three beats in the first line and two beats in the second line in 16:20. Gächter has been the most thoroughgoing in his quest for a rhythm of stressed syllables in John. He worked with the Greek text, although occasionally he reconstructed the Aramaic original. He preferred short lines of two beats each, and did not believe that the poetic division of a line must necessarily constitute a sense unit—the line is one of stress rhythm and need not convey a complete thought. This feature made Gächter's reconstruction of the poetry quite unique, with very little resemblance to the wisdom poetry of the OT. Gächter also insisted on a highly complicated system of strophic arrangement.

As mentioned, Bultmann maintained that the Greek form of the discourses in John had for the most part preserved the poetic format of the original Revelatory Discourse Source. D. M. Smith's isolation and printing of the material that Bultmann attributed to this source shows at a

---

14. Parallelism is not peculiar to the Fourth Gospel. Burney, *Poetry*, 63–99, shows that the same forms of parallelism are found in the words of Jesus recorded by the Synoptics.

15. Burney, *Poetry*, 174–75.

glance how good a case can be made for casting John in poetic format.[16] This holds true even without resort to putative Aramaic originals or to counting off accentual beats. In the various discourse sections of the Greek Gospel there is a constant rhythmic effect of lines of approximately the same length, each constituting a clause. Two features of Bultmann's arrangement are more open to question. He joined the Prologue with the rest of the discourse material, but the "staircase" parallelism of the Prologue represents a far more carefully worked out poetic style than any passage of length in the discourses. In my opinion, the Prologue was a hymn, while the discourses were not. Second, in his reconstruction of the poetic format, Bultmann was rather arbitrary in his excision of glosses that he attributed to the final redactor. The poetic format is not so fixed or strict that awkward lines can be diagnosed as additions.

In his French translation of John (SB), D. Mollat set up the discourses in a poetic format. Without formulating his principles, like Burney and Bultmann he divided according to sense lines. At times, in a struggle to present balanced lines in the French translation, Mollat sacrificed the balance of the Greek lines.[17] It is a very interesting exercise to make a comparative study of these various attempts at setting the Johannine discourses in a poetic format. Perhaps two-thirds of the time Bultmann and Mollat will be in agreement on the number of lines into which a verse should be divided. Yet, even with one-third variation, they are much closer to one another than to Gächter.[18] We lack conclusive proof that a poetic format is justified; but, when one has worked with the material for a while, searching to find a format, one does get caught up into the pattern.

Perhaps it is worthwhile to insist once more that the use of poetic format means only that there is a quasi-poetic balance to the prose of the discourses. I do not believe that one can consistently find rhyme, strict parallelism, or exact stress patterns. If the prose is solemn, it is far from lyrical. The language of the discourses achieves a monotonous grandeur

---

16. Smith, *Composition*, 23–34.

17. Bultmann, who printed the Gospel verses in Greek, did not have to face the translation problem. Mollat adopted a block form for his poetic lines, while Bultmann indented subordinate lines.

18. E.g., in 6:35 both Mollat and Bultmann have three lines, while Gächter has five.

by repetition of simple words and not by the use of highly literary vocabulary.[19]

Notable Characteristics in Johannine Style[20]

Inclusion. At the end of a passage, the Gospel will often mention a detail or make an allusion that recalls something recorded in the opening of the passage. This feature, well attested in other biblical books, for example, the Wisdom of Solomon, can serve as a means of packaging a unit or a subunit by tying together the beginning and the end. Note the references to the two Cana miracles in 2:11 and 4:46, 54; the references to the Transjordan in 1:28 and 10:40; the implicit references to the paschal lamb in 1:29 and 19:36.

Chiasm or inverted parallelism. In two units which share a number of parallel features, the first verse of I corresponds to the last verse of II, the second verse of I corresponds to the next to the last verse of II, etc.

I		II
v. 1	=	v. 7
v. 2	=	v. 6
v. 3	=	v. 5
	v. 4	

Good examples may be seen in 6:36–40 and in the organization of the trial before Pilate in 18:28–19:16.[21]

---

19. *Editor's Note:* In the original script, Brown repeats his words from *John,* cxxxiv: "With some hesitation, we have decided to use poetic format in our own translation in order to offer the English reader an opportunity to judge for himself whether or not there is a rhythmic balance in the Johannine lines." I suspect that Brown would have largely reproduced the "poetic format" in a new translation that would be very similar to that of the 1966–70 edition of *John.* Readers of this new Introduction might refer to the 1966–70 translation and make their own judgment.

20. For a fuller list and description of these characteristics, see BINT, 333–36.

21. See *John,* 275–76 (6:36–40), 857–59 (18:28–19:16).

Twofold or double meaning. The Gospel often plays on the double mean-ings of words, whether in Aramaic or Greek, for example, in 3:3–5 on *anôthen* as "from above" and "again"; in 4:10–11 on the twofold meaning "living" and "flowing" to describe the water; in 7:8 on the ambiguity of "going up" (to Jerusalem or to the Father?).[22] This leads into the next feature.

Misunderstanding, ambivalence, and/or riddles. Because of double mean-ing or symbolic usage, language used in John may be misunderstood or not understood at all. This feature has been the subject of much scholarly discussion. Already Bernard sought to isolate distinctive aspects of mis-understanding;[23] and Gingrich, Bultmann, Clavier, and Cullmann pur-sued the study. Leroy devoted a major book to bringing more precision into the discussion. He notes ten instances where those outside Jesus' circle of followers express their misunderstanding of what he means and, although Jesus offers no explanation, the readers are expected to understand.[24] For instance, when Jesus speaks of water and bread, his di-alogue partners may think of corporeal drink and food (4:10–15; 6:32–34), but readers know he is speaking of the revelation he brings. Leroy distinguishes from such misunderstandings examples where Jesus speaks to his followers who do not understand him (13:33 + 36–38; 14:2–9) but no explicit misunderstanding is expressed. In these instances Leroy contends that John is closer to riddle language (as found in the an-cient Greek oracles), for Jesus has to explain what he means. Others

---

22. *Editor's Note:* I would add the important double-meaning word *hypsothênai* to this brief list. It can mean both "to lift up physically" (as the serpent was lifted up on a stake in 3:14), or "to exalt." For a misunderstanding (see next section) that flows from this double-meaning, see 12:32–33 + v. 34. Jesus speaks of his exaltation on the cross, which is the moment of his crucifixion (vv. 32–33), but "the crowds" under-stand it only to mean his death (v. 34).

23. Bernard, *St John*, 1.cxi–cxii.

24. John 2:19–22; 3:3–4; 4:10; 6:41–42; 6:51–52; 7:33–35; 8:21–22, 31–33, 51–53, 56–58. In an eleventh (4:31–34) the disciples of Jesus are involved, and Jesus himself gives the correct interpretation to them. In 2:19–22, the hearers wrongly think of the Jerusalem Temple building as the Temple sanctuary to be destroyed and raised up; and the commenting evangelist explains that Jesus was talking about the sanctuary of his body, for he reports that his disciples did not understand at the time and seem-ingly he does not trust the readers to understand even after the resurrection.

would find the situation even more complicated. Sometimes the misunderstanding/nonunderstanding is related to double meanings; in other instances it is related to the symbolic language of the Johannine Jesus. In 13:5–7, Peter does not understand an *action* of Jesus; and in 11:17–24, without a clear play on a specific word, Martha misunderstands the eternal life that Jesus has come to give, wishing that their brother could be spared death by preserved or restored natural life. Richard sees double meaning in many instances that are never explained (and on which modern commentators disagree, usually choosing one meaning), e.g, "gave" in 3:16 ("sent into the world" or "handed over to death"); *katalambanein* 1:5 ("receive, understand" or "overcome"); *ekathisen epi* in 19:13 "sat on" or "set [Jesus] on."[25]

Some scholars would relate all this to the in-language of the Johannine community, highlighting its sectarian character and isolation from other Christians (e.g., Petersen). However, one should qualify that claim by the recognition that some of this symbolism is the Johannine equivalent of the parabolic language of the Synoptics, and that misunderstanding/nonunderstanding is partially the Johannine equivalent of the failure to understand that greets the parables in the Synoptic tradition (Mark 4:12). Other interpreters (myself included) primarily relate misunderstanding/nonunderstanding to the Johannine Christology. As background for double meaning, symbolic, and ambivalent language, one must recognize that Jesus belongs to another world above (17:16; 3:31) and has come below as a stranger. When he wishes to speak of the heavenly world of his origin, he has only the language of this world to use. In the flow of the Gospel story readers are meant to understand what the *dramatis personae* of the Johannine stories misunderstand; Jesus wishes his disciples to understand him although often that is not possible without his further explanation; but finally there are more things that Jesus has to tell that the disciples cannot bear until the Spirit of Truth comes to guide them along the way to all truth (16:12–13). In any case, whether John narrates the misunderstanding of outsiders or the nonunderstanding of disciples, readers of the Gospel can find themselves confused by Jesus. That may well be intentional on the part of the evangelist, for Jesus always remains the stranger from above (to use M. de Jonge's term). Readers of all time must encounter him to receive eternal life, and in-

---

25. Richard, "Expressions."

evitably in that encounter they will have their own misunderstandings parallel to those of the Johannine characters.

Irony. This feature is related to misunderstanding. The opponents of Jesus are given to making statements about him that are derogatory, sarcastic, incredulous, or at least inadequate in the sense they intend. However, by way of irony these statements are often true or more meaningful in a sense they do not realize. The evangelist simply presents such statements and leaves them unanswered (or answered with eloquent silence), for he is certain that his believing readers will see the deeper truth. For example, as "the Jews" question the man born blind, they make a solemn announcement: "We know that God has spoken to Moses, but as for this man, we do not know where he comes from" (9:29). The believing reader recognizes the irony in this statement, and sides with the cured man, who suggests that Jesus might be "from God" (v. 33). Further good examples are 4:12; 7:35, 42; 8:22; 11:50.

Explanatory notes. In the Gospel we often find explanatory comments, inserted into the running narrative of the story. They explain names (1:38, 42) and symbols (2:21; 12:33; 18:9); they correct possible misapprehensions (4:2; 6:6); they remind the readers of related events (3:24; 11:2) and reidentify for them the characters of the plot (7:50; 21:20). Tenney, "Footnotes," has counted some fifty-nine such notes; and if it would not lead to confusion, they might well be placed at the bottom of the page as footnotes, as E. V. Rieu does in his NT translations. It is difficult to decide whether these notes reflect an editing process, wherein the same writer at a later time or a later writer decides that (new?) readers/hearers need help in order to understand. There is some evidence that in its history (part of?) the Johannine community may have moved from Palestine to a site in the Gentile world (7:35: Ephesus?), and that may have made it necessary to explain words with Semitic roots (1:38, 41, 42). Narrative critics insist upon the essential function of these so-called "notes" *within the text* as "explicit" or "implicit" commentary upon the discourse of the story.[26]

---

26. *Editor's Note:* The "story" is the sequence of events along a timeline, during which characters interact and develop as a plot unfolds, etc. "Discourse" is the underlying meaning the storyteller wishes to communicate to a reader *by means of* the

Relecture and réécriture.[27] Closely related to the remarks just made, J. Zumstein and his student A. Dettwiler have developed an approach to the Gospel that is helpful for an understanding of its development and some of its literary features. It begins from the obvious literary feature of "repetitions" in the narrative. They suggest that, as the Gospel developed, the author(s) deliberately read and reread (*relecture*) earlier traditions. The final form of the Gospel is deliberately composed of these various traditions and their rereading. Dettwiler has suggested that there are six basic principles involved in recognizing this process and interpreting the Johannine text.[28]

1. *Relecture* is an intertextual phenomenon that has to be analyzed both synchronically and diachronically.
2. The reread (*der Rezeptionstext*) text looks back upon the original text (*der Bezugstext*) for its original meaning that it has further developed.
3. *Relecture* happens in the twofold action of further developing the original text, and applying it to a different context.
4. The final text is always to be understood as a rereading of the original text.
5. The reasons for *Relecture* can, on the one hand, be a need for the further theological development of an original theological position within the narrative itself (*synchrony*), or on the other hand, called for because of a new historical or social situation of the community (*diachrony*).
6. The question of authorship plays little or no part in understanding the process of *Relecture*.

The process has been carefully examined for the interpretation of ch. 21 (Zumstein) and in chs. 13–17 (Dettwiler). It has long been recognized that the final discourse contains both an earlier tradition (14:1–31) and a later rereading (*Relecture*) (16:4b–33).

---

story. See S. Chatman, *Story and Discourse: Narrative Structure in Fiction and Film* (Ithaca: Cornell University Press, 1968). On implicit commentary in the Fourth Gospel, see Culpepper, *Anatomy*, 151–202.

27. *Editor's Note:* This paragraph has been added to Brown's text.

28. Dettwiler, *Gegenwart*, 46–52. See also Scholtissek, *In ihm sein*, 131–39; Idem, "Relecture und Réécriture," 1–29.

The process of *réédition* is purely synchronic. The interpeter starts from the presupposition that the Fourth Gospel has a central message, and that this message is taken up again and again, rewritten and reexpressed in a number of different ways throughout the story. "The Gospel as a whole has a unified style and language. . . . This is the result of continual reworking over decades of the Johannine community's telling and re-telling (in this context one should also say writing and re-writing) of the story of Jesus."[29] The two processes of *Relecture* and *réédition* have been used in a recent fine study of the Johannine use of the language of "immanence" in the Johannine Writings,[30] and merit the further attention of Johannine scholarship.

BIBLIOGRAPHY

ORIGINAL LANGUAGE

Brown, S., "From Burney to Black: The Fourth Gospel and the Aramaic Question," *CBQ* 26 (1964): 323–39.

Gundry, R. H., "The Language Milieu of First-century Palestine," *JBL* 83 (1964): 404–8.

GREEK TEXT

Aland, K. and Aland, B., *The Text of the New Testament. An Introduction to the Critical Editions and to the Theory and Practice of Modern Textual Criticism* (Grand Rapids: Eerdmans, 1987).

Fee, G. D., "Codex Sinaiticus in the Gospel of John. A Contribution to Methodology in Establishing Textual Relationships," *NTS* 15 (1968–69): 23–44.

The New Testament in Greek IV: The Gospel According to St. John, Vol. One: The Papyri (eds. W. J. Elliott and D. C. Parker; New Testament Tools and Studies 20; Leiden: E. J. Brill, 1995).

Parker, D. C., "The International Greek New Testament Project: The Gospel of John," *NTS* 36 (1990): 157–60.

Bodmer Papyri: P[66] or Bodmer Papyrus II, dating from ca. 200, was published by V. Martin, with chs. i–xiv appearing in 1956 and the rest in 1958.

---

29. Moloney, *Belief in the Word,* 241, n. 22. Parenthesis added to original.

30. Scholtissek, *In ihm sein.*

For corrections of the 1956 ed., see H. M. Teeple and F. A. Walker in "Notes on the Plates in Papyrus Bodmer II," *JBL* 78 (1959): 148–52; and G. D. Fee in "Corrections of Papyrus Bodmer II and the Nestle Greek Testament," *JBL* 84 (1965): 66–72. A revised ed. of P⁶⁶ was published by V. Martin and J. W. Barns in 1962. For subsequent corrections, see Barns, "Bodmer Papyrus II. Some Corrections and Remarks," *Le Muséon* 75 (1962): 327–29; E. F. Rhodes, "The Corrections of Papyrus Bodmer II," *NTS* 14 (1967–68): 271–81. For new fragments, K. Aland, "Neue Neutestamentliche Papyri II," *NTS* 20 (1973–74): 357–81. For analysis, see H. Zimmermann, "Papyrus Bodmer II und seine Bedeutung für die Textgeschichte des Johannesevangeliums," *BZ* 2 (1958): 214–43; G. D. Fee, *Papyrus Bodmer II (P⁶⁶): Its Textual Relationships and Scribal Characteristics* (Salt Lake: University of Utah Press, 1968).

P⁷⁵ or Bodmer Papyrus XV, dating from slightly after 200, was published by V. Martin and R. Kasser in 1961. K. Aland has analyzed the relations of these two papyri and collated their readings: "Neue Neutestamentliche Papyri II," *NTS* 9 (1962–63): 303–16; "Neue Neutestamentliche Papyri II," *NTS* 10 (1963–64): 62–79, dealing particularly with P⁶⁶; *NTS* 11 (1964–65): 1–21, dealing particularly with P⁷⁵. See S. A. Edwards, "P⁷⁵ under the Magnifying Glass," *NovT* 18 (1976): 190–212.

Clark, K. W., "The Text of the Gospel of John in Third-century Egypt," *NovT* 5 (1962): 17–24.

Comfort, P. W., "The Greek Text of the Gospel of John according to the Early Papyri," *NTS* 36 (1990): 625–29.

Delobel, J., "The Bodmer Papyri of John," in de Jonge, *L'Évangile*, 317–23.

Martini, C. M., *Il problema della recensionalità del Codice B alla luce del papiro Bodmer XIV* (AnBib 26; Rome: PBI, 1966).

Mees, M., "Erhöhung und Verherrlichung Jesu im Johannesevangelium nach dem Zeugnis neutestamentlicher Papyri," *BZ* 18 (1974): 32–44.

Metzger, B. M., *The Text of the New Testament. Its Transmission, Corruption, and Restoration* (2nd ed.; Oxford: Clarendon Press, 1968).

Porter, C. L., "Papyrus Bodmer XV (P⁷⁵) and the Text of Codex Vaticanus," *JBL* 81 (1962): 363–76.

———, "An Analysis of the Textual Variations between P⁷⁵ and Codex Vaticanus," in *Studies in the History and Text of the New Testament in Honor of Kenneth Willes Clark* (eds. B. L. Daniels and M. J. Suggs; Studies and Documents 29; Salt Lake: University of Utah, 1967), 71–80.

Tasker, R.V.G., "The Chester Beatty Papyrus and the Caesarean Text of John," *HTR* 30 (1967): 157–64.

In 1958 R. Kasser published Papyrus Bodmer III, a 4th-century Bohairic (Coptic) version of John rendered directly from the Greek. In "Le Papyrus

Bodmer III et les Versions Bibliques Coptes," *Le Muséon* 74 (1961): 423–33, Kasser studies this ms. in relation to the other Coptic witnesses to John. See also his *L'Évangile de Jean et les versions coptes de la Bible* (Neuchatel: Delachaux et Niestlé, 1966).

PATRISTIC EVIDENCE FOR THE GREEK TEXT

Birdsall, J. N., "Photius and the Text of the Fourth Gospel," *NTS* 4 (1957–58): 61–63.

Boismard, M.-É., "Critique textuelle et citations patristiques," *RB* 57 (1950): 388–408.

————, "Lectio Brevior, Potior," *RB* 58 (1951): 161–68.

————, "Problèmes de critique textuelle concernant le quatrième évangile," *RB* 60 (1953), 347–71.

————, (and A. Lamouille for vol. 1), *Un évangile pré-johannique* (many projected vols., with 2 tomes each; Paris: Gabalda, 1993–).

Ehrman, B. D., "Heracleon, Origen, and the Text of the Fourth Gospel," *VigChr* 47 (1993): 105–18.

————, "Heracleon and the 'Western' Textual Tradition," *NTS* 40 (1994): 161–79.

————, et al., *The Text of the Fourth Gospel in the Writings of Origen* (Atlanta: Scholars Press, 1992).

POETIC OR SPECIAL FORMAT

Breck, J., *The Shape of Biblical Language. Chiasmus in the Scriptures and Beyond* (New York: St. Vladimir's Seminary Press, 1994).

Burney, C. F., *The Poetry of Our Lord* (Oxford: Clarendon, 1925).

Ellis, P. F., *The Genius of John* (Collegeville: The Liturgical Press, 1984).

Gächter (Gaechter), P., [Both spellings are used by the author in his own published works.] in a series of articles, has treated individual passages.

  John 1:1–18: "Strophen im Johannesevangelium," *ZKT* 60 (1936): 99–111.

  John 5:19–30: "Zur Form von Joh 5,19–30," in *NTAuf,* 65–68.

  John 5:19–47: *ZKT* 60 (1936): 111–20.

  John 6:35–58: "Die Form der eucharistischen Rede Jesu," *ZKT* 59 (1935): 419–41.

  John 8:12–59: *ZKT* 60 (1936): 402–12.

  John 10:11–39: *ZKT* 60 (1936): 412–15.

  John 13–16: "Der formale Aufbau der Abschiedsreden Jesu," *ZKT* 58 (1934): 155–207.

Lund, N. W., "The Influence of Chiasmus upon the Structure of the Gospels," *ATR* 13 (1931): 27–48, 405–33.

————, *Chiasmus in the New Testament* (Chapel Hill: University of North Carolina Press, 1942).

Menken, M. J. J., *The Fourth Evangelist's Use of Numbers of Words and Syllables* (NovTSup 55; Leiden: E. J. Brill, 1985).

Mlakushyil, G., *The Christocentric Literary Structure of the Fourth Gospel* (AnBib 117; Rome: Biblical Institute Press, 1987).

CHARACTERISTICS OF STYLE

Abbott, E. A., *Johannine Grammar* (London: Black, 1906).

Belle, G. van, *Les parenthèses dans l'évangile de Jean* (Leuven: Peeters, 1985).

————, "Les parenthèses johanniques," FGFN, 3.1901–33.

Black, C. C., " 'The Words That You Gave to Me I have Given to Them': The Grandeur of Johannine Rhetoric," CBEGJ, 220–39.

Born, J. B., "Literary Features in the Gospel of John [3:1–21]," *Direction* 17 (1988): 3–17.

Boismard, M.-É., "Un procédé rédactionnel dans le quatrième évangile: la *Wiederaufnahme*," in de Jonge, *L'Évangile*, 235–41.

Carson, D. A., "Understanding Misunderstandings in the Fourth Gospel," *Tyndale Bulletin* 33 (1982): 59–91.

Clavier, H., "Les sens multiples dans le nouveau testament," *NovT* 2 (1957): 185–98.

————, "L'ironie dans le quatrième évangile," *StEv,* 1.261–76.

Cullmann, O., "Der johanneische Gebrauch doppeldeutiger Ausdrücke als Schlüssel zum Verständnis des vierten Evangeliums," *TZ* 4 (1948): 360–72.

Culpepper, R. A., *Anatomy of the Fourth Gospel.*

————, "Reading Johannine Irony," CBEGJ, 193–207.

Dettwiler, A., *Die Gegenwart des Erhöhten. Eine exegetische Studie zu den johanneischen Abschiedsreden (Joh 13,31–16,33) unter besonderer Berücksichtigung ihres Relekture-Charakters* (FRLANT 169; Göttingen: Vandenhoeck & Ruprecht, 1995).

————, "Fragile compréhension: L'hermeneutique de l'usage johannique du malentendu," *RTP* 131 (1999): 371–84.

————, "Le phénomène de la relecture dans la tradition johannique: une proposition de typologie," in *Intertextualité: Le Bible en échos* (Le monde de la Bible 10; Geneva: Labor et Fides, 2000), 185–200.

Domeris, W. R., "The Johannine Drama," *Journal of Theology for Southern Africa* 42 (1983): 29–36.

Duke, P. D., *Irony in the Fourth Gospel* (Atlanta: Knox, 1985).

Fee, G. D., "The Use of the Definite Article with Personal Names in the Gospel of John," *NTS* 17 (1970–71): 168–83.

Flanagan, N., "The Gospel of John as Drama," *BibTod* 19 (1981): 264–70.

Freed, E. W., "Variations in the Language and Thought of John," *ZNW* 55 (1964): 167–97.

Jansen, H. L., "Typology in the Gospel according to John," in *The Many and the One. Essays on Religion in the Greco-Roman World Presented to Herman Ludin Jansen on his 80th Birthday* (Relieff 15; Trondheim: Tapir, 1985), 125–43.

Léon-Dufour, X., "Trois chiasmes johanniques," *NTS* 7 (1960–61): 249–55.

Leroy, H., *Rätsel und Missverständnis. Ein Beitrag zur Formgeschichte des Johannesevangeliums* (BBB 30; Bonn: Hanstein, 1968).

———, "Das johanneische Missverständnis als literarische Form," *BibLeb* 9 (1968): 196–207.

Louw, J. P., "On Johannine Style," *Neotestamentica* 20 (1986): 5–12.

MacRae, G. W., "Theology and Irony in the Fourth Gospel," in *The Word in the World. Essays in Honor of F. L. Moriarty, S.J.* (eds. R. J. Clifford and G. W. MacRae; Cambridge, MA: Weston College Press, 1973), 83–96.

Menken, M. J. J., *Numerical Literary Techniques in John* (NovTSup 55; Leiden: Brill, 1985).

Morris, L., "Variation—A Feature of Johannine Style," in his *Studies*, 293–319.

Neirynck, F., "L'*epanalepsis* et la critique littéraire. À propos de l'évangile de Jean," *ETL* 56 (1980): 303–38.

———, "Parentheses in the Fourth Gospel," *ETL* 65 (1989): 119–23.

O'Rourke, J. J., "Asides in the Gospel of John," *NovT* 21 (1979): 210–19.

Pamment, M., "Path and Residence Metaphors in the Fourth Gospel," *Theology* 88 (1985): 118–24.

Petersen, N. R., *The Gospel of John and the Sociology of Light. Language and Characterization in the Fourth Gospel* (Valley Forge: Trinity International Press, 1993).

Rahner, J., "Missverstehen um zu verstehen: Zur Funktion der Missverständnisse im Johannesevangelium," *BZ* 43 (1999): 212–19.

Richard, E., "Expressions of Double Meaning and Their Function in the Gospel of John," *NTS* 31 (1985): 96–112.

Riesenfeld, H., "Zu den johanneischen *hina*-Sätzen," *ST* 19 (1965): 213–20.

Roberge, M., "Notices de conclusion et rédaction du quatrième Évangile," *Laval Théologique et Philosophique* 71 (1975): 49–53.

Scholtissek, K., "Ironie und Rollenwechsel im Johannesevangelium," *ZNW* 89 (1998): 235–55.

———, "Relecture und réécriture: Neue Paradigmen zu Methode und Inhalt," *Theologie und Philosophie* 75 (2000): 1–29.

Shedd, R., "Multiple Meanings in the Gospel of John," in *Current Issues in Biblical and Patristic Interpretation. Studies in Honor of Merill C. Tenney Presented by His Former Students* (Grand Rapids: Eerdmans, 1975), 247–58.

Tenney, M. C., "The Footnotes of John's Gospel," *BSac* 117 (1960): 350–64.

Wahlde, U. C. von, "A Redactional Technique in the Fourth Gospel," *CBQ* 38 (1976): 520–33.

Wead, D. W., *The Literary Devices in John's Gospel* (Basel: Reinhardt, 1970).

———, "Johannine Irony as a Key to Author," *SBL Proceedings 1974*, 33–44.

———, "The Johannine Double Meaning," *Restoration Quarterly* 13 (1970): 106–20.

Zumstein, J., *Kreative Erinnerung. Relecture und Auslegung im Johannesevangelium* (Zürich: Pano Verlag, 1999).

———, "La rédaction finale de l'évangile de Jean (à l'exemple du chapitre 21)," in Kaestli, Poffet and Zumstein, eds., *La communauté*, 207–30.

———, "Der Prozess der Relecture in der johanneischen Literatur," *NTS* 42 (1996): 394–411.

9

The Outline of the Gospel

◆

The General Outline of the Gospel

THE FOLLOWING DIVISION is suggested by the Gospel itself:

1:1–18: THE PROLOGUE. An early Christian hymn, probably stemming from Johannine circles, which has been adapted to serve as an overture to the Gospel narrative of the career of the incarnate Word.

1:19–12:50: THE BOOK OF SIGNS. The public ministry of Jesus where in sign and word he shows himself to his own people as the revelation of his Father, only to be rejected.

13:1–20:29: THE BOOK OF GLORY. To those who accept him Jesus shows his glory by returning to the Father in "the hour" of his crucifixion, resurrection, and ascension. Fully glorified, he communicates the Spirit of life.

20:30–31: CONCLUDING STATEMENT. Turning to the readers, the evangelist tells them this narrative was written so that they may come to life through ever-deeper faith in Jesus, the Christ, the Son of God.

21:1–25: THE EPILOGUE. An added account of postresurrectional appearances in Galilee.

It is quite clear that the end of ch. 12 and the beginning of 13 specifically mark a break in the narrative. In 12:37–43 there is a summary description and analysis of Jesus' public ministry and its effect on the people; 12:44–50 are the last words of Jesus directed to the people in general. In 13:1–3 there is a shift in emphasis, marked by the words, "It was before the Passover feast, and Jesus was aware that the hour had come for him to pass from this world to the Father." All Jesus' words in chs. 13–17 are directed to "his own" (13:1), his disciples whom he loves and who have come to believe in him. The spirit of these two main divisions of the Gospel is summed up in two verses of the Prologue (1:11–12) that contrast his own people who did not accept him and those who did accept him, thus becoming God's children. The second division of the Gospel comes to an end in 20:30–31, a conclusion which comments on the content and purpose of the Gospel. Several reasons, both internal and external, suggest that one should treat ch. 21 as an Epilogue.[1]

I have designated 1:19–12:50 as "The Book of Signs" because these chapters largely concern Jesus' miracles, referred to as "Signs," and discourses that interpret the signs. By contrast, the word "sign" occurs in the second division of the Gospel only in the summary statement of 20:30. The second division, which narrates what happened from the Thursday evening of the Last Supper until Jesus' appearance to his disciples after the resurrection, has all through it the theme of Jesus' return to his Father (13:1; 14:2, 28; 15:26; 16:7, 28; 17:5, 11; 20:17). This return means the glorification of Jesus (13:31; 16:14; 17:1, 5, 24), so that the resurrected Jesus appears to his disciples as Lord and God (20:25, 28)—whence our title "The Book of Glory."[2] The signs of the first book anticipated the glory of Jesus in a figurative way for those who had the faith to see

---

1. See *John*, 1077–82. *Editor's Note:* By "internal" is meant the uniqueness of the language and syntax of ch. 21, and by "external" is meant the relationship between the argument of ch. 21 with 1:1–20:31. See Moloney, *John*, 545–68.

2. *Editor's Note:* Two functions of "glory" and "glorification" are involved in the Johannine theology of the cross. *On the cross,* Jesus reveals the glory of God by his unconditional gift of self in love (the *doxa tou theou*), but *by means of the cross* ("the hour of Jesus") he is glorified in his perfect fulfillment of the task given him by the Father (see 19:30) and his return to where he was before the world was made. See especially 11:4: "This sickness is not unto death, but for the glory of God, and so that the Son of God may be gloried by means of it." See also 13:31–32; 17:5.

through the signs to their significance (2:11; 11:4, 40), but many greeted these signs with only limited perception and inadequate belief. The action of the second book, directed to those who believed in the signs of the first, accomplishes in reality what was anticipated by the signs of the first book, so that the Prologue can exclaim: "We have seen his glory, the glory of an only Son coming from the Father" (1:14).

The General Outline of the Book of Signs

WHAT ARE THE INDICATIONS within the Gospel itself that can serve as a guide for subdividing the Book of Signs? The many disputes among scholars about how this book of the Gospel should be divided suggest that the indications are not absolutely clear. After the Prologue, there is a relatively continuous narrative from 1:19 to 12:50. The Gospel gives us some indications of the passing of time, for example, the three Passovers mentioned in 2:13, 6:4; and 11:55; but these are merely by way of setting for a particular narrative, and there is nothing to suggest that they are signposts for a division of the Gospel. The idea of dividing Jesus' ministry into two or three years does not come from the Gospel itself.

If one speaks of a Book of Signs, it is not impossible that the signs may represent a key to the division of the book. The following miraculous signs are narrated in some detail:

1. Changing water to wine at Cana (2:1–11).
2. Curing the royal official's son at Cana (4:46–54).
3. Curing the paralytic at the pool of Bethesda (5:1–15).
4. Multiplication of the loaves in Galilee (6:1–15).
5. Walking upon the Sea of Galilee (6:16–21).
6. Curing a blind man in Jerusalem (9).
7. Raising Lazarus from the dead at Bethany (11).

Division of the Book of Signs (1:19–12:50)

Part One: The Opening Days of the Revelation of Jesus (1:19–51, plus 2:1–11)

A. 1:19–34: The Testimony of John the Baptist:
   (vv. 19–28): Concerning his role in relation to one to come;
   (vv. 29–34): Concerning Jesus.

B. 1:35–51: The Baptist's disciples come to Jesus as he manifests himself: (vv. 35–42):

a. Two disciples—Jesus acknowledged as rabbi;

b. Simon Peter—Jesus as Messiah;

(vv. 43–51):

a. Philip—Jesus as the fulfillment of the Law and the prophets;

b. Nathanael—Jesus as Son of God and King of Israel;—A saying about the Son of Man (v. 51).

Bridge Scene: 2:1–11: The disciples come to believe in Jesus as he manifests his glory at Cana. This scene both closes Part One and opens Part Two, and can thus be termed a "bridge scene."

Part Two: From Cana to Cana—Various responses to Jesus' ministry in the regions of Palestine (2–4)

A. 2:1–11: The first sign at Cana in Galilee—water to wine.

v. 12: Transition—Jesus goes to Capernaum.

B. 2:13–22: Cleansing of the Temple in Jerusalem.

vv. 23–25: Transition—Reaction to Jesus in Jerusalem.

C. 3:1–21: Discourse with Nicodemus in Jerusalem.

vv. 22–30: The Baptist's final witness to Jesus.

vv. 31–36: Discourse of Jesus completing the preceding.

4:1–3: Transition—Jesus leaves Judea.

D. 4:4–42: Discourse with the Samaritan woman at Jacob's Well.

43–45: Transition—Jesus enters Galilee.

E. 4:46–54: The second sign at Cana in Galilee—healing the official's son; the household become believers.

Part Three: Jesus and the principal feasts of the Jews (5–10, introduced by 4:46–54)

Bridge Scene: 4:46–54 Jesus gives life to the official's son at Cana. This scene both closes Part Two and opens Part Three.

A. 5:1–47: THE SABBATH. Jesus performs works that only God can do on the Sabbath:

vv. 1–15: Gift of life [healing] to the man at Bethesda pool in Jerusalem;

vv. 16–47: Discourse explaining the giving of life and his work on the Sabbath.

B. 6:1–71: PASSOVER. Jesus gives bread replacing the manna of the Exodus:[3]

vv. 1–21: Multiplication of the loaves; walking on the sea.

vv. 22–24: Transition—the crowd comes to Jesus.

vv. 25–71: Discourse explaining the multiplication.

C. 7:1–8:59: TABERNACLES. Jesus replaces the water and light ceremonies:

vv. 7:1–13: Introduction: Will Jesus go up to the feast?

vv. 14–36: Scene 1: Discourse on the middle day of the festival week.

vv. 37–52: Scene 2: The last day of the feast.

[7:53–8:11: Adulteress, a non-Johannine interpolation]

8:12–59: Scene 3: Miscellaneous discourses.

9:1–10:21: AFTERMATH OF TABERNACLES.[4]

9:1–41: Healing of the man born blind—Jesus as the light.

10:1–21: Jesus as sheep gate and shepherd.

D. 10:22–39: DEDICATION. Jesus, the Messiah and Son of God. consecrated in place of the Temple altar:

vv. 22–31: Jesus as the Messiah.

vv. 32–39: Jesus as the Son of God.

vv. 40–42: Apparent conclusion to the public ministry.

Part Four: Jesus moves toward the hour of death and glory (11–12)

A. 11:1–54: Jesus gives men life; men condemn Jesus to death:

vv. 1–44: Jesus gives life to Lazarus—Jesus as the life.

vv. 45–54: The Sanhedrin condemns Jesus to die. Withdrawal to Ephraim.

vv. 55–57: Transition: Will Jesus come to Jerusalem for Passover?

---

3. *Editor's Note:* As the reader would expect, I continue to object to Brown's use of the expression "replace." See earlier notes, and Brown's own use of the expression "fulfillment" from time to time.

4. *Editor's Note:* I have left this section as an "aftermath," as Brown had it in the script. There is increasing unanimity, however, that 9:1–10:21 brings Tabernacles to a close: Jesus is the light, the living water and the messianic Good Shepherd. See Moloney, *John*, 290–91, 300–301, 306–8, and the literature cited there.

B. 12:1–36: Scenes preparatory to Passover and death:
  vv. 1–4: At Bethany, Jesus is anointed for death.
  vv. 9–19: The crowds acclaim Jesus as he enters Jerusalem.
  vv. 20–36: The coming of the Greeks marks the coming of the hour.

Conclusion: Evaluation and summation of Jesus' ministry (12:37–50):
  12:37–43: An evaluation of Jesus' ministry to his own people.
  vv. 44–50: An unattached discourse of Jesus used as a summary proclamation.

Even a cursory glance at the distribution of these signs throughout the chapters of John indicates that they scarcely form an adequate basis for the division of the Gospel. And indeed we should emphasize that these are not the only signs mentioned in the Book of Signs, for there are passing (sometimes implicit) references to signs in 2:23, 4:45, 7:4, 12:37 (and see 20:30). The fact that there are seven signs narrated at length has fascinated some, for a pattern of sevens is clear in another work generally regarded to have come from the Johannine school, Revelation.[5] Boismard has perfected to a fine art the discovery of sevens in the Fourth Gospel: seven miracles, seven discourses, seven similes used by Jesus, seven titles in ch. 1, seven days in chs. 1–2, seven periods in Jesus' life, etc.[6] But a closer look leads one to suspect that this ingenuity is being imposed on the evangelist, who never once gives the slightest indication that he has such numerical patterns in mind and never uses the word "seven" (contrast Revelation). For instance, does the evangelist intend (4) and (5) above to be treated as two separate signs?

Dodd divides Book One into seven episodes, which form a somewhat more satisfactory apportionment than the seven signs:

1. The New Beginning (2:1–4:42)
2. The Life-giving Word (4:46–5:47)
3. The Bread of Life (6)

---

5. *Editor's Note:* Increasingly, however, critical scholarship is disassociating Revelation from the school (community and/or communities) that produced the Gospel and 1, 2 and 3 John. See my comment on Brown's inconsistent use of Revelation in relation to the Johannine corpus in the Conclusion.
6. Boismard, "L'Évangile."

4. Light and Life (7–8)
5. Judgment by the Light (9:1–10:21) and Appendix (10:22–39)
6. The Victory of Life over Death (11:1–53)
7. Life through Death (12:1–36).[7]

Dodd's general principle of joining sign with interpretative discourse is valid, and the brilliance of his analysis of many of these units has left a permanent mark on Johannine studies. But there is a problem of overall apportionment. There is a certain unity in chs. 2–4, but is this "unit" to be put on an equal footing with a single chapter like 11? Chapters 2–4 are composed of at least five different stories set in different locales; ch. 11 consists substantially of one well-knit narrative. Has not Dodd too been hypnotized by a desire to find a pattern of seven in the Gospel?

We propose our own division with hesitation, realizing the danger of imposing insights on the evangelist. But we do claim that there are certain indications in the Gospel itself for the broad lines of this division. For instance, the theme of John the Baptist and his disciples who become Jesus' disciples holds together 1:19–2:11, our Part One. The Gospel itself makes the connection between the first sign at Cana and the second sign at Cana, the two scenes that are the demarcation of our Part Two. The emphasis on feasts as the occasion and indeed subject matter of Jesus' discourses is underlined by the evangelist in chs. 5–10, our Part Three. And not only the theme of Lazarus, but also certain stylistic peculiarities bind together chs. 11–12, Part Four.[8]

There is, moreover, in this division an earnest effort to respect the fluidity of the Gospel writer's thought. In Revelation it is clear that the last member of one series of seven items is at the same time the beginning of the next series, for example, in Revelation 8:1 the seventh seal opens the seven trumpets. While we are reluctant to transfer features that are peculiar to Revelation as a book of apocalyptic (e.g., numerical patterns) to the different literary form of the Gospel, nevertheless we suggest that this feature of overlapping thought may help in dividing the Gospel as well.[9]

---

7. Dodd, *Interpretation,* 297–379.

8. *Editor's Note:* For a fuller discussion of the unity that exists between chs. 11 and 12, see Moloney, *Signs and Shadows,* 200–201.

9. *Editor's Note:* In the light of my earlier notes, Brown's suggestion here does not necessarily indicate that there is any literary association to be made between the Gospel of John and Revelation. He is uncovering a pattern common to both. There is no

For instance, the evangelist clearly ties the Cana scene to what has preceded by stressing the role of the disciples (2:2, 11); yet by emphasizing that this was the first of Jesus' signs, the evangelist also looks forward to what is to follow. The same problem faces us with the second Cana miracle (4:46–54), which looks backward in recalling the first Cana miracle, and yet looks forward with its theme of life, which is taken up in ch. 5. The endless arguments about how to place such scenes in a division of the Gospel may find a solution if we recognize that these scenes have a double role of concluding one part and opening the next. They are so-called "bridge scenes."

The Themes of the Individual Parts of the Book of Signs[10]

Part One: The themes here are obvious in our table of division. The suggestion (Boismard and others) that this part is held together by the theme of the seven days of the new creation is questionable, at best. Although not absent, the theme of creation (so important to other parts of the NT, especially Paul) is subordinated to the theme of revelation in John.

Part Two: There are at least two principal themes that run through this part. While the evangelist suggests these themes rather clearly, one cannot find them worked out consistently in every subdivision; and the desire for logical development has led interpreters to force these themes beyond the expressed intention of the Gospel. The first theme is that of replacing Jewish institutions and religious views: In A, the replacement of the water for Jewish purifications, in B, the replacement of the Temple, in D, the replacement of worship at Jerusalem and Gerizim. However, in C there is no clear reference to replacement; the suggestion that Jesus is replacing birth into the Chosen People by begetting from above is forced. Possibly, in E one might find a replacement of inadequate faith in signs, but this is scarcely a particularly Jewish religious view.[11]

---

need for a literary association between the two documents, the Gospel of John and the Book of Revelation.

10. For a fuller decsription of the themes of 1:19–12:50, see BINT, 338–51.

11. *Editor's Note:* Again, I must express dissatisfaction with Brown's use of "replacement," and suggest that a better expression can be found to speak of John's christological program in which Jesus perfects (rather than "replaces") Jewish practices, theology and institutions.

The second theme is that of the different reactions of individuals and groups to Jesus. In A, the disciples believe at Cana in Galilee. In the transition of 2:23–25, many at Jerusalem believe inadequately in his signs. In C, Nicodemus at Jerusalem believes inadequately. In D, the Samaritan woman believes with doubts (4:29) while the Samaritan populace believes more fully (4:42). In the transition of 4:43–45, many of the Galileans believe inadequately in his signs, while in E, the royal official and his household come to believe on the basis of Jesus' word and sign. The temptation is to find a logical development in this sequence. One that has been suggested is a growth of faith from Nicodemus, a Jew, through the Samaritan woman (a half-Jew) to the royal official, a Gentile. However, the designation of the official as a Gentile is on the basis of his identification with the Synoptic centurion; John does not mention it, and the evangelist can scarcely have expected the readers to guess it. Other scholars see a geographical progression: faith gets stronger as Jesus moves away from Jerusalem through Samaria into Galilee. But the faith of the Galileans in 4:43–45 is the same as the faith of those at Jerusalem in 2:23–25; and there is no significant difference of faith between the Samaritan populace of 4:42 and the official's household of 4:53. We must beware of being more ingenious than the evangelist himself.

Part Three: This is dominated by Jesus' actions and discourses on the occasion of great Jewish feasts. However, the relation of what is said to a theme of the feast is less obvious in some cases than in others. Subdivisions B and C are the clearest, but in D the reference to the theme of dedication is subtle and confined to only one verse (10:36).[12] There are subthemes: the exodus symbolism of manna and of water from the rock uniting 6 and 7; opposition to the Pharisees uniting 9 and 10. The theme of light illustrated in 9 is matched in the next part by an enactment of the theme of life in 11, and there are many parallels between these two chapters.

Part Four: The theme of life and death that dominates this part is centered around Lazarus. However, especially in the light of the crucial 11:4,

---

12. *Editor's Note:* It could be suggested that Jesus' twofold claim to oneness with the Father in 10:30, 38, within the context of dedication, is a further indication that the Temple as the dwelling place of God in Jerusalem has now been perfected (after the loss of the Temple for the readers of the gospel) in the presence of the divine in Jesus Christ.

chs. 11–12 indicate that Jesus has turned definitively toward his own death, a death that reveals the glory of God, is the means by which he returns to the glory that was his before the world was made, and a death that gives life to others, prefigured in the Lazarus episode (see esp. 11:25–26), its aftermath (see 11:51–52), and Jesus' final public discourse in 12:23–36 (see vv. 24, 32–33).

The General Outline of the Book of Glory [13]

BROWN COMMENTED THAT THE INDICATIONS in the text for the subdivision of the Book of Signs were not absolutely clear. For that reason, there have been many disputes and suggestions concerning the shape of John 1:19–12:50. This is not the case for the Book of Glory. It would be rash to claim universal agreement, but the vast majority of scholars would accept a fourfold general outline of the Book of Glory, with an epilogue to the gospel as a whole:

1. Jesus' final encounter with "his own" (13:1–17:26).[14]
2. The arrest, trials, passion and death of Jesus (18:1–19:42).
3. The empty tomb and encounters with the risen Jesus (20:1–29).

---

13. *Editor's Note:* The script left by Brown finished at this point, with a note indicating that he would deal with this question at the beginning of his second volume. What follows is entirely my work, on the basis of Brown's 1970 second volume of *John,* 545–47 (John 13:1–17:26); 785–86 (John 18:1–19:42); 965 (John 20:1–29); 1065 (John 21:1–25), and especially his more recent BINT, 334–35. Readers should be aware, however, that the literary and theological suggestions that follow are more mine than Brown's. I feel free to do this in the light of Brown's own streamlining and slight retouching of his outline of the Book of Signs between the 1966 edition and this new Introduction, and his deeper concern for a reading of the Gospel as a unity, a literary whole (see above, pp. 44–45, 63–64). All subsequent notes are mine, and thus will not be prefaced with the rubric of *Editor's Note.*

14. This section of the Book of Glory is widely and popularly called "the last discourse." I avoid that title because it really only applies to 14:1–16:33. John 13:1–38 is composed of narrative (footwashing and gift of the morsel), predictions (the betrayal of Judas and the denials of Peter), and discourse. After the discourses of 14:1–16:33, 17:1–26 has the literary form of a prayer, not discourse. Other "encounters" between Jesus and the disciples take place in chs. 20–21, but 13:1–17:26 is his final encounter with them before his passion and resurrection.

4. Conclusion (20:30–31).

5. Epilogue. A chapter has been added to the obvious conclusion to the Book of Glory in 20:30–31. No manuscript of the complete gospel exists which did not have this chapter attached to it. It forms part of the Johannine tradition, and adds some important reflections upon the Christian community and its leadership.

The second half of the gospel moves toward the fulfillment of Jesus' promises, made during the Book of Signs, that he would be "lifted up" (see 3:14; 8:28; 12:32–33) on a cross. In the Johannine theology, this act of self-gift is a consummate act of love (13:1; see also 15:13) and is thus the time and the place where the glory of God can be seen, and the means by which the Son of God is glorified (see 11:4). The focus on "glory" emerges from the events, discourses and prayer of Jesus' final evening with the disciples, and then from the unique Johannine narrative of Jesus' death and resurrection.

Division of the Book of Glory (13:1–21:25)

Part One: The Last Encounter (13:1–17:26). This carefully constructed description of events and words of Jesus from his last night with the disciples states and restates themes around the command to love (15:12–17), in the midst of rejection and hatred (15:1–11, 15:18–16:4a).

A. 13:1–38: *Making God known:* the footwashing (13:1–17) and the morsel (13:21–38) set around Jesus' words on the purpose of his gestures that the disciples may know that they may believe "that I AM HE" (vv. 18–20).

B. 14:1–31: *Jesus' departure and its consequences.* He will not leave his own orphans. They are to love and believe and obey the commandments of Jesus, guided and strengthened by another Paraclete, a further gift of Jesus from the Father.

C. 15:1–11: To abide in Jesus.

D. 15:12–17: To love as Jesus has loved.

C'. 15:18–16:4a: To be rejected, hated and even slain, as Jesus has been rejected, hated and slain.

B'. 16:4b–33: *Jesus' departure and its consequences.* He will not leave his own orphans. They are to love and believe and obey the commandments of Jesus, guided and strengthened by the Paraclete who will continue Jesus' revealing action and lay bare sin, false righteousness and judgment.

A'. 17:1–26: *Making God known:* Jesus' final prayer asks the Father for his own glorification.

(vv. 1–11), that the Holy Father make his followers holy and protect them as their Father.

(vv. 12–19), that all may be swept up into the union of love that existed before all time between the Father and the Son, so that the God who sent Jesus will be made known (20–26).

Part Two: The Arrest, Trials and Passion of Jesus (18:1–19:42). A further carefully constructed narrative tells the traditional story of the arrest, trials, crucifixion, death and burial of Jesus, but focuses upon this moment as Jesus' royal enthronement, making God known and establishing a community.

A. 18:1–11: Jesus and his enemies in a garden. He is lord of the situation, revealing himself as "I am" and protecting his disciples, the future community.

B. 18:12–27: Jesus' appearance before "the Jews." As Peter denies Jesus (vv. 12–18, 25–27), Jesus tells his interrogators that they are to ask those who have heard him (vv. 19–24: the Christian community) if they wish to discover his teaching.

C. 18:28–19:16a: Jesus before Pilate. At the center of the passion narrative, the trial before Pilate, with its introduction and conclusion, ironically proclaims and crowns Jesus as King. On the basis of movement from outside the praetorium to inside, the following divisions can be suggested:

   a. 18:28: INTRODUCTION: JESUS IS LED TO PILATE.

     b. 18:29–32: Jesus' accusers present him to Pilate (outside).

       c. 18:33–38: Jesus and Pilate: Jesus as King (inside).

         d. 18:39–40: Jesus' accusers reject their King, and ask Pilate for Barabbas (outside).

           e. 19:1–3: Jesus is ironically crowned and dressed as a King (inside).

         d'. 19:4–7: Pilate presents Jesus as "the Man." His accusers reject him and ask for crucifixion (outside).

       c'. 19:8–11: Jesus and Pilate: Jesus as the Son of God (inside).

     b'. 19:12–15: Jesus' opponents reject their innocent King and ask Pilate for crucifixion (outside).

   a'. 19:16: CONCLUSION: PILATE HANDS JESUS OVER FOR CRUCIFIXION.

D. 19:16b–37: The crucifixion of Jesus (19:16b–37). The "lifting up" of Jesus is briefly reported, but a series of five scenes develops the theme of what the crucified Jesus does for the Christian community. The following scenes can be suggested:

   a. 19:17–22: Jesus is crucified and proclaimed King of the Jews by the title on the cross.

      b. vv. 23–25a: The fulfillment of Scripture as Jesus' garment is not torn apart.

         c. vv. 25b–27: The mother of Jesus is given to the Beloved Disciple, and a new community is founded at the cross.

      b'. vv. 28–30: Jesus' death brings to perfection the task he was given by the Father, and he pours down the Spirit on the community.

   a'. vv. 31–37: Blood and water flow from the pierced side of the crucified Passover Lamb, so that those who read the gospel may also believe. They shall gaze upon the pierced one.

E. 19:38–42: Jesus buried as a King in a garden with his newly established companions.

Part Three: 20:1–29: The Resurrection. The theme of the faith response of those who encounter Jesus returns (see 2:1–4:54) in scenes at the tomb, and then in the house.

A. 20:1–18: Scenes at the tomb.

   vv. 1–10: Visits to the empty tomb.

   vv. 11–18: Jesus appears to Mary Magdalene.

B. 20:19–29: Scenes in the house.

   vv. 19–23: Jesus appears to the disciples, but not Thomas.

   vv. 24–29: Jesus appear to the disciples, including Thomas.

The Conclusion of the Gospel (20:30–31): "These things have been written that you may go on believing."

Epilogue (21:1–25): Further resurrection appearances deal with matters left unresolved by the original Gospel: who belongs to the community of Jesus, and the respective roles of Peter and the BD.

   21:1–14: The miraculous draft of fishes on the Sea of Tiberias.

   21:15–24: Jesus, Peter, and the BD.

   21:25: A second conclusion to the Gospel.

I must repeat Brown's reservations, as he concluded his survey of the outline of the Book of Signs. I am proposing my own division with hesitation, realizing the danger of imposing insights on the evangelist. I have further cause for hesitation, insofar as I am only broadly following Brown's 1970 outlines. My main differences are my inclusion of 13:31–38 with the narrative of the footwashing and the morsel,[15] and my attempt to recognize a carefully constructed literary and theological pattern behind 13:1–17:26. In the outlines for the Passion and Resurrection, despite slight differences, we are largely in agreement.[16] I have taken the liberty of proceeding in this way because of Brown's statement earlier in the Introduction, and his acceptance of a criterion stated by R. A. Culpepper: "At the end of the hypothesizing, however, let me remind readers what I wrote at the beginning of this subsection before advancing my theory of composition: primary consideration must be given to the Gospel as it now stands. I agree fully with Culpepper: 'In its present form, if not in its origin, the Gospel must be approached as a unity, a literary whole.' "[17]

My division attempts to respect the indications of the present text, while not disregarding the achievements of an earlier generation, including Brown, that made divisions on the basis of the reconstruction of sources. This issue is critical in the division of Jesus' final encounter with his disciples before going to the cross (13:1–17:26). Different themes and different literary forms have led most earlier scholars to posit a source (at least one) for the narrative of 13:1–30, and a different source for what was probably the most primitive form of a Johannine final discourse (paralleling the many examples of final discourses in the Bible, and in Jewish and classical literature) in 13:31–14:31. The words of Jesus, "Rise, let us go hence," indicate closure. But the message of 13:31–14:31 has been adapted and further developed in the community to form a further parallel (but not identical) discourse in 16:4b–33.[18] The material now

---

15. I am also doing this, however, on the basis of BINT, 335, 351–52, where Brown also presents and surveys 13:1–38 as a literary unit, beginning the "discourse" with 14:1. However, he continues to regard the prayer of 17:1–26 as discourse.

16. See BINT, 351–60.

17. See above, p. 86, with reference to Culpepper, *Anatomy,* 49.

18. See the excellent chart showing the parallels between 13:31–14:31 and 16:4b–33 in *John,* 589–93. It is interesting to notice, however, that parallels with 13:31–38 are scarce in this scheme.

found in 15:1–16:4a presented even more difficulty, with most suggesting two different sources. A discourse using the allegory of the vine and the command to love was the source for 15:1–17. Behind 15:18–16:4a lay another source, closely related with the experience of expulsion from the synagogue(s). Perhaps the most refined and latest addition to the growth of 13:1–17:26 was the final prayer (17:1–26), another literary form widespread across a number of literatures—biblical, Jewish and classical—from antiquity. I have no quibble with these suggestions, and the many variations upon them. No doubt 13:1–17:26 had a long literary history before it reached its final form, and there are a number of indications in the text that such was the case (most clearly, 14:31, but there are many other tensions and difficulties).[19]

But these more archaeological investigations support the division of 13:1–17:26 proposed above. The question that my division attempts to answer is, What was the overarching Johannine theological motif that led the evangelist to produce 13:1–17:26 *as we now have it?* The narrative of 13:1–38 and the prayer of 17:1–26 stand apart from the literary form of the discourse, and have as their central theme the revelation of the love of God, initially in Jesus, and subsequently through the commissioning and sending out of the disciples. John 14:1–31 and 16:4b–33 have long been recognized as a statement and a more developed restatement of the same themes, all of which depend upon Jesus' departure. That leaves 15:1–16:4a as the centerpiece of this section. The highlight of vv. 1–11 is not the allegory of the vine, but the steady use of the verb "to abide." There is an obvious literary inclusion between Jesus' love command in v. 12 and v. 17 that makes vv. 12–17 the centerpiece of the central 15:1–16:4a. Disciples are urged to love one another as Jesus, has loved them, and are reminded that they did not choose him, but he chose them (v. 16). The other part of 15:1–16:4a, in an elegant oppositional balance to the insistence upon abiding in Jesus, is his instruction that as Jesus has been hated and eventually slain, such will also be the destiny of the disciple, for "a servant is not greater than his master" (v. 20). The Johannine theological motivation for the architecture and message of 13:1–17:26,

---

19. For a schematic presentation of these difficulties, and theories adopted to resolve them, see Brown, *John,* 582–86. For a more detailed survey, see Segovia, *Farewell,* 1–58. The process of "relecture" (Zumstein, Dettwiler) has obvious applications to this section of the Gospel.

therefore, is a statement and restatement of central Johannine themes found elsewhere in the Gospel. Jesus is the unique revelation of a God who is love. His leaving them to return to the Father is itself an act of love, but he will not leave his disciples orphans. He instructs them in the need for faith and love, promising them the gift of another Paraclete who will continue the presence of Jesus, the first Paraclete, among them, even during the time of his physical absence. But the disciples are not only recipients. They are summoned to love as he has loved. However, the ultimate goal of the love of the disciples for one another is not their security within a closed sectarian movement. The love of the Johannine believer is to make known the God and Father of Jesus, that others may recognize Jesus as the sent one of the Father (see 13:34–35; 15:12, 17; 17:23). In his departure through death, Jesus reveals the love of God, glorifies God, and is himself glorified. The disciples are exhorted to the glory of loving.[20]

The Themes of the Remaining Individual Parts of the Book of Glory

The description above of the history, background and process that led me to my division of Jesus' final encounter with "his own" (13:1–17:26) already provides the reader with the major themes that are developed in that major (and longest) section of the Book of Glory. It remains necessary now only to highlight briefly the key themes of the remaining three sections.

The Arrest, Trials, Death and Burial of Jesus. The Johannine gospel continues the traditional sequence of events: arrest, Jewish trial, Roman trial, crucifixion, death and burial. However, as the division already indicates, the evangelist has introduced a unique perspective into the story. As Brown wrote of 19:16b–37: "The Johannine crucifixion scene is, in a certain way, less concerned with the fate of Jesus than with the significance of that fate for his followers."[21] The series of events from the garden of

---

20. I take this expression from the title of a study that has been most formative in my reading of John 13:1–17:26: Y. Simoens, *La gloire d'aimer. Structures stylistiques et interprétatives dans la Discours de la Cène* (AnBib 90: Rome: Biblical Institute Press, 1981). For my own extended development of these issues, see Moloney, *Glory not Dishonor*, 1–126.

21. *John*, 912. See also F. J. Moloney, "The Johannine Passion and the Christian Community," *Salesianum* 57 (1995): 25–61.

Gethsemane (18:1–11) to the garden of his burial (19:38–42) tells of Jesus' arrest, death and burial. However, Jesus is always in command of the situation, insisting on the importance of his followers (see 18:8–9), even announcing to his Jewish interrogators, as Peter denied him three times, that it is to the disciples of Jesus that they must now turn if they wish to know his teaching (18:12–27).[22] Before Pilate, he is proclaimed as a King, crowned as a King, dressed as a King, and he goes to the cross still bearing the royal clothing (18:28–19:16a). All of this is irony. Jesus dies as an innocent crucified criminal, but on the cross he is proclaimed as King (19:16b–22), and the theme of the "gathering" of many in his moment of being "lifted up" (see 10:16; 11:51–52; 12:11, 19, 24, 32–33) is brought to completion as a new community is founded (19:25b–27), given the Spirit (19:30) and nourished so that even in his absence they might believe in him (19:31–37). In the end, he is buried by formerly "hidden" disciples of Jesus who publicly ask for his body and lay him to rest as a King (19:38–42).

The Resurrection of Jesus. It has been said (C. H. Dodd), that so much happens on the cross in the Johannine story that there is hardly any need for a resurrection account. Again, one must recognize that the author's major interest is the Johannine believers, not what happened to Jesus. As with the passion account, the basic tradition is still found in the Fourth Gospel: a woman at an empty tomb (20:1), lack of faith (20:11–15, 27), appearances (20:11–18, 19–23, 26–29), and a commission (20:21–23).[23] But the tradition has been reshaped within the Johannine tradition to tell of three journeys to faith. The BD, who does not see Jesus, nevertheless recognizes the action of God in the tomb and the clothes of death, now empty. He saw and believed. Mary Magdalene moves from darkness and ignorance through a desire to hold Jesus to obediently announce, "I have seen the Lord" (20:1–2, 11–18). Thomas will not believe unless he can also (like Mary Magdalene) experience the fleshly presence of Jesus. But the presence of the risen Jesus leads him to confess, "My Lord and my

---

22. See Moloney, "John 18:15–27: A Johannine View of the Church," in *"A Hard Saying,"* 131–47.

23. See C. H. Dodd, "The Appearances of the Risen Christ: a Study in Form-Criticism of the Gospels," in *More New Testament Studies* (Manchester: Manchester University Press, 1968), 102–33.

God" (20:28). Each of these episodes addresses the readers, who are blessed by Jesus because—like the BD—they believe without seeing (v. 29). They have the Scriptures (v. 10), they have the founding commission given to the disciples (vv. 21–23), and they have the things "written in this book" (v. 30).

The Conclusion. As the original disciples, the BD, Mary Magdalene, and Thomas made their journey to faith in the risen Lord, so must the readers of "this book" (see 20:30). They are living in a period of time when Jesus is no longer with them. Yet, like the BD, they are blessed because they do not hanker for the flesh of Jesus, as did Mary and Thomas. They have the Scriptures, the community with its authority, and most of all, they have this book, written that they may ever deepen their faith in Jesus as the Christ, the Son of God. They will have life in his name (20:30–31).

The Epilogue. A community based only upon the commandments to believe and love would eventually encounter internal difficulties. The three Epistles of John are clear proof that this was the case for the Johannine community. However, so also is the Epilogue, which raises two questions and provides answers to both. Who belongs to the community? Who is the leading authority in the community? By means of the story of the miraculous haul of fish (21:1–14), the Johannine community is instructed that, under the guidance of Jesus (and both Peter and the BD [see vv. 7, 8, 11]), the community is to gather all and sundry. Peter is made the pastor of the community by means of his threefold profession of love, and the promise that he will follow Jesus into death (21:15–19), but what of the BD (v. 21)? By the time ch. 21 was penned and added to 1:1–20:31, the BD is already deceased (see vv. 22–23), but he is the figure who has given the community their story of Jesus, and he remains for them the model of discipleship because of his unique relationship with Jesus. The Johannine Epilogue contributes importantly to Christianity by making a clear distinction between the bearer of authority (vv. 15–19) and the best of all disciples (vv. 20–24). Leaders have responsibilities entrusted to them by the Lord, and they are called to be shepherds, and even to die in his service. But the disciple—who may not necessarily be the leader—is called to love, listen, and transmit the tradition. The Epilogue ends with a rather prosaic statement about all the books of this world, matched by similar conclusions in other Jewish and classical literature.

BIBLIOGRAPHY

Balmforth, H., "The Structure of the Fourth Gospel," *StEv*, 2.25–33.

Boismard, M.-É., "L'Evangile à quatre dimensions," *LumVie* 1 (1951): 94–114.

Bussche, H. van den, "De Structuur van het vierde Evangelie," *Collationes Brugenses et Gandavenses* 2 (1956): 23–42, 182–99.

Deeks, D., "The Structure of the Fourth Gospel," *NTS* 15 (1968–69): 107–29.

Devillers, L., "Les trois témoins: Une structure pour le quatrième évangile," *RB* 104 (1997): 40–87.

Ellis, P. F., "Inclusion, Chiasm and Division of the Fourth Gospel," *St. Vladimir's Theological Quarterly* 43 (1999): 269–338.

Feuillet, A., "Essai sur la composition littéraire de Joh. IX–XII," *Mélanges Bibliques rédigés en l'honneur de André Robert* (Paris: Bloud et Gay, 1957), 478–93. Now in English in *JohSt*, 129–47.

Giblin, C. H., "The Tripartite Structure of John's Gospel," *Biblica* 71 (1990): 449–68.

Hoare, F. R., *The Original Order and Chapters of St. John's Gospel* (London: Burns and Oates, 1944).

Hull, W. E., "A Teaching Outline of the Gospel of John," *RExp* 62 (1965): 405–16.

Lohmeyer, E., "The Structure and Organization of the Fourth Gospel," *Journal of Higher Criticism* 5 (1998): 113–38. Translated from the 1928 original by C. Brown.

Rodríguez-Ruiz, M., "Estructura del Evangelio de san Juan desde el punto di vista christológico y ecclesiológico," *EstBib* 56 (1998): 75–96.

Segalla, G., *Vangelo secondo Giovanni: Traduzione strutturata* (Sussidi biblici 56; Reggio Emilia: Edizioni San Lorenzo, 1997).

Segovia, F. F., "The Journey(s) of the Word of God: A Reading of the Plot of the Fourth Gospel," *Semeia* 53 (1991): 23–54.

Simoens, Y., *Selon Jean*. Vol. 1: *Une traduction*.

Talbert, C. H., "Artistry and Theology: An Analysis of the Architecture of Jn 1,19–5,47," *CBQ* 32 (1970): 341–66.

Thomas, W. H. G., "The Plan of the Fourth Gospel," *BSac* 15 (1968): 313–23.

Wyller, E. A., "In Solomon's Porch: A Henological Analysis of the Architectonic of the Fourth Gospel," *ST* 42 (1988): 151–67.

EDITOR'S CONCLUSION

RAYMOND BROWN's *Introduction to the Gospel of John* is masterly, clear, and comprehensive. By way of a brief conclusion, there are several suggestions—one may even call them queries—that come to me from my longtime close association with this now completed script. It has sometimes been claimed that one of the reasons the Gospel of John has its present shape, and its infamous tensions and difficulties, is because it was published in an unfinished form.[1] In my introduction, I already hinted that Brown may have been moving his understanding of the Gospel of John in new directions. What follows will suggest that the *Introduction* in its finished form may have marked a watershed as a great Johannine scholar moved into waters he had hitherto not charted. Brown's untimely death cut short this movement. I can do no more than trace "hints," aware that I may be misreading them because of my own lenses.

Brown committed himself to develop what he called in 1966 "a moderately critical theory of the composition of the Gospel."[2] He claims to have altered his original theory of Five Stages to a newer theory of Three Stages. He suggests that his proposed three stages could be posited for the development of all four Gospels. However, there is some sleight of hand here. Brown draws into his new First Stage (the activity of Jesus and the

---

1. After listing the apparent tensions and non sequiturs in the Gospel, Painter, *Quest*, 62, remarks: "It is a moot point whether these tensions exist because the evangelist has failed to assimilate his sources successfully or because the text became disordered and was finally redacted by another hand (or hands), or because Jn has come to us unpolished and to a degree unfinished."

2. *John*, vi.

witness of a disciple) what were originally two different preliterary stages. He then has *two* figures playing a crucial role in his present Third Stage: the evangelist and the redactor. When one adds all this up, one returns to the Five Stages of 1966. I have no objection to that. It is Brown's way of making more acceptable what was always (even in 1966), to his mind, a three-stage composition history that produced the Gospel of John. In this, it needs to be said that those who objected to the complexity of Brown's original five stages had not really understood its simplicity.

What struck me, however, as I worked through Brown's own text, was that his partially completed script, spanning only 30 years (1966–98), was itself highlighted by a number of tensions and non sequiturs. I was aware that Brown had his 1966 text in front of him, rewriting it here and there, adding bibliography. In some places he retouched the original stylistically, or brought up to date something he had said earlier, but nuanced it in the light of more recent Johannine scholarship. Then there are several places (e.g., the discussion of the identification and the function of "the Jews," and the section on "the Son of Man") where completely new material was added to the original text. Necessarily, this process of reworking an older text in a somewhat piecemeal fashion creates literary and even theological tensions. I have tried to cover most of them by means of editor's notes, and there are places where, respectfully, I altered Brown's text. Some will be obvious to a careful reader. I will give two examples. Brown declares he is not prepared to make use of Revelation as support for a Johannine idea or literary pattern, but there are times when he continues to do so.[3] Secondly, there are some occasions when he speaks of the Johannine Christology "replacing" the Jewish institutions. Yet there are one or two places where he (more correctly) speaks of Jesus' perfecting or fulfilling the possibilities of the Jewish institutions.[4] There are other examples, but I wish to make a single point. If Brown's own work— obviously the work of a single author working on the same material across a span of 30 years—can reflect these (and other) tensions and internal contradictions, is it necessary to develop a hypothesis involving a series of different authors (BD, evangelist, redactor) to explain the com-

---

3. See my remarks above, on p. 237, n. 39.

4. Yet, it must be recognized that Brown continues to use "replacement" language in BINT, 344–49.

position history of the Gospel of John that will demonstrate these tensions and internal contradictions?

In terms of the composition history of Brown's *Introduction*, there is but one author. The physical writer of the original work (1966) is the same writer (and in some ways the same person acting as a redactor) who produced a different, and at times, contradictory, text (1998).[5] I am aware that we are dealing with two written texts, and this separates the process of Brown's writing and rewriting from the development of the Gospel of John. The Gospel text (one must speculate) had a long preliterary history. It must always be remembered that respect for received traditions may have caused a certain awkwardness in an evangelist's use of them.[6] But what was the relationship between the evangelist and the BD, whose traditions he forged into a narrative? Jesus, the tradition, an evangelist and a redactor must surely be posited (although many scholars would question the redactor). The enigma remains, however, of the function of the BD in the development of the Johannine tradition. I am personally attracted to Brown's understanding of his role as the chief witness and storyteller in the preliterary stage of the Gospel. But, in the light of Brown's three decades of work on the major introductory questions that surround the Gospel of John, could the BD and the evangelist be one and the same figure? What must be admitted is that all such reconstructions lie outside our scientific control—a reservation that Brown levels against many of his colleagues who have also attempted to reconstruct the composition history of the Gospel.

I wonder how a second edition of Brown's commentary would have looked. In a way untypical of the first edition of his work, Brown regularly insists on the need to comment upon the Gospel of John as we now have it. Almost paralleling C. H. Dodd's classical description of

---

5. This is even more remarkable when one follows Brown's work from his 1966 commentary via his 1967 work for the *New Catholic Encyclopedia*, to his BINT of 1997, and this present script. Across 30 years Brown uses a rigid "grid" in all his "introductions" to the Gospel of John. Given the "sameness" of these 30 years of scholarship, I strongly suspect a new commentary from Brown would have broken that mold, and contend that this unfinished *New Introduction* already shows signs of this.

6. In my opinion, this is the case for the clumsy Johannine use of Isaiah 6:9–10 in 12:37–43. See Moloney, *John*, 363–65, 367–68

the final author's being, at worst, "a scribe doing his best," Brown has written:

> Even though I think there was both an evangelist and a redactor, the duty of the commentator is not to decide what was composed by whom, or in what order it originally stood, nor whether these composers drew on a written source or an oral tradition. One should deal with the Gospel of John as it now stands, for that is the only form that we are certain has ever existed.[7]

Yet in many of the introductory questions, Brown has recourse to the various stages of his composition history to explain tensions within the text. Major examples are: the levels of the redaction to which one must look to trace the historicity of the data in the narrative; the stage at which other influences impacted upon the development (and the reception) of the Gospel; apologetics, especially the question of "the Jews"; the possibility that one can trace several "purposes" for the Gospel, depending upon which stage in the development of the Gospel is under consideration; the explanation of features in the narrative that possibly indicate a presence of the Johannine community in northern Transjordan. The list could be extended.

It could be objected that these issues are properly part of the science of an "introduction" to a New Testament book, and there is truth in that. But I can only speculate on Brown's answer to the following questions. Would Brown have provided a commentary on 1:1–18 *without* discussing the influence of the *later* (and perhaps apologetic) addition of vv. 6–8 and 15 into a hymn that (for Brown) was itself a late addition from the hand of the redactor?[8] Would he have explained 6:25–59 *without* recourse to the suggestion that vv. 51c–58 were a late insertion (obvious from the contradictory meaning of "flesh" [*sarx*] in vv. 51c–58 and v. 63)?[9] Would he have accepted the synchronic reading of 13:1–17:26 proposed above, in my contribution to the outline of the Book of Glory?[10] He, and the bulk of Johannine scholars, are surely correct in identifying a parallel between 14:1–31 and 16:4b–33. John 15 is different,

---

7. See above, pp. 44–45. See Dodd, *Interpretation*, 290.
8. See *John*, 18–23.
9. See *John*, 284–91.
10. See *John*, 581–604.

as are the narratives and the prayer in 13:1–38 and 17:1–26. But what would have determined the understanding of the meaning of Jesus' final encounter with his disciples: the tradition history or "the Gospel as it now stands, for that is the only form that we are certain has ever existed"?

Finally, as Brown left his text in 1998, one finds only a brief mention of Johannine symbolism in his treatment of the issue of sacramental material in the Fourth Gospel. Brown maintains his stature as a giant among those who have used historical criticism to read the Gospel of John. But contemporary commentary on the Fourth Gospel must face the challenge, vigorously argued over several decades by Sandra Schneiders,[11] of the pervasive use of sign, metaphor and symbol at every level of this rich narrative. Xavier Léon-Dufour and Günther Stemberger have ventured into this field, but that has not been the major feature of their work.[12] Craig Koester produced a very helpful systematic approach to the question in 1995,[13] but it will be interesting to observe how contemporary Johannine scholarship will deal with the recent stunning study of my Australian colleague, Dorothy Lee: *Symbolism, Gender and Theology in the Gospel of John.* This volume, an amazing balance of historical-critical insights, a deep awareness of the power and depth of the Johannine use of symbolism, and the impact such readings have made upon the Christian tradition, must not go unobserved.[14] Would the meticulous Raymond

---

11. See S. M. Schneiders, "History and Symbolism in the Fourth Gospel," in *L'Évangile de Jean. Sources, redaction, théologie* (ed. M. de Jonge; BETL 44; Leuven: Leuven University Press, 1977), 371–76; Idem, "Symbolism and Sacramental Principle in the Fourth Gospel," in *Segni e Sacramenti nel Vangelo di Giovanni* (ed. P.-R. Tragan; Studia Anselmiana 66; Rome: Editrice Anselmiana, 1977), 221–35; Idem, "The Footwashing (John 13:1–20): An Experiment in Hermeneutics," *CBQ* 43 (1981): 76–92; Idem, *Written That You May Believe: Encountering Jesus in the Fourth Gospel* (New York: Crossroads, 1999).

12. X. Léon-Dufour, "Towards a Symbolic Reading of the Fourth Gospel," *NTS* 27 (1980–81): 439–56. There are occasions when Léon-Dufour has recourse to his understanding of Johannine symbolic writing in his four-volume *Lecture de l'évangile selon Jean* (4 vols.; Paris; Editions du Seuil, 1988–96). For Stemberger, see G. Stemberger, *La symbolique du bien et du mal selon saint Jean* (Paris: Editions du Seuil, 1970).

13. C. Koester, *Symbolism in the Fourth Gospel: Meaning, Mystery, Community* (Minneapolis: Fortress, 1995).

14. D. Lee, *Flesh and Glory. Symbolism, Gender and Theology in the Gospel of John* (New York: Herder & Herder, 2002).

Brown have turned his mind to such questions in a commentary for the third millennium?

We will never know the answers to these questions, but the more I ponder them, the more I suspect Brown was moving in a direction that may have surprised his many outstanding colleagues who did so much for the establishment of the historical-critical method in the English-speaking world. One of the major contributions of this *Introduction* motivates this suspicion. Despite the eight "riders" that Brown adds to his final solution to the question of "the Jews" in the Gospel of John, he proposes that they are to be understood in terms of *their role* in the narrative, rather than (ultimately) their historical identity.[15]

A fundamental question may be asked in conclusion. As in his 1966 edition, but with more detail, erudition, experience and lightness of touch, Brown insists that the Gospel of John is the product of "traditional Judaism" rejects any direct influence from Gnosticism, Mandean thought, the *Hermetica,* or extrabiblical Hellenistic thought.[16] Nevertheless, one traces here an important, however small, shift of position. I would like to force that issue further. Brown's carefully articulated argument reflects a middle-of-the-road position, taken by most scholars of his generation. Yet, as I indicated in my Introduction, and as Brown admits in the text, he has chosen to shift away from his original identification of "Palestinian Judaism" to the more *broadly based* "traditional Judaism" as his basic point of reference for the background to the Gospel of John. This not insignificant shift of position opens the door—ever so slightly—on another possibility that was not articulated in the text as we have it.

Let me explain further, and what follows is speculation on my part, perhaps the result of a vain hope that the distance between Brown's understanding of the Gospel of John and my own is closer than might be first imagined. Brown's work on the history of the Johannine community enabled him to develop the theory that the Gospel of John was not influenced by Gnostic thought, but that as the community fell into disunity, one direction some members of the Johannine community took was into

---

15. Brown is correct to attempt, via his eight-point "riders," to link his identification of the literary "role" of "the Jews" in the narrative with the world that produced the text. Some narrative critics (e.g., Caron, *Qui sont?*) disregard this task.

16. See above, Chapter Four.

Gnosticism. Thus, Gnosticism played no role in the formation of the Gospel, but was an important *recipient* of the Gospel. In his analysis of the possible influence of Philonic-type Jewish-Hellenistic thinking, Brown concludes that Philo and the evangelist shared a common way of working out biblical motifs in a partially Jewish, partially Greek world where Hellenistic thought had taken root. This theme is developed further by means of Brown's careful listing of the many parallels between the Wisdom tradition and the Johannine thought-world, imagery and terminology. The Wisdom tradition, as we have seen, reflects the presence of Jewish-Hellenistic thinking and writing in the pre-Christian era. But as he closes his reflections upon Wisdom, Brown returns to his earlier reflections on the various possible influences on the Gospel. He adds, in a note:

> What John shows in common with these latter bodies of literature (Gnostic, Mandean or Hermetic) often represents a common but independently received heritage from the Jewish Wisdom Literature.[17]

As with his earlier suggestions concerning the Gnostic *reception* of the Johannine tradition, the Gospel and the many other non-Jewish and non-biblical literatures and "cultures" contemporaneous with the emergence of the Gospel of John are regarded as *recipients* of common traditions.

Might I suggest that the person(s) responsible for the final form of the Gospel of John was well aware that this story of Jesus was very different from the Jewish traditions that formed it? The existence of a Philonic-like Jewish approach to the life and practices of Israel in the first Christian century is obvious, and Philo himself is evidence of it. But he would not have been alone. It happens that we have his written work, and we tend to think that he must have been something of a unique and lone voice. Such was surely not the case. Similarly, by Brown's own admission (and it is commonplace among all scholars of early Christianity),[18] a profound Hellenization of Judaism had been going on for some centuries before the Christian movement.

---

17. See above, p. 263, n. 99.

18. The work of M. Hengel, *Judaism and Hellenism: Studies in Their Encounter i n Palestine During the Early Hellenistic Period* (London: SCM Press, 1974), marked a watershed in these discussions. See also the briefer, but lucid treatment of L. I. Levine, *Judaism and Hellenism in Antiquity* (Peabody: Hendrickson, 1999).

So much has been said and written about a pre-Christian Gnosticism. Did it, or did it not exist? This is to ask the wrong question in a discussion of the factors that may have influenced the formation of the Gospel of John as we now have it. Clearly the great Gnostic systems that we know from the second century owe a great deal to the Christian tradition, and especially to the Gospel of John. However, did these powerful intellectual movements, which almost took the young Christian church by storm, and aroused anger and voluminous writing from people like Irenaeus, Hippolytus and Epiphanius, come from nowhere? Did they suddenly appear on the scene in the second century as fully developed systems? As Giovanni Filoramo poses the question: "Related, if not prior to Christianity, it had arisen independently, based on oriental texts and ideas, a genuine religion in which the *logos* (word/reason) was the son of the *mythos* (myth) and Christianity one of several elements that came together to make a difficult puzzle." [19] It would be better, in the light of Filoramo's comment and the evidence of the second century, to speak of a *"pre-Gnostic Gnosticism."* If Brown is correct that the Gospel saw the light of day in its present form at Ephesus,[20] the world *into which* the Gospel of John told its story of Jesus was marked by a maelstrom of religious thoughts and practices, however eclectic and primitive they may have been. It would have been impossible, to my mind, for the author(s) of the Gospel of John *not* to shape the Johannine story of Jesus so that it might address the confused and confusing religious world of one of the great cosmopolitan cities of Asia Minor.[21]

The Gospel of John told the old story of Jesus in a radically different fashion, without betraying the roots of the original Christian tradition: the life, teaching, death and resurrection of Jesus of Nazareth. One of the reasons for these remarkable differences, might I suggest (and hope that

---

19. G. Filoramo, *A History of Gnosticism* (Oxford: Blackwell, 1990), 11–12.

20. See Moloney, *John*, 5–6.

21. Some contemporary Markan scholars are suggesting that the Gospel of Mark, however Jewish its origins, was shaped to speak to a Greco-Roman audience. See, for example, T. H. Kim, "The Anarthrous υἱὸς Θεοῦ in Mark 15,39," *Bib* 79 (1998): 221–41; A. Y. Collins, "Mark and His Readers: The Son of God among Jews," *HTR* 92 (1999): 393–408. See also her "Mark and His Readers: The Son of God among Greeks and Romans," *HTR* 93 (2000): 85–100; C. A. Evans, "Mark's Incipit and the Priene Calendar Inscription: From Jewish Gospel to Greco-Roman Gospel," *Journal of Greco-Roman Christianity and Judaism* 1 (2000): 67–81.

Ray Brown is nodding approvingly), was an awareness of the new world into which Jesus' story had to be announced. Only of recent times have literary critics and people interested in the newer science of hermeneutics begun to speak about the worlds behind, within and in front of the text.[22] However, in all ages, anyone who tells a story (the world in the text) is influenced by both the material he or she receives (the world behind the text) and the people for whom the story is being written (the world in front of the text). Surely this was the case for the author(s) of the Gospel of John. If so, then the "pre-Gnostic Gnostic" and Hellenistic world of the first century (the world in front of the text), side by side with the formative elements from the story of Jesus and the traditional Judaism within which it was originally told (the world behind the text), also played *a formative role* in the development of the Gospel of John (the world in the text). This preparedness to shape a new story of Jesus to address a new world is one of the many reasons, in my opinion, for the perennial fascination of the Gospel of John. Into these worlds also steps the remarkable *personae* of Brown's BD and evangelist if, indeed, they are to be separated. They have inscribed themselves into these inspired and inspiring pages.[23] The Gospel of John builds bridges from one socio-cultural and religious world (traditional Judaism) into another (the Gnostic-Hellenistic world of Asia Minor), and in doing so serves as a paradigm for all who seek to tell and retell the story of Jesus.[24]

---

22. The influence of Gadamer, and his "fusion of horizons" (*Horizontsver-schmelzung*) has been very influential here. See H.-G. Gadamer, *Truth and Method* (New York: Seabury, 1975), 269–74. See p. 273: "Understanding . . . is always a fusion of these horizons which we *imagine* to exist by themselves" (my emphasis).

23. On the *inevitable* presence of the *persona* of an author in a narrative, see F. J. Moloney, "Adventure with Nicodemus. An Exercise in Hermeneutics," in *"A Hard Saying,"* 259–79.

24. For the same sentiments, see the summary of K. Scholtissek, *In ihm sein und bleiben. Die Sprache der Immanenz in den johanneischen Schriften* (Herders Biblische Studien 21; Freiburg: Herder, 2000), 23–130, esp. p. 23. This has been elegantly stated by Dodd, *Interpretation*, 9: "We are to think of the work as addressed to a wide public consisting primarily of devout and thoughtful persons . . . in the varied and cosmopolitan society of a great Hellenistic city such as Ephesus under the Roman Empire." See also R. J. Cassidy, *John's Gospel in New Perspective. Christology and the Realities of Roman Power* (New York: Maryknoll, 1992).

AUTHOR INDEX

Aarde, A. G. van, 193
Abbott, E. A., 128
Achtemeier, P. J., 52
Aland, B., 209, 283
Aland, K., 209, 283
Albright, W. F., 91, 284
Allen, E. L., 174
Anderson, Paul N., 4, 98, 107
Andrews, Mary, 207
Arendt, Hannah, 158
Argyle, A. W., 129
Ashton, L., 162, 164, 166, 167, 169, 171
Aune, D. E., 247

B

Backhaus, K., 153
Bacon, B. W., 27, 104, 207
Bailey, J. A., 95, 102
Balabanski, V., 204, 246
Baldensperger, W., 153
Balmforth, H., 91
Balzac, Honoré de, 39
Barclay, W., 27
Barrett, C. K., 28, 30, 36, 44, 91, 95, 117, 133, 161, 179, 193, 208, 210, 220, 230, 249
Bauckham, R., 55, 195
Bauer, W., 1, 116, 203
Baum-Bodenbender, R., 96
Baur, F. C., 207
Becker, H., 53, 55, 56, 120
Becker, J., 28, 230, 266
Becker, J. J., 98
Belle, G. van, 57, 96

Benoit, P., 266
Bernard, J. H., 4, 28, 43, 44, 45, 46, 288
Beutler, J., 133, 138, 224
Bieringer, R., 158, 161, 169, 171
Billerbeck, P., 139
Birdsall, J. N., 284
Bittner, J., 57
Black, C. C., 279, 280, 281
Black, M., 137, 254
Blackburn, B., 57
Blank, J., 245
Blinzler, J., 95
Bloch, R., 137
Böcher, O., 140
Boer, M. C. de, 161
Boismard, M.-É., 7, 43, 55, 59–62, 78, 81, 82, 95, 96, 98, 103, 208, 230, 241, 245, 279–84, 303, 305
Borgen, Peder, 52, 57, 83, 96, 127, 130, 139, 231, 258, 261
Bornhäuser, K., 173
Bornkamm, G., 105, 231, 247
Borsch, F., 255, 258
Bousset, W., 116
Bouyer, L., 229
Braun, F.-M., 117, 127, 130, 131, 134, 140, 208, 259
Brown, Raymond E., xi–xvii, xix, 1–14, 30, 31, 37–39, 69, 73–76, 100, 101, 102, 104, 108, 116, 125, 126, 140, 152, 155, 161, 165, 177, 178, 191, 196, 227, 230, 231, 237, 256, 261, 266, 283, 287, 291, 302–7, 311–13, 317–25
Brownlee, W. H., 202

Büchsel, F., 116
Bühner, J.-A., 258
Bultmann, R., 1, 4, 5, 28, 43, 44, 46, 47–53,
   55, 56, 59, 82, 85, 97–98, 104, 105, 116,
   119, 120, 121, 153, 170, 183, 221, 223,
   231, 232, 236, 241, 245–47, 250, 258,
   279, 280, 285, 286, 288
Burkett, D., 253, 255, 257
Burney, C. F., 203, 279, 280, 281, 285,
   286
Burrows, F., 279
Busse, U., 224

C

Caron, G., 172, 322
Carson, D. A., 27, 54, 55, 106, 152
Cassem, N. H., 182
Cassidy, J., 325
Charlesworth, J. H., 169, 208
Chatman, S., 39, 291
Clark, D. K., 262
Clavier, H., 288
Cohen, Shaye, 158
Collins, R. F., 161
Colpe, C., 119
Comfort, P. W., 283
Conzelmann, H., 105
Cook, M. J., 166, 168
Cook, W. R., 235
Coppens, J., 257
Corell, A., 229, 236
Corsani, B., 55
Cothenet, É., 133, 136
Cribbs, F. L., 95, 102, 173, 212
Crossan, J. D., 98
Cullmann, O., 98, 127, 191, 203, 221, 229,
   232, 233, 236, 252, 258, 288
Culpepper, R. A., 31, 44, 84, 86, 158, 166,
   182, 191, 196, 208, 231, 291, 311
Cuming, G. J., 162

D

Dahl, N. A., 171
Daly-Denton, M., 135
D'Aragon, J.-L., 222
Das, A. A., 249
Daube, D., 139
Dauer, A., 96, 97
Davey, D. M., 208

Davies, William David, 179, 264, 265
de Boer, M. C., 161
de Jonge, H. J., 161
de Jonge, M., 70, 166, 167, 171, 173, 214,
   244, 247, 248, 261, 289
de Solages, B., 96
Déaut, R. Le, 137, 280
Delafosse, H., 207
Delobel, J., 96
Dettwiler, A., 291, 312
Dietzfelbinger, C., 134
Dion, H.-M., 259
Dodd, C. H., 1, 6, 7, 28, 44, 50, 51, 91, 97,
   100, 106, 121, 124, 130, 131, 139, 191,
   208, 236, 238, 239, 241, 245, 258, 303,
   304, 314, 319, 320, 325
Donovan, J., 27
Drower, Lady E. S., 121
Dschulnigg, P., 51, 57
Dubois, J.-D., 120, 123
Dunderberg, J., 4, 55, 56, 62, 63, 86, 99
Dunne, J. D. G., 158

E, F

Easton, B. S., 46, 49
Ehrman, B. D., 282
Enz, J. J., 134, 135
Evans, C. A., 133, 324
Fee, G. D., 152
Festugière, A. J., 131
Feuillet, A., 129, 130, 225, 264
Filoramo, Giovanni, 119, 324
Fischer, K. M., 120, 126
Fish, Stanley, 35
Fitzmyer, J. A., 140, 176, 254
Fortna, R. T., 53–54, 55, 56, 58, 78, 98,
   224
Freed, E. D., 133
Freedman, David Noel, 260, 283
Frenchowski, M., 202
Frey, J., 235
Fridrichser, A., 266

G

Gächter (also Gaechter), P., 285, 286
Gadamer, H.-G., 325
Gardner-Smith, P., 6, 7, 97
Gärtner, E. G. B., 139
Gingrich, F.W., 288

Giversen, S., 57
Glasswell, M. E., 95, 98
Goodenough, E. R., 97, 207, 212
Goodwin, C., 77, 99, 136
Grelot, P., 158, 160, 162, 166
Griffiths, D.R., 135
Guilding, Aileen., 139
Guthrie, D., 95

H

Haenchen, E., 28, 126, 231
Hamerton-Kelly, R., 179
Hanson, A. T., 134, 137
Hare, D. R. A., 258
Hartingsveld, L. van, 241
Heekerens, H.-P., 51, 55, 56, 57, 99
Heidegger, Martin, 110
Hengel, M., 96, 122, 125, 137, 138, 196, 204, 208, 210, 323
Hickling, C. J. A., 161
Higgins, A. J. B., 91, 255, 258
Hilgenfeld, A., 250
Hirsch, E., 47, 207
Hoare, F. R., 45, 46
Hoegen-Rohls, C., 247
Hofrichter, P., 117, 122
Holladay, C. H., 57
Holland, H. S., 94
Horbury, W., 213
Horst, P. W. van der, 69, 172, 213
Hoskyns, E. C., 1, 28, 44, 110, 134, 229
Hufmann, R. J., 133

I, J

Inge, W. R., 128
Iser, Wolfgang, 83
Janssens, Y., 117, 122
Jeremias, J., 51
Johnson, L. T., 159
Jonas, H., 120
Jonge, H. J. de, 161
Jonge, M. de, 70, 166, 167, 171, 173, 214, 244, 247, 248, 261, 289
Jülicher, A., 95

K

Käsemann, E., 28, 98, 123, 221, 251
Kaufman, S. A., 280
Kemper, F., 202

Kilpatrick, G. D., 131, 132
Kim, S., 257
Kim, T. H., 324
Kimelman, R., 213
Klauck, H.-J., 203
Kleinknecht, K. T., 96
Koester, Craig, 69, 321
Koester, H., 98, 122, 123, 203, 205, 231
Kügler, J., 195
Kuhn, K. G., 140
Kümmel, W. G., 95
Kundsin, K., 200
Kurz, W., 193
Kysar, R., 55, 98, 167, 168, 246

L

Labahn, Michael, 3, 4, 7, 57, 63, 101, 104
Lacomara, A., 135
Lagrange, M.-J., 1
Lamouille, A., 7, 61, 230
Lang, Manfred, 4, 95, 96
Langbrandtner, Wolfgang, 57, 72–74, 122
Layton, B., 117, 123
Le Déaut, R., 137, 280
Leal, J., 91
Lee, Dorothy, 321
Lee, E. K., 79, 95
Léon-Dufour, Xavier, 230, 321
Leroy, H., 288
Levine, L. I., 323
Licht, J., 242
Lichtenberger, H., 154
Lieu, J. M., 69, 122, 158
Lightfoot, R. H., 1, 28, 95, 229
Lindars, B., 28, 54, 57, 77, 230, 258
Loader, W., 252
Locher, C., 169
Logan, A. H. B., 118, 122
Lohse, E., 231
Loisy, A., 1, 207
Lowe, M., 162

M

Macgregor, G. H. C., 47, 279
MacRae, G. W., 116, 182, 259
Maddox, R., 103, 255, 259
Maier, G., 95

Manns, F., 204
Marguerat, D., 57
Martyn, J. Louis, 68, 70–71, 73, 74, 98, 172, 202, 208, 257
Matera, F. J., 249
Mattill, A. J., 71
Maurer, Christian, 208
McGrath, J. F., 67
McLeman, J., 47
Meeks, W. A., 162, 200, 221, 259
Mees, M., 282
Meier, J. P., 65, 66, 93
Mendner, S., 95
Menken, M. J. J., 133, 136
Menoud, P.-H., 51
Michaelis, W., 232, 233
Moeller, H. R., 259
Moffatt, J., 95
Mollat, D., 286
Moloney, Francis J., xiii, xv, xvi, 10–14, 30, 31, 44, 67, 75, 77, 81, 84, 92, 98, 156, 168, 191, 201, 213, 214, 224, 226, 230, 231, 247, 249, 255–61, 292, 299, 302, 304, 311, 313, 314, 319, 325
Morris, L., 27, 94, 98, 109
Morton, A. Q., 47
Motyer, S., 158
Mussner, F., 110

N, O

Neirynck, F., 6, 7, 55, 61, 96, 97, 99
Neusner, J., 142
Nicol, W., 55, 56, 98
Niemand, C., 155
Niewalda, P., 229, 232
Noack, B., 46, 57, 77
Nock, A. D., 118, 131
Obermann, A., 133, 137, 138
O'Grady, J. F., 221
Olsson, B., 137
O'Neill, J. C., 157
Ong, Walter, 101
O'Rourke, J., 133
Osiek, C., 116
Osty, E., 95, 102

P, Q

Painter, John, 4, 63, 69, 79, 82, 126, 213, 317

Pamment, M., 254
Parker, P., 52, 59, 82, 95, 96, 103
Percy, E., 116
Perkins, P., 116, 117, 120
Perrin, N., 96
Pervo, R. I., 125, 126
Pesch, R., 55
Petersen, N. R., 221, 289
Pietrantonio, R., 162
Pilgaard, A., 55
Poffet, J.-M., 124, 208
Pollefeyt, D., 158
Porsch, F., 170, 172
Pratscher, W., 170
Pryor, J. W., 124, 208
Quispel, G., 117

R

Rehm, G., 98
Reim, G., 203, 204
Reinhartz, A., 161
Reitzenstein, R., 116
Rhea, R., 255
Ricca, P., 236, 243, 248
Richard, E., 289
Richmond, W. J., 94
Richter, Georg, 71–72, 73, 74, 124
Ridderbos, H. N., 27, 98
Rieu, E. V., 290
Robert, R., 61
Robinson, J. A. T., 152, 173, 180, 212, 213, 241
Robinson, J. M., 117, 122
Romanides, J. S., 208
Rossé, G., 223
Ruckstuhl, E., 51, 52, 53, 86, 123, 143
Rudolph, K., 121

S

Sabbe, M., 96, 97
Salmon, V., 63
Sanday, W., 27
Sanders, E. P., 213
Sanders, J. N., 28, 96, 110, 202, 208
Sanders, J. T., 242
Sanders, W., 98
Sasse, M., 10, 11
Schäfer, P., 158
Schenke, H. M., 119

Schenke, L., 54
Schlatter, A., 139
Schmithals, W., 207, 245
Schnackenburg, R., 8, 28, 55, 56, 98, 151, 152, 153, 180, 205, 225, 230, 232, 254, 255, 259
Schneider, H., 28, 230
Schneiders, Sandra M., 31, 321
Schnelle, Udo, 4, 7, 9, 57, 69, 95, 96, 100, 177, 266
Schniewind, J., 103
Scholtissek, K., 3, 30, 37, 291, 292
Schottroff, L., 122, 123
Schuchard, B. G., 133, 136
Schultz, S., 120
Schulz, S., 28, 57, 98, 230
Schwank, B., 28, 201
Schwartz, E., 58
Schweitzer, A., 238
Schweizer, E., 51, 52, 53, 86, 116, 221, 222, 226, 228, 231
Scobie, C. H. H., 200
Scott, M., 259
Scroggs, R., 179
Segovia, F. F., 312
Sevrin, J.-M., 123, 124
Sidebottom, E. M., 255
Simoens, Y., 313
Smalley, S. S., 57, 255
Smiga, G. M., 162, 166
Smith, D. M., 48, 49, 52, 69, 95, 97, 98, 153, 285
Smith, R. H., 134, 135, 137
Soards, M. L., 54
Solages, B. de, 96
Spicq, C., 266, 267
Spitta, F., 47, 55
Stählin, G., 246
Stanley, D., 229
Stauffer, E., 91, 241
Steiner, George, 33–34
Stemberger, Günther, 321
Stibbe, M. W. G., 31, 44
Stimpfle, A., 244
Stowasser, M., 153
Strack, F., 139
Strecker, G., 96, 124, 241
Streeter, B., 95
Stuhlmacher, P., 96

T

Talbert, C. H., 258
Tarelli, C. C., 208
Taylor, M. J., 101
Teeple, H. M., 40, 55, 56, 141
Temple, S., 55
Tenney, M. C., 290
Thomas, J. C., 142, 209
Thüsing, W., 10, 28
Thyen, H., 57, 58, 96, 99, 162
Tomson, P. J., 161
Torrey, F., 279, 281
Townsend, J. T., 170
Tracy, David, 37, 38
Trocmé, E., 153, 154
Trumbower, J. A., 250
Turner, G. A., 211

V

van Aarde, A. G., 193
van Belle, G., 57, 96
van der Horst, P. W., 69, 172, 213
van Hartingsveld, L., 241
van Unnik, W. C., 152, 173, 180, 241
Vandecasteele-Vanneuville, F., 158
Vawter, B., 135, 229
Vermes, G., 253
Vernette, J., 119
Vogler, W., 95
von Wahlde, U. C., 4, 55, 56, 58, 62, 63, 98, 126, 157, 165, 166, 182
Vouga, F., 124, 127, 161, 169

W

Wahlde, U. C. von, 4, 55, 56, 58, 62, 63, 98, 126, 157, 165, 166, 182
Wedderburg, A. J. M., 258
Wellhausen, J., 58
Wendt, H. H., 47, 58
Wengst, K., 68, 162, 169, 203, 204
Westcott, B. F., 27, 28
Whitacre, R. A., 151
Wikenhauser, A., 43
Wilkens, W., 43, 58–59, 82, 85, 98, 176
Willett, M. E., 261
Williams, M. L., 97
Wilson, R. McL., 130
Windisch, H., 12, 95, 100

Wisse, F., 121
Witherup, Ronald, 2

Y
Yamauchi, E. M., 117
Yarbro-Collins, Adela, 36, 77, 324

Z
Zahn, T., 95
Ziener, G., 262
Zumstein, J., 171, 291, 312
Zwaan, De, 279

SUBJECT INDEX

abstract or symbolic language attributed to Jesus, 92–93, 289–90
accidental displacement theories, 43–46, 50, 62–64
Acts, 98, 157, 161, 205, 225, *see also* Biblical Citations Index
Acts of John (5th century), 194
Acts of John (Leucian), 118, 123, 125, 194, 203
Adversus Haereses. (Irenaeus), 124, 175, 176, 199
Aenon, 201
Agrippa II, 203
Alexandria, 125, 127, 129, 202, 260, 282
Alexandria, Philo of, 28, 129–30, 140, 202, 258, 259, 323
Alexandrinus (A) (Codex), 282
the Alogoi, 126
anachronisms, 92–93
Andrew, 178
Annas, 93, 103
anti-Jewish/anti-Semitic/anti-Judaic, John as, 158, 159, 167–69
Antichrists, 227
Antioch, 101, 203, 205
antithetic parallelism, 284–85
aorist subjunctive *(hina pisteusête)*, use of, 152, 182
Apocalypse of James, 125
apocalyptic material: future eschatology, 183, 238–48; Judaism's influence on Gospel, 140; Revelation, 225, 237, 303, 304, 305, 318; Son of Man, 258; structure and outline of Gospel, 305

Apocryphon of John, 122, 125
Apollonius of Tyana, 52
Apollos, 129, 153, 205
apologetics, 8–9, 92, 151–88, 320; Christians of inadequate faith, 177–80; crypto-Christians or "Jewish Christians," 173–75; heretical groups, 175–77; "the Jews" *(Ioudaios)*, 157–73; John the Baptist, adherents of, 153–57; lifetime of Jesus, conflicts with "the Jews" during, 159–60, 167; Petrine followers, 177–79, 244; refusal of belief in Jesus by Jews, 153–72; *testimonia*, 136
Apology (Justin Martyr), 124
aporias, 53, 64
apostles, 178–79, 202, 220, 223, 224, 228
Aramaic: composition of Gospel, 48, 52, 60, 61, 81; evangelists, original languages of, 279; Greek text, Aramaisms in, 279; original language of John's Gospel, 278–81; patristic texts, evidence in, 284; place of composition of Gospel, 201, 204; poetic/quasi-poetic format, 48, 50, 51, 284–87; rhyme in, 285; Son of Man terminology, 253–54
archetypal primordial man myth and Son of Man concept, 258
Arimathea, Joseph of, 174
ascending/descending motif, 10–11, 257–59, 258, 261
Asia Minor, 208, 210, 212
Augustine, 26

333

authorities *(archontes),* "the Jews"
(Ioudaios) used to mean, 163–66, 171
authority behind style of literature, 190
authority within church/community, 228
authorship, concept of, 189–90
authorship of Gospel, 9, 32–34, 39,
189–99, 318–20, *see also* "the
evangelist"; "the redactor"; BD as
author, 190–96; eyewitness as author,
194–96; identity of author(s), 40,
189–99, 215; *relecture* process, 291;
Revelation author and, 204; unity of
authorship, 40–42, 86; "we," authorial
significance of, 193–95; writer
distinguished from, 189–90
authorship of Johannine epistles, 198–99,
207

B

baptism, 155–56, 183, 223, 230–34,
240
bar nasha (Son of Man), 253
Baruch, *see* Biblical Citations Index
Batanea, 203
Bathyra, 203–4
belief and faith: ecclesiology, 222–23,
227; eschatology, 234; geographical
symbolism, 201; purpose of Gospel,
faith and belief as, 152, 166, 179–83;
structure and outline of Gospel
addressing, 300, 306, 313, 314–15
Beloved Disciple (BD), 5, 6, 26, 318–19,
325; apostles' Synoptic role, 224; author
of Gospel, 190–96; Book of Glory, 310,
314–15; death of, 194, 214–15, 244;
disciples of, 190, 194, 197; Essene,
viewed as, 143; "the evangelist," 78, 82,
192–96, 225; eyewitness to Gospel
account, as, 194–96, 198; first stage of
Brown's three-stage theory, 65, 86;
Johannine community (stage two) and,
73, 74, 77, 86, 191, 310, 314–15; mother
of Jesus given to, 310; multiple editions
theories, 59, 60, 62; narrator of Gospel,
191; other apostles/disciples compared
to, 177–80, 203; Paraclete-Spirit, as
instrument of, 81, 236; personal
thought, influence of, 115–16, 143–44;
Qumran literature's Righteous Teacher,

141; "the redactor," 78, 82, 192, 194,
225; Synoptic knowledge of, 97
Bethany, 201, 303
Bethel, 204
Bethesda, pool of, 92, 200, 300, 301
Bethsaida, 204
Bezae (D) (Codex), 282
Birkat ha-mînîm, 69, 70, 73–74, 172, 205,
213
birth of Jesus, 212
blind man story, 163, 173–74, 256, 290,
300, 302
Bodmer papyri, 210, 283, 292–94
Bohairic (Coptic) versions of Gospel, 282,
293–94
book (codex) as form of Gospel text,
45–46
Book of Glory, 12, 298, 320;
disciples/Johannine community,
directed at, 299, 309, 310; parts of,
308–13; structure and outline, 307–15;
themes of individual parts, 311–15
Book of Signs, 298–300; parts of, 300–305;
public ministry of Jesus, 298–99, 302,
303; Son of Man passages, 255, 256;
structure and outline, 300–307; themes
of individual parts, 305–7
Bread of Life Discourse, 42, 50, 81, 229,
303
bronze serpent on pole, 10, 135, 137, 233,
256, 288, 308

C

Cana miracles, 41, 51, 155, 163, 230, 282,
300, 301, 304, 306
Cerinthus, 124, 175–76, 205
Chenoboskion, 117
Christology, 9–11, 26, 249, 318; conflicting
statements regarding, 250–51; dating of
Gospel, 207; *Ego Eimi (see Ego Eimi* ("I
am")); epistles of John, 84; eschatology
and, 244, 248; "the evangelist," 79; JBap,
presentation of, 156; "the Jews," use of,
166, 171–72; Johannine community,
theories of, 72, 73, 74, 75; keys, words
and motifs as, 251–52; multiple edition
theories, 60, 61; multiple source
theories, 55–57; OT citations, 134;
perfection *vs.* replacement, 305;

Pseudo-Clementine writings, low Christology of, 179; Son of God (*see* Son of God); Son of Man (*see* Son of Man); sources and influences, 115; symbolic language and, 289; Synoptic tradition, 115; theocentrism of, 249, 250; Wisdom tradition, 252, 258–65

christos vs. messias, use of, 160

Chronicle (Eusebius), 203

chronological inconsistencies, 41–42, 46, 94–91, 108

Chrysostom (John), 26, 61, 283–84

Church Fathers, writings of, *see* patristic texts

cleansing of the Temple, 108, 249, 301

Clement of Alexandria, 27, 193

Clement of Rome, 124, 208, 209

codex (book) as form of Gospel text, 45–46, 283

codices, great, 193, 210, 282, 283

Colossians, 197, 205, 260, 266

commandment, Johannine concept of, 135

commentaries on John, historiography of, 26–30

Commentary on the Diatessaron (Ephraem), 154

composition of Gospel, 1, 4–6, 42 et seq., 317–21; accidental displacement theories, 43–46, 50, 62–64; BD stage (stage two) (*see* Beloved Disciple (BD)); Christological stages, 250–51; ecclesiology and, 222; "the evangelist" (stage three) (*see* "the evangelist"); five-stage theory, 4–5, 64, 317–18; historical origins (stage one) (*see* historical origins of Gospel); Johannine community (stage two) (*see* Johannine community.); multiple edition theories, 46, 58–62, 81–82, 165, 168; multiple source theories, 46–48; "the redactor" (stage three) (*see* "the redactor"); three-stage theory, 5–6, 64 et seq., 317–18; written stage (stage 3) (*see* written stage of Gospel)

Contra Celsum (Origen), 126

Coptic texts: Nag-Hammadi, 53, 117–18, 121–23, 125, 208; versions of John's Gospel, 282, 293–94

copyists' mistakes and deliberate changes, 157, 281–83

Corinthians, First and Second Epistles to, 68, 205, 224, 228, 243

covenant theme, 223

creation theme, 245, 305

cross-influence between John and Synoptics, 101–4

crucifixion and cross, 10, 11, 36

crypto-Christians ("Jewish Christians"), 9, 70–71, 74, 79, 173–75, 179

cult, 247

Cynics, 128

D

Damascus Document (CD), 139

Daniel, 226, 254, 255, 256, 258

darkness and light, *see* light and darkness

dating of Gospel, 9, 28, 60, 62, 173, 206–15

David, 135, 160, 190, 204, 259

Dead Sea Scrolls (DSS), xii, 8, 28, 65–66, 93, 136, 139, 142, 254, 278

death and life, theme of, 238–40, 242, 243, 305, 306–7

death of apostolic generation, crisis of, 214

death of BD, 194, 214–15, 244

death of Peter, 214

Dedication, 161, 302, 306

Delos, 205

"demiurge," 131

descending/ascending motif, 10–11, 257–59, 258, 261

Deutero-Isaiah, 135

Deuteronomy, 68, 71, 135, 190

diachrony, 37, 291

Dialogue against Trypho (Justin Martyr), 68, 124, 173, 213

Dialogue of the Savior, 118, 123

Diatessaron (Tatian), 109, 154, 210, 283

Diodorus of Tarsus, 284

Diotrephes of 3 John, 73, 123, 202

disciples of BD/author of Gospel, 190, 194, 197

disciples of JBap, 143, 154, 201, 203, 204

disciples of Jesus: "apostle" and "disciple," Gospel's use of, 178; Book of Glory directed at, 299, 309, 310, 314; last encounter between Jesus and, 307,

disciples of Jesus *(continued)*
308–9, 311–13; Moses' disciples, contrasted with, 164; responsibility for Johannine community, 314–15; resurrected Jesus appearing to, 310; sending forth of, 223

disciples of Paul as authors of post-Pauline writings, 197

discourse *vs.* story, 290–91

discourses: Bread of Life Discourse, 42, 50, 81, 229, 303; edition theories, 59, 61, 62; Last (Final) Discourse, 42, 80, 84, 171, 255, 291, 307, 311; Last Supper Discourse, 41, 84, 85, 178, 211, 231, 234, 248, 299; poetic/quasi-poetic format, 285–86; Rabbinic Judaism, 139; Revelatory Discourse Source *(Offenbarungsreden)*, 48–49, 51, 52, 54, 121, 279, 285; signs, interpreting, 304; source theories, 48–49, 50–51, 53, 54; structure and outline of Gospel, 301, 302, 303, 307, 311–12; Wisdom Tradition, influence of, 136, 262

displacement of parts of Gospel, accidental, 43–46, 50, 62–64

"The Divine" *(ho theologos)*, John known as, 27, 30, 107, 220, 267

Docetism, 72, 75, 122, 123, 124, 176–77, 205, 251

Document C, 60, 78, 136

Dositheus of Shechem, 154

double meanings, 256, 288–89

dualism, 73, 118–19, 120, 122, 123, 140, 172, 176

duplications and repetitions, 42, 46, 61, 291

E

early/primitive traditions distinguished from historical traditions, 106

Eastern textual tradition, 125, 282

Ebion and the Ebionites, 176

Ecclesiastes, 190, 260

"Ecclesiastical Redactor" (Bultmann), 49, 52, 82, 224, 231, 241, 286

ecclesiology, 9, 73, 125–26, 202, 221–29, 266

editions, multiple, 46, 58–62, 81–82, 165, 168, 211

Egerton Papyrus 2, 98, 210

Ego Eimi ("I am"), 251, 252; composition of Gospel, 74; eschatology, 240; Gnosticism, 115, 119, 123, 125; Judaism's influence on Gospel, 135; Wisdom tradition, 259, 262

Egypt, 208, 210, *see also* Alexandria

Eighteen Benedictions *(Shemoneh 'Esreh),* 172, 213

eisegesis, 232, 233

I Enoch, 254, 255, 262

Ephesians (Biblical Epistle), 178, 190, 197, 205, 228, 243, 260

Ephesians (Ignatius), 179, 205, 208, 246

Ephesus, 9, 60–61, 82, 101, 129, 153, 177, 194, 198, 204–6, 290

Ephraem, 154

Ephraim, 201, 302

Epilogue, 12, 298, 299, 307, 308, 310, 315

Epiphanius, 324

Epistle to the Philippians (Polycarp), 205

Erasmus, 282

eschatology, 9, 234–48; composition of Gospel and, 42, 49–50, 75; dating of Gospel, 214; defining, 235; development in New Testament, 242–44; diversity of approaches, 244–48, 266; Johannine logion, 265; OT background, 134, 137, 235; Qumran literature, 141; realized and future/apocalyptic, 183, 214, 238–48, 255; "vertical" and "horizontal," 235–38, 248

Essenes, 93, 127, 132, 139–40, 143, 159, 169, *see also* Qumran literature and community

Estius, 233

eternal life, 239–40, 243, 249, 250

ethics, 75

Ethiopic versions of Gospel, 282

ethnic categories, loss of significance of, 170, 181

ethnic usage of "the Jews" *(Ioudaios),* 158, 159, 161–62, 169, 170

Eucharist, 177, 183, 212, 223, 230–34, 240

Eusebius, 203

"the evangelist," 5–6, 79–82, 197–98, 318–20, 325; BD and, 78, 82, 192–96, 225; Christological stages, 250; dating of Gospel, 206–15; historical value of stage three, 108–10; identity of, 189; "the Jews" *(Ioudaios),* use of, 160, 168; Johannine school, 196–97; movement of Johannine community after work of, 200, 204, 206; multiple editions of, 81–82, 211; OT Wisdom literature's influence, 143; personal thought influencing Gospel, 115–16, 143–44; preaching of, 79, 83; purpose of, 79; "the redactor" regarded as, 99; relationship to BD and "redactor," 225; sacramental passages attributed to, 232; signs, theological function of, 80–81; structure, 80; Synoptic tradition and, 7

existential qualities of Gospel, 183, 245, 265

Exodus story, 44, 134, 135, 137, 259, 302, 306

explanatory notes, 286, 290

expulsion of Johannine community from synagogue: composition of Gospel, 62, 69, 70, 73–74, 75–77, 79; dating of Gospel, 213–14; eschatology, 244; "the Jews," hostility towards and separation from, 123, 152, 166, 169, 171–72; Johannine school, 197; place of composition of Gospel, 201; Roman religious tolerance, loss of, 169

eyewitness sources, 94, 104, 194–96

Ezekiel, 135.253

F

faith, *see* belief and faith

Fathers of the Church, writings of, *see* patristic texts

feasts, Jewish: apologetics, 161–63, 166; composition of Gospel, 69, 76; eschatology, 237; historical value of Johannine information, 92, 108; Judaism's influence on Gospel, 135, 139; place of composition of Gospel, 201; structure and outline of Gospel, 301, 302, 304, 306

Final (Last) Discourse, 42, 80, 84, 171, 255, 291, 307, 311

format of Gospel, *see* composition of Gospel; structure and outline of Gospel

French translation of John (SB), 284, 286

fulfillment theme, 133, 137, 177, 230, 237, 302, 308

fundamentalist Christianity, 31

future/apocalyptic eschatology, 183, 238–48

G

Gaius, 126, 202

Galatians, 180, 203, 205

Galilean influences, 59, 65, 82, 162–63, 201, 278

Gamaliel II, 213

gardens, 309, 310, 313–14

Gaulanitis, 203, 204

Genesis, 134, 245, 258

Gentile/Greco-Roman Christians, 170, 180–81, 201–2, 203

geographical inconsistencies, 41–42, 46, 91–94

geographical location of composition of John's Gospel, 9, 28, 60, 61, 82, 101, 199–206, 290

geographical usage of "the Jews" *(Ioudaios),* 158, 159, 162–63, 169

Gerizim, 92, 200

glory and glorification, 10, 11, 36, 125, 240, 254, 261, 299, 305, 307–13, *see also* Book of Glory

glosses, 286, 290

Gnosticism, 8, 26–29, 116–19, 322–25; anti-Gnosticism of John, 122–24, 126, 155, 175–76, 205; Christian, Jewish, and pagan expressions of, 116, 118, 122; Christology, 250; dating of Gospel, 208; defining, 116–17; descending/ascending motif, 259; Docetism, 123; dualism, 118–19, 120, 122, 123; ecclesiology, 221; eschatology, 236, 244, 245; first century A.D., 117; gnosis and gnosticism, distinguishing, 116; Hermetic literature, 131; influence on religious thought in John, 116–26; JBap, 153–55; "the Jews" *(Ioudaios),* 170; Johannine community's development, 73, 75, 122–26; Johannine material reflecting, 119–26; modern gnosticizing movements, 119; multiple source theories, 48–50, 52–53; place of composition of Gospel, 202, 203;

Gnosticism *(continued)*
　post-Gospel relationship of John to,
　　124–26; pre-Christian, 118, 122; pre-
　　Gospel relationship of John to, 120–22;
　　redeemer myth, 119, 121; Samarian
　　origins, 154; second century A.D.,
　　117–18; Son of Man concept, 254, 258;
　　Valentinian school, 117, 125–26, 176,
　　202, 250; Wisdom literature, 260, 263;
　　"the world," 170
Gospel of Peter, 98
Gospel of the Nazoreans, 279
Gospel of Thomas, 118, 123
Gospel of Truth, 117
grammatical tenses, significance of, 152,
　182
"Great Church," 126
great codices, 282–84
Greco-Roman/Gentile Christians, 170,
　180–81, 201–2, 203
Greco-Roman thought, *see* Hellenistic
　thought
Greek language and text, 12, 35–36, 38,
　281–84; "the evangelist," 82; Aramaisms
　in, 279; authorship of Gospel and,
　40–41; evangelists, original languages
　of, 279; Judaism, Greek-speaking, 279;
　LXX (Septuaguint), 136–37, 201, 204,
　226, 253, 280; mistranslations into,
　279–81; multiple source theories,
　48–49, 52; number of early surviving
　mss. of, 281; original language of
　Gospel, 278–81; OT used by John, 136;
　place of composition of Gospel, 201;
　Synoptic cross-influences, 102; Textus
　Receptus, 282; translation of
　Hebrew/Aramaic terms into Greek, 136,
　180, 201; variant versions, 280, 281–84
Greek oracles, 154, 288

H
Hanina, 52
Hebrew (language), 136–37, 201, 253–254,
　278–280
Hebrews (epistle), 99, 266–67
Hegelian thesis, antithesis, and synthesis,
　207, 265
Hellenistic thought, 8, 28, 92–93, 322–25;
　Cynics, 128; eschatology, 235–36, 238;

Gospel written to appeal to, 128, 182;
　Hermetic literature, 132; influence on
　religious thought in John, 127–32;
　Jesus and, 128; neo-Pythagoreans, 127;
　neoplatonism, 28; oracles, riddle
　language of, 288; Platonism, 128–29,
　131, 143, 235, 236; Pythagoreans, 196;
　Son of Man terminology, 258; Stoicism,
　128–29, 131; Wisdom tradition, 122,
　127, 252, 260
Hellenists, 127, 181, 205
Heracleon, 125, 250, 282
heretical groups, 175–77, 221, *see also*
　specific sects
Hermas, Shepherd of, 124
Hermes Trismegistus, 131
Hermetic literature, 53, 127–32, 139, 142,
　202, 258, 260, 263, 322, 323
Herod Antipas, tetrarchy of, 162
Herod the Great, 168
hidden Messiah, 139, 241
Hierapolis, 205
hina pisteusête/hina pisteuête, 152, 182
Hippolytus, 324
historical-critical approach, 1, 3–4, 7,
　13, 27–31, 62–64, 110–11, 320–
　322
historical origins of Gospel, 5, 27–30,
　90–91, 104–11, 324; conflicts with "the
　Jews" during lifetime of Jesus, 159–60,
　167; eschatology, 242, 244–45; first stage
　of Brown's three-stage theory, 64–66,
　105, 106, 108; information found only
　in John, 91–94; language spoken by
　Jesus, 278; multiple source theories and,
　48, 49, 51; order of Synoptic and
　Johannine Gospels dictated by, 80;
　primitive/early traditions distinguished
　from historical, 106; purpose of Gospel
　and, 151, 183; second stage of Brown's
　three-stage theory, 106–7; Son of Man
　terminology, 253, 255; Synoptic and
　Johannine parallels, significance of, 80,
　106–7, 109; third stage of Brown's
　three-stage theory, 108–10; Wisdom
　literature, 143, 264–65
historiography of Johannine
　commentaries, 26–30
hokma, 260

Holy Spirit, *see* Paraclete-Spirit
Homilies, 154
Honi, 52
"horizontal" eschatology, 235–38, 248
hu huios tou anthrôpou (Son of Man), 253
hypostatization *vs.* personalization of
    Wisdom tradition, 260

I

"I am," *see* Ego Eimi ("I am")
Ignatius of Antioch, 75, 124, 176, 177, 179,
    203, 205, 208, 209, 246
imagery of community, lack of, 222
immanence, language of, 292
inclusion, 287
independent Johannine tradition, 99–101
individual relationship with Jesus *vs.*
    concept of community, 226–27
influences, *see* sources and influences
inverted parallelism, 287
Irenaeus of Lyons, 26, 117, 124, 126, 175,
    176, 199, 208, 215, 324
irony, 290, 314
Isaiah, 135, 190, *see also* Biblical Citations
    Index
Ithiel, 253

J

Jacob's Well, Samaritan Woman at, 81,
    301, 306
James, Apocalypse of, 125
James (Biblical Epistle), 260, 261, 266
James (brother of Jesus and bishop of
    Jerusalem), 74, 179
Jamnia, 165, 203, 205, 213
Jeremiah, 82
Jerome, 176, 203, 279
Jerusalem, destruction of (A.D. 70), 164,
    204, 209, 210–13, 243–44
"Jewish Christians" (crypto-Christians), 9,
    70–71, 74, 79, 173–75, 179
"the Jews" (*Ioudaios*), 9, 318, 320, 322;
    anachronistic terminology, 92; anti-
    Jewish/anti-Semitic/anti-Judaic, John
    as, 158, 159, 167–69; apologetic against,
    157–73; authorities (*archontes*), used to
    mean, 163–66, 171; blood continuity
    with Israel, no stress on, 227; ethnic
    usage, 158, 159, 161–62, 169, 170; "the

evangelist," 80, 85; geographical usage,
    158, 159, 162–63, 169; hostility to Jesus,
    as generalized reference to those
    showing, 158, 166; Johannine
    community, development of, 74, 79,
    160–72; lifetime of Jesus, conflicts with
    "the Jews" during, 159–60, 167; man
    born blind story, 290; mob or crowd, as
    reference to, 165–66; multiple edition
    theories, 60, 62; OT citations and, 133,
    134, 138; place issues in use of, 166;
    place of composition of Gospel and,
    201; political usage, 162; reader-
    response criticism, 167–68; "the
    redactor," 80, 85; refusing belief in Jesus,
    157–72; religious usage, 166–67, 169;
    Samaritan influence, 67–68; singular *vs.*
    plural usage, 161; structure and outline
    of Gospel, 309; time issues in use of,
    166; "the world, identification with,
    170–71; written Gospel, conflicts with
    "the Jews" during time of, 160–72
Job, Book of, 261, 262
Job, Targum of, 280
Johannine comma, 281
Johannine community, 9, 13, 28–29,
    35–39, 320, 322, 325; backwater, viewed
    as, 266; BD's role in, 73, 74, 77, 86, 191,
    310, 314–15; Book of Glory directed at,
    299, 309, 310, 314; crises of, Gospel
    written to address, 182–83; cross,
    founded at, 310; crypto-Christians or
    "Jewish Christians," 9, 70–71, 74, 79;
    disciples' responsibility for, 314–15;
    ecclesiology and, 221–29; Epilogue
    addressing issues of authority and
    belonging, 315; expulsion from
    synagogue (*see* expulsion of Johannine
    community from synagogue);
    Gnosticism/anti-Gnosticism of, 73,
    75, 122–26; in-language of, 289; "the
    Jews" and, 74, 79, 160–72; Johannine
    school, whole community as, 197;
    Langbrandtner's theory of, 72–74; last
    encounter between Jesus and disciples,
    307, 308–9, 311–13; location of
    composition of Gospel and, 199–200;
    Martyn's theory of, 69–71; movement
    of, 199–200, 204, 206, 290; OT citations,

Johannine community *(continued)*
137–38; OT Wisdom literature's
influence, 143; passion/resurrection
narrative and belief without seeing, 315;
relecture, réécriture, and *réédition*
(telling and retelling), 292; Revelation's
relationship to, 303; Richter's theory of,
71–72; Roman religious tolerance, loss
of, 169; signs, attitude towards, 73, 123,
125; stage two of Brown's three-stage
theory, 66–69, 74–78, 79, 215;
synagogue, expulsion from *(see*
expulsion of Johannine community
from synagogue); Wisdom literature
and, 261; world, apartness from, 60, 71,
74, 170–71, 181–82, 237, 289
Johannine epistles, 315, *see also* 1 John, 2
John, 3 John; authorship, 198–99, 207;
community problems displayed by, 315;
composition of Gospel, 68, 73–75, 94;
dating, 215; ecclesiology, 225, 228;
eschatology, 245
Johannine logion, 265
Johannine school of thought and writing,
196–97
John, Acts of (5th century), 194
John, Acts of (Leucian), 118, 123, 125, 194,
203
John, Apocryphon of, 122, 125
John the Baptist (JBap), 9, 28; apologetic
against adherents of, 153–57; Book of
Signs, 300–301, 304; composition of
Gospel, 41, 42, 48, 49, 60, 64–66, 74, 80;
disciples of, 143, 154, 201, 203;
Gnosticism, 121; "the Jews" sending
emissaries to, 163; location of
composition of Gospel, 200, 201, 203;
Mandaeans and, 121, 154; Messiah,
regarded as, 154; Qumran and, 156;
Synoptic tradition, 91, 94, 98, 109, 110
John Chrysostom, 26, 61, 283–84
John, First Letter of, *see also* Biblical
Citations Index: apologetic, 175, 177;
author of, 195, 198; composition of
Gospel, 62, 68, 73; dating, 215;
ecclesiology, 225; *Epistle to the
Philippians* (Polycarp) showing
knowledge of, 205; eschatology, 245,
247; Gnosticism, 26, 125, 126; "I,"

authorial use of, 195; Matthew and,
203; members leaving community, 202;
patristic understanding of, 127;
Revelation and, 303
John, Gospel of, *see* more specific entries,
and see also Biblical Citations Index
John, Second Letter of, *see also* Biblical
Citations Index: author of, 195, 198;
community, members leaving, 202;
composition of Gospel, 68, 72, 73, 84;
dating, 207, 215, 241; Gnosticism, 124,
125, 126; Presbyter, 195, 198–99, 207,
288; Revelation and, 303
John son of Zebedee, 27, 40, 59, 60, 94,
191, 193, 204
John *ho theologos* ("the Divine"), 27, 30,
107, 220, 267
John, Third Letter of, *see also* Biblical
Citations Index: author of, 195, 198;
composition of Gospel, 68, 73; dating,
207, 215; Diotrephes, 73, 123, 202;
ecclesiology, 227, 228; Gnosticism, 124;
Presbyter, 195, 198–99, 207, 288;
Revelation and, 303
Joseph of Arimathea, 174
Josephus, 127, 132, 140, 154, 203
Joshua, 168
Judaism's influence on Gospel, 8, 132–44,
318, 322–25; blood continuity with
Israel, 227; dating, 212; eschatology,
236–38, 242; OT, 133–38, 280;
Palestinian Judaism *(see* Palestine and
Palestinian Judaism); Platonism,
128–29; Qumran literature, 139–42;
Rabbinic Judaism, 138–39, 238; Son of
Man concept, 253–55, 258–59;
"traditional" Judaism, 132, 136
Judas (apostle), 48, 62, 307
Judas the Galilean, 132
Judean version, 59
Judeans, "the Jews" *(Ioudaios)* used to
mean, 162–63
Judges, Johannine reference to, 135
Justin Martyr, 68, 124, 173, 208, 213

K
Kidron, 200
King, Jesus as, 134, 137, 160, 162, 229, 257,
309, 310, 314

"kingdom of God" *(basileia tou theou),* 222, 228–29, 238–39, 242, 243, 254

L

lamb, Jesus as, 160, 201, 282, 310

language, *see also* Aramaic; Greek language and text: Hebrew, 136–37, 201, 253–54, 278–80; original language of Gospel, 278–81

last encounter with disciples, 307, 308–9, 311–13

Last (Final) Discourse, 42, 80, 84, 171, 255, 291, 307, 311

Last Supper Discourse, 41, 84, 85, 178, 211, 231, 234, 248, 299

Latin versions, 282

the Law: "horizontal" eschatology, 236; Jesus as one fulfilling, 257, 258; OT influence on Gospel, 134; unified acceptance of interpretation of, 227; Wisdom identified with, 263; "your Law," references to, 92, 159, 160, 162

Lazarus as author of *Document C,* 60

Lazarus story, 84–85, 95–96, 103, 246, 289, 300, 302, 304, 306–7

lectionary mss. of John's Gospel, 281

Leucian *Acts of John,* 118, 123, 125, 194, 203

Levites, 163

Leviticus, 168

life and death, theme of, 238–40, 242, 243, 305, 306–7

light and darkness: apologetic and, 155, 157, 172; eschatology, 236; Gnosticism, 117, 118–19; Hermetic literature, 132; Qumran literature, 140, 141; realized eschatology, 183; Wisdom literature, 261

location of composition of John's Gospel, 9, 28, 60, 61, 82, 101, 199–206, 290

logos (Word), 41; Christological significance, 250, 251; Gnosticism, 117, 125; Hermetic literature, 132; OT citations, 137; Philo of Alexandria, 129–30; Rabbinic Judaism, 139; sacramentalism of, 230; Son of Man identified with, 258; Stoicism, 129; Wisdom literature, 260, 261

Louvain school, 6, 96, 98

love, 141, 227, 308, 309, 312–13, 315

Luke, 7, 91, 95–104, *see also* Synoptic tradition, and Biblical Citations Index; Acts used with, 225; authorship, 191; birth stories, 212; composition of Gospel, 65, 67; dating, 209, 211; division between Jesus' ministry and period of church in, 236; final redactor of John's Gospel, Luke as, 60, 103; OT citations, 133; rabbi, Jesus never referred to as, 165; scene from Matt 28:19 not in, 233; Wisdom literature and, 264

LXX (Septuaguint), 136–37, 201, 204, 226, 253, 280

M

Magnesians (Ignatius), 179

man born blind story, 163, 173–74, 256, 290, 300, 302

Manda d'Hayye, 121, 154

Mandean thought and literature: apologetics, 154; composition of Gospel, 48, 53; Gnosticism, 121; Hellenistic thought, 132; Judaism, 139, 142; relationship of Gospel to, 322, 323; Son of Man, 258; Wisdom tradition, 263, 323

Manichaean texts, 258

manna, 44, 135, 302, 306

Marcion, 194

Mark, 91, 94–104, 106, 109, 324, *see also* Synoptic tradition, and Biblical Citations Index; authorship, 191; birth story, ignorance of, 212; composition of Gospel, 60, 65, 67, 77; dating, 211, 212; distinction between Gospel and tradition, 98–99; Matthew's dependence on, 195; OT citations, 133; parallels of John with, 212; Peter as eyewitness source for, 196; rabbi, Jesus as, 165; scene from Matt 28:19 not in, 233; Son of Man terminology, 253; teacher, Jesus addressed as, 264; Wisdom literature and, 264

Mark, Secret Gospel of, 98, 125, 210

Martha and Mary, 95–96, 103, 289

Mary Magdalene, 310, 314, 315

Matthew (the apostle), 118

Matthew, Gospel of, *see also* Synoptic
    tradition, and Biblical Citations Index:
    authorship, 191; birth stories, 212;
    composition of Gospel, 65, 67; dating,
    209, 211; eyewitness, not written by,
    195; Hebrew and Aramaic, 279; Mark,
    dependence on, 195; OT citations, 133;
    OT formula references, 134; rabbi,
    forbidden title in, 165; Wisdom
    literature and, 264

Melito of Sardis, 208

Messiah, Jesus as: apologetics, 154, 155,
    160, 173, 174, 178, 179, 180;
    Christology, 249, 253, 254, 255, 257;
    Judaism's influence on Gospel, 134, 139;
    Son of Man, 253, 254, 255, 257

messias vs. christos, use of, 160

metaphor, sign, and symbol, 92–93,
    289–90, 321

midrashim, 137

miracles, *see* signs

missionary purpose of Gospel, 151, 152,
    172–75, 181–82, 183

mistakes by copyists, 281–83

mistranslations (confused Greek
    passages), 279–81

misunderstanding as stylistic device,
    288–90

monotheism, 60

Montanus and Montanism, 125, 208

the morsel, 308, 311

Moses, 68, 134, 135, 164, 190, 204, 236,
    252, 258, 259

mother of Jesus given to care of BD, 310

multiple edition theories, 46, 58–62,
    81–82, 165, 168, 211

multiple source theories, 46–58

multiplication of the loaves, 107, 109, 300,
    302

Muratorian Fragment, 126, 193

mysticism, 238, 260

N

Nag-Hammadi texts, 53, 117–18, 121–23,
    125, 208

narrative-critical approach, 3, 13, 29–39,
    191, 193, 248, 251, 322

narrator of Gospel, 191

Nathanael, 161, 227, 256, 301

Nazoreans, Gospel of the, 279

neo-Pythagoreans, 127

Neofiti (Targum), 280

neoplatonism, 28

Nestorians, 121

Nicodemus, 174, 233, 301, 306

Nicolaitans, 124, 205

northern Transjordan, 203–4

numerical patterns, 303–4

O

Odes of Solomon, 48, 52, 121, 122, 203,
    208

Offenbarungsreden (Revelatory Discourse
    Source), 51, 52, 54, 121, 279, 285

Old Testament (OT), 133–42, 212, 235,
    258–59, 280

Onqelos (Targum), 280

oracles, 154, 288

oral tradition, 46, 77, 97, 101, 108, 281

Origen, 26, 126, 282

Original Man, 48

orthodoxy of John, acceptance of, 124–26

outline of Gospel, *see* structure and
    outline of Gospel

P, Q

Pachomius, 117

Palestine and Palestinian Judaism, 8, 9, 28,
    116, 136, 322; birth tradition, 212;
    dating of Gospel, 209; geographical use
    of "the Jews," 162; Hellenistic thought,
    influence of, 127–29; Johannine
    independent knowledge of, 92;
    Mandaeans, 121; multiple edition
    theories, 60, 61, 82; place of
    composition of Gospel, 200–201, 204,
    206

Papias, 60, 193–94, 279

papyri copies of John, 98, 202, 209–10,
    282–83

Paraclete-Spirit: authorship of Gospel
    and, 198; BD as instrument of, 81, 236;
    children of God begotten of water and,
    227; Christology, 252; church order
    and, 228; composition of Gospel, 75,
    81; dating of Gospel, 214; eschatology,
    234, 236, 247; Ezekiel as background

for, 135; Gnosticism, 120, 125; Jesus' followers who do not know of, 153–54, 177; last encounter between Jesus and disciples, promise made at, 308, 313; purposes of Gospel and, 183; Qumran literature, 140, 141; Son of Man terminology, 257; Wisdom literature, 263; the world and, 181

parallelism, 170, 256, 284–87, 311

Paraphrase of Shem, 121

parousia, 214, 235, 246, 266, *see also* eschatology

passion and resurrection narratives: ascending/descending motif, 10; composition of Gospel, 49, 54, 80; glory and glorification, and theology of cross, 299; OT citations, 138; structure and outline of Gospel, 299, 307, 309–11, 313–15; Synoptic tradition, 10

Passover: apologetics, 161, 166; composition of Gospel, 59, 85; Judaism's influence on Gospel, 139; place of composition of Gospel, 201; Quartodeciman discussions, 208; structure and outline of Gospel, 300, 302, 303, 310; Synoptic tradition, 93, 109

Pastoral Epistles, 190, 197, 205, 207

Patmos, 194, 204

patristic texts: baptism, institution of, 233; Gnosticism, 117, 124–26, 154–55, 175–76; Greek text of Gospel, 282, 283–84; JBap's followers, 154–55; knowledge of John, 124–25; orthodoxy of John, 124–26; understanding of John, 127

Paul and Pauline writings: apologetics, 154, 161, 180; birth story, ignorance of, 212; composition of Gospel and, 60; disciples of Paul as authors of post-Pauline writings, 197; dispute with Antioch, 203; ecclesiology, 222, 227, 228; Ephesus area, Christians in, 205; eschatology, 243; Eucharist, 212; Hegelian thesis, antithesis, and synthesis, 207; importance in theology of NT, 30, 207, 220, 265, 266; relationship of John to, 90, 266, 267; structure and outline of Gospel, 305

Pella, 204

"people of God," 222

Perea, 162

Perfect Mind, 125

perfecting *vs.* replacing, 305, 306

pericopes, 281

pesharim, 137

Peter: apologetic against followers of, 177–79, 244; blame shifted to Judas from, 62; confession of faith, 94, 178, 301; death by crucifixion, 214; denials of, 307, 309, 314; eschatology, 242; Johannine community, role regarding, 315; Last Supper Discourse, 41; Mark, as eyewitness source for, 196; Matthew, Petrine source for, 104; misunderstanding by, 289; pastoral role of, 84, 223, 310, 315; place of composition of Gospel and portrayal of, 203; structure and outline of Gospel, 301, 307, 309, 310, 314, 315

Peter, First and Second Epistles of, 178, 214, 243, 267

Peter, Gospel of, 98

Pharisees: apologetic against, 157–60, 163–65, 169, 171; dating of Gospel, 213; ecclesiology, 224; exaggerated role of, 92; Hellenistic thought, 127; Judaism's influence on Gospel, 132, 138, 140, 142

Philadelphians (Ignatius), 208

Philemon, 205

Philip, 118, 128, 178, 204, 205, 301

Philippians (Biblical Epistle), 10, 205, 256, 266

Philippians, Epistle to (Polycarp), 205

Philo of Alexandria, 8, 28, 129–30, 140, 202, 258, 259, 323

Philostratus, 52

Photius, 284

Pilate, trial before, 42, 110, 160–63, 194, 287, 309, 314

place of composition of John's Gospel, 9, 28, 60, 61, 82, 101, 199–206, 290

Platonism, 128–29, 131, 143, 235, 236

plêrôma, 41

Pliny, 140, 169

pneumatology, *see* Paraclete-Spirit

poetic/quasi-poetic format, 48, 50, 51, 259, 284–87

Poimandres, 258, 259

polemic purpose of Gospel, 151, 152, 165

political usage of "the Jews" *(Ioudaios),* 162

Polycarp (Ignatius), 246

Polycarp of Smyrna, 126, 205

prayer as literary form, 307, 309, 312

preaching, 69, 79, 83, 90–91, 142, 278, 279

predestination, 250

preexistence, 212, 257–59, 261

Presbyter John (Papias), 60

Presbyter of 2 and 3 John, 195, 198–99, 207, 288

present subjunctive *(hina pisteuête),* use of, 152, 182

primitive/early traditions distinguished from historical traditions, 106

primordial man myth and Son of Man concept, 254, 258

Prochorus, 194

Prologue: apologetic, 153, 160, 170; author of Gospel, 193; composition of Gospel, 41, 48, 52, 60, 76, 80, 84; eschatology, 236, 239; Gnosticism, 122, 125; Hellenistic thought, 129; poetic/quasi-poetic format, 285, 286; structure and outline of Gospel, 298, 299, 300

prophets, 134, 167, 224, 228, 252, 257

Proverbs, 190, *see also* Biblical Citations Index

Psalms, 133, 136, 141, 190, 226

Pseudo-Clementine writings, 154, 155, 179, 203, 208

Pseudo-Jonathan (Targum), 280

"pseudo-Judaism," 172

purposes of Gospel, 8–9, 79, 151–53, 180–83, 323

Pythagoreans, 196

Q, 65, 67, 100–101, 106, 253, 264, 265

Quartodeciman discussions, 208

quasi-poetic format, 48, 50, 51, 259, 284–87

Qumran literature and community: apologetics, 169; composition of Gospel, 60, 66; Ebionites, 176; eschatology, 242, 244; Hellenistic thought, 127, 128; hostility between

Jerusalem high-priestly family and, 169; JBap, 156; place of composition of Gospel, 205; Targum of Job, 280; theology of Gospel influenced by, 93, 132, 136, 137, 139–42, 143; *yahad* (oneness) as name for community, 227

R

Rabban Gamaliel II, 213

rabbi, Jesus as, 165

Rabbinic Judaism, 130, 137, 138–39, 142, 164, 165, 213, 238, 253

reader-response criticism, 30, 32–39, 64, 111, 167–68, 246, 248, 290, 291–92, 312, 315

realized eschatology, 183, 214, 238–48, 255

rearrangement of parts of Gospel, 43–46, 62–64, 96

Recognitions (Pseudo-Clementine), 154, 208

"the redactor," 5–6, 79, 80, 82–85, 199, 318–20; anti-Gnosticism, 122; BD and, 78, 82, 192, 194, 225; Bultmann's "Ecclesiastical Redactor," 49, 52, 82, 224, 231, 241, 286; Christological stages, 250; dating of Gospel, 206–15; eschatological passages, 246; "the evangelist," regarded as, 99; historical value of stage three, 108–10; "the Jews" *(Ioudaios),* use of, 160, 168; Luke as final redactor of John's Gospel, 60, 103; movement of Johannine community prior to work of, 200, 204, 206; OT citations, 138; OT Wisdom literature's influence, 143; relationship to BD and "evangelist," 225; sacramental and ecclesiological passages attributed to, 224–25, 231–32; Synoptic tradition and, 7, 85, 99; variant theories of, 54, 57, 73

Reformation, 27

relecture, réécriture, and *réédition,* 37, 291–92, 312, 315

religious usage of "the Jews" *(Ioudaios),* 166–67, 169

repetitions and duplications, 42, 46, 61, 291

replacement motif, 76, 77, 108, 161, 237, 302, 305, 318

resurrection, *see* passion and resurrection narratives

return to the Father, 10, 256, 262, 299

Revelation (Book of), 225, 237, 303, 304, 305, 318, *see also* Biblical Citations Index

revelation of glory of God, 10, 11, 36, 125, 240, 254, 261, 299, 305, 307–13, *see also* Book of Glory

revelation of love of God, 141, 227, 308, 309, 312–13, 315

Revelatory Discourse Source (*Offenbarungsreden*), 48–49, 51, 52, 54, 121, 279, 285

rhetorical criticism, 29, 32

rhyme and rhythm, 285–87

riddle language, 288

Righteous Teacher (Qumran literature), 141

Roman persecutions, 169, 244

Roman textual tradition, 125, 202, 208, 282

Romans (Epistle), 205, 257

Romans (Ignatius), 208

royal official's son, 300, 301, 306

royal shepherd, Johannine reference to, 135

Rufinus, 203

Rule of the Community (QS), 139

Rylands Papyrus (p52), 209

S

sacraments and sacramentalism, 9, 27, 229–34, 321; anti-sacramentalism of Gospel, 230–31; apologetics, 155, 177, 183; composition of Gospel, 49–50, 81, 85; dating of Gospel, 207, 214; eschatology, 240; Johannine cultic structures, formation of, 123; Wisdom tradition, 266

Sadducees, 127, 132, 140, 159, 169

Salim, 201

salvation, 73, 134, 141, *see also* eschatology

Samarian origins of Gnosticism, 154

Samaritan Woman at Jacob's Well, 81, 301, 306

Samaritans: apologetics, 159, 163, 170; Christology derived from, 252; composition of Gospel and, 60, 67–69,

74; Delos, 205; Hellenistic thought, 127; Johannine community's contact with, 28, 91, 92, 197, 201; missionary activities amongst, 28, 181, 201

Samuel the Small, 213

Sanhedrin, 92, 110, 163, 164, 174, 302

Sayings Tradition, 123

scribal mistakes and deliberate changes, 281–83

Scripture (OT), 133–42, 212, 235, 258–59, 280

scroll as form of Gospel text, 45–46

Secret Gospel of Mark, 98, 125, 210

Seder service, 139

Semitic languages, *see* Aramaic; Hebrew

Semitizing Greek, 48, 49, 52

Seneca, 202

Septuaguint (LXX), 136–37, 201, 204, 226, 253, 280

sequential inconsistencies, 41–42, 46

Sermon on the Mount, 108

serpent on pole, 10, 135, 137, 233, 256, 288, 308

Servant of God, Jesus as, 134, 160

sevens, pattern of, 303–4

Shechem, 200, 204

sheep, church/community as flock of, 222, 227, 229, 237

Shem, Paraphrase of, 121

Shemoneh 'Esreh (Eighteen Benedictions), 172, 213

Shepherd of Hermas, 124

Sibylline Oracles 4, 154

signs, 92–93, 289–90, 321, *see also* Book of Signs; edition theories, 59, 62; eschatology, 248; historical value, 105; interpretative discourses, 304; JBap's failure to perform, 153, 155; Johannine community and, 73, 123, 125; OT citations, 135; sacramentalism and, 230; source theories, 47–48, 50–51, 53, 54–57, 78, 98, 153; theological function for "the evangelist," 80–81; Wisdom literature, 261–62

silence, argument from, 221–25, 228

Siloam, 92, 200

Simeon, 168

Simon Magus, 154, 176

Simon Peter, *see* Peter

Sinaiticus (S) (Codex), 210, 282, 283

Sirach, 127, 201, 252, *see also* Biblical Citations Index

Smyrnaeans (Ignatius), 177

Solomon as "author" of Wisdom literature, 190

Solomon, Odes of, 48, 52, 121, 122, 203, 208

Solomon's Portico, 92, 200

Son of God: apologetics, 164–65, 174, 178, 180; Christology, 72, 73, 249; *logos,* identification with, 258; OT influence, 137; Son of Man, 253, 256, 257, 258

Son of Man, 9–11, 251–59, 301, 318; *bar nasha,* 253; composition of Gospel, 48; diversity of views on, 266; eschatology, 234, 236, 239, 243; Gnosticism, 48, 119; *hu huios tou anthrôpou,* 253; Judaism's influence on Gospel, 135, 253–55, 258–59; number of passages in John, 255; origins of concept, 135, 253–55, 258–59; Son of God, 253, 256, 257, 258; Synoptic tradition, 253, 255–56, 258; vine allegory, 226; Wisdom tradition, joined with, 259, 261

Sophia, 259, 260

soteriology, 73, 134, 141, *see also* eschatology

sources and influences, 8, 28–30, 320–25; Christological stages, 250–51; cross-influence between John and Synoptics, 101–4; Gnosticism, 116–26; Hellenistic thought, 127–32; independent tradition, 99–101; Judaism *(see* Judaism's influence on Gospel); Last (Final) Discourse and last encounter between Jesus and disciples, 311–12; multiple source theories, 46–48; nonhistorical/fictional, 97–98, 99; OT, 133–38, 212; pre-Christian theological motifs in Prologue, 122; Qumran literature and community, 139–42; signs source theories, 47–48, 50–51, 53, 54–57, 78, 98, 153; Son of Man concept, 135, 253–55, 258–59; Synoptic tradition, 48, 49, 51, 65, 99–104; theology and religious thought, 115–50

Spirit, *see* Paraclete-Spirit

stages of composition of Gospel, 5–6, 64

et seq., 317–18, *see also* composition of Gospel; stage one *(see* historical origins of Gospel); stage two *(see* Johannine community); stage three *(see* written stage of Gospel)

"staircase" parallelism, 285, 286

Stoicism, 128–29, 131

story *vs.* discourse, 290–91

"stranger from above," Jesus as, 289

stress patterns, 286

structure and outline of Gospel, 12; Book of Glory, 307–15; Book of Signs, 300–307; bridge scenes, 301, 305; ecclesiology and, 222; general structure and outline, 298–300; unity and literary wholeness of Gospel, 311

stylistic features of Gospel, 12, 29, 32, 33, 287–92; abstract language attributed to Jesus, 92–93; chapters 11–12, stylistic peculiarities of, 304; composition of Gospel, 40–41, 46, 86; Johannine peculiarities, 51–52; poetic/quasi-poetic format, 48, 50, 51, 284–87; storytelling techniques, 79

supplementation of Synoptic Gospels, John viewed as, 94

Sychar (Shechem), 200, 204

symbol, metaphor, and sign, 92–93, 289–90, 321, *see also* signs

symbolic geographical references, 201

symbolic or abstract language attributed to Jesus, 92–93, 289–90

symbolic references to sacraments, 230–34

synagogue, expulsion of Johannine community from, *see* expulsion of Johannine community from synagogue

synchrony, 37, 291, 320

synonymous parallelism, 284

Synoptic tradition, 6–7, 27, 29; Christian community shaping, 66–67; Christology of, 115; dating of Gospel, 209–11; dependence theories, 95–97; dissimilarities of Gospel of John to, 100; ecclesiological imagery, 222, 223; eschatology, 244; eternal life, 239; eyewitnesses, 195; geographical and chronological arrangements, 93; harmonization with John, danger of attempting, 109; Hegelian thesis,

antithesis, and synthesis, 207; historicity of Synoptic parallels with John, 80, 106–7, 109; independence theories, 97–104; JBap, presentation of, 156; "the Jews" *(Ioudaios)*, 157, 163–64; Johannine Gospel and tradition, relationship to, 90–91, 94–104, 207; "kingdom of God" *(basileia tou theou)*, 229, 238; location of action in, 201; love, 141; multiple edition theories, 60, 62; parabolic language, 289; parallelism, 285; preaching, shaped by, 69; redactional passages of, Johannine dependence on, 96; "the redactor" and, 7, 85, 99; religious disputes between Jews shown in, 159; royal official/Synoptic centurion, 306; sacramental passages, 233–34; similarities of Gospel of John to, 100; Son of Man terminology, 253, 255–56, 258; sources and influences, 48, 49, 51, 65, 99–104; supplementation, John viewed as, 94; theological emphasis, difference from John in, 100, 107, 207, 265–66; Wisdom Literature, use of, 66, 68, 142, 143, 264–65
synthetic parallelism, 285
Syria, 137, 203, 208
Syriac, 48, 52, 282
Syrian Christianity, 121

T

Tabernacles, Feast of, 92, 135, 161, 201, 302
Targums, 136, 137, 204, 280
Tatian, 43, 109, 154, 208, 210, 283
teachers, 202, 224, 228, 262, 263, 264
Temple in Jerusalem: cleansing of the Temple, 108, 249, 301; dating of Gospel, 213; destruction of, 138; festal ceremonies, 92; Jesus as replacement for Temple, 137, 305; Jesus' disputes with Temple practices, 159, 171; "the Jews" used to describe authorities of, 163–65, 167; nonconformist Judaism opposing, 127; place of composition of Gospel, 201
tense of verbs used, 152, 182
Tertullian, 126

Testaments of the Twelve Patriarchs, 140
testimonia, 136
Textus Receptus, 282
theocentrism of Johannine Christology, 249, 250
Theodotus, 125
"The Theologian" *(ho theologos),* John known as, 27, 30, 107, 220, 267
theological issues: dating of Gospel, 207, 211–13, 214; geological and chronological anachronisms, 92; glory and glorification, 10, 11, 36, 125, 240, 254, 261, 299, 305, 307–13; Hermetic literature, 131–32; importance of John regarding, 207, 220, 265–67; "the Jews," use of, 166; John *ho theologos* ("the Divine"), 27, 30, 107, 220, 267; John the Baptist (JBap), adherents of, 154–55; last encounter with disciples, theological pattern to, 307, 308–9, 311–13; love, 141, 227, 308, 309, 312–13, 315; OT usage, 137; personal thought of BD/evangelist, 115–16, 143–44; purposes of Gospel and, 183; Qumran literature, 141; separation of pre-Johannine tradition from "the evangelist's" theology, 97; simple *vs.* sophisticated thought and expression, 143–44; sources and influences, 115–50; Synoptic Gospels, Johannine difference from, 100, 107, 207, 265–66; tone and language, distinctiveness of, 65–66; variant versions, 281, 282
Theophilus bishop of Antioch, 124, 208
Thessalonians, First and Second Epistles to, 197, 243, 248
Thomas (apostle), 178, 240, 310, 314, 315
Thomas, Gospel of, 118, 123
Thoth, 131
The Thunder, 125
Timothy, First and Second Epistles to, 190, 197, 205, 207
Titus, 190, 197, 207
Toletanus (Codex), 193
Torah, 139
Trachonitis, 203
"traditional" Judaism, 132, 136, *see also* Judaism's influence on Gospel
Trallians (Ignatius), 246

Transjordan, 9, 136–37, 154, 162, 203–4, 282, 320
Trimorphic Protennoia, 117, 122, 125
Trinity, 26
Tripartite Tractate, 125
Truth, Gospel of, 117
Trypho, Dialogue against (Justin Martyr), 68, 124, 173, 213
twofold meanings, 288–89
typology, 230

U, V, W

unity of authorship, 40–42, 86
Valentinian Gnosticism, 117, 125–26, 176, 202, 250
variant versions of John's Gospels, 280, 281–84
Vaticanus (B) (Codex), 210, 282, 283
"vertical" eschatology, 235–38, 248
Victorinus of Pettau, 176
vine and its branches, allegory of, 222, 226–29, 248, 312
vocabulary comparisons, 131, 141
Vulgate, 193–94
War Scroll (1QM), 242
water themes, 44, 135, 227, 230, 234, 236, 305, 306
Western textual tradition, 125, 282
Wisdom of Solomon, 127, 252, 260, 287, *see also* Biblical Citations Index
Wisdom tradition, 9, 258–65, 323; Christology, 252, 258–65; ecumenism of, 260; eschatology, 238, 244; female

figure of Wisdom, 259, 260; Gnosticism, 122; Hellenistic thought, 122, 127, 252, 260; Hermetic literature, 132; historical origins of Gospel, 143, 264–65; hypostatization *vs.* personalization, 260; *Jean II-A,* 60; OT influence on John, 135–36, 142, 143; Philo, 130; poetic/quasi-poetic format of Gospel, 50, 79, 259, 284; Solomon as "author" of, 190; Son of Man, joined with, 259, 261; Synoptic tradition and, 66, 68, 142, 143, 264–65
the Word, *see logos* (Word)
the world: apartness of Johannine community from, 60, 71, 74, 170–71, 181–82, 237, 289; Gnosticism, 170; Jesus not from, 236, 259, 289; missionary purpose of Gospel, 183; persons addressed by Gospel, 181–82
written stage of Gospel, 78–85, *see also* "the evangelist" and "the redactor"; "the Jews," conflicts with, 160–72; lapse of time between Stage two and, 210–11, 215; original language, 281; Synoptic tradition, 107, 108–10

X, Y, Z

Xenophon, 143
yahad (oneness), 227
Zebedee, John son of, 27, 40, 59, 60, 94, 191, 193, 204
Zechariah, Johannine citations from, 135
Zoroastrian dualism, 119, 140

BIBLICAL CITATIONS INDEX

See also Subject Index for topical reference to Biblical texts.

Genesis
  1:26, 258
  2:7, 245
  28:10–17, 134
Leviticus 27:28–29,
  168
Deuteronomy
  6:4, 68
  18:18, 71
  34:1–2, 190
Joshua
  6:21, 168
  8:22, 168
  10:38–39, 168
Job
  11:6–7, 262
  ch. 28, 261
Psalms
  27:1, 141
  42:7, 133
  80:14–15, 226
Proverbs, 190
  1–9, 261
  1:20–21, 262
  1:24–25, 262
  1:28, 263
  4:13, 262
  8:1–4, 262
  8:3–36, 262
  8:7, 262
  8:17, 262, 263
  8:22–23, 261

  8:31, 261
  8:32–33, 262
  9:2–5, 262
  30:1–4, 253
Isaiah
  6:9–10, 319
  9:1, 141
  29:13, 133
  31:3, 128
  42:6–7, 141
  55:1–2, 128
  55:1–3, 262
  60:1–3, 141
Daniel 7:13, 226, 254, 255,
  256, 258
Wisdom of Solomon
  chs. 6–10, 261
  6:12, 263
  6:16, 262
  6:17–18, 262
  6:17–19, 262
  6:18–19, 262
  6:22, 261, 262
  7:10, 261
  7:14, 262
  7:24, 263
  7:25, 261
  7:26, 261
  7:27, 262, 263
  7:29, 261
  8:4, 262
  9:9–10, 262

  9:10, 261
  9:16–17, 261
  9:16–18, 262
  ch. 10, 263
  10:15–17, 262
  chs. 11–19, 262
Sirach, 127, 201, 252
  ch. 1, 261
  1:29, 261
  4:11, 262
  4:11–19, 261
  4:12, 262
  4:13, 261
  6:18, 262
  6:18–31, 261
  6:20–26, 262
  6:27, 263
  ch. 10, 261
  14:20–15, 261
  ch. 24, 261, 262
  24:3, 261
  24:8, 261
  24:9, 261
  24:19, 265
  24:19–21, 262
  24:21, 133
  24:23, 263
  51:23–27, 265
Baruch
  3:9–4:4, 261
  3:12, 262
  3:29, 261

Baruch (*cont.*)
  3:37, 261
  4:1, 262, 263

Matthew
  1:19, 168
  1:41–42, 102
  2:3–4, 168
  2:20, 168
  3:1–12, 156
  chs. 5–8, 108
  6:2, 205
  6:68–69, 102
  7:24, 264
  10:5, 67
  10:17, 205
  10:23, 242
  11:11, 156
  11:19, 264
  11:25–27, 265
  11:25–30, 102
  11:28–30, 265
  12:42, 264
  16:16, 178
  16:18, 178, 222
  18:8–9, 239
  18:17, 222
  21:15–17, 102
  21:43, 229
  23:34, 160, 205, 264
  25:31–46, 239
  26:64, 242
  27:25, 157
  28:15, 157
  28:19, 231, 233

Mark
  1:5, 162
  2:10, 253
  2:17, 264
  2:19–20, 222
  3:13 ff., 223
  4:12, 289
  5:41, 278
  6:7 ff., 223
  6:37, 85, 102
  7:3, 157
  7:6, 133
  7:24, 200
  7:31, 200

  7:34, 278
  8:31, 11
  9:1, 242
  9:31, 11
  9:38–41, 177
  10:24, 264
  10:30, 239
  10:33–35, 11
  11:1, 94
  13:9, 68
  13:30, 242
  13:32–33, 242
  14:3, 85, 102
  14:5, 85, 102
  14:13–14, 93
  14:24f, 223
  14:36, 278
  15:34, 278

Luke
  1:5–6, 168
  2:25, 168
  2:36, 168
  4:29, 168
  5:4–9, 103
  6:35, 240
  6:47, 264
  7:3, 157
  7:28, 156
  7:35, 264
  9:49–50, 177
  9:52–54, 67
  10:21–22, 102, 265
  10:38–42, 95
  11:31, 264
  11:49, 264
  13:34, 93
  16:27–31, 103
  16:31, 95
  17:22, 242
  20:36, 240
  21:15, 264
  21:20, 243
  22:67, 103
  22:70, 103
  23:13, 165
  23:51, 157
  24:12, 103
  24:20, 165
  24:40, 103

John
  ch. 1, 303
  chs. 1–2, 303
  chs. 1–9, 62
  chs. 1–13, 47
  1:1, 68, 119, 250, 261
  1:1–2, 134
  1:1–13, 72, 73
  1:1–18, 84, 298, 320
  1:1–20:31, 299, 315
  1:3, 175
  1:4–5, 140, 261
  1:5, 289
  1:6, 76, 156
  1:6–7, 140
  1:6–8, 84, 320
  1:8, 76
  1:9, 119, 140, 181
  1:9–13, 153
  1:10, 134
  1:10–11, 170
  1:11, 71, 163, 170, 226
  1:11–12, 80, 181, 299
  1:12, 227
  1:12–13, 182, 245, 250
  1:13, 227
  1:14, 76, 119, 135, 176,
    193, 236, 239, 261,
    300
  1:14–18, 72
  1:15, 320
  1:16, 193
  1:17, 68, 77, 135, 160,
    164, 227, 236, 258
  1:19, 84, 163, 164
  1:19–2:11, 304
  1:19–12:50, 80, 298, 299,
    300–5, 307
  1:19–22, 163
  1:19–27, 69
  1:19–28, 300
  1:19–34, 56, 300
  1:19–51, 36, 300–301
  1:20, 124, 155
  1:23, 124, 137
  1:24, 163
  1:26, 155
  1:28, 287
  1:29, 160, 181, 287

1:29–34, 41, 72, 156, 300
1:30, 155
1:31, 156, 160
1:35–42, 301
1:35–49, 48, 56, 70, 178
1:35–50, 223
1:35–51, 56, 301
1:36–38, 262
1:38, 82, 290
1:40–42, 178
1:40–49, 227
1:41, 160, 290
1:42, 82, 278, 290
1:43, 262
1:43–51, 301
1:45, 133
1:47, 134, 204, 227
1:49, 160, 256, 257
1:50, 257
1:50–51, 178
1:51, 11, 134, 204, 247,
    255, 256, 257, 301
ch. 2, 56, 85
chs. 2–4, 161, 301, 304
chs. 2–12, 50
2:1–4:54, 310
2:1–11, 50, 300–301, 301
2:1–12, 56, 59
2:1–42, 303
2:2, 305
2:4, 237
2:5, 155
2:6, 36
2:11, 41, 48, 50, 140, 287,
    300, 305
2:12, 301
2:12–13, 193
2:13, 108, 162, 300
2:13–22, 59, 94, 301
2:18, 164
2:19–22, 76, 288
2:20, 164
2:21, 290
2:22, 133
2:23, 41, 303
2:23–25, 301, 306
2:26–30, 41
2:27, 228
ch. 3, 41, 43, 73

3:1, 165, 258
3:1–21, 44, 301
3:2, 174
3:3, 36, 222, 228, 236,
    250
3:3–4, 288
3:3–5, 35, 124, 288
3:5, 36, 49, 141, 155, 222,
    227, 228, 234, 240,
    250
3:5–6, 181
3:6, 236
3:11, 284, 285
3:13, 10, 11, 236, 253,
    255, 256, 257, 261
3:13–14, 68
3:14, 10, 11, 35, 36, 135,
    136, 137, 233, 255,
    256, 288, 308
3:14, 261
3:14–15, 250
3:14–16, 256
3:16, 134, 257, 289
3:16–21, 181
3:17, 181
3:18, 239, 285
3:19, 236, 239
3:19–21, 140, 250
3:21, 140
3:22, 41, 155
3:22–30, 44, 301
3:23, 154
3:24, 290
3:25–26, 76
3:26, 155
3:28, 155
3:29, 76, 156, 222, 227
3:30, 76, 155
3:31, 236, 261, 289
3:31–36, 42, 44, 83, 301
3:39, 156
ch. 4, 47, 56, 59, 92
4:1–3, 301
4:2, 290
4:3, 162
4:4–40, 56
4:4–42, 81, 301
4:5, 204
4:5–6, 134

4:6., 136
4:9, 161, 170
4:10, 208, 250, 288
4:10–11, 288
4:10–14, 236
4:10–15, 288
4:11–12, 134
4:12, 136, 290
4:13–14, 234, 262
4:21–23, 181, 237
4:22, 134, 161
4:23, 221, 240
4:25, 160
4:25–26, 155
4:29, 306
4:31–34, 288
4:35–38, 237
4:36, 284, 285
4:38, 67
4:39–42, 181, 227
4:42, 67, 181, 306
4:43–45, 301, 306
4:45, 303
4:46, 287
4:46–5:47, 303
4:46–54, 56, 91, 94, 97,
    300, 301, 305
4:47, 162
4:48, 201
4:53, 306
4:54, 41, 48, 50, 162, 287
ch. 5, 41, 44, 56, 92, 305
chs. 5–10, 77, 108, 161,
    301–2, 304
5:1, 69, 162
5:1–15, 300, 301
5:1–47, 301–2
5:2, 36
5:2–18, 56
5:9, 36
5:10, 76, 164
5:14, 262
5:16, 164
5:16–18, 171
5:16–47, 302
5:18, 68, 164, 249
5:19–20, 256
5:19–25, 42, 245
5:19–30, 256

John *(continued)*
5:20–21, 76
5:22–23, 256
5:24, 239, 240, 250
5:25, 240
5:26–30, 42, 245
5:27, 11, 255, 256
5:28–29, 49, 241, 255,
    256
5:30, 256
5:31–40, 156
5:31–47, 69
5:35, 157
5:39, 160, 237
5:40, 264
5:45–46, 68, 227
5:46, 135, 160, 263
5:46–47, 158
ch. 6, 44, 47, 50, 56, 59,
    73, 91, 94, 95, 102,
    231, 303, 306
6:1–15, 300
6:1–21, 302
6:1–25, 56
6:1–71, 302
6:4, 36, 69, 76, 108, 162,
    300
6:6, 290
6:7, 85
6:14, 72
6:16–21, 106, 300
6:22–24, 302
6:25–59, 320
6:25–71, 302
6:27, 11, 236, 240, 255
6:31, 137, 231
6:31–32, 137, 227
6:31–33, 69
6:31–35, 76
6:31–58, 135
6:32, 68
6:32–34, 288
6:32–35, 81
6:33, 181, 208
6:35, 133, 262, 264, 284,
    286
6:35–50, 42, 83
6:36–40, 287
6:37, 285

6:38, 261
6:39–40, 241
6:39–54, 241
6:41, 163, 165
6:41–42, 201, 288
6:42, 163
6:45, 137, 264
6:51, 63, 240
6:51–52, 288
6:51–58, 36, 42, 49, 59,
    83, 85, 177, 207, 212,
    231, 234
6:51 ff., 262
6:51c–58, 231, 320
6:52, 163, 165, 201
6:53, 255
6:53–54, 11
6:54, 240, 255
6:55, 284
6:59, 163
6:60–66, 76, 179
6:62, 10, 11, 255, 257
6:63, 236, 263, 320
6:64, 179
6:67, 223, 262
6:68, 244
6:69, 160
6:70, 223
ch. 7, 43, 306
chs. 7–8, 42, 92, 304
7:1, 159, 162, 163, 164
7:1–8:59, 302
7:1–13, 302
7:2, 36, 76, 162
7:2–10, 56
7:3, 162
7:3–5, 41, 179, 201
7:4, 303
7:8, 288
7:14–36, 302
7:15, 165
7:19, 158
7:19–23, 56
7:22–23, 227
7:24, 158
7:26, 165
7:28, 262
7:31, 72, 201
7:32, 165

7:33–35, 288
7:34, 263, 284
7:35, 165, 180, 290
7:37, 262
7:37–38, 44, 76, 141
7:37–38., 135
7:37–39, 234
7:37–52, 302
7:38, 135, 136, 208
7:38–39, 177
7:39, 154, 240, 247
7:42, 68, 212, 290
7:48, 165
7:50, 290
7:50–52, 174
7:53–8:11, 40, 302
8:12, 43, 76, 119, 140,
    181, 261
8:12–59, 302
8:13, 163
8:15, 158
8:17, 92, 159, 164
8:20, 237
8:21, 263
8:21–22, 288
8:22, 163, 165, 290
8:23, 236
8:24, 158
8:27–28, 72
8:28, 10, 11, 35, 36, 240,
    255, 256
8:30, 201
8:31, 165
8:31–32, 120
8:31–33, 288
8:31–38, 134
8:31 ff., 76, 179, 180
8:32, 285
8:35, 285
8:41, 158
8:44, 158, 170, 285
8:46, 262
8:47, 158
8:48, 67, 68, 165
8:50, 261
8:51–53, 288
8:52, 165
8:55, 158
8:56, 160, 263

8:56–58, 288
8:57, 165
8:59, 165
ch. 9, 42, 56, 79, 171, 233, 300, 306
chs. 9–11, 47
9:1–10:21, 302, 304
9:1–38, 56
9:1–41, 81, 302
9:5, 63, 181, 261
9:7, 92
9:15–16, 163–64
9:18, 164
9:22, 68, 172, 173, 213
9:22–23, 76
9:27, 174
9:27–28, 76
9:28, 164
9:28–29, 35
9:29, 290
9:30, 174
9:33, 290
9:33–34, 174
9:33–38, 81
9:35, 255, 256, 262
9:35–36, 256
9:35–38, 11
9:39, 285
9:39–41, 224
9:41, 43, 158
ch. 10, 43, 222, 227
10:1, 224
10:1–3, 179
10:1–5, 285
10:1–6, 224
10:1–21, 302
10:1 ff., 135
10:3, 250
10:7, 208
10:7–8, 179
10:16, 67, 71, 178, 227, 237, 314
10:19, 165
10:22, 36, 76
10:22–23, 92
10:22–31, 302
10:22–39, 302, 304
10:24, 165
10:24–25, 103

10:25, 262
10:26, 250
10:28–29, 71
10:30, 249, 306
10:31, 165
10:31–36, 172
10:31–39, 80
10:32–39, 302
10:33, 68, 103, 165
10:34, 92, 137, 160, 162, 164
10:34–35, 134
10:34–36, 69
10:35, 133, 135
10:36, 76, 306
10:38, 306
10:40, 154, 204, 287
10:40–42, 41, 56, 84, 302
10:41, 153, 155
10:42, 80
ch. 11, 56, 95, 162, 300, 304, 306
chs. 11–12, 80, 81, 84–85, 168, 302–3, 304, 307
11:1–44, 81, 302
11:1–53, 304
11:1–54, 302
11:2–19, 56
11:4, 10, 36, 261, 299, 300, 306, 308
11:7, 162
11:8, 163, 165
11:17–24, 289
11:17–40, 168
11:19, 168
11:25, 236, 240
11:25–26, 81, 240, 307
11:27, 201
11:31, 168
11:33, 168
11:33–35, 133
11:33–44, 56
11:36, 168
11:40, 300
11:42, 201
11:45, 168, 201
11:45–54, 302
11:46–47, 92

11:49, 92
11:50, 290
11:51–52, 181, 227, 307, 314
11:52, 227, 237
11:54, 163, 165, 169
11:55, 108, 162, 300
11:55–57, 302
ch. 12, 43, 94, 299
12:1–4, 303
12:1–7, 59, 103, 195
12:1–8, 230
12:1–36, 303, 304
12:3, 85, 102
12:4, 102
12:5, 85
12:9, 168
12:9–19, 303
12:11, 168, 201, 314
12:13, 137
12:15, 137
12:16, 72
12:19, 314
12:20, 180
12:20–23, 180
12:20–36, 303
12:23, 10, 11, 36, 237, 255, 256
12:23–36, 307
12:24, 307, 314
12:27, 11, 48, 133
12:28, 240
12:31–32, 181
12:32, 10, 35, 36, 181, 236
12:32–33, 11, 288, 307, 308, 314
12:33, 10, 290
12:34, 253, 255, 256, 288
12:35–36, 140
12:36, 42
12:37, 48, 303
12:37–38, 56
12:37–40, 319
12:37–41, 80, 180
12:37–43, 41, 56, 303
12:37–50, 303
12:38, 137
12:40., 136

John *(continued)*
  12:41, 136, 263
  12:42, 165, 172, 213
  12:42–43, 70, 74, 76, 173
  12:44, 43, 262
  12:44–50, 42, 83, 299,
    303
  12:46, 181
  12:48, 49, 241
  12:50, 12
  ch. 13, 299
  chs. 13–17, 255, 291, 299
  13:1, 80, 178, 299, 308
  13:1–3, 299
  13:1–11, 233
  13:1–16:33, 171
  13:1–17, 308
  13:1–17:26, 307, 308–
    9, 311, 312, 313, 320
  13:1–20:29, 298
  13:1–20:31, 80 (*see* Book
    of Glory [13:1–
    20:31])
  13:1–21:25, 13, 308–13
  13:1–30, 311
  13:1–38, 307, 308, 311,
    312, 321
  13:5–7, 289
  13:6, 178
  13:7, 72
  13:14, 228
  13:16, 228, 284
  13:18, 137, 223
  13:18–20, 308
  13:20, 285
  13:21, 133
  13:24, 178
  13:31, 240, 255, 299
  13:31–14:31, 80, 311
  13:31–17:26, 80
  13:31–32, 10, 11, 256,
    299
  13:31–38, 311
  13:33, 159, 165, 262,
    263, 288
  13:34, 141
  13:34–35, 313
  13:36, 41, 178
  13:36–38, 288

ch. 14, 84, 133, 283
chs. 14–16, 47, 171
14:1–3, 120
14:1–10, 285
14:1–16:33, 307
14:1–31, 42, 291, 308,
  312, 320
14:2, 299
14:2–3, 240
14:2–9, 288
14:5, 41
14:6, 119, 169, 262
14:8–10, 118
14:9, 249
14:17, 140, 171
14:20, 72
14:21, 285
14:23, 263
14:26, 72, 140
14:28, 299
14:31, 41, 84, 182, 249,
  312
ch. 15, 43, 222, 320
chs. 15–17, 62, 80, 84
15:1–11, 308, 312
15:1–16:4a, 312
15:1–17, 312
15:3, 262
15:9, 227
15:12, 141, 227, 312, 313
15:12–17, 308, 312
15:13, 308
15:15, 262
15:16, 223, 312
15:17, 312, 313
15:18, 71
15:18–16:3, 71
15:18–16:4a, 308, 312
15:19, 181
15:20, 312
15:25, 69, 137, 160, 164
15:26, 299
15:26–27, 183, 228
ch. 16, 43
16:2, 68, 71, 169, 172,
  173
16:2–13, 289
16:4, 69
16:4–33, 42, 84

16:4b–33, 291, 308–9,
  311, 312, 320
16:5, 41
16:7, 240, 299
16:8, 237
16:8–11, 171
16:13, 181, 228
16:14, 299
16:20, 213, 285
16:27, 262
16:28, 261, 299
16:32, 240
16:33, 71
17:1, 299
17:1–11, 309
17:1–26, 71, 307, 309,
  311, 312, 321
17:3, 60, 120, 249
17:5, 11, 68, 258, 261,
  299
17:6, 250
17:11, 299
17:12, 48
17:12–19, 309
17:14, 181, 237
17:16, 120, 171, 289
17:17, 262
17:18, 182
17:20, 166, 227, 237
17:20–26, 309
17:21, 182, 223
17:21–22, 178
17:22, 182
17:22–23, 183, 227
17:23, 223, 313
17:24, 10, 240, 247,
  299
17:34, 131
chs. 18–19, 42, 163
18:1, 36, 41, 84
18:1–11, 309, 314
18:1–19:42, 307, 309
18:3, 163
18:8–9, 314
18:9, 290
18:12, 162, 163
18:12–18, 309
18:12–27, 309, 314
18:15–27, 314